GO!

with Microsoft®

Office 2016

Getting Started

**Shelley Gaskin,
Alicia Vargas, Nancy Graviett,
and Debra Geoghan**

PEARSON

Boston   Columbus   Indianapolis   New York   San Francisco
Amsterdam   Cape Town   Dubai   London   Madrid   Milan   Munich   Paris   Montréal   Toronto
Delhi   Mexico City   São Paulo   Sydney   Hong Kong   Seoul   Singapore   Taipei   Tokyo

Vice President, Career Skills: Andrew Gilfillan
Executive Editor: Jenifer Niles
Project Manager: Holly Haydash
Team Lead, Project Management: Laura Burgess
Development Editor: Ginny Munroe
Editorial Assistant: Michael Campbell
Director of Product Marketing: Maggie Waples
Director of Field Marketing: Leigh Ann Sims
Field Marketing Managers: Molly Schmidt and Joanna Conley
Marketing Coordinator: Susan Osterlitz
Operations Specialist: Maura Zaldivar-Garcia

Senior Art Director: Diane Ernsberger
Cover Photos: GaudiLab, Rawpixel.com, Pressmaster, Eugenio Marongiu, Boggy, Gajus, Rocketclips, Inc
Associate Director of Design: Blair Brown
Director of Media Development: Blaine Christine
Media Project Manager, Production: John Cassar
Full-Service Project Management: Lumina Datamatics, Inc.
Composition: Lumina Datamatics, Inc.
Printer/Binder: RR Donnelley/Menasha
Cover Printer: RR Donnelley/Menasha
Text Font: Times LT Pro

Library of Congress Control Number: 2016930970

10 9 8 7 6 5 4 3 2 1

ISBN 10: 0-13-449706-6
ISBN 13: 978-0-13-449706-8

Brief Contents

Table of Contents

Excel   Introducing Microsoft Excel 2016   121

Chapter 1   Creating a Worksheet and Charting Data......................... 123

Introduction to Microsoft Access 2016   **189**

Chapter 1   Getting Started with Microsoft Access 2016.......... 191

Introducing Microsoft PowerPoint 2016   271

Chapter 1   Getting Started with Microsoft PowerPoint 273

About the Authors

Shelley Gaskin, Series Editor, is a professor in the Business and Computer Technology Division at Pasadena City College in Pasadena, California. She holds a bachelor's degree in Business Administration from Robert Morris College (Pennsylvania), a master's degree in Business from Northern Illinois University, and a doctorate in Adult and Community Education from Ball State University (Indiana). Before joining Pasadena City College, she spent 12 years in the computer industry, where she was a systems analyst, sales representative, and director of Customer Education with Unisys Corporation. She also worked for Ernst & Young on the development of large systems applications for their clients. She has written and developed training materials for custom systems applications in both the public and private sector, and has also written and edited numerous computer application textbooks.

This book is dedicated to my students, who inspire me every day.

Alicia Vargas is a faculty member in Business Information Technology at Pasadena City College. She holds a master's and a bachelor's degree in business education from California State University, Los Angeles, and has authored several textbooks and training manuals on Microsoft Word, Microsoft Excel, and Microsoft PowerPoint.

This book is dedicated with all my love to my husband Vic, who makes everything possible; and to my children Victor, Phil, and Emmy, who are an unending source of inspiration and who make everything worthwhile.

Debra Geoghan is a Professor of Computer Science in the STEM department at Bucks County Community College, teaching computer classes ranging from basic computer literacy to cybercrime, computer forensics, and networking. She has certifications from Microsoft, CompTIA, and Apple. Deb has taught at the college level since 1996 and also spent 11 years in the high school classroom. She holds a B.S. in Secondary Science Education from Temple University and an M.A. in Computer Science Education from Arcadia University.

Throughout her teaching career Deb has worked with educators to integrate technology across the curriculum. At BCCC she serves on many technology committees, presents technology workshops for BCCC faculty, and heads the Computer Science Area. Deb is an avid user of technology, which has earned her the nickname "gadget lady."

This book is dedicated to my colleagues and students at Bucks County Community College: for your suggestions and encouragement throughout this process. You inspire me every day. And most importantly—my family. My husband and sons for your patience, help, and love—I couldn't have done this without your love and support.

Nancy Graviett is a professor and department chair in Business Technology at St. Charles Community College in Cottleville, Missouri. She holds a bachelor's degree in marketing and a master's degree in business education from the University of Missouri and has completed a certificate in online education. Nancy has authored textbooks on WordPerfect, Google, Microsoft Outlook and Microsoft Access.

This book is dedicated to my husband, Dave, and my children, Matthew and Andrea. I cannot thank my family enough for the love and support they share everyday.

GO! with Office 2016

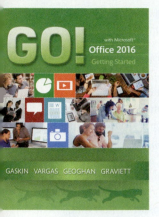

GO! with Office 2016 is the right approach to learning for today's fast-moving, mobile environment. The GO! Series focuses on the job and *success* skills students need to succeed in the workforce. Using job-related projects that put Microsoft Office into context, students learn the *how* and *why* at the moment they need to know, and because the GO! Series uses Microsoft procedural syntax, students never get lost in the instruction. For Office 2016, the hallmark GO! *guided practice-to-skill mastery pathway* is better than ever. Not only do students have multiple opportunities to work live in Microsoft Office to practice and apply the skills they have learned, but also, the *instructional* projects are now Grader projects, so students can work live in Office and receive auto-graded feedback as they learn!

By combining these new instructional Grader projects with the variety of existing Grader projects and the high-fidelity simulations that match the text, students have an effective pathway for learning, practicing, and assessing their abilities. After completing the instructional projects, students are ready to apply the skills with a wide variety of progressively challenging projects that require them to solve problems, think critically, and create projects on their own. The new *GO! with Google* projects also enable students to apply what they have learned in a different environment, and the integrated MOS objectives make this the one resource needed to learn Office, gain critical productivity skills, and prepare to get MOS certified!

What's New

Coverage of new features of Office 2016 ensures that students are learning the skills they need to work in today's job market.

NEW MyITLab 2016 Grader Projects In addition to the homework and assessment Graders already available, the A and B *instructional* projects are now Graders, enabling students to *learn by doing* live in the application *and* receive the instant feedback they need to ensure understanding.

MyITLab HTML 5 Training & Assessment Simulations for Office 2016 These simulations are rewritten by the authors to match the pedagogical approach of the textbook projects and to provide a direct one-to-one learning experience.

NEW Windows 10 Coverage Students practice and learn everything necessary to get up and running with Windows 10, including *GO! Learn How* videos and MyITLab simulation trainings for the Windows 10 skills covered in the textbook.

NEW Google Projects For each A and B instructional project, students construct a parallel project using Google productivity tools. This gives students the opportunity to think critically and apply what they are learning about Microsoft Office to *other* productivity tools, which is an essential job skill.

NEW MOS Preparation MOS objectives are integrated into the text for easy review and reference for students who are preparing for a MOS certification exam. A MOS appendix is also included to provide a comprehensive list of the exam objectives.

NEW Lessons on the GO! How do you teach software that is constantly updated and getting new features all the time? This new project type will cover newer Microsoft apps such as Sway and MIX and things yet to come! These lessons are found in MyITLab and the Instructor Resource Center, and come with instructional content, student data files, solutions files, and rubrics for grading.

GO! To Work Page Here, students can review a summary of the chapter items focused on employability, including a MOS Objective summary, Build Your ePortfolio guidelines, and the GO! For Job Success soft skills videos and discussions.

Application Capstone Projects MyITLab grader Capstone projects for each application provide a variety of opportunities for students to ensure they have reached proficiency.

FOUR Types of Videos Students enjoy video learning, and these videos help students learn and gain skills and insight needed to succeed in the workforce.

- *(NEW) GO! Walk Thru:* Give students a quick 30-second preview of what they will do and create—from beginning to end—by completing each of the A and B Instructional Projects. These videos increase the student's confidence by letting the student see the entire project built quickly.
- *GO! Learn How (formerly Student Training):* Students learn visually by viewing these instructor-led videos that are broken down by Objective for direct guidance. This is the personal instruction students need—especially outside of the classroom—to answer the *How do I?* questions.
- *GO! to Work:* These videos provide short interviews with real business information workers showing how they use Office in the workplace.
- *GO! for Job Success:* These videos relate to the projects in the chapter and cover important career topics such as *Dressing for Success*, *Time Management*, and *Making Ethical Choices*.

Expanded Project Summary chart This easy-to-use guide outlines all the instructional and end-of-chapter projects by category, including Instruction, Review, Mastery and Transfer of Learning, and Critical Thinking.

In-text boxed content for easy navigation *Another Way*, *Notes*, *More Knowledge*, *Alerts*, and *By Touch* instructions are included in line with the instruction—not in the margins—so students won't miss this important information and will learn it in context with what is on their screen.

MyITLab 2016 for GO! Let MyITLab do the work by giving students instantaneous feedback and saving hours of grading with GO!'s extensive Grader Project options. And the HTML5 Training and Assessment simulations provide a high-fidelity environment that provide step-by-step summary of student actions and include just-in-time learning aids to assist students: Read, Watch, Practice.

All other end-of-chapter projects, C, D, H, I, J, K, L, M, N, and O, have grading rubrics and solution files for easy hand grading. These are all Content-based, Outcomes-based, Problem-Solving, and Critical Thinking projects that enable you to add a variety of assessments—including authentic assessments—to evaluate a student's proficiency with the application.

IT Innovation Station Stay current with Office and Windows updates and important Microsoft and office productivity news and trends with help from your Pearson authors! Now that Microsoft Office is in the cloud, automatic updates occur regularly. These can affect how you to teach your course and the resources you are using. To keep you and your students completely up to date on the changes occurring in Office 2016 and Windows 10, we are launching the *IT Innovation Station*. This website will contain monthly updates from our product team and our author-instructors with tips for understanding updates, utilizing new capabilities, implementing new instructional techniques, and optimizing your Office use.

Why the GO! Approach Helps Students Succeed

GO! Provides Personalized Learning

MyITLab from Pearson is an online homework, training, and assessment system that will improve student results by helping students master skills and concepts through immediate feedback and a robust set of tools that allows instructors to easily gauge and address the performance of individuals and classrooms.

MyITLab learning experiences engage students using both realistic, high-fidelity simulations of Microsoft Office as well as auto-graded, live-in-the-application assignments, so they can understand concepts more thoroughly. With the ability to approach projects and problems as they would in real life—coupled with tutorials that adapt based on performance—students quickly complete skills they know and get help when and where they need it.

For educators, MyITLab establishes a reliable learning environment backed by the Pearson Education 24/7, 99.97 percent uptime service level agreement, and that includes the tools educators need to track and support both individual and class-wide student progress.

GO! Engages Students by Combining a Project-Based Approach with the Teachable Moment

GO!'s project-based approach clusters the learning objectives around the projects rather than around the software features. This tested pedagogical approach teaches students to solve real problems as they practice and learn the features.

GO! instruction is organized around student learning outcomes with numbered objectives and two instructional projects per chapter. Students can engage in a wide variety of end-of-chapter projects where they apply what they have learned in outcomes-based, problem-solving, and critical thinking projects—many of which require students to create the project from scratch.

GO! instruction is based on the teachable moment where students learn important concepts at the exact moment they are practicing the skill. The explanations and concepts are woven into the steps—not presented as paragraphs of text at the beginning of the project before students have even seen the software in action.

Each Project Opening Page clearly outlines Project Activities (what the student will do in this project), Project Files (what starting files are needed and how the student will save the files), and Project Results (what the student's finished project will look like). Additionally, to support this page, the GO! Walk Thru video gives students a 30-second overview of how the project will progress and what they will create.

GO! Demonstrates Excellence in Instructional Design

Student Learning Outcomes and Objectives are clearly defined so students understand what they will learn and what they will be able to do when they finish the chapter.

Clear Instruction provided through project steps written following Microsoft® Procedural Syntax to guide students where to go *and then* what to do, so they never get lost!

Teachable moment approach has students learn important concepts when they need to as they work through the instructional projects. No long paragraphs of text.

Clean Design presents textbook pages that are clean and uncluttered, with screenshots that validate the student's actions and that engage visual learners.

Sequential Pagination displays the pages sequentially numbered, like every other textbook a student uses, instead of using letters or abbreviations. Student don't spend time learning a new numbering approach.

Important information is boxed within the text so that students won't miss or skip the Another Way, By Touch, Note, Alert, or More Knowledge details so there are no distracting and "busy-looking" marginal notes.

Color-Coded Steps guide students through the projects with colors coded by project.

End-of-Project Icon helps students know when they have completed the project, which is especially useful in self-paced or online environments. These icons give students a clearly identifiable end point for each project.

GO! Learn How Videos provide step-by-step visual instruction for the A and B instructional projects—delivered by a real instructor! These videos provide the assistance and personal learning students may need when working on their own.

GO! Delivers Easy Course Implementation

Instructor Page

Teach the Course You Want in Less Time

The *GO!* series' one-of-a-kind instructional system provides you with everything you need to prepare for class, teach the material, and assess your students.

Prepare

- **Office 2013 to 2016 Transition Guide** provides an easy-to-use reference for updating your course for Office 2016 using GO!
- **Annotated Instructor Tabs** provide clear guidance on how to implement your course.
- **MyITLab Implementation Guide** is provided for course planning and learning outcome alignment.
- **MyITLab content folders** now organized by *Instruction*, *Practice*, *Review*, and *Assessment*.
- **Syllabus templates** outline various plans for covering the content in an 8-, 12-, or 16-week course.
- **List of Chapter Outcomes and Objectives** is provided for course planning and learning outcome alignment.
- **Student Assignment Tracker** for students to track their own work.
- **Assignment Planning Guide** Description of the *GO!* assignments with recommendations based on class size, delivery method, and student needs.
- **Solution Files** Examples of homework submissions to serve as examples for students.
- **Online Study Guide for Students** Interactive objective-style questions based on chapter content.

Teach

- **The Annotated Instructors Edition** includes the entire student text, spiral-bound and wrapped with teaching notes and suggestions for how to implement your course.
- **Scripted Lectures** present a detailed guide for delivering live in-class demonstrations of the A and B Instructional Projects.
- **PowerPoint Presentations** provide a visual walk-through of the chapter with suggested lecture notes included.
- **Audio PowerPoint Presentations** provide a visual walk-through of the chapter with the lecture notes read out loud.
- **Walk Thru Videos** provide a quick 30-second preview of what the student will do and create—from beginning to end—by completing each of the A and B Instructional projects. These videos increase the student's confidence by letting the student see the entire project built quickly.

Assess

- **A scoring checklist, task-specific rubric, or analytic rubric** accompanies every assignment.
- **Prepared Exams** provide cumulative exams for each project, chapter, and application that are easy to score using the provided scoring checklist and point suggestions for each task.
- **Solution Files** are provided in three formats: native file, PDF, and annotated PDF.
- **Rubrics** provide guidelines for grading open-ended projects.
- **Testbank questions** are available for you to create your own objective-based quizzes for review.

Grader Projects

- **Projects A & B** (Guided Instruction)
- **Project E Homework** (Formative) and Assesment (Summative) (Cover Objectives in Project A)
- **Project F Homework** (Formative) and Assesment (Summative) (Cover Objectives in Project B)
- **Project G Homework** (Formative) and Assesment (Summative) (Cover Objectives in Projects A and B)
- **Application Capstone Homework** (Formative review of core objectives covered in application)
- **Application Capstone Exam** (Summative review of core objectives covered in application— generates badge with 90 percent or higher)

GO! Series Hallmarks

Teach the Course You Want in Less Time

A Microsoft® Office textbook designed for student success!

- **Project-Based** – Students learn by creating projects that they will use in the real world.

- **Microsoft Procedural Syntax** – Steps are written to put students in the right place at the right time.

- **Teachable Moment** – Expository text is woven into the steps—at the moment students need to know it—not chunked together in a block of text that will go unread.

- **Sequential Pagination** – Students have actual page numbers instead of confusing letters and abbreviations.

Clearly defined Learning Outcomes and Objectives

Visual Design – Engages students and provides a clear learning pathway.

GO! To Work videos – Provide real-work examples of how Office is used in various careers.

Application Introductions – Provide an overview of the application to prepare students for the upcoming chapters.

Scenario – Each chapter opens with a job-related scenario that sets the stage for the projects the student will create.

Simulation Training and Assessment – Give your students the most realistic Office 2016 experience with realistic, high-fidelity simulations.

Project Activities – A project summary stated clearly and quickly.

Project Files – Clearly shows students which files are needed for the project and the names they will use to save their documents.

Build from Scratch icons – Indicate which projects students build from scratch.

NEW GO! Walk Thru videos – Give students a 30-second overview of what they will create in the project.

NEW MyITLab Grader projects for Instructional A & B projects – Allow students to work live in the application to learn by doing.

Project Results – Shows students what successful completion looks like.

In-text Features
Another Way, Notes, More Knowledge, Alerts, and By Touch Instructions

Color Coding – Each chapter has two instructional projects, which is less overwhelming for students than one large chapter project. The projects are differentiated by different colored numbering and headings.

MOS Objectives – Are highlighted throughout the text to provide a review and exam prep reference.

FIGURE 1.7

Microsoft Procedural Syntax – Steps are written to put the student at the right place at the right time.

Teachable Moment – Expository text is woven into the steps—at the moment students need to know it—not chunked together in a block of text that will go unread.

Intext Callouts – Ensure that students will read this important material—Another Way, Notes, More Knowledge, Alerts, and By Touch instructions.

Sequential Pagination – Students are given actual page numbers to navigate through the textbook instead of confusing letters and abbreviations.

End-of-Chapter

MOS Skills Summary – List all the MOS objectives covered in the chapter.

Build Your ePortfolio – Provides guidelines for creating an effective representation of your course work.

GO! For Job Success – Soft skills, videos, and discussions to prepare students with the soft skills needed for today's work environment.

Review and Assessment Chart – Provides an easy-to-use guide to all the instructional and end-of-chapter projects by category from Mastery and Transfer of Knowledge to Critical Thinking.

End-of-Chapter Glossary – Gives students an easy way to review key terms.

End-of-Chapter

Objective List – Every end-of-chapter project includes a listing of covered Objectives from Projects A and B.

Grader Projects – In addition to the two Grader Projects for the instructional portion of the chapter (Projects A and B), each chapter has six MyITLab Grader projects within the end-of-chapter material—three homework and three assessment—clearly indicated by the MyITLab logo.

Task-Specific Rubric – A matrix specific to the GO! Solve It projects that states the criteria and standards for grading these defined-solution projects.

End-of-Chapter

Outcomes-Based Assessments – Assessments with open-ended solutions.

Outcomes-Based Assessments – Assessments with open-ended solutions.

Outcomes Rubric – A standards-based analytic rubric specific to the GO! Think projects that states the criteria and standards for grading these open-ended assessments. For these authentic assessments, an analytic rubric enables the instructor to judge and the student to self assess.

Sample Solution – Outcomes-based assessments include a sample solution so the instructor can compare student work with an example of expert work.

Google Projects for each A & B instructional project – Provide students the opportunity to think critically and apply what they are learning about Microsoft Office to other productivity tools—an essential job skill.

Student Materials

Student Data Files – All student data files are available in MyITLab for Office 2016 or at **www.pearsonhighered.com/go**

FOUR Types of Videos help students learn and gain skills and insight needed to succeed in the workforce.

- **(NEW)** *GO! Walk Thru* is a brief overview of the A & B instructional projects to give students the context of what they will be doing in the projects
- *GO! Learn How (formerly Student Training)* instructor-led videos are broken down by Objective for direct guidance; this personal instruction answers the "how-do-I" questions students ask.
- *GO! to Work* videos provide short interviews with workers showing how they use Office in the workplace.
- *GO! for Job Success* videos relate to the projects in the chapter and cover important career topics such as *Dressing for Success*, *Time Management*, and *Making Ethical Choices*.

Matching and multiple choice questions provide a variety of review options for content in each chapter.

MOS Objective quiz provides a quick assessment of student understanding of the MOS objectives covered in the chapter. Helpful for courses focused on the pathway to MOS certification.

Available in MyITLab for Office 2016.

GO! with MyITLab
Gives you a completely integrated solution

Instruction ▪ Training ▪ Assessment

All of the content in the book and MyITLab is written by the authors, who are instructors, so the instruction works seamlessly with the simulation trainings and grader projects—
true 1:1. eText, Training & Assessment Simulations, and Grader Projects.

Instructor Resources

All Instructor Resources found in MyITLab or at pearsonhighered.com/go

Annotated Instructor Edition – This instructor tool includes a full copy of the student textbook and a guide to implementing your course depending on the emphasis you want to place on digital engagement. Also included are teaching tips, discussion topics, and other useful pieces for teaching each chapter.

Assignment Sheets – Lists all the assignments for the chapter. Just add the course information, due dates, and points. Providing these to students ensures they will know what is due and when.

Scripted Lectures – A script to guide your classroom lecture of each instructional project.

Annotated Solution Files – Coupled with the scorecards, these create a grading and scoring system that makes grading easy and efficient.

PowerPoint Lectures – PowerPoint presentations for each chapter.

Audio PowerPoints – Audio versions of the PowerPoint presentations for each chapter.

Scoring Rubrics – Can be used either by students to check their work or by you as a quick check-off for the items that need to be corrected.

Syllabus Templates – For 8-week, 12-week, and 16-week courses.

Test Bank – Includes a variety of test questions for each chapter.

Instruction

Instruction: General

Syllabi templates demonstrate different approaches for covering the content in an 8-, 12-, or 16-week course.

Application Intro Videos provide a quick overview of what the application is and its primary function.

GO! to Work Videos put each chapter into context as related to how people use productivity software in their daily lives and work.

GO! For Success videos and discussions provide real-life scenarios exploring the essential soft skills needed to succeed in the workplace and professional settings.

Instruction: Hands-On *using one or more of the following:*

- **Interactive eText** allows students to read the narrative and instruction and also link directly to the various types of videos included.
- **(NEW) Walk Thru Videos** provide a quick 30-second overview of what students will do in the A & B instructional projects.
- **Scripted Lectures** are a detailed guide through the A & B projects from the book for you to use for in-class demonstration.
- **GO! Learn How** (previously Student Training) videos are instructor-led videos that provide guided instruction through each Objective and the related Activities.
- **PowerPoint Presentations** provide a visual walk-through of the chapter with suggested lecture notes included.
- **Audio PowerPoint Presentations** provide the visual walk-through of chapters with the lecture notes read aloud.
- **(NEW) A & B Instruction Projects** assigned to students. Students can complete the Instructional Projects 1A and 1B and submit for instructor review or manual grading. They can also submit as a MyITLab Grader project, which allows the students to work live in the application starting with files downloaded from MyITLab and then submitted for automatic grading and feedback.
- **(NEW) MOS Objectives** are covered throughout the chapter and are indicated with the **MOS** icon. Instructors use these to point students to content they would encounter on a MOS exam. If a course is focused on MOS preparation, this content would be emphasized in the instruction.

Practice

MyITLab Skill-based Training Simulation provides students with hands-on practice applying the skills they have learned in a simulated environment where they have access to Learning Aids to assist if needed (READ, WATCH, PRACTICE). All of the student's keystrokes are recorded so that instructors can review and provide support to the students. Instructor can set the number of times the students can complete the simulation.

MyITLab Homework Grader Projects (E, F, or G) provide students with live-in-the-application practice with the skills they learned in Projects A and B. These projects provide students with detailed reports showing them where they made errors and also provide "live comments" explaining the details.

Student Assignment Tracker for students to track their work.

Review

GO! Online activities (multiple choice and matching activities) provide objective-based quizzing to allow students to review how they are doing.

Testbank questions are available for instructors to create their own quizzes for review or assessment.

End-of-chapter online projects H–O provide Content-based, Outcome-based, and Critical Thinking projects that you can assign for additional review, practice, or assessments. These are graded manually by the instructor using the provided Solution Files and Grading Scorecards or Rubrics.

MOS Quizzes provide an objective-based quiz to review the MOS objective-related content covered in the chapter. Provides students with review to help if they plan to take a MOS Certification exam.

Assessment

MyITLab Skill-based Exam Simulation provides students with an assessment of their knowledge and ability to apply the skills they have learned. In the Simulated Exams, students do not have access to the Learning Aids. All of the student's keystrokes are recorded so that instructors can review and provide support to the students. Instructors can set the number of times the students can complete the simulation exam.

MyITLab Assessment Grader Projects (E, F, or G) provide students with live-in-the-application practice with the skills they learned in Projects A and B. These projects provide students with detailed reports showing the student where they made errors and also provides "live comments" explaining the details.

Prepared Exams – these are additional projects created specifically for use as exams that the instructor will grade manually. They are available by Project, by Chapter, and by Unit.

Pre-built Chapter quizzes provide objective-based quizzing to allow students to review how they are doing.

Testbank questions are available for instructors to create their own quizzes for review or assessment.

Reviewers Of The GO! Series

Abul Sheikh	Abraham Baldwin Agricultural College	Kenneth A. Hyatt	Lonestar College - Kingwood
John Percy	Atlantic Cape Community College	Glenn Gray	Lonestar College North Harris
Janette Hicks	Binghamton University	Gene Carbonaro	Long Beach City College
Shannon Ogden	Black River Technical College	Betty Pearman	Los Medanos College
Karen May	Blinn College	Diane Kosharek	Madison College
Susan Fry	Boise State University	Peter Meggison	Massasoit Community College
Chigurupati Rani	Borough of Manhattan Community College / CUNY	George Gabb	Miami Dade College
Ellen Glazer	Broward College	Lennie Alice Cooper	Miami Dade College
Kate LeGrand	Broward College	Richard Mabjish	Miami Dade College
Mike Puopolo	Bunker Hill Community College	Victor Giol	Miami Dade College
Nicole Lytle-Kosola	California State University, San Bernardino	John Meir	Midlands Technical College
Nisheeth Agrawal	Calhoun Community College	Greg Pauley	Moberly Area Community College
Pedro Diaz-Gomez	Cameron	Catherine Glod	Mohawk Valley Community College
Linda Friedel	Central Arizona College	Robert Huyck	Mohawk Valley Community College
Gregg Smith	Central Community College	Kevin Engellant	Montana Western
Norm Cregger	Central Michigan University	Philip Lee	Nashville State Community College
Lisa LaCaria	Central Piedmont Community College	Ruth Neal	Navarro College
Steve Siedschlag	Chaffey College	Sharron Jordan	Navarro College
Terri Helfand	Chaffey College	Richard Dale	New Mexico State University
Susan Mills	Chambersburg	Lori Townsend	Niagara County Community College
Mandy Reininger	Chemeketa Community College	Judson Curry	North Park University
Connie Crossley	Cincinnati State Technical and Community College	Mary Zegarski	Northampton Community College
Marjorie Deutsch	City University of New York - Queensborough Community College	Neal Stenlund	Northern Virginia Community Colege
		Michael Goeken	Northwest Vista College
Mary Ann Zlotow	College of Dupage	Mary Beth Tarver	Northwestern State University
Christine Bohnsak	College of Lake County	Amy Rutledge	Oakland University
Gertrude Brier	College of Staten Island	Marcia Braddock	Okefenokee Technical College
Sharon Brown	College of The Albemarle	Richard Stocke	Oklahoma State University - OKC
Terry Rigsby	Columbia College	Jane Stam	Onondaga Community College
Vicki Brooks	Columbia College	Mike Michaelson	Palomar College
Donald Hames	Delgado Community College	Kungwen (Dave) Chu	Purdue University Calumet
Kristen King	Eastern Kentucky University	Wendy Ford	CUNY - Queensborough CC
Kathie Richer	Edmonds Community College	Lewis Hall	Riverside City College
Gary Smith	Elmhurst College	Karen Acree	San Juan College
Wendi Kappersw	Embry-Riddle Aeronautical University	Tim Ellis	Schoolcraft College
Nancy Woolridge	Fullerton College	Dan Combellick	Scottsdale Community College
Abigail Miller	Gateway Community & Technical College	Pat Serrano	Scottsdale Community College
Deep Ramanayake	Gateway Community & Technical College	Rose Hendrickson	Sheridan College
Gwen White	Gateway Community & Technical College	Kit Carson	South Georgia College
Debbie Glinert	Gloria K School	Rebecca Futch	South Georgia State College
Dana Smith	Golf Academy of America	Brad Hagy	Southern Illinois University Carbondale
Mary Locke	Greenville Technical College	Mimi Spain	Southern Maine Community College
Diane Marie Roselli	Harrisburg Area Community College	David Parker	Southern Oregon University
Linda Arnold	Harrisburg Area Community College - Lebanon	Madeline Baugher	Southwestern Oklahoma State University
Daniel Schoedel	Harrisburg Area Community College - York Campus	Brian Holbert	St. Johns River State College
Ken Mayer	Heald College	Bunny Howard	St. Johns River State College
Xiaodong Qiao	Heald College	Stephanie Cook	State College of Florida
Donna Lamprecht	Hopkinsville Community College	Sharon Wavle	Tompkins Cortland Community College
Kristen Lancaster	Hopkinsville Community College	George Fiori	Tri-County Technical College
Johnny Hurley	Iowa Lakes Community College	Steve St. John	Tulsa Community College
Linda Halverson	Iowa Lakes Community College	Karen Thessing	University of Central Arkansas
Sarah Kilgo	Isothermal Community College	Richard McMahon	University of Houston-Downtown
Chris DeGeare	Jefferson College	Shohreh Hashemi	University of Houston-Downtown
David McNair	Jefferson College	Donna Petty	Wallace Community College
Diane Santurri	Johnson & Wales	Julia Bell	Walters State Community College
Roland Sparks	Johnson & Wales University	Ruby Kowaney	West Los Angeles College
Ram Raghuraman	Joliet Junior College	Casey Thompson	Wiregrass Georgia Technical College
Eduardo Suniga	Lansing Community College	DeAnnia Clements	Wiregrass Georgia Technical College

Introduction to Microsoft Office 2016 Features

1

PROJECT 1A

OUTCOMES
Create, save, and print a Microsoft Office 2016 document.

OBJECTIVES

1. Explore Microsoft Office 2016
2. Enter, Edit, and Check the Spelling of Text in an Office 2016 Program
3. Perform Commands from a Dialog Box
4. Create a Folder and Name and Save a File
5. Insert a Footer, Add Document Properties, Print a File, and Close a Desktop App

---

PROJECT 1B

OUTCOMES
Perform commands, apply formatting, and install apps for Office in Microsoft Office 2016

OBJECTIVES

6. Open an Existing File and Save it with a New Name
7. Sign in to Office and Explore Options for a Microsoft Office Desktop App
8. Perform Commands from the Ribbon and Quick Access Toolbar
9. Apply Formatting in Office Programs and Inspect Documents
10. Compress Files and Get Help with Office
11. Install Apps for Office and Create a Microsoft Account

Imagewell10/Fotolia

In This Chapter

 GO! to Work with Office Features

In this chapter, you will practice using features in Microsoft Office 2016 that work similarly across Word, Excel, Access, and PowerPoint. These features include managing files, performing commands, adding document properties, signing in to Office, applying formatting to text, and searching for Office commands quickly. You will also practice installing apps from the Office Store and setting up a free Microsoft account so that you can use OneDrive.

The projects in this chapter relate to **Skyline Metro Grill**, which is a chain of 25 casual, full-service restaurants based in Boston. The Skyline Metro Grill owners are planning an aggressive expansion program. To expand by 15 additional restaurants in Chicago, San Francisco, and Los Angeles by 2020, the company must attract new investors, develop new menus, develop new marketing strategies, and recruit new employees, all while adhering to the company's quality guidelines and maintaining its reputation for excellent service. To succeed, the company plans to build on its past success and maintain its quality elements.

PROJECT ACTIVITIES

In Activities 1.01 through 1.08, you will create a note form using Microsoft Word 2016, save it in a folder that you create by using File Explorer, and then print the note form or submit it electronically as directed by your instructor. Your completed note form will look similar to Figure 1.1.

 PROJECT FILES

 If your instructor wants you to submit Project 1A in the MyITLab Grader system, log in to MyITLab, locate Grader Project1A, and then download the files for this project.

For Project 1A, you will need the following file:
New blank Word document

You will save your file as:
Lastname_Firstname_1A_Note_Form

 PROJECT RESULTS

Build From Scratch

GO! Walk Thru Project 1A

Skyline Metro Grill, Chef's Notes
Executive Chef, Sarah Jackson

Lastname_Firstname_1A_Note_Form

Word 2016, Windows 10, Microsoft Corporation

FIGURE 1.1 Project 1A Note Form

NOTE	If You Are Using a Touchscreen
	Tap an item to click it.
	Press and hold for a few seconds to right-click; release when the information or commands display.
	Touch the screen with two or more fingers and then pinch together to zoom out or stretch your fingers apart to zoom in.
	Slide your finger on the screen to scroll—slide left to scroll right and slide right to scroll left.
	Slide to rearrange—similar to dragging with a mouse.
	Swipe to select—slide an item a short distance with a quick movement—to select an item and bring up commands, if any.

Objective 1 | Explore Microsoft Office 2016

NOTE	Creating a Microsoft Account

Use a free Microsoft account to sign in to Office 2016 so that you can work on different PCs and use your OneDrive. If you already sign in to a Windows PC, tablet, or phone, or you sign in to Xbox Live, Outlook.com, or OneDrive, use that account to sign in to Office. To create a Microsoft account, you can use *any* email address as the user name for your new Microsoft account—including addresses from Outlook.com, Yahoo! or Gmail.

GO! Learn How
Video OF1.1

The term *desktop application* or *desktop app* refers to a computer program that is installed on your PC and that requires a computer operating system such as Microsoft Windows. The programs in Microsoft Office 2016 are considered to be desktop apps. A desktop app typically has hundreds of features and takes time to learn.

An *app* refers to a self-contained program usually designed for a single purpose and that runs on smartphones and other mobile devices—for example, looking at sports scores or booking a flight on a particular airline. Microsoft's Windows 10 operating system supports both desktop apps that run only on PCs and *Windows apps* that run on all Windows device families—including PCs, Windows phones, Windows tablets, and the Xbox gaming system.

ALERT!	Is Your Screen More Colorful and a Different Size Than the Figures in This Textbook?

Your installation of Microsoft Office 2016 may use the default Colorful theme, where the ribbon in each application is a vibrant color and the ribbon tabs display with white text. In this textbook, figures shown use the White theme, but you can be assured that all the commands are the same. You can keep your Colorful theme, or if you prefer, you can change your theme to White to match the figures here. To do so, open any application and display a new document. On the ribbon, click the File tab, and then on the left, click Options. With General selected on the left, under Personalize your copy of Microsoft Office, click the Office Theme arrow, and then click White.

Additionally, the figures in this book were captured using a screen resolution of 1280 x 768. If that is not your screen resolution, your screen will closely resemble, but not match, the figures shown. To view or change your screen's resolution on a Windows 10 PC, on the desktop, right-click in a blank area, click Display settings, and then on the right, click Advanced display settings. On a Windows 7 PC, right-click on the desktop, and then click Screen resolution.

Activity 1.01 | Exploring Microsoft Office 2016 and Creating a Blank Word Document

> **ALERT!**   **To submit as an autograded project, log into MyITLab, download the files for this project, and then begin with those files instead of a new blank document.**

1 On the computer you are using, start Microsoft Word 2016, and then compare your screen with Figure 1.2.

Depending on which operating system you are using and how your computer is set up, you might start Word from the taskbar in Windows 7, Windows 8, or Windows 10, or from the Start screen in Windows 8, or from the Start menu in Windows 10. On an Apple Mac computer, the program will display in the dock.

Documents that you have recently opened, if any, display on the left. On the right, you can select either a blank document or a *template*—a preformatted document that you can use as a starting point and then change to suit your needs.

Word 2016, Windows 10, Microsoft Corporation

FIGURE 1.2

2 Click **Blank document**. Compare your screen with Figure 1.3, and then take a moment to study the description of these screen elements in the table in Figure 1.4.

> **NOTE**   Displaying the Full Ribbon
>
> If your full ribbon does not display, click any tab, and then at the right end of the ribbon, click 📌 to pin the ribbon to keep it open while you work.

FIGURE 1.3

Word 2016, Windows 10, Microsoft Corporation

SCREEN ELEMENT	DESCRIPTION
File tab	Displays Microsoft Office Backstage view, which is a centralized space for all of your file management tasks such as opening, saving, printing, publishing, or sharing a file—all the things you can do *with* a file.
Group names	Indicate the name of the groups of related commands on the displayed tab.
Quick Access Toolbar	Displays buttons to perform frequently used commands and resources with a single click. The default commands include Save, Undo, and Redo. You can add and delete buttons to customize the Quick Access Toolbar for your convenience.
Ribbon	Displays a group of task-oriented tabs that contain the commands, styles, and resources you need to work in an Office 2016 desktop app. The look of your ribbon depends on your screen resolution. A high resolution will display more individual items and button names on the ribbon.
Ribbon Display Options	Displays three ways you can display the ribbon: Auto-hide Ribbon, Show Tabs, or Show Tabs and Commands.
Ribbon tabs	Display the names of the task-oriented tabs relevant to the open program.
Share button	Opens the Share pane from which you can save your file to the cloud—your OneDrive—and then share it with others so you can collaborate.
Signed-in user	Identifies the signed-in user.
Status bar	Displays file information on the left; on the right displays buttons for Read Mode, Print Layout, and Web Layout views; on the far right displays Zoom controls.
Tell Me box	Provides a search feature for Microsoft Office commands that you activate by typing what you are looking for in the Tell Me box; as you type, every keystroke refines the results so that you can click the command as soon as it displays.
Title bar	Displays the name of the file and the name of the program; the window control buttons are grouped on the right side of the title bar.
Window control buttons	Displays buttons for commands to change the Ribbon Display Options, Minimize, Restore Down, or Close the window.

Word 2016, Windows 10, Microsoft Corporation

FIGURE 1.4

GO! Learn How
Video OF1.2

All of the programs in Office 2016 require some typed text. Your keyboard is still the primary method of entering information into your computer. Techniques to enter text and to *edit*—make changes to—text are similar across all of the Office 2016 programs.

1.4.6

Activity 1.02 | Entering and Editing Text in an Office 2016 Program

1 On the ribbon, on the **Home tab**, in the **Paragraph group**, if necessary, click **Show/Hide** ¶ so that it is active—shaded. If necessary, on the **View tab**, in the **Show group**, select the **Ruler** check box so that rulers display below the ribbon and on the left side of your window, and then redisplay the **Home tab**.

The *insertion point*—a blinking vertical line that indicates where text or graphics will be inserted—displays. In Office 2016 programs, the mouse *pointer*—any symbol that displays on your screen in response to moving your mouse device—displays in different shapes depending on the task you are performing and the area of the screen to which you are pointing.

When you press ⌨Enter, ⌨Spacebar, or ⌨Tab on your keyboard, characters display to represent these keystrokes. These screen characters do not print, and are referred to as *formatting marks* or *nonprinting characters*.

> **NOTE** | **Activating Show/Hide in Word Documents**
>
> When Show/Hide is active—the button is shaded—formatting marks display. Because formatting marks guide your eye in a document—like a map and road signs guide you along a highway—these marks will display throughout this instruction. Many expert Word users keep these marks displayed while creating documents.

2 Type **Skyline Grille Info** and notice how the insertion point moves to the right as you type. Point slightly to the right of the letter *e* in *Grille* and click one time to place the insertion point there. Compare your screen with Figure 1.5.

A *paragraph symbol* (¶) indicates the end of a paragraph and displays each time you press ⌨Enter. This is a type of formatting mark and does not print.

Word 2016, Windows 10, Microsoft Corporation

FIGURE 1.5

3 On your keyboard, locate and then press the ⌨Backspace key to delete the letter *e*.

Pressing ⌨Backspace removes a character to the left of the insertion point.

4 Press ⟶ one time to place the insertion point to the left of the *I* in *Info*. Type **Chef's** and then press ⌨Spacebar one time.

By *default*, when you type text in an Office program, existing text moves to the right to make space for new typing. Default refers to the current selection or setting that is automatically used by a program unless you specify otherwise.

5 Press Del four times to delete *Info* and then type **Notes**

Pressing Del removes a character to the right of the insertion point.

6 With your insertion point blinking after the word *Notes*, on your keyboard, hold down the Ctrl key. While holding down Ctrl, press ← three times to move the insertion point to the beginning of the word *Grill*. Release Ctrl.

This is a ***keyboard shortcut***—a key or combination of keys that performs a task that would otherwise require a mouse. This keyboard shortcut moves the insertion point to the beginning of the previous word.

A keyboard shortcut is indicated as Ctrl + ← (or some other combination of keys) to indicate that you hold down the first key while pressing the second key. A keyboard shortcut can also include three keys, in which case you hold down the first two and then press the third. For example, Ctrl + Shift + ← selects one word to the left.

7 With the insertion point blinking at the beginning of the word *Grill*, type **Metro** and press Spacebar.

8 Press Ctrl + End to place the insertion point after the letter *s* in *Notes*, and then press Enter one time. With the insertion point blinking, type the following and include the spelling error:
Exective Chef, Madison Dunham

9 With your mouse, point slightly to the left of the *M* in *Madison*, hold down the left mouse button, and then ***drag***—hold down the left mouse button while moving your mouse—to the right to select the text *Madison Dunham* but not the paragraph mark following it, and then release the mouse button. Compare your screen with Figure 1.6.

The ***mini toolbar*** displays commands that are commonly used with the selected object, which places common commands close to your pointer. When you move the pointer away from the mini toolbar, it fades from view.

Selecting refers to highlighting—by dragging or clicking with your mouse—areas of text or data or graphics so that the selection can be edited, formatted, copied, or moved. The action of dragging includes releasing the left mouse button at the end of the area you want to select.

The Office programs recognize a selected area as one unit to which you can make changes. Selecting text may require some practice. If you are not satisfied with your result, click anywhere outside of the selection, and then begin again.

BY TOUCH Double-tap on *Madison* to display the gripper—a small circle that acts as a handle—directly below the word. This establishes the start gripper. If necessary, with your finger, drag the gripper to the beginning of the word. Then drag the gripper to the end of *Dunham* to select the text and display the end gripper.

FIGURE 1.6

10 With the text *Madison Dunham* selected, type **Sarah Jackson**

> In any Windows-based program, such as the Microsoft Office 2016 programs, selected text is deleted and then replaced when you begin to type new text. You will save time by developing good techniques for selecting and then editing or replacing selected text, which is easier than pressing the [Del] key numerous times to delete text.

Activity 1.03 | Checking Spelling

Office 2016 has a dictionary of words against which all entered text is checked. In Word and PowerPoint, words that are not in the dictionary display a wavy red line, indicating a possible misspelled word, a proper name, or an unusual word—none of which are in the Office 2016 dictionary.

In Excel and Access, you can initiate a check of the spelling, but red underlines do not display.

1 Notice that the misspelled word *Exective* displays with a wavy red underline.

2 Point to *Exective* and then **right-click**—click your right mouse button one time.

> A **shortcut menu** displays, which displays commands and options relevant to the selected text or object. These are **context-sensitive commands** because they relate to the item you right-clicked. These shortcut menus are also referred to as **context menus**. Here, the shortcut menu displays commands related to the misspelled word.

🔄 **BY TOUCH** Tap and hold a moment—when a square displays around the misspelled word, release your finger to display the shortcut menu.

3 Press [Esc] to cancel the shortcut menu, and then in the lower left corner of your screen, on the status bar, click the **Proofing** icon 📖, which displays an *X* because some errors are detected. Compare your screen with Figure 1.7.

> The Spelling pane displays on the right. Here you have many more options for checking spelling than you have on the shortcut menu. The suggested correct word, *Executive*, is highlighted.

> You can click the speaker icon to hear the pronunciation of the selected word. If you have not already installed a dictionary, you can click *Get a Dictionary*—if you are signed in to Office with a Microsoft account—to find and install one from the online Office store; or if you have a dictionary app installed, it will display here and you can search it for more information.

> In the Spelling pane, you can ignore the word one time or in all occurrences, change the word to the suggested word, select a different suggestion, or add a word to the dictionary against which Word checks.

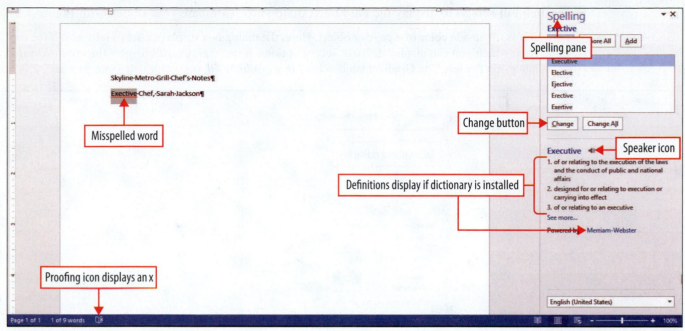

FIGURE 1.7

Word 2016, Windows 10, Microsoft Corporation

 ANOTHER WAY Press `F7` to display the Spelling pane; or, on the Review tab, in the Proofing group, click Spelling & Grammar.

4 In the *Spelling* pane, click **Change** to change the spelling to *Executive*. In the message box that displays, click **OK**.

Objective 3 | Perform Commands from a Dialog Box

In a dialog box, you make decisions about an individual object or topic. In some dialog boxes, you can make multiple decisions in one place.

GO! Learn How
Video OF1.3

Activity 1.04 | Performing Commands from a Dialog Box

MOS
1.3.6

1 On the ribbon, click the **Design tab**, and then in the **Page Background group**, click **Page Color**.

2 At the bottom of the menu, notice the command *Fill Effects* followed by an **ellipsis** (…). Compare your screen with Figure 1.8.

An *ellipsis* is a set of three dots indicating incompleteness. An ellipsis following a command name indicates that a dialog box will display when you click the command.

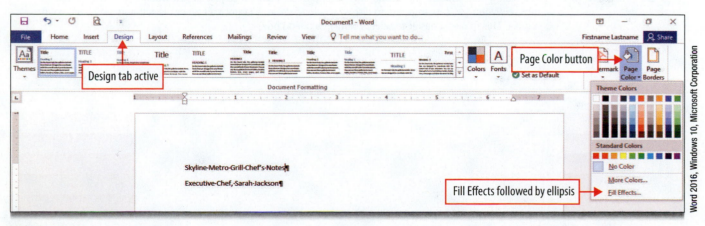

FIGURE 1.08

Word 2016, Windows 10, Microsoft Corporation

3 Click **Fill Effects** to display the **Fill Effects** dialog box. Compare your screen with Figure 1.9.

Fill is the inside color of a page or object. Here, the dialog box displays a set of tabs across the top from which you can display different sets of options. Some dialog boxes display the option group names on the left. The Gradient tab is active. In a *gradient fill*, one color fades into another.

FIGURE 1.9

4 Under **Colors**, click the **One color** option button.

The dialog box displays settings related to the One color option. An *option button* is a round button that enables you to make one choice among two or more options.

5 Click the **Color 1 arrow**—the arrow under the text *Color 1*—and then in the third column, point to the second color to display the ScreenTip *Gray-25%, Background 2, Darker 10%*.

When you click an arrow in a dialog box, additional options display. A *ScreenTip* displays useful information about mouse actions, such as pointing to screen elements or dragging.

6 Click **Gray-25%, Background 2, Darker 10%**, and then notice that the fill color displays in the **Color 1** box. In the **Dark Light** bar, click the **Light arrow** as many times as necessary until the scroll box is all the way to the right. Under **Shading styles**, click the **Diagonal down** option button. Under **Variants**, click the **upper right variant**. Compare your screen with Figure 1.10.

This dialog box is a good example of the many different elements you may encounter in a dialog box. Here you have option buttons, an arrow that displays a menu, a slider bar, and graphic options that you can select.

🔄 BY TOUCH In a dialog box, you can tap option buttons and other commands just as you would click them with a mouse. When you tap an arrow to display a color palette, a larger palette displays than if you used your mouse. This makes it easier to select colors in a dialog box.

FIGURE 1.10

7 ▶ At the bottom of the dialog box, click **OK**, and notice the subtle page color.

In Word, the gray shading page color will not print—even on a color printer—unless you set specific options to do so. However, a subtle background page color is effective if people will be reading the document on a screen. Microsoft's research indicates that two-thirds of people who open Word documents on a screen never print them; they only read them.

MOS

2.2.6

Activity 1.05 │ Using Undo and Applying a Built-In Style to Text

1 ▶ Point to the *S* in *Skyline*, and then drag down and to the right to select both paragraphs of text and include the paragraph marks. On the mini toolbar, click **Styles**, and then *point to* but do not click **Title**. Compare your screen with Figure 1.11.

A ***style*** is a group of ***formatting*** commands, such as font, font size, font color, paragraph alignment, and line spacing that can be applied to a paragraph with one command. Formatting is the process of establishing the overall appearance of text, graphics, and pages in an Office file— for example, in a Word document.

Live Preview is a technology that shows the result of applying an editing or formatting change as you point to possible results—before you actually apply it.

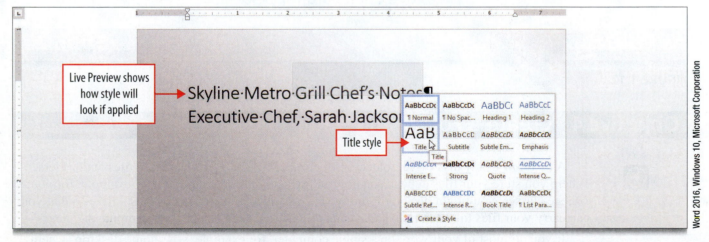

FIGURE 1.11

2 ▶ In the **Styles** gallery, click **Title**.

A ***gallery*** is an Office feature that displays a list of potential results.

3 On the ribbon, on the **Home tab**, in the **Paragraph group**, click **Center** to center the two paragraphs.

> *Alignment* refers to the placement of paragraph text relative to the left and right margins. *Center alignment* refers to text that is centered horizontally between the left and right margins. You can also align text at the left margin, which is the default alignment for text in Word, or at the right.

🔄 ANOTHER WAY   Press [Ctrl] + [E] as the keyboard shortcut for the Center command.

4 With the two paragraphs still selected, on the **Home tab**, in the **Font group**, click **Text Effects and Typography** to display a gallery.

5 In the second row, click the first effect—**Gradient Fill – Gray**. Click anywhere to *deselect*—cancel the selection—the text and notice the text effect.

6 Because this effect might be difficult to read, in the upper left corner of your screen, on the *Quick Access Toolbar*, click **Undo**.

> The *Undo* command reverses your last action.

🔄 ANOTHER WAY   Press [Ctrl] + [Z] as the keyboard shortcut for the Undo command.

7 With all of the text still selected, display the **Text Effects and Typography** gallery again, and then in the second row, click the second effect—**Gradient Fill – Blue, Accent 1, Reflection**. Click anywhere to deselect the text and notice the text effect. Compare your screen with Figure 1.12.

> As you progress in your study of Microsoft Office, you will practice using many dialog boxes and commands to apply interesting effects such as this to your Word documents, Excel worksheets, Access database objects, and PowerPoint slides.

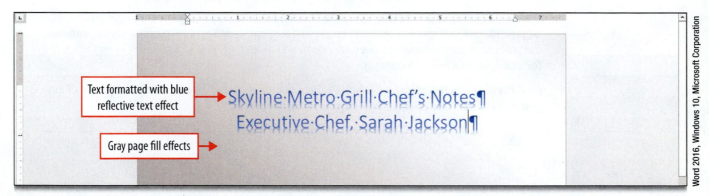

FIGURE 1.12

Objective 4   Create a Folder and Name and Save a File

GO! Learn How
Video OF1.5

A *location* is any disk drive, folder, or other place in which you can store files and folders. Where you store your files depends on how and where you use your data. For example, for your college classes, you might decide to store your work on a removable USB flash drive so that you can carry your files to different locations and access your files on different computers.

If you do most of your work on a single computer, for example, your home desktop system or your laptop computer that you take with you to school or work, then you can store your files in one of the folders—Documents, Music, Pictures, or Videos—on your hard drive provided by your Windows operating system.

The best place to store files if you want them to be available anytime, anywhere, from almost any device is on your **OneDrive**, which is Microsoft's free **cloud storage** for anyone with a free Microsoft account. Cloud storage refers to online storage of data so that you can access your data from different places and devices. **Cloud computing** refers to applications and services that are accessed over the Internet, rather than accessing applications installed on your local computer.

If you have an **Office 365** account—one of the versions of Microsoft Office to which you subscribe for an annual fee—your storage capacity on OneDrive is a terabyte or more, which is more than most individuals would ever require.

Because many people now have multiple computing devices—desktop, laptop, tablet, smartphone—it is common to store data *in the cloud* so that it is always available. **Synchronization**, also called **syncing**—pronounced SINK-ing—is the process of updating computer files that are in two or more locations according to specific rules. So if you create and save a Word document on your OneDrive using your laptop, you can open and edit that document on your tablet in OneDrive. When you close the document again, the file is properly updated to reflect your changes. Your OneDrive account will guide you in setting options for syncing files to your specifications.

You need not be connected to the Internet to access documents stored on OneDrive because an up-to-date version of your content is synched to your local system and available on OneDrive. You must, however, be connected to the Internet for the syncing to occur. Saving to OneDrive will keep the local copy on your computer and the copy in the cloud synchronized for as long as you need it. You can open and edit Office files by using Office apps available on a variety of device platforms, including iOS, Android, and Windows.

The Windows operating system helps you to create and maintain a logical folder structure, so always take the time to name your files and folders consistently.

Activity 1.06 | Creating a Folder and Naming and Saving a File

A Word document is an example of a file. In this Activity, you will create a folder in the storage location you have chosen to use for your files and then save your file. This example will use the Documents folder on the PC at which you are working. If you prefer to store on your OneDrive or on a USB flash drive, you can use similar steps.

1 Decide where you are going to store your files for this Project.

As the first step in saving a file, determine where you want to save the file, and if necessary, insert a storage device.

2 At the top of your screen, in the title bar, notice that *Document1 – Word* displays.

The Blank option on the opening screen of an Office 2016 program displays a new unsaved file with a default name— *Document1, Presentation1*, and so on. As you create your file, your work is temporarily stored in the computer's memory until you initiate a Save command, at which time you must choose a file name and a location in which to save your file.

3 In the upper left corner of your screen, click the **File tab** to display **Backstage** view. Compare your screen with Figure 1.13.

Backstage view is a centralized space that groups commands related to *file* management; that is why the tab is labeled *File*. File management commands include opening, saving, printing, publishing, or sharing a file. The **Backstage tabs**—*Info*, *New*, *Open*, *Save*, *Save As*, *Print*, *Share*, *Export*, and *Close*—display along the left side. The tabs group file-related tasks together.

Here, the **Info tab** displays information—*info*—about the current file, and file management commands display under Info. For example, if you click the Protect Document button, a list of options that you can set for this file that relate to who can open or edit the document displays.

On the right, you can also examine the **document properties**. Document properties, also known as **metadata**, are details about a file that describe or identify it, such as the title, author name, subject, and keywords that identify the document's topic or contents. To close Backstage view and return to the document, you can click ⊖ in the upper left corner or press Esc.

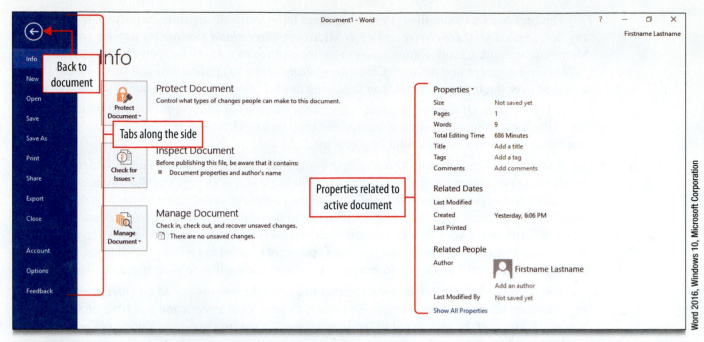

FIGURE 1.13

4 On the left, click **Save As**, and notice that the default location for storing Office files is your **OneDrive**—if you are signed in. Compare your screen with Figure 1.14.

When you are saving something for the first time, for example, a new Word document, the Save and Save As commands are identical. That is, the Save As commands will display if you click Save or if you click Save As.

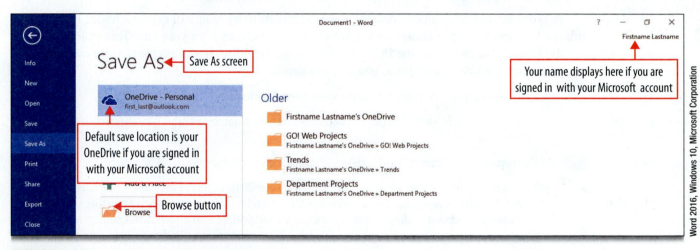

FIGURE 1.14

NOTE   Saving After Your File Is Named

After you name and save a file, the Save command on the Quick Access Toolbar saves any changes you make to the file without displaying Backstage view. The Save As command enables you to name and save a *new* file based on the current one—in a location that you choose. After you name and save the new document, the original document closes, and the new document—based on the original one—displays.

---

5 To store your Word file in the **Documents** folder on your PC, click **Browse** to display the **Save As** dialog box. On the left, in the **navigation pane**, scroll down; if necessary click > to expand This PC, and then click **Documents**, or navigate to your USB flash drive or other location. In a college lab, your work may be lost if you store in the Documents folder. Compare your screen with Figure 1.15.

In the Save As dialog box, you must indicate the name you want for the file and the location where you want to save the file. When working with your own data, it is good practice to pause at this point and determine the logical name and location for your file.

In the Save As dialog box, a *toolbar* displays, which is a row, column, or block of buttons or icons, that displays across the top of a window and that contains commands for tasks you perform with a single click.

FIGURE 1.15

6 On the toolbar, click **New folder**.

In the file list, Windows creates a new folder, and the text *New folder* is selected.

7 Type **Office Features Chapter 1** and press Enter. Compare your screen with Figure 1.16.

In Windows-based programs, the Enter key confirms an action.

FIGURE 1.16

8 In the **file list**, double-click the name of your new folder to open it and display its name in the **address bar**.

9 In the lower portion of the dialog box, click in the **File name** box to select the existing text. Notice that as the suggested file name, Office inserts the text at the beginning of the document.

10 On your keyboard, locate the [-] key, to the right of zero on the number row. Notice that the [Shift] of this key produces the underscore character. With the text still selected and using your own name, type **Lastname_Firstname_1A_Note_Form** Compare your screen with Figure 1.17.

> You can use spaces in file names, however, some people prefer not to use spaces. Some programs, especially when transferring files over the Internet, may insert the extra characters *%20* in place of a space. In general, however, unless you encounter a problem, it is OK to use spaces. In this instruction, underscores are used instead of spaces in file names.

FIGURE 1.17

11 In the lower right corner, click **Save** or press [Enter]. Compare your screen with Figure 1.18.

> The Word window redisplays and your new file name displays in the title bar, indicating that the file has been saved to the location that you have specified.

FIGURE 1.18

12 In the first paragraph, click to place the insertion point after the word *Grill* and type **,** (a comma). In the upper left corner of your screen, on the **Quick Access Toolbar**, click **Save** 🖫.

> After a document is named and saved in a location, you can save any changes you have made since the last Save operation by using the Save command on the Quick Access Toolbar. When working on a document, it is good practice to save your changes from time to time.

GO! Learn How
Video OF1.5

MOS
1.3.4, 1.4.5

For most of your files, especially in a workplace setting, it is useful to add identifying information to help in finding files later. You might also want to print your file on paper or create an electronic printout. The process of printing a file is similar in all of the Office applications.

Activity 1.07 | Inserting a Footer, Inserting Document Info, and Adding Document Properties

> **NOTE** What Does Your Instructor Require for Submission? A Paper Printout, an Image That Looks Like a Printed Document, or Your Word File?
>
> In this Activity, you can produce a paper printout or an electronic image of your document that looks like a printed document. Or, your instructor may want only your completed Word file.

1 On the ribbon, click the **Insert tab**, and then in the **Header & Footer group**, click **Footer**.

2 At the bottom of the list, click **Edit Footer**. On the ribbon, notice that the **Header & Footer Tools** display.

The *Header & Footer Tools Design* tab displays on the ribbon. The ribbon adapts to your work and will display additional tabs like this one—referred to as **contextual tabs**—when you need them.

A *footer* is a reserved area for text or graphics that displays at the bottom of each page in a document. Likewise, a *header* is a reserved area for text or graphics that displays at the top of each page in a document. When the footer (or header) area is active, the document area is dimmed, indicating it is unavailable.

3 On the ribbon, under **Header & Footer Tools**, on the **Design tab**, in the **Insert group**, click **Document Info**, and then click **File Name** to insert the name of your file in the footer, which is a common business practice. Compare your screen with Figure 1.19.

Ribbon commands that display ▼ will, when clicked, display a list of options for the command.

FIGURE 1.19

Project 1A: Note Form | Office   **17**

Word 2016, Windows 10, Microsoft Corporation

4 At the right end of the ribbon, click **Close Header and Footer**.

🔄 **ANOTHER WAY**   Double-click anywhere in the dimmed document to close the footer.

5 Click the **File tab** to display **Backstage** view. On the right, at the bottom of the **Properties** list, click **Show All Properties**.

🔄 **ANOTHER WAY**   Click the arrow to the right of Properties, and then click Advanced Properties to show and edit properties at the top of your document window.

6 On the list of **Properties**, click to the right of *Tags* to display an empty box, and then type **chef, notes, form**

> *Tags*, also referred to as *keywords*, are custom file properties in the form of words that you associate with a document to give an indication of the document's content. Adding tags to your documents makes it easier to search for and locate files in File Explorer, on your OneDrive, and in systems such as Microsoft *SharePoint* document libraries. SharePoint is collaboration software with which people in an organization can set up team sites to share information, manage documents, and publish reports for others to see.

🔄 **BY TOUCH**   Tap to the right of Tags to display the Tags box and the onscreen keyboard.

7 Click to the right of *Subject* to display an empty box, and then type your course name and section #; for example, *CIS 10, #5543*.

8 Under **Related People**, be sure that your name displays as the author. If necessary, right-click the author name, click Edit Property, type your name, click outside of the Edit person dialog box, and then click OK. Compare your screen with Figure 1.20.

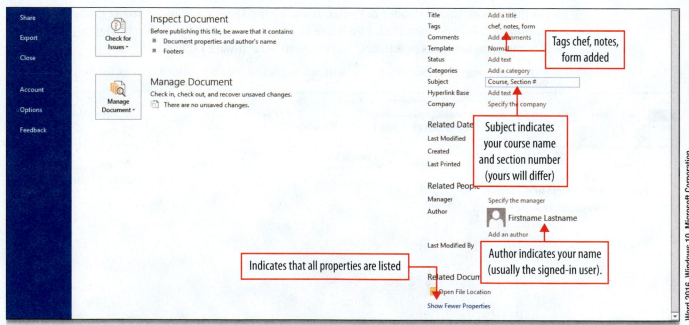

FIGURE 1.20

Activity 1.08 | Printing a File and Closing a Desktop App

1 In **Backstage** view, in the upper left corner, click **Back** ⊙ to return to the Word window. On the **Design tab**, in the **Page Background group**, click **Page Color**, and then click **No Color** to remove the fill effects.

> It's easy to remove formatting from your documents if you change your mind about how you want your document to look.

2 ▶ Click the **File tab** to return to **Backstage** view, on the left click **Print**, and then compare your screen with Figure 1.21.

Here you can select any printer connected to your system and adjust the settings related to how you want to print. On the right, the *Print Preview* displays, which is a view of a document as it will appear on paper when you print it.

At the bottom of the Print Preview area, in the center, the number of pages and page navigation arrows with which you can move among the pages in Print Preview display. On the right, the Zoom slider enables you to shrink or enlarge the Print Preview. *Zoom* is the action of increasing or decreasing the viewing area of the screen.

 ANOTHER WAY   From the document screen, press Ctrl + P or Ctrl + F2 to display Print in Backstage view.

FIGURE 1.21

3 ▶ To create an electronic image of your document that looks like a printed document, skip this step and continue to Step 4. To print your document on paper using the default printer on your system, in the upper left portion of the screen, click **Print**.

The document will print on your default printer; if you do not have a color printer, the blue text will print in shades of gray. Backstage view closes and your file redisplays in the Word window.

4 ▶ To create an electronic image of your document that looks like a printed document, in **Backstage** view, on the left click **Export**. On the right, click the **Create PDF/XPS** button to display the **Publish as PDF or XPS** dialog box.

PDF stands for *Portable Document Format*, which is a technology that creates an image that preserves the look of your file. This is a popular format for sending documents electronically, because the document will display on most computers.

XPS stands for *XML Paper Specification*—a Microsoft file format that also creates an image of your document and that opens in the XPS viewer.

5 On the left in the **navigation pane**, if necessary expand > This PC, and then navigate to your **Office Features Chapter 1** folder in your **Documents** folder—or in whatever location you have created your Office Features Chapter 1 folder. Compare your screen with Figure 1.22.

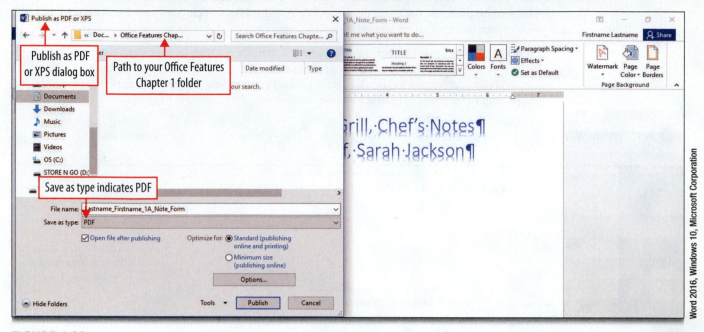

FIGURE 1.22

6 In the lower right corner of the dialog box, click **Publish**; if a program installed on your computer displays your PDF, in the upper right corner, click Close ⊠. If your PDF displays in Microsoft Edge (on a Windows 10 computer), in the upper right corner click Close ⊠. Notice that your document redisplays in Word.

🔄 **ANOTHER WAY**   In Backstage view, click Save As, navigate to the location of your Chapter folder, click the Save as type arrow, on the list click PDF, and then click Save.

7 Click the **File tab** to redisplay **Backstage** view. On the left, click **Close**, click **Save** to save the changes you have made, and then compare your screen with Figure 1.23.

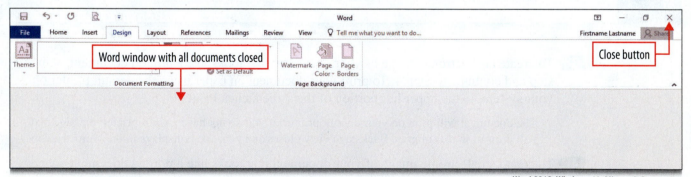

FIGURE 1.23   Word 2016, Windows 10, Microsoft Corporation

8 In the upper right corner of the Word window, click **Close** ⊠. If directed by your instructor to do so, submit your paper printout, your electronic image of your document that looks like a printed document, or your original Word file.

> **END | You have completed Project 1A**

PROJECT ACTIVITIES

In Activities 1.09 through 1.24, you will open, edit, and then compress a Word file. You will also use the Tell Me help feature and install an app for Office. Your completed document will look similar to Figure 1.24.

PROJECT FILES

MyITLab
grader

If your instructor wants you to submit Project 1B in the MyITLab Grader system, log in to MyITLab, locate Grader Project1B, and then download the files for this project.

For Project 1B, you will need the following file:

of01B_Rehearsal_Dinner

You will save your file as:

Lastname_Firstname_1B_Rehearsal_Dinner

PROJECT RESULTS

GO!
Walk Thru
ect 1B

Skyline Metro Grill

TO:	Sarah Jackson, Executive Chef
FROM:	Laura Mabry Hernandez, General Manager
DATE:	February 17, 2019
SUBJECT:	Wedding Rehearsal Dinners

In the spring and summer months, wedding rehearsal dinners provide a new marketing opportunity for Skyline Metro Grill at all of our locations. A rehearsal dinner is an informal meal following a wedding rehearsal at which the bride and groom typically thank those that have helped them make their wedding a special event.

Our smaller private dining rooms with sweeping city views are an ideal location for a rehearsal dinner. At each of our locations, I have directed the Sales and Marketing Coordinator to partner with local wedding planners to promote Skyline Metro Grill as a relaxed yet sophisticated venue for rehearsal dinners. The typical rehearsal dinner includes the wedding party, the immediate family of the bride and groom, and out-of-town guests.

Please develop six menus—in varying price ranges—to present to local wedding planners so that they can easily promote Skyline Metro Grill to couples who are planning a rehearsal dinner. In addition to a traditional dinner, we should also include options for a buffet-style dinner and a family-style dinner.

This marketing effort will require extensive communication with our Sales and Marketing Coordinators and with local wedding planners. Let's meet to discuss the details and the marketing challenges, and to create a promotional piece that begins something like this:

Skyline Metro Grill for Your Rehearsal Dinner

Lastname_Firstname_1B_Rehearsal_Dinner

Word 2016, Windows 10, Microsoft Corporation

FIGURE 1.24 Project 1B Memo

GO! Learn How
Video OF1.6

In any Office program, you can display the *Open dialog box*, from which you can navigate to and then open an existing file that was created in that same program.

The Open dialog box, along with the Save and Save As dialog boxes, is a common dialog box. These dialog boxes, which are provided by the Windows programming interface, display in all Office programs in the same manner. So the Open, Save, and Save As dialog boxes will all look and perform the same regardless of the Office program in which you are working.

ALERT! **To Complete This Project, You Will Need the Student Data Files That Accompany This Chapter**

To complete this project, you will need the Student Data Files that accompany this chapter. Possibly your instructor has provided these to you already; for example, in the learning management system used by your college. Alternatively, to download the files, go to **www.pearsonhighered.com/go** On the left, narrow your choice by selecting the appropriate topic, and then on the right, locate and click the image of this book. In the window that displays, click Download Data Files, and then click the chapter name. Using the commands for your browser, store the zipped file in your storage location, and then use the Extract tools in File Explorer to extract the zipped folder. Instructions for extracting can be found in the Getting Started with Windows 10 chapter.

Activity 1.09 | Opening an Existing File and Saving It with a New Name

In this Activity, you will display the Open dialog box, open an existing Word document, and then save it in your storage location with a new name.

ALERT! **To submit as an autograded project, log into MyITLab, download the files for this project, and begin with those files instead of the student data file.**

1 Be sure you have saved the folder **of01_student_data_files** for this chapter in your storage location; you can download this folder from **www.pearsonhighered.com/go** or it may have been provided to you by your instructor.

2 Start Word, and then on Word's opening screen, on the left, click **Open Other Documents**. Under **Open**, click **Browse**.

3 In the **Open** dialog box, on the left in the **navigation pane**, navigate to the location where you stored the **of01_student_data_files** folder for this chapter, and then in the **file list**, double-click the folder name **of01_student_data_files** to open the folder.

4 In the **file list**, double-click the file **of01B_Rehearsal_Dinner** to open it in Word. If **PROTECTED VIEW** displays at the top of your screen, in the center click **Enable Editing**.

In Office 2016, a file will open in *Protected View* if the file appears to be from a potentially risky location, such as the Internet. Protected View is a security feature in Office 2016 that protects your computer from malicious files by opening them in a restricted environment until you enable them. *Trusted Documents* is another security feature that remembers which files you have already enabled.

You might encounter these security features if you open a file from an email or download files from the Internet; for example, from your college's learning management system or from the Pearson website. So long as you trust the source of the file, click Enable Editing or Enable Content—depending on the type of file you receive—and then go ahead and work with the file.

5 With the document displayed in the Word window, be sure that **Show/Hide** is active; if necessary, on the Home tab, in the Paragraph group, click Show/Hide to activate it; on the View tab, be sure that Rulers are active. Compare your screen with Figure 1.25.

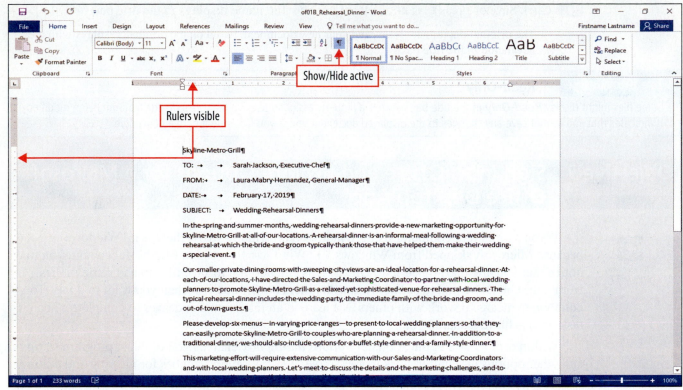

FIGURE 1.25

Word 2016, Windows 10, Microsoft Corporation

6 Click the **File tab** to display **Backstage** view, and then on the left, click **Save As**. Under **Save As**, click **Browse**.

7 In the **Save As** dialog box, use the **navigation pane** to navigate to and open the **Office Features Chapter 1** folder that you created to store your work from this chapter.

> In Backstage view, on the right, you might also see your Office Features Chapter 1 folder listed, and if so, you can open it directly from there. The common dialog boxes Open, Save, and Save As remember your recently used locations and display them in Backstage view.

ANOTHER WAY From the Word window, press F12 to display the Save As dialog box.

8 Click in the **File name** box to select the existing text, and then, using your own name, type **Lastname_Firstname_1B_Rehearsal_Dinner** Compare your screen with Figure 1.26.

FIGURE 1.26

Word 2016, Windows 10, Microsoft Corporation

9 Click **Save** or press Enter; notice that your new file name displays in the title bar.

The original document closes, and your new document, based on the original, displays with the new name in the title bar.

> **More Knowledge** | **Read-Only**
>
> Some files might display **Read-Only** in the title bar, which is a property assigned to a file that prevents the file from being modified; it indicates that you cannot save any changes to the displayed document unless you first save it with a new name.

Objective 7 | Sign In to Office and Explore Options for a Microsoft Office Desktop App

GO! Learn How
Video OF1.7

If you sign in to a computer using Windows 8 or Windows 10—there is no Windows 9, because Microsoft skipped from Windows 8 to Windows 10—with a Microsoft account, you may notice that you are also signed in to Office. This enables you to save files to and retrieve files from your OneDrive and to *collaborate* with others on Office files when you want to do so. To collaborate means to work with others as a team in an intellectual endeavor to complete a shared task or to achieve a shared goal.

Within each Office application, an *Options dialog box* enables you to select program settings and other options and preferences. For example, you can set preferences for viewing and editing files.

Activity 1.10 | Signing In to Office and Viewing Application Options

1 In the upper right corner of your screen, if you are signed in with a Microsoft account, click your name, and then compare your screen with Figure 1.27.

Here you can change your photo, go to About me to edit your profile, examine your Account settings, or switch accounts to sign in with a different Microsoft account.

> **A L E R T !** | **Not Signed In to Office or Have Not Yet Created a Microsoft Account?**
>
> In the upper right corner, click Sign in, and then enter your Microsoft account. If you have not created a free Microsoft account, click Sign in, type any email address that you currently use, click Next, and then click Sign up now. If you are working in a college lab, this process may vary.

FIGURE 1.27

2 Click the **File tab** to display **Backstage** view. On the left, click **Options**.

3 In the **Word Options** dialog box, on the left, click **Display**, and then on the right, locate the information under **Always show these formatting marks on the screen**.

> The Word Options dialog box—or the similar Options dialog box in any of the Office applications—controls nearly every aspect of the application. Next to many of the items, you will see small *i* icons, which when you point to them display a ScreenTip.

> If you click each of the categories on the left side of the dialog box, you will see that the scope of each application is quite large and that you have a great deal of control over how the application behaves. For example, you can customize the tab names and group names in the ribbon.

> If you are not sure what a setting or option does, in the upper right corner of the title bar, click the Help button—the question mark icon.

4 Under **Always show these formatting marks on the screen**, be sure the last check box, **Show all formatting marks**, is selected—select it if necessary. Compare your screen with Figure 1.28.

FIGURE 1.28

5 In the lower right corner of the dialog box, click **OK**.

Objective 8 Perform Commands from the Ribbon and Quick Access Toolbar

GO! Learn How
Video OF1.8

The ribbon that displays across the top of the program window groups commands in the way that you would most logically use them. The ribbon in each Office program is slightly different, but all contain the same three elements: *tabs*, *groups*, and *commands*.

Tabs display across the top of the ribbon, and each tab relates to a type of activity; for example, laying out a page. Groups are sets of related commands for specific tasks. Commands—instructions to computer programs—are arranged in groups and might display as a button, a menu, or a box in which you type information.

You can also minimize the ribbon so only the tab names display, which is useful when working on a smaller screen such as a tablet computer where you want to maximize your screen viewing area.

Activity 1.11 | **Performing Commands from and Customizing the Quick Access Toolbar**

1.4.3

1 Take a moment to examine the document on your screen. If necessary, on the ribbon, click the View tab, and then in the Show group, click to place a check mark in the Ruler check box. Compare your screen with Figure 1.29.

This document is a memo from the General Manager to the Executive Chef regarding a new restaurant promotion for wedding rehearsal dinners.

When working in Word, display the rulers so that you can see how margin settings affect your document and how text and objects align. Additionally, if you set a tab stop or an indent, its location is visible on the ruler.

FIGURE 1.29

2 In the upper left corner of your screen, above the ribbon, locate the **Quick Access Toolbar**.

Recall that the Quick Access Toolbar contains commands that you use frequently. By default, only the commands Save, Undo, and Redo display, but you can add and delete commands to suit your needs. Possibly the computer at which you are working already has additional commands added to the Quick Access Toolbar.

3 At the end of the **Quick Access Toolbar**, click the **Customize Quick Access Toolbar** button [▼], and then compare your screen with Figure 1.30.

A list of commands that Office users commonly add to their Quick Access Toolbar displays, including New, Open, Email, Quick Print, and Print Preview and Print. Commands already on the Quick Access Toolbar display a check mark. Commands that you add to the Quick Access Toolbar are always just one click away.

Here you can also display the More Commands dialog box, from which you can select any command from any tab to add to the Quick Access Toolbar.

 BY TOUCH   Tap once on Quick Access Toolbar commands.

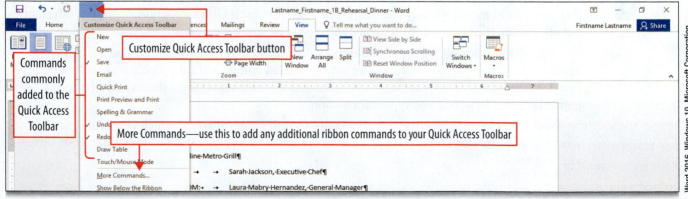

FIGURE 1.30

4 On the list, click **Print Preview and Print**, and then notice that the icon is added to the **Quick Access Toolbar**. Compare your screen with Figure 1.31.

The icon that represents the Print Preview command displays on the Quick Access Toolbar. Because this is a command that you will use frequently while building Office documents, you might decide to have this command remain on your Quick Access Toolbar.

⟳ **ANOTHER WAY**   Right-click any command on the ribbon, and then on the shortcut menu, click Add to Quick Access Toolbar.

Icon for Print Preview and Print added to Quick Access Toolbar

FIGURE 1.31   Word 2016, Windows 10, Microsoft Corporation

MOS
5.2.5

Activity 1.12 | Performing Commands from the Ribbon

1 In the first line of the document, if necessary, click to the left of the *S* in *Skyline* to position the insertion point there, and then press Enter one time to insert a blank paragraph. Press ↑ one time to position the insertion point in the new blank paragraph. Compare your screen with Figure 1.32.

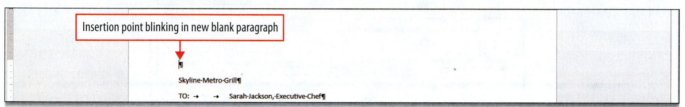

Insertion point blinking in new blank paragraph

Skyline·Metro·Grill¶

TO: →   →   Sarah·Jackson,·Executive·Chef¶

FIGURE 1.32   Word 2016, Windows 10, Microsoft Corporation

2 On the ribbon, click the **Insert tab**. In the **Illustrations group**, *point* to **Online Pictures** to display its ScreenTip.

Many buttons on the ribbon have this type of *enhanced ScreenTip*, which displays useful descriptive information about the command.

3 Click **Online Pictures**, and then compare your screen with Figure 1.33.

In the Insert Pictures dialog box, you can search for online pictures using Bing Image Search, and, if you are signed in with your Microsoft account, you can also find images on your OneDrive by clicking Browse. At the bottom, you can click a logo to download pictures from your Facebook and other types of accounts if you have them.

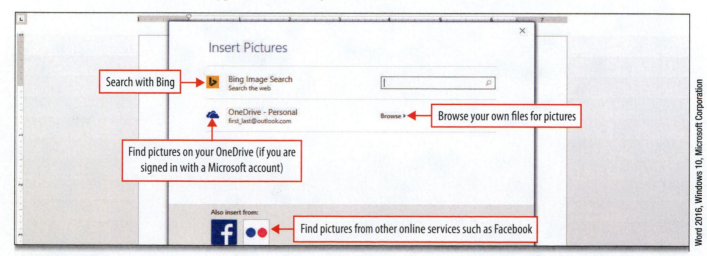

Search with Bing

Browse your own files for pictures

Find pictures on your OneDrive (if you are signed in with a Microsoft account)

Find pictures from other online services such as Facebook

FIGURE 1.33

4 ▸ With the insertion point positioned in the **Bing Image Search** box, type **salad** and press ⏎. Point to any of the results, and notice that keywords display. Compare your screen with Figure 1.34.

You can use various keywords to find images that are appropriate for your documents. The results shown indicate the images are licensed under *Creative Commons*, which, according to **www.creativecommons.org** is "a nonprofit organization that enables the sharing and use of creativity and knowledge through free legal tools."

Creative Commons helps people share and use their photographs, but does not allow companies to sell them. For your college assignments, you can use these images so long as you are not profiting by selling the photographs.

To find out more about Creative Commons, go to **https://creativecommons.org/about** and watch the video.

FIGURE 1.34

5 ▸ Locate an attractive picture of a salad on a plate or in a bowl that has a horizontal orientation—the picture is wider than it is tall—and then click that picture to select it. In the lower right corner, click **Insert**. In the upper right corner of the picture, point to the **Layout Options** button to display its ScreenTip, and then compare your screen with Figure 1.35.

Layout Options enable you to choose how the *object*—in this instance an inserted picture—interacts with the surrounding text. An object is a picture or other graphic such as a chart or table that you can select and then move and resize.

When a picture is selected, the Picture Tools become available on the ribbon. Additionally, *sizing handles*—small circles or squares that indicate an object is selected—surround the selected picture.

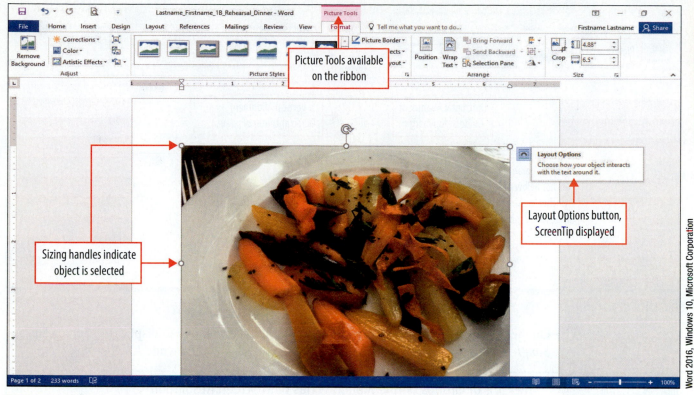

Picture Tools available on the ribbon

Sizing handles indicate object is selected

Layout Options
Choose how your object interacts with the text around it.

Layout Options button, ScreenTip displayed

Word 2016, Windows 10, Microsoft Corporation

FIGURE 1.35

6 ▶ With the image selected, click **Layout Options** 🖼, and then under **With Text Wrapping**, in the second row, click the first layout—**Top and Bottom**.

7 ▶ On the ribbon, with the **Picture Tools Format tab** active, at the right, in the **Size group**, click in the **Shape Height** box to select the existing text. Type **2** and press Enter.

8 ▶ Point to the image to display the pointer, hold down the left mouse button to display a green line at the left margin, and then drag the image to the right and slightly upward until a green line displays in the center of the image and at the top of the image, as shown in Figure 1.36, and then release the left mouse button. If you are not satisfied with your result, on the Quick Access Toolbar, click Undo 🔄 and begin again.

Alignment guides are green lines that display to help you align objects with margins or at the center of a page.

Inserted pictures anchor—attach to—the paragraph at the insertion point location—as indicated by an anchor symbol.

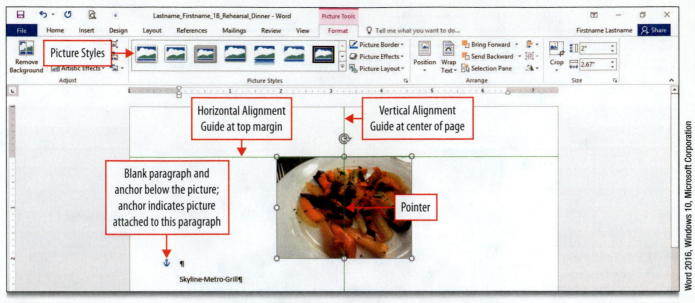

FIGURE 1.36

Word 2016, Windows 10, Microsoft Corporation

9 On the ribbon, in the **Picture Styles group**, point to the first style to display the ScreenTip *Simple Frame, White,* and notice that the image displays with a white frame.

> **NOTE** The Size of Groups on the Ribbon Varies with Screen Resolution
>
> Your monitor's screen resolution might be set higher than the resolution used to capture the figures shown here. At a higher resolution, the ribbon expands some groups to show more commands than are available with a single click, such as those in the Picture Styles group. Or, the group expands to add descriptive text to some buttons, such as those in the Arrange group. Regardless of your screen resolution, all Office commands are available to you. In higher resolutions, you will have a more robust view of the ribbon commands.

10 Watch the image as you point to the second picture style, and then to the third, and then to the fourth.

Recall that Live Preview shows the result of applying an editing or formatting change as you point to possible results—*before* you actually apply it.

11 In the **Picture Styles group**, click the second style—**Beveled Matte, White**—and then click anywhere outside of the image to deselect it. Notice that the Picture Tools no longer display on the ribbon. Compare your screen with Figure 1.37.

Contextual tabs on the ribbon display only when you need them.

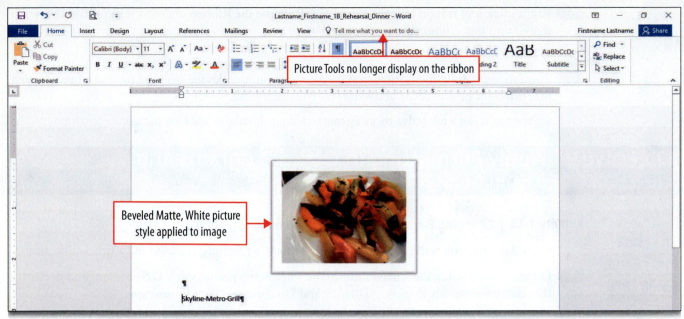

FIGURE 1.37

Word 2016, Windows 10, Microsoft Corporation

12 On the **Quick Access Toolbar**, click **Save** 🖫 to save the changes you have made.

Activity 1.13 | Minimizing the Ribbon and Using the Keyboard to Control the Ribbon

Instead of a mouse, some individuals prefer to navigate the ribbon by using keys on the keyboard.

1 On your keyboard, press Alt, and then on the ribbon, notice that small labels display on the tabs. Press N to activate the commands on the **Insert tab**, and then compare your screen with Figure 1.38.

Each label represents a *KeyTip*—an indication of the key that you can press to activate the command. For example, on the Insert tab, you can press F to open the Online Pictures dialog box.

FIGURE 1.38

Word 2016, Windows 10, Microsoft Corporation

2 Press Esc to redisplay the KeyTips for the tabs. Then, press Alt or Esc again to turn off keyboard control of the ribbon.

3 Point to any tab on the ribbon and right-click to display a shortcut menu.

Here you can choose to display the Quick Access Toolbar below the ribbon or collapse the ribbon to maximize screen space. You can also customize the ribbon by adding, removing, renaming, or reordering tabs, groups, and commands, although this is not recommended until you become an expert Word user.

4 Click **Collapse the Ribbon**. Notice that only the ribbon tabs display. Click the **Home tab** to display the commands. Click anywhere in the document, and notice that the ribbon goes back to the collapsed display.

5 Right-click any ribbon tab, and then click **Collapse the Ribbon** again to remove the check mark from this command.

> Most expert Office users prefer the full ribbon display.

6 Point to any tab on the ribbon, and then on your mouse device, roll the mouse wheel. Notice that different tabs become active as you roll the mouse wheel.

> You can make a tab active by using this technique, instead of clicking the tab.

Objective 9 Apply Formatting in Office Programs and Inspect Documents

GO! Learn How
Video OF1.9

MOS
1.4.2

Activity 1.14 | Changing Page Orientation and Zoom Level

In this Activity, you will practice common formatting techniques used in Office applications.

1 On the ribbon, click the **Layout tab**. In the **Page Setup group**, click **Orientation**, and notice that two orientations display—*Portrait* and *Landscape*. Click **Landscape**.

> In *portrait orientation*, the paper is taller than it is wide. In *landscape orientation*, the paper is wider than it is tall.

2 In the lower right corner of the screen, locate the **Zoom slider**.

> Recall that to zoom means to increase or decrease the viewing area. You can zoom in to look closely at a section of a document, and then zoom out to see an entire page on the screen. You can also zoom to view multiple pages on the screen.

3 Drag the **Zoom slider** to the left until you have zoomed to approximately *60%*. Compare your screen with Figure 1.39.

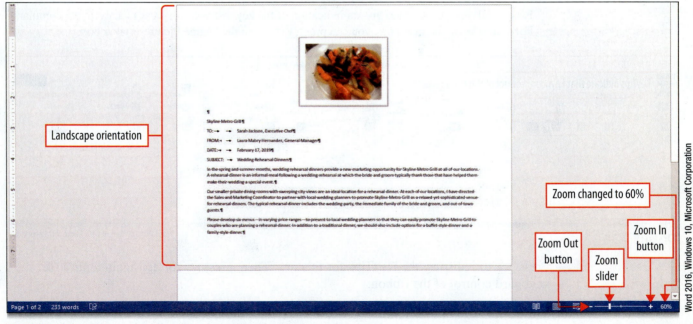

Landscape orientation

Zoom changed to 60%

Zoom Out button

Zoom slider

Zoom In button

Word 2016, Windows 10, Microsoft Corporation

FIGURE 1.39

🔄 **BY TOUCH**   Drag the Zoom slider with your finger.

4 Use the technique you just practiced to change the **Orientation** back to **Portrait**.

The default orientation in Word is Portrait, which is commonly used for business documents such as letters and memos.

5 In the lower right corner, click the **Zoom In** button ⊞ as many times as necessary to return to the **100%** zoom setting.

Use the zoom feature to adjust the view of your document for editing and for your viewing comfort.

> 🔄 **ANOTHER WAY**   You can also control Zoom from the ribbon. On the View tab, in the Zoom group, you can control the Zoom level and also zoom to view multiple pages.

6 On the **Quick Access Toolbar**, click **Save** 🖫.

More Knowledge   **Zooming to Page Width**

Some Office users prefer *Page Width*, which zooms the document so that the width of the page matches the width of the window. Find this command on the View tab, in the Zoom group.

Activity 1.15 | Formatting Text by Using Fonts, Alignment, Font Colors, and Font Styles

1 If necessary, on the right edge of your screen, drag the vertical scroll box to the top of the scroll bar. To the left of *Skyline Metro Grill*, point in the margin area to display the ⟰ pointer and click one time to select the entire paragraph. Compare your screen with Figure 1.40.

Use this technique to select complete paragraphs from the margin area—drag downward to select multiple-line paragraphs—which is faster and more efficient than dragging through text.

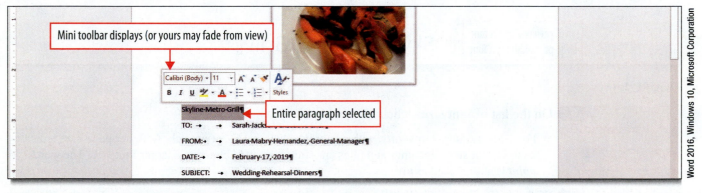

Mini toolbar displays (or yours may fade from view)

Entire paragraph selected

Word 2016, Windows 10, Microsoft Corporation

FIGURE 1.40

2 On the ribbon, click the **Home tab**, and then in the **Paragraph group**, click **Center** ▤ to center the paragraph.

3 On the **Home tab**, in the **Font group**, click the **Font button arrow** Calibri (Body) ▾. On the alphabetical list of font names, scroll down and then locate and *point to* **Cambria**.

A *font* is a set of characters with the same design and shape. The default font in a Word document is Calibri, which is a *sans serif font*—a font design with no lines or extensions on the ends of characters.

The Cambria font is a *serif font*—a font design that includes small line extensions on the ends of the letters to guide the eye in reading from left to right.

The list of fonts displays as a gallery showing potential results. For example, in the Font gallery, you can point to see the actual design and format of each font as it would look if applied to text.

4 ▶ Point to several other fonts and observe the effect on the selected text. Then, scroll back to the top of the **Font** gallery. Under **Theme Fonts**, click **Calibri Light**.

A *theme* is a predesigned combination of colors, fonts, line, and fill effects that look good together and is applied to an entire document by a single selection. A theme combines two sets of fonts— one for text and one for headings. In the default Office theme, Calibri Light is the suggested font for headings.

5 ▶ With the paragraph *Skyline Metro Grill* still selected, on the **Home tab**, in the **Font group**, click the **Font Size button arrow** ⊞ ⊟, point to **36**, and then notice how Live Preview displays the text in the font size to which you are pointing. Compare your screen with Figure 1.41.

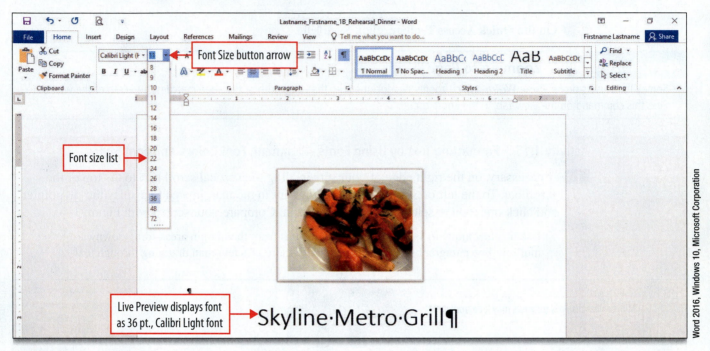

FIGURE 1.41

6 ▶ On the list of font sizes, click **20**.

Fonts are measured in *points*, with one point equal to 1/72 of an inch. A higher point size indicates a larger font size. Headings and titles are often formatted by using a larger font size. The word *point* is abbreviated as *pt*.

7 ▶ With *Skyline Metro Grill* still selected, on the **Home tab**, in the **Font group**, click the **Font Color button arrow** ⊞ ⊟. Under **Theme Colors**, in the last column, click the last color— **Green, Accent 6, Darker 50%**. Click anywhere to deselect the text.

8 ▶ To the left of *TO:*, point in the left margin area to display the ⊞ pointer, hold down the left mouse button, drag down to select the four memo headings, and then release your mouse button. Compare your screen with Figure 1.42.

Use this technique to select complete paragraphs from the margin area—drag downward to select multiple paragraphs—which is faster and more efficient than dragging through text.

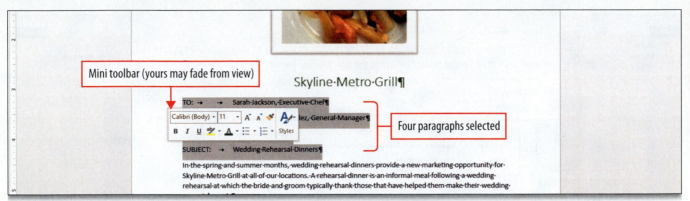

Mini toolbar (yours may fade from view)

Skyline·Metro·Grill¶

Four paragraphs selected

FIGURE 1.42

Word 2016, Windows 10, Microsoft Corporation

9 With the four paragraphs selected, on the mini toolbar, click the **Font Color** button [A], and notice that the text color of the four paragraphs changes.

> The font color button retains its most recently used color—Green, Accent 6, Darker 50%. As you progress in your study of Microsoft Office, you will use other commands that behave in this manner; that is, they retain their most recently used format. This is commonly referred to as *MRU*—most recently used.

> Recall that the mini toolbar places commands that are commonly used for the selected text or object close by so that you reduce the distance that you must move your mouse to access a command. If you are using a touch screen device, most commands that you need are close and easy to touch.

10 On the right edge of your screen, if necessary drag the vertical scroll box down slightly to position more of the text on the screen. Click anywhere in the paragraph that begins *In the spring*, and then *triple-click*—click the left mouse button three times—to select the entire paragraph. If the entire paragraph is not selected, click in the paragraph and begin again.

11 With the entire paragraph selected, on the mini toolbar, locate and then click the **Font Color button arrow** [A], and then under **Theme Colors**, in the sixth column, click the last color—**Orange, Accent 2, Darker 50%**.

12 In the memo headings, select the guide word **TO:** and then on the mini toolbar, click **Bold** [B] and **Italic** [I].

> *Font styles* include bold, italic, and underline. Font styles emphasize text and are a visual cue to draw the reader's eye to important text.

13 On the mini toolbar, click **Italic** [I] again to turn off the Italic formatting.

> A *toggle button* is a button that can be turned on by clicking it once, and then turned off by clicking it again.

2.2.2

Activity 1.16 | Using Format Painter

Use the Format Painter to copy the formatting of specific text or of a paragraph and then apply it in other locations in your document.

1 With TO: still selected, on the mini toolbar, click **Format Painter** [✔]. Then, move your mouse under the word *Sarah*, and notice the [I] mouse pointer. Compare your screen with Figure 1.43.

> The pointer takes the shape of a paintbrush, and contains the formatting information from the paragraph where the insertion point is positioned. Information about the Format Painter and how to turn it off displays in the status bar.

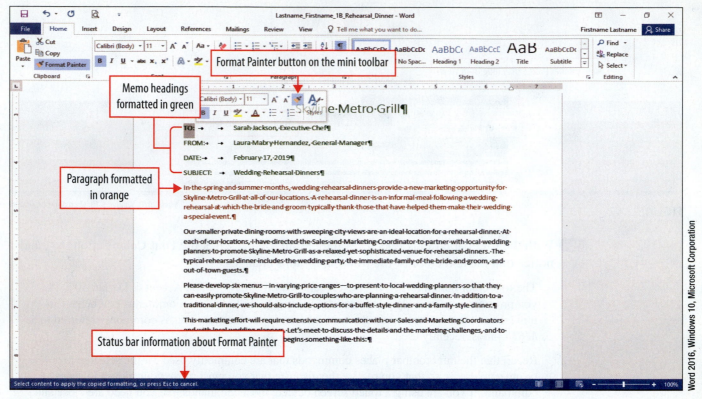

FIGURE 1.43

> 2 With the ⬛I pointer, drag to select the guide word **FROM:** and notice that Bold formatting is applied. Then, point to the selected text *FROM:* and on the mini toolbar, *double-click* **Format Painter** ⬛.

> 3 Select the guide word **DATE:** to copy the Bold formatting, and notice that the pointer retains the ⬛I shape.

When you *double-click* the Format Painter button, the Format Painter feature remains active until you either click the Format Painter button again, or press Esc to cancel it—as indicated on the status bar.

> 4 With **Format Painter** still active, select the guide word **SUBJECT:**, and then on the ribbon, on the **Home tab**, in the **Clipboard group**, notice that **Format Painter** ⬛ is selected, indicating that it is active. Compare your screen with Figure 1.44.

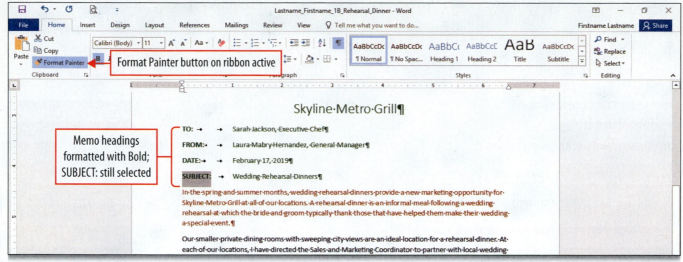

FIGURE 1.44

Word 2016, Windows 10, Microsoft Corporation

5 On the ribbon, click **Format Painter** to turn the command off.

🔄 **ANOTHER WAY**   Press Esc to turn off Format Painter.

6 In the paragraph that begins *In the spring*, triple-click again to select the entire paragraph. On the mini toolbar, click **Bold** B and **Italic** *I*. Click anywhere to deselect.

7 On the **Quick Access Toolbar**, click **Save** 🖫 to save the changes you have made to your document.

2.1.2

Activity 1.17 | Using Keyboard Shortcuts and Using the Clipboard to Copy, Cut, and Paste

The *Clipboard* is a temporary storage area that holds text or graphics that you select and then cut or copy. When you *copy* text or graphics, a copy is placed on the Clipboard and the original text or graphic remains in place. When you *cut* text or graphics, a copy is placed on the Clipboard, and the original text or graphic is removed—cut—from the document.

After copying or cutting, the contents of the Clipboard are available for you to *paste*—insert—in a new location in the current document, or into another Office file.

1 On your keyboard, hold down Ctrl and press Home to move to the beginning of your document, and then take a moment to study the table in Figure 1.45, which describes similar keyboard shortcuts with which you can navigate quickly in a document.

TO MOVE	PRESS
To the beginning of a document	Ctrl + Home
To the end of a document	Ctrl + End
To the beginning of a line	Home
To the end of a line	End
To the beginning of the previous word	Ctrl + ←
To the beginning of the next word	Ctrl + →
To the beginning of the current word (if insertion point is in the middle of a word)	Ctrl + ←
To the beginning of the previous paragraph	Ctrl + ↑
To the beginning of the next paragraph	Ctrl + ↓
To the beginning of the current paragraph (if insertion point is in the middle of a paragraph)	Ctrl + ↑
Up one screen	PgUp
Down one screen	PgDn

Word 2016, Windows 10, Microsoft Corporation

FIGURE 1.45

2 ▶ To the left of *Skyline Metro Grill*, point in the left margin area to display the pointer, and then click one time to select the entire paragraph. On the **Home tab**, in the **Clipboard group**, click **Copy** 🗐.

Because anything that you select and then copy—or cut—is placed on the Clipboard, the Copy command and the Cut command display in the Clipboard group of commands on the ribbon. There is no visible indication that your copied selection has been placed on the Clipboard.

🔄 **ANOTHER WAY**   Right-click the selection, and then click Copy on the shortcut menu; or, use the keyboard shortcut Ctrl + C.

3 ▶ On the **Home tab**, in the **Clipboard group**, to the right of the group name *Clipboard*, click the **Dialog Box Launcher** button ⬚, and then compare your screen with Figure 1.46.

The Clipboard pane displays with your copied text. In any ribbon group, the *Dialog Box Launcher* displays either a dialog box or a pane related to the group of commands. It is not necessary to display the Clipboard in this manner, although sometimes it is useful to do so.

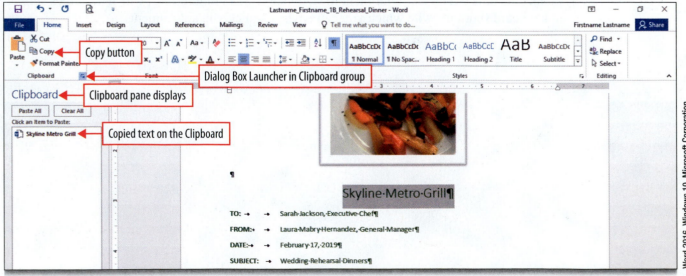

Word 2016, Windows 10, Microsoft Corporation

FIGURE 1.46

4 ▶ In the upper right corner of the **Clipboard** pane, click **Close** ☒.

5 ▶ Press Ctrl + End to move to the end of your document. Press Enter one time to create a new blank paragraph. On the **Home tab**, in the **Clipboard group**, point to **Paste**, and then click the *upper* portion of this split button.

> The Paste command pastes the most recently copied item on the Clipboard at the insertion point location. If you click the lower portion of the Paste button, a gallery of Paste Options displays. A *split button* is divided into two parts; clicking the main part of the button performs a command, and clicking the arrow displays a list or gallery with choices.

🔄 **ANOTHER WAY**   Right-click, on the shortcut menu under Paste Options, click the desired option button; or, press Ctrl + V.

6 ▶ Below the pasted text, click **Paste Options** 🗐 as shown in Figure 1.47.

> Here you can view and apply various formatting options for pasting your copied or cut text. Typically you will click Paste on the ribbon and paste the item in its original format. If you want some other format for the pasted item, you can choose another format from the ***Paste Options gallery***.
>
> The Paste Options gallery provides a Live Preview of the various options for changing the format of the pasted item with a single click. The Paste Options gallery is available in three places: on the ribbon by clicking the lower portion of the Paste button—the Paste button arrow; from the Paste Options button that displays below the pasted item following the paste operation; or on the shortcut menu if you right-click the pasted item.

FIGURE 1.47

7 ▶ In the **Paste Options** gallery, *point* to each option to see the Live Preview of the format that would be applied if you clicked the button.

> The contents of the Paste Options gallery are contextual; that is, they change based on what you copied and where you are pasting.

8 Press Esc to close the gallery; the button will remain displayed until you take some other screen action.

9 On your keyboard, press Ctrl + Home to move to the top of the document, and then click the **salad image** one time to select it. While pointing to the selected image, right-click, and then on the shortcut menu, click **Cut**.

> Recall that the Cut command cuts—removes—the selection from the document and places it on the Clipboard.

ANOTHER WAY   On the Home tab, in the Clipboard group, click the Cut button; or use the keyboard shortcut Ctrl + X.

10 Press Del one time to remove the blank paragraph from the top of the document, and then press Ctrl + End to move to the end of the document.

11 With the insertion point blinking in the blank paragraph at the end of the document, right-click, and notice that the **Paste Options** gallery displays on the shortcut menu. Compare your screen with Figure 1.48.

Paste Options on the shortcut menu

FIGURE 1.48

12 On the shortcut menu, under **Paste Options**, click the first button—**Keep Source Formatting**.

13 Point to the picture to display the pointer, and then drag to the right until the center green **Alignment Guide** displays and the blank paragraph is above the picture, as shown in Figure 1.49. Release the left mouse button.

BY TOUCH   Drag the picture with your finger to display the Alignment Guide.

Word 2016, Windows 10, Microsoft Corporation

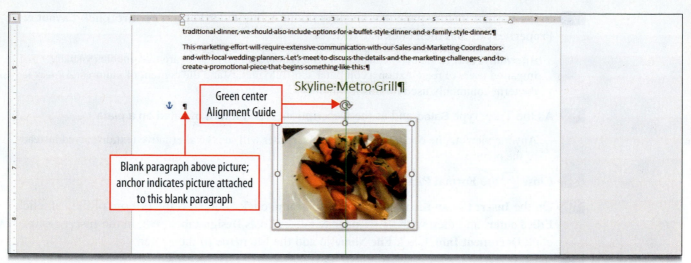

Green center
Alignment Guide

Skyline·Metro·Grill¶

Blank paragraph above picture;
anchor indicates picture attached
to this blank paragraph

FIGURE 1.49

Word 2016, Windows 10, Microsoft Corporation

MOS

2.2.7, 5.2.8

Activity 1.18 | Changing Text to WordArt and Adding Alternative Text for Accessibility

1 Above the picture, click to position the insertion point at the end of the word *Grill*, press [Spacebar] one time, and then type **for Your Rehearsal Dinner**

2 Select the text *Skyline Metro Grill for Your Rehearsal Dinner*, and then on the **Insert tab**, in the **Text group**, click **Insert WordArt** [4 ▾].

> *WordArt* is an Office feature available in Word, Excel, and PowerPoint that enables you to change normal text into decorative stylized text.

3 In the displayed gallery, use the ScreenTips to locate and then click **Fill - Gold, Accent 4, Soft Bevel**.

4 With the WordArt surrounded with a solid line, on the **Home tab**, in the **Font group**, change the font size to **16**.

5 Point to the solid line surrounding the WordArt to display the [🖑] pointer, and then drag the WordArt slightly to the right until the green center alignment guides display, as shown in Figure 1.50, and then release the mouse button to center the WordArt above your picture. Click outside of the WordArt to deselect.

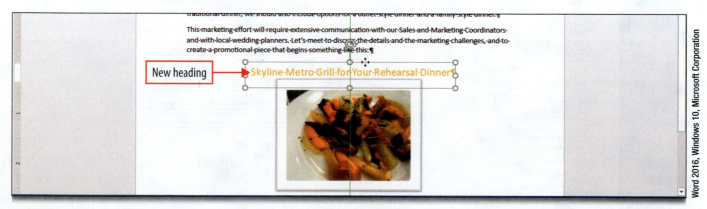

New heading

FIGURE 1.50

Word 2016, Windows 10, Microsoft Corporation

6 Point to the picture of the salad and right-click. On the shortcut menu, click **Format Picture**.

7 In the **Format Picture** pane that displays on the right, under **Format Picture**, click **Layout & Properties** 📊, and then click **Alt Text**.

Alternative text helps people using a *screen reader*, which is software that enables visually impaired users to read text on a computer screen to understand the content of pictures. *Alt text* is the term commonly used for this feature.

8 As the Title, type **Salad** and as the Description, type **Picture of salad on a plate**

Anyone viewing the document with a screen reader will see the alternative text displayed instead of the picture.

9 Close ✕ the **Format Picture** pane.

10 On the **Insert tab**, in the **Header & Footer group**, click **Footer**. At the bottom of the list, click **Edit Footer**, and then with the **Header & Footer Tools Design tab** active, in the **Insert group**, click **Document Info**. Click **File Name** to add the file name to the footer.

11 On the right end of the ribbon, click **Close Header and Footer**.

12 On the **Quick Access Toolbar**, point to the **Print Preview and Print icon** 🔍 you placed there, right-click, and then click **Remove from Quick Access Toolbar**.

If you are working on your own computer and you want to do so, you can leave the icon on the toolbar; in a college lab, you should return the software to its original settings.

13 Click **Save** 💾 and then click the **File tab** to display **Backstage** view. With the **Info tab** active, in the lower right corner, click **Show All Properties**. As **Tags**, type **weddings, rehearsal dinners, marketing**

14 As the **Subject**, type your course name and number—for example, *CIS 10, #5543*. Under **Related People**, be sure your name displays as the author (edit it if necessary), and then on the left, click **Print** to display the Print Preview. Compare your screen with Figure 1.51.

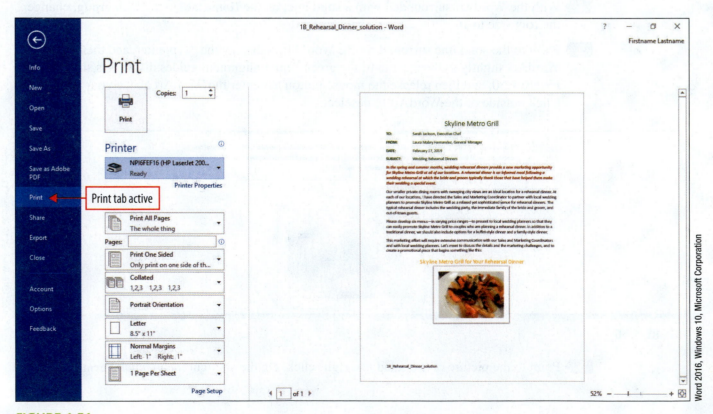

FIGURE 1.51

15 ▶ On the left side of **Backstage** view, click **Save**. In the upper right corner of the Word window, click **Close** ☒. If a message indicates *Do you want to keep the last item you copied?* click **No**.

> This message displays if you have copied some type of image to the Clipboard. If you click Yes, the items on the Clipboard will remain for you to use in another program or document.

16 ▶ As directed by your instructor, create and submit a paper printout or an electronic image of your document that looks like a printed document; or, submit your completed Word file. If necessary, refer to Activity 1.08 in Project 1A.

1.5.4, 1.5.5,
1.5.6

Activity 1.19 | Inspecting a Document

Word, Excel, and PowerPoint all have the same commands to inspect a file before sharing it.

1 ▶ If necessary, open your **Lastname_Firstname_1B_Rehearsal_Dinner** document.

2 ▶ Click the **File tab**, on the left, if necessary, click **Info**, and then on the right, click **Check for Issues**.

3 ▶ On the list, click **Inspect Document**.

> The *Inspect Document* command searches your document for hidden data or personal information that you might not want to share publicly. This information could reveal company details that should not be shared.

4 ▶ In the lower right corner of the **Document Inspector** dialog box, click **Inspect**.

> The Document Inspector runs and lists information that was found and that you could choose to remove.

5 ▶ Click **Close**, click **Check for Issues** again, and then click **Check Accessibility**.

> The *Check Accessibility* command checks the document for content that people with disabilities might find difficult to read. The Accessibility Checker pane displays on the right and lists two objects that might require attention: a text box (your WordArt) and your picture.

6 ▶ **Close** ☒ the **Accessibility Checker** pane, and then click the **File tab**.

7 ▶ Click **Check for Issues**, and then click **Check Compatibility**.

> The *Check Compatibility* command checks for features in your document that may not be supported by earlier versions of the Office program. This is only a concern if you are sharing documents with individuals with older software.

8 ▶ Click **OK**. Leave your Word document displayed for the next Activity.

1.2.3

Activity 1.20 | Inserting a Bookmark

A *bookmark* identifies a word, section, or place in your document so that you can find it quickly without scrolling. This is especially useful in a long document.

1 ▶ In the paragraph that begins *Please develop*, select the text *six menus*.

2 ▶ On the **Insert tab**, in the **Links group**, click **Bookmark**.

3 ▶ In the Bookmark name box, type **menus** and then click **Add**.

4 ▶ Press Ctrl + Home to move to the top of your document.

5 ▶ Press Ctrl + G, which is the keyboard shortcut for the Go To command.

6 ▶ Under **Go to what**, click **Bookmark**, and then with menus selected, click **Go To**. **Close** the **Find and Replace** dialog box, and notice that your bookmarked text is selected for you.

7 ▶ **Close** ☒ Word, and then click **Save**. Close any open windows.

GO! Learn How
Video OF1.10

A *compressed file* is a file that has been reduced in size. Compressed files take up less storage space and can be transferred to other computers faster than uncompressed files. You can also combine a group of files into one compressed folder, which makes it easier to share a group of files.

Within each Office program, you will see the *Tell Me* feature at the right end of the ribbon tabs, which is a search feature for Microsoft Office commands that you activate by typing what you are looking for in the Tell Me box.

Another method to get help with an Office command is to point to the command on the ribbon, and then at the bottom of the displayed ScreenTip, click Tell me more, which will display step-by-step assistance.

Activity 1.21 | Compressing Files

In this Activity, you will combine the two files you created in this chapter into one compressed file.

1 On the Windows taskbar, click **File Explorer** 📁. On the left, in the **navigation pane**, navigate to your storage location, and then open your **Office Features Chapter 1** folder. If you have been using this folder, in might appear under Quick access. Compare your screen with Figure 1.52.

Word 2016, Windows 10, Microsoft Corporation

FIGURE 1.52

2 In the **file list**, click your **Lastname_Firstname_1A_Note_Form** Word file one time to select it. Then, hold down Ctrl, and click your **Lastname_Firstname_1B_Rehearsal_Dinner** file to select both files in the list.

In any Windows-based program, holding down Ctrl while selecting enables you to select multiple items.

3 On the **File Explorer** ribbon, click **Share**, and then in the **Send group**, click **Zip**. Compare your screen with Figure 1.53.

Windows creates a compressed folder containing a *copy* of each of the selected files. The folder name is selected—highlighted in blue—so that you can rename it. The default folder name is usually the name of the first file in the group that you select.

BY TOUCH   Tap the ribbon commands.

FIGURE 1.53

Word 2016, Windows 10, Microsoft Corporation

↻ ANOTHER WAY   Point to the selected files in the File List, right-click, point to Send to, and then click Compressed (zipped) folder.

4 ▸ With the folder name selected—highlighted in blue—using your own name, type **Lastname_Firstname_Office_Features_Chapter_1** and press Enter.

> The compressed folder is ready to attach to an email or share in some other format.

5 ▸ In the upper right corner of the folder window, click **Close** ⊠.

Activity 1.22 | Using Microsoft Office Tell Me and Tell Me More to Get Help

In this Activity, you will use Tell Me to find information about formatting currency in Excel.

1 ▸ Start Excel and open a **Blank workbook**. With cell **A1** active, type **456789** and press Enter. Click cell **A1** again to make it the active cell.

2 ▸ At the top of the screen, click in the **Tell me what you want to do** box, and then type **format as currency** In the displayed list, point to **Accounting Number Formats**, and then click **$ English (United States)**.

> As you type, every keystroke refines the results so that you can click the command as soon as it displays. This feature helps you apply the command immediately; it does not explain how to locate the command.

3 ▸ On the **Home tab**, in the **Alignment group**, *point to* **Merge & Center**, and then at the bottom of the displayed ScreenTip, click **Tell me more**. At the right edge of the displayed **Excel 2016 Help** window, use the scroll bar to scroll about halfway down the window, and then compare your screen with Figure 1.54.

> The *Tell me more* feature opens the Office online Help system with explanations about how to perform the task.

FIGURE 1.54

4 If you want to do so, at the top of the **Excel Help** window, click Print 🖶 to print a copy of this information for your reference.

5 In the upper right corner of the Help window, click **Close** ⊠.

6 Leave Excel open for the next Activity.

Objective 11   Install Apps for Office and Create a Microsoft Account

ALERT!   **Working with Web-Based Applications and Services**

Computer programs and services on the web receive continuous updates and improvements. Thus, the steps to complete the following web-based activities may differ from the ones shown. You can often look at the screens and the information presented to determine how to complete the activity.

GO! Learn How
Video OF1.11

Apps for Office are a collection of downloadable apps that enable you to create and view information within your familiar Office programs. Apps for Office combine cloud services and web technologies within the user interface of Office. Some of these apps are developed by Microsoft, but many more are developed by specialists in different fields. As new apps are developed, they will be available from the online *Office Store*—a public marketplace that Microsoft hosts and regulates on Office.com.

A *task pane app* works side-by-side with an Office document by displaying a separate pane on the right side of the window. For example, a task pane app can look up and retrieve product information from a web service based on the product name or part number selected in the document.

A *content app* integrates web-based features as content within the body of a document. For example, in Excel, you can use an app to look up and gather search results for a new apartment by placing the information in an Excel worksheet, and then use maps to determine the distance of each apartment to work and to family members. *Mail apps* display next to an Outlook item. For example, a mail app could detect a purchase order number in an email message and then display information about the order or the customer.

Activity 1.23 | Installing Apps for Office

1 With cell **A1** active, on your keyboard, press Delete to clear the cell. On the Excel ribbon, click the **Insert tab**. In the **Add-ins group**, click **Store**.

2 In the **Office Add-ins** dialog box, in the upper right, click in the **Search the Office Store** box, type **bing maps** and then press Enter.

3 Click the **Bing logo**, and then in the lower right corner, click **Trust It**.

4 If necessary, click Update. On the Welcome message, click **Insert Sample Data**.

Here, the Bing map displays information related to the sample data—this is a *content app*. Each city in the sample data displays a small pie chart that represents the two sets of data—revenue and expenses. Compare your screen with Figure 1.55.

This is just one example of many apps downloadable from the Office Store.

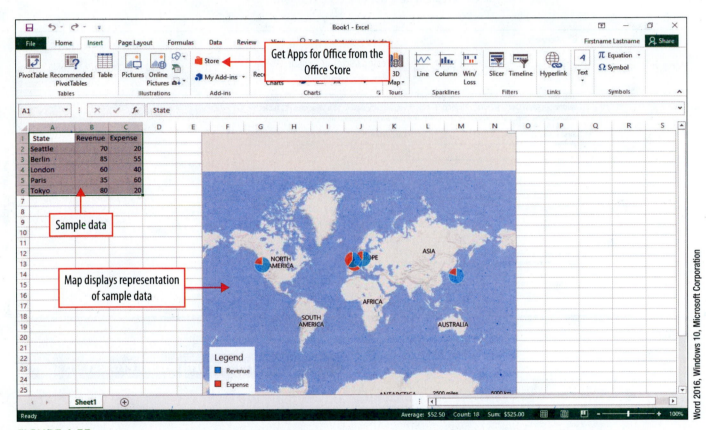

FIGURE 1.55

5 In the upper right corner of your screen, **Close** ☒ Excel without saving.

Activity 1.24 | Creating a Microsoft Account

ALERT! **This is an optional activity.**

You will find both Windows and Office to be much more useful if you sign in with a Microsoft account. If you already have an email account from **msn.com**, **hotmail.com**, **live.com**, or **outlook.com**, then you already have a Microsoft account. If you do not, you can create a free Microsoft account by following the steps in this activity.

In Windows 8 and Windows 10, you can use a Microsoft account to sign in to *any* Windows PC. Signing in with a Microsoft account is recommended because you can:

- Download Windows apps from the Windows Store.
- Get your online content—email, social network updates, updated news—automatically displayed in an app when you sign in.
- Synch settings online to make every Windows computer you use look and feel the same.
- Sign in to Office so that you can store documents on your OneDrive.

1 Use an Internet search engine to search for **create a microsoft account** or go to **signup.live.com** and at the bottom click **Sign up now**. You will see a screen similar to Figure 1.56. Complete the form to create your account.

You can use any email address that you currently have for your Microsoft account. Or, on this screen, you can create a new outlook.com account.

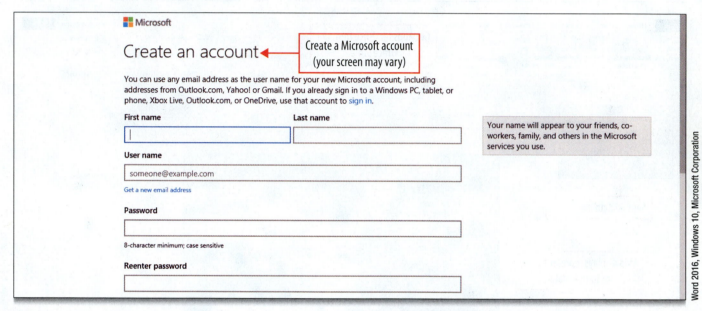

FIGURE 1.56

END | You have completed Project 1B

Word 2016, Windows 10, Microsoft Corporation

GO! To Work

MICROSOFT OFFICE SPECIALIST (MOS) SKILLS IN THIS CHAPTER	
PROJECT 1A	**PROJECT 1B**
1.1.1 Create a blank document	**1.2.3** Create bookmarks
1.3.4 Insert headers and footers	**1.4.2** Customize views by using zoom settings
1.3.6 Format page background elements	**1.4.3** Customize the Quick Access toolbar
1.4.5 Add document properties	**1.5.4** Inspect a document for hidden properties or personal information
1.4.6 Show or hide formatting symbols	**1.5.5** Inspect a document for accessibility issues
2.2.6 Apply built-in styles to text	**1.5.6** Inspect a document for compatibility issues
	2.1.2 Cut, copy, and paste text
	2.2.2 Apply formatting by using Format Painter
	2.2.7 Change text to WordArt
	5.2.5 Apply a picture style
	5.2.8 Add alternative text to objects for accessibility

BUILD YOUR E-PORTFOLIO

An E-Portfolio is a collection of evidence, stored electronically, that showcases what you have accomplished while completing your education. Collecting and then sharing your work products with potential employers reflects your academic and career goals. Your completed documents from the following projects are good examples to show what you have learned: 1A and 1B.

END OF CHAPTER

SUMMARY

Many Office features and commands, such as accessing the Open and Save As dialog boxes, performing commands from the ribbon and from dialog boxes, and using the Clipboard are the same in all Office desktop apps.

A desktop app is installed on your computer and requires a computer operating system such as Microsoft Windows or Apple's Mac OS-X to run. The programs in Microsoft Office 2016 are considered to be desktop apps.

An app refers to a self-contained program usually designed for a single purpose and that runs on smartphones and other mobile devices—for example, looking at sports scores or booking a flight on a particular airline.

Within an Office app, you can add Apps for Office from the Office Store, which combine cloud services and web technologies within the Office user interface. Apps can be task pane apps, content apps, or mail apps.

GO! LEARN IT ONLINE

Review the concepts, key terms, and MOS skills in this chapter by completing these online challenges, which you can find at **MyITLab**.

Matching and Multiple Choice: Answer matching and multiple-choice questions to test what you learned in this chapter.

Lessons on the GO!: Learn how to use all the new apps and features as they are introduced by Microsoft.

MOS Prep Quiz: Answer questions to review the MOS skills that you practiced in this chapter.

GLOSSARY

GLOSSARY OF CHAPTER KEY TERMS

Alignment The placement of text or objects relative to the left and right margins.

Alignment guides Green lines that display when you move an object to assist in alignment.

Alt text Another name for alternative text.

Alternative text Text added to a picture or object that helps people using a screen reader understand what the object is.

App A self-contained program usually designed for a single purpose and that runs on smartphones and other mobile devices.

Apps for Office A collection of downloadable apps that enable you to create and view information within Office programs, and that combine cloud services and web technologies within the user interface of Office.

Backstage tabs The area along the left side of Backstage view with tabs to display screens with related groups of commands.

Backstage view A centralized space for file management tasks; for example, opening, saving, printing, publishing, or sharing a file. A navigation pane displays along the left side with tabs that group file-related tasks together.

Bookmark A command that identifies a word, section, or place in a document so that you can find it quickly without scrolling.

Center alignment The alignment of text or objects that is centered horizontally between the left and right margin.

Clipboard A temporary storage area that holds text or graphics that you select and then cut or copy.

Check Accessibility A command that checks the document for content that people with disabilities might find difficult to read.

Check Compatibility A command that searches your document for features that may not be supported by older versions of Office.

Cloud computing Applications and services that are accessed over the Internet, rather than accessing applications that are installed on your local computer.

Cloud storage Online storage of data so that you can access your data from different places and devices.

Collaborate To work with others as a team in an intellectual endeavor to complete a shared task or to achieve a shared goal.

Commands Instructions to a computer program that cause an action to be carried out.

Compressed file A file that has been reduced in size and thus takes up less storage space and can be transferred to other computers quickly.

Content app An app for Office that integrates web-based features as content within the body of a document.

Context menus Menus that display commands and options relevant to the selected text or object; also called *shortcut menus*.

Context-sensitive commands Commands that display on a shortcut menu that relate to the object or text that you right-clicked.

Contextual tabs Tabs that are added to the ribbon automatically when a specific object, such as a picture, is selected, and that contain commands relevant to the selected object.

Copy A command that duplicates a selection and places it on the Clipboard.

Creative Commons A nonprofit organization that enables sharing and use of images and knowledge through free legal tools.

Cut A command that removes a selection and places it on the Clipboard.

Default The term that refers to the current selection or setting that is automatically used by a computer program unless you specify otherwise.

Deselect The action of canceling the selection of an object or block of text by clicking outside of the selection.

Desktop app A computer program that is installed on your PC and requires a computer operating system such as Microsoft Windows; also known as a *desktop application*.

Desktop application A computer program that is installed on your PC and requires a computer operating

system such as Microsoft Windows; also known as a *desktop app*.

Dialog Box Launcher A small icon that displays to the right of some group names on the ribbon and that opens a related dialog box or pane providing additional options and commands related to that group.

Document properties Details about a file that describe or identify it, including the title, author name, subject, and keywords that identify the document's topic or contents; also known as *metadata*.

Drag The action of holding down the left mouse button while moving your mouse.

Edit The process of making changes to text or graphics in an Office file.

Ellipsis A set of three dots indicating incompleteness; an ellipsis following a command name indicates that a dialog box will display if you click the command.

Enhanced ScreenTip A ScreenTip that displays more descriptive text than a normal ScreenTip.

Fill The inside color of an object.

Font A set of characters with the same design and shape.

Font styles Formatting emphasis such as bold, italic, and underline.

Footer A reserved area for text or graphics that displays at the bottom of each page in a document.

Formatting The process of establishing the overall appearance of text, graphics, and pages in an Office file—for example, in a Word document.

Formatting marks Characters that display on the screen, but do not print, indicating where the Enter key, the Spacebar, and the Tab key were pressed; also called *nonprinting characters*.

Gallery An Office feature that displays a list of potential results instead of just the command name.

Gradient fill A fill effect in which one color fades into another.

Groups On the Office ribbon, the sets of related commands that you might need for a specific type of task.

Header A reserved area for text or graphics that displays at the top of each page in a document.

Info tab The tab in Backstage view that displays information about the current file.

Inspect Document A command that searches your document for hidden data or personal information that you might not want to share publicly.

Insertion point A blinking vertical line that indicates where text or graphics will be inserted.

Keyboard shortcut A combination of two or more keyboard keys, used to perform a task that would otherwise require a mouse.

KeyTip The letter that displays on a command in the ribbon and that indicates the key you can press to activate the command when keyboard control of the Ribbon is activated.

Keywords Custom file properties in the form of words that you associate with a document to give an indication of the document's content; used to help find and organize files. Also called *tags*.

Landscape orientation A page orientation in which the paper is wider than it is tall.

Layout Options A button that displays when an object is selected and that has commands to choose how the object interacts with surrounding text.

Live Preview A technology that shows the result of applying an editing or formatting change as you point to possible results—*before* you actually apply it.

Location Any disk drive, folder, or other place in which you can store files and folders.

Mail app An app for Office that displays next to an Outlook item.

Metadata Details about a file that describe or identify it, including the title, author name, subject, and keywords that identify the document's topic or contents; also known as *document properties*.

Mini toolbar A small toolbar containing frequently used formatting commands that displays as a result of selecting text or objects.

MRU Acronym for *most recently used*, which refers to the state of some commands that retain the characteristic most recently applied; for example, the Font Color button retains the most recently used color until a new color is chosen.

Nonprinting characters Characters that display on the screen, but do not

print, indicating where the Enter key, the Spacebar, and the Tab key were pressed; also called *formatting marks*.

Object A text box, picture, table, or shape that you can select and then move and resize.

Office 365 A version of Microsoft Office to which you subscribe for an annual fee.

Office Store A public marketplace that Microsoft hosts and regulates on Office.com.

OneDrive Microsoft's free cloud storage for anyone with a free Microsoft account.

Open dialog box A dialog box from which you can navigate to, and then open on your screen, an existing file that was created in that same program.

Option button In a dialog box, a round button that enables you to make one choice among two or more options.

Options dialog box A dialog box within each Office application where you can select program settings and other options and preferences.

Page Width A view that zooms the document so that the width of the page matches the width of the window. Find this command on the View tab, in the Zoom group.

Paragraph symbol The symbol ¶ that represents the end of a paragraph.

Paste The action of placing text or objects that have been copied or cut from one location to another location.

Paste Options gallery A gallery of buttons that provides a Live Preview of all the Paste options available in the current context.

PDF The acronym for *Portable Document Format*, which is a file format that creates an image that preserves the look of your file, but that cannot be easily changed; a popular format for sending documents electronically, because the document will display on most computers.

Pointer Any symbol that displays on your screen in response to moving your mouse.

Points A measurement of the size of a font; there are 72 points in an inch.

Portable Document Format A file format that creates an image that preserves the look of your file, but that cannot be easily changed; a popular format for sending documents electronically, because the document

will display on most computers; also called a *PDF*.

Portrait orientation A page orientation in which the paper is taller than it is wide.

Print Preview A view of a document as it will appear when you print it.

Protected View A security feature in Office 2016 that protects your computer from malicious files by opening them in a restricted environment until you enable them; you might encounter this feature if you open a file from an e-mail or download files from the Internet.

pt The abbreviation for *point*; for example, when referring to a font size.

Quick Access Toolbar In an Office program window, the small row of buttons in the upper left corner of the screen from which you can perform frequently used commands.

Read-only A property assigned to a file that prevents the file from being modified or deleted; it indicates that you cannot save any changes to the displayed document unless you first save it with a new name.

Right-click The action of clicking the right mouse button one time.

Sans serif font A font design with no lines or extensions on the ends of characters.

Screen reader Software that enables visually impaired users to read text on a computer screen to understand the content of pictures.

ScreenTip A small box that that displays useful information when you perform various mouse actions such as pointing to screen elements or dragging.

Selecting Highlighting, by dragging with your mouse, areas of text or data or graphics, so that the selection can be edited, formatted, copied, or moved.

Serif font A font design that includes small line extensions on the ends of the letters to guide the eye in reading from left to right.

Share button Opens the Share pane from which you can save your file to the cloud—your OneDrive—and then share it with others so you can collaborate.

SharePoint Collaboration software with which people in an organization can set up team sites to share information, manage documents, and publish reports for others to see.

Shortcut menu A menu that displays commands and options relevant to the selected text or object; also called a *context menu*.

Sizing handles Small squares or circles that indicate a picture or object is selected.

Split button A button divided into two parts and in which clicking the main part of the button performs a command and clicking the arrow opens a menu with choices.

Status bar The area along the lower edge of an Office program window that displays file information on the left and buttons to control how the window looks on the right.

Style A group of formatting commands, such as font, font size, font color, paragraph alignment, and line spacing that can be applied to a paragraph with one command.

Synchronization The process of updating computer files that are in two or more locations according to specific rules—also called *syncing*.

Syncing The process of updating computer files that are in two or more locations according to specific rules—also called *synchronization*.

Tabs (ribbon) On the Office ribbon, the name of each task-oriented activity area.

Tags Custom file properties in the form of words that you associate with a document to give an indication of the document's content; used to help find and organize files. Also called *keywords*.

Task pane app An app for Office that works side-by-side with an Office document by displaying a separate pane on the right side of the window.

Tell Me A search feature for Microsoft Office commands that you activate by typing what you are looking for in the Tell Me box.

Tell me more A prompt within a ScreenTip that opens the Office online Help system with explanations about how to perform the command referenced in the ScreenTip.

Template A preformatted document that you can use as a starting point and then change to suit your needs.

Theme A predesigned combination of colors, fonts, and effects that looks good together and is applied to an entire document by a single selection.

Title bar The bar at the top edge of the program window that indicates the name of the current file and the program name.

Toggle button A button that can be turned on by clicking it once, and then turned off by clicking it again.

Toolbar In a folder window, a row of buttons with which you can perform common tasks, such as changing the view of your files and folders.

Triple-click The action of clicking the left mouse button three times in rapid succession.

Trusted Documents A security feature in Office that remembers which files you have already enabled; you might encounter this feature if you open a file from an e-mail or download files from the Internet.

Windows apps An app that runs on all Windows device families—including PCs, Windows phones, Windows tablets, and the Xbox gaming system.

WordArt An Office feature in Word, Excel, and PowerPoint that enables you to change normal text into decorative stylized text.

XML Paper Specification A Microsoft file format that creates an image of your document and that opens in the XPS viewer.

XPS The acronym for XML Paper Specification—a Microsoft file format that creates an image of your document and that opens in the XPS viewer.

Zoom The action of increasing or decreasing the size of the viewing area on the screen.

Introducing Microsoft Word 2016

devrim_pinar/fotolia

Word 2016: Introduction

Content! Defined by Merriam-Webster's online dictionary as "the topic or matter treated in a written work" and also as "the principal substance (as written matter, illustrations, or music) offered by a World Wide Web site," content is what you consume when you read on paper or online, when you watch video, or when you listen to any kind of music—live or recorded.

Content is what you *create* when your own words or performances are recorded in some form. For creating content in the form of words, Microsoft Office 2016 is a great choice. Rather than just a tool for word processing, Word is now a tool for you to communicate and collaborate with others. When you want to communicate with pictures or images in your Word document, Office 2016 has many features to help you do so. You can use Microsoft Word 2016 on a Windows desktop, laptop, or tablet. If your PC is touch-enabled, you will be able to use your fingers to work with Word. For example, the ribbon expands to make it easy to tap commands and you can resize images by moving your fingers on the screen.

Best of all, Microsoft Word 2016 is integrated into the cloud. If you save your documents to your cloud-based storage that comes with any free Microsoft account, you can retrieve them from any device and continue to work with and share your documents. Enjoy learning Word 2016!

Creating Documents with Microsoft Word 2016

PROJECT 1A

OUTCOMES
Create a flyer with a picture.

OBJECTIVES

1. Create a New Document and Insert Text
2. Insert and Format Graphics
3. Insert and Modify Text Boxes and Shapes
4. Preview and Print a Document

PROJECT 1B

OUTCOMES
Format text, paragraphs, and documents.

OBJECTIVES

5. Change Document and Paragraph Layout
6. Create and Modify Lists
7. Set and Modify Tab Stops
8. Insert a SmartArt Graphic and an Online Video

IvicaNS/Fotolia

In This Chapter

In this chapter, you will begin your study of Microsoft Word, one of the most popular computer software applications and one that almost everyone has a reason to use. You will use many of the tools and features in Word 2016, such as applying attractive styles to your documents. You can use Microsoft Word to perform basic word processing tasks such as writing a memo, a report, or a letter. You can also use Word to complete complex tasks, such as creating sophisticated tables, embedding graphics, writing blogs, and creating publications. Word is a program that you can learn gradually, and then add more advanced skills one at a time.

The projects in this chapter relate to **Sturgeon Point Productions**, an independent film company based in Miami with offices in Detroit and Milwaukee. The film professionals produce effective broadcast and branded content for many industries, and provide a wide array of film and video production services. Sturgeon Point Productions has won awards for broadcast advertising, business media, music videos, and social media. The mission of the company is to help clients tell their stories—whether the story is about a social issue, a new product, a geographical location, a company, or a person.

PROJECT
1A

PROJECT ACTIVITIES

In Activities 1.01 through 1.16, you will create a flyer announcing two internships for a short documentary by Sturgeon Point Productions. Your completed document will look similar to Figure 1.1.

PROJECT FILES

MyITLab
grader

If your instructor wants you to submit Project 1A in the MyITLab Grader system, log in to MyITLab, locate Grader Project 1A, and then download the files for this project.

For Project 1A, you will need the following files:

New blank Word document
w01A_Text
w01A_Bird

You will save your document as:

Lastname_Firstname_1A_Flyer

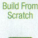 PROJECT RESULTS

Build From
Scratch

GO!
Walk Thru
Project 1A

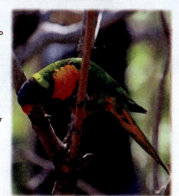

Internships Available

Interviews will be held:

Friday and Saturday, January 14 and 15

In the Career Services Conference Room

This summer, Sturgeon Point Productions will be filming a short documentary in Costa Rica about its native birds and has positions available for two interns. The filming will begin the first week of July and will last approximately two weeks. Payment will be by Day Rate of $100 per day. Transportation, food, and lodging will be provided.

The First Assistant Director will work with the second film crew, which will be filming background video. The Assistant Script Supervisor will work with the Script Supervisor and will be responsible for coordinating communication between the two camera crews.

You must have a valid U. S. passport; no inoculations are necessary. Details are available on the company website.

To set up an interview, apply online at:

www.SturgeonPointProductions.com

Word 2016, Windows 10, Microsoft Corporation

Lastname_Firstname_1A_Flyer

FIGURE 1.1 Project 1A Internship Flyer

Objective 1 Create a New Document and Insert Text

GO! Learn How
Video W1-1

When you start Word, documents you have recently opened, if any, display on the left. On the right, you can select a *template*—a preformatted document that you can use as a starting point and then change to suit your needs. If you want to start a new, blank document, you can select the blank document template. When you create a new document, you can type all of the text, or you can type some of the text and then insert additional text from another source.

MOS
1.1.1, 1.4.6

Activity 1.01 | Starting a New Word Document

> **ALERT!**   **To submit as an autograded project, log into MyITLab and download the files for this project, and begin with those files instead of a new blank document.**

1 ▸ Start Word and then click **Blank document**. On the **Home tab**, in the **Paragraph group**, if necessary click **Show/Hide** ¶ so that it is active and the formatting marks display. If the rulers do not display, click the View tab, and then in the Show group, select the Ruler check box.

2 ▸ Type **Internships Available** and then press Enter two times. Then type the following text: **This summer, Sturgeon Point Productions will be filming a short documentary in Costa Rica about its native birds and has positions available for two interns.**

As you type, the insertion point moves to the right, and when it approaches the right margin, Word determines whether the next word in the line will fit within the established right margin. If the word does not fit, Word moves the entire word down to the next line. This is *wordwrap* and means that you press Enter *only* when you reach the end of a paragraph—it is not necessary to press Enter at the end of each line of text.

> **NOTE**   Spacing Between Sentences
>
> Although you might have learned to add two spaces following end-of-sentence punctuation, the common practice now is to space only one time at the end of a sentence. Be sure to press Spacebar only one time following end-of-sentence punctuation.

3 ▸ Press Spacebar and then take a moment to study the table in Figure 1.2 to become familiar with the default document settings in Microsoft Word. Compare your screen with Figure 1.3.

When you press Enter, Spacebar, or Tab on your keyboard, characters display in your document to represent these keystrokes. These characters do not print and are referred to as *formatting marks* or *nonprinting characters*. These marks will display throughout this instruction.

DEFAULT DOCUMENT SETTINGS IN A NEW WORD DOCUMENT	
SETTING	**DEFAULT FORMAT**
Font and font size	The default font is Calibri, and the default font size is 11 points.
Margins	The default left, right, top, and bottom page margins are 1 inch.
Line spacing	The default line spacing is 1.08, which provides slightly more space between lines than single spacing does.
Paragraph spacing	The default spacing after a paragraph is 8 points, which is slightly less than the height of one blank line of text.
View	The default view is Print Layout view, which displays the page borders and displays the document as it will appear when printed.

FIGURE 1.2

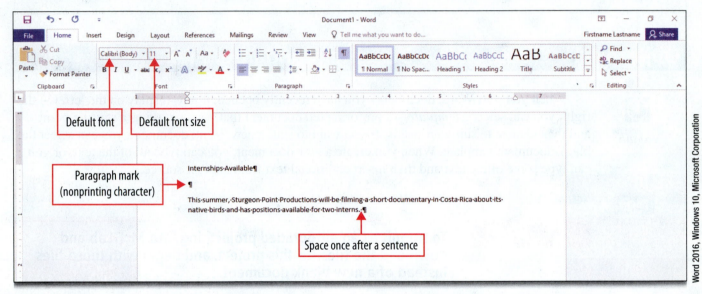

FIGURE 1.3

More Knowledge **Word's Default Settings Are Easier to Read Online**

Until just a few years ago, word processing programs used single spacing, an extra blank paragraph to separate paragraphs, and 12 pt Times New Roman as the default formats. Now, studies show that individuals find the Word default formats described in Figure 1.2 to be easier to read online, where many documents are now viewed and read.

1.1.4

Activity 1.02 | **Inserting Text from Another Document**

1 ▶ On the ribbon, click the **Insert tab**. In the **Text group**, click the **Object button arrow**, and then click **Text from File**.

ALERT! **Does the Object dialog box display?**

If the Object dialog box displays, you probably clicked the Object *button* instead of the Object *button arrow*. Close the Object dialog box, and then in the Text group, click the Object button arrow, as shown in Figure 1.4. Click *Text from File*, and then continue with Step 2.

2 ▶ In the **Insert File** dialog box, navigate to the student files that accompany this textbook, locate and select **w01A_Text**, and then click **Insert**. Compare your screen with Figure 1.4.

A *copy* of the text from the w01A_Text file displays at the insertion point location; the text is not removed from the original file.

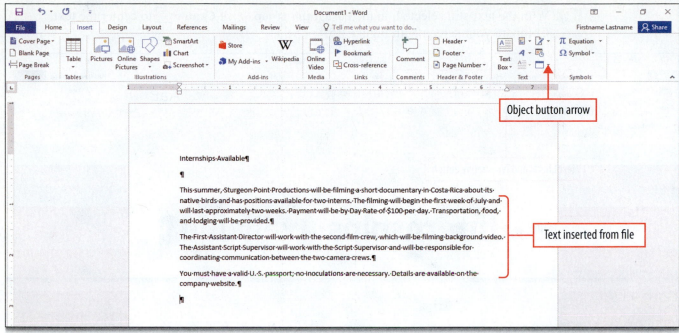

FIGURE 1.4

Word 2016, Windows 10, Microsoft Corporation

🔄 **ANOTHER WAY**   Open the file, copy the required text, close the file, and then paste the text into the current document.

> **3** ▶ On the **Quick Access Toolbar**, click **Save** 💾, and then under **Save As**, click **Browse**. Navigate to the location where you are saving your files for this chapter, and then create and open a new folder named **Word Chapter 1** In the **File name** box, using your own name, replace the existing text with **Lastname_Firstname_1A_Flyer** and then click **Save**.

Objective 2   Insert and Format Graphics

GO! Learn How
Video W1-2

To add visual interest to a document, insert *graphics*. Graphics include pictures, online pictures, charts, and *drawing objects*—shapes, diagrams, lines, and so on. For additional visual interest, you can apply an attractive graphic format to text; add, resize, move, and format pictures; and add a page border.

2.2.6 and 2.2.10

Activity 1.03 │ Formatting Text by Using Text Effects

Text effects are decorative formats, such as shadowed or mirrored text, text glow, 3-D effects, and colors that make text stand out.

> **1** ▶ Including the paragraph mark, select the first paragraph of text—*Internships Available*. On the **Home tab**, in the **Font group**, click **Text Effects and Typography** 🅰️▾.

> **2** ▶ In the **Text Effects and Typography** gallery, in the third row, point to the first effect to display the ScreenTip *Fill – Black, Text 1, Outline – Background 1, Hard Shadow – Background 1*, and then click this effect.

> **3** ▶ With the text still selected, in the **Font group**, click in the **Font Size** box 11 ▾ to select the existing font size. Type **52** and then press Enter.

When you want to change the font size of selected text to a size that does not display in the Font Size list, type the number in the Font Size box and press Enter to confirm the new font size.

4 With the text still selected, in the **Paragraph group**, click **Center** to center the text. Compare your screen with Figure 1.5.

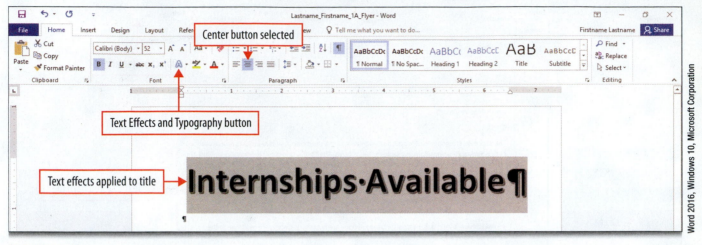

FIGURE 1.5

5 With the text still selected, in the **Font group**, click the **Font Color button arrow**. Under **Theme Colors**, in the sixth column, click the first color—**Orange, Accent 2**.

6 With the text still selected, in the **Font group**, click **Text Effects and Typography**. Point to **Shadow**, and then under **Outer**, in the second row, click the third style—**Offset Left**.

7 Click anywhere in the document to deselect the text, click **Save**, and then compare your screen with Figure 1.6.

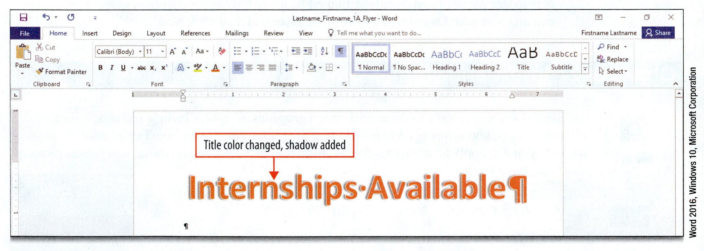

FIGURE 1.6

More Knowledge | **Clear Existing Formatting**

If you do not like your text effect, you can remove all formatting from any selected text. To do so, on the Home tab, in the Font group, click Clear All Formatting.

MOS
5.1.2

Activity 1.04 | **Inserting Pictures**

1 In the paragraph that begins *This summer*, click to position the insertion point at the beginning of the paragraph.

2 On the **Insert tab**, in the **Illustrations group**, click **Pictures**. In the **Insert Picture** dialog box, navigate to your student data files, locate and click **w01A_Bird**, and then click **Insert**.

> Word inserts the picture as an ***inline object***; that is, the picture is positioned directly in the text at the insertion point, just like a character in a sentence. The Layout Options button displays to the right of the picture. You can change the ***Layout Options*** to control the manner in which text wraps around a picture or other object. Sizing handles surround the picture indicating it is selected.

3 Notice the round sizing handles around the selected picture, as shown in Figure 1.7.

> The corner sizing handles resize the graphic proportionally. The center sizing handles resize a graphic vertically or horizontally only; however, sizing with these will distort the graphic. A ***rotation handle***, with which you can rotate the graphic to any angle, displays above the top center sizing handle.

FIGURE 1.7

5.2.6

Activity 1.05 | Wrapping Text Around a Picture Using Layout Options

> Recall that Layout Options enable you to control ***text wrapping***—the manner in which text displays around an object.

1 Be sure the picture is selected—you know it is selected if the sizing handles display.

2 To the right of the picture, click **Layout Options** 🖾 to display a gallery of text wrapping arrangements. Point to each icon layout option to view its ScreenTip.

> Each icon visually depicts how text will wrap around an object.

ANOTHER WAY   On the Format tab, in the Arrange group, click Wrap Text.

3 From the gallery, under **With Text Wrapping**, click the first layout—**Square**. Compare your screen with Figure 1.8.

> Select Square text wrapping when you want to wrap the text to the left or right of an image. To the left of the picture, an *object anchor* displays, indicating that the selected object is anchored to the text at this location in the document.

FIGURE 1.8

4 **Close** ☒ the **Layout Options**, and then **Save** 🖫 your document.

Activity 1.06 | Resizing Pictures and Using Live Layout

When you move or size a picture, *Live Layout* reflows text as you move or size an object so that you can view the placement of surrounding text.

1 If necessary, scroll your document so the entire picture displays. At the lower right corner of the picture, point to the sizing handle until the ⬉ pointer displays. Drag slightly upward and to the left. As you drag, a green alignment guide may display at the left margin. Compare your screen with Figure 1.9.

> *Alignment guides* may display when you are moving or sizing a picture to help you with object placement, and Live Layout shows you how the document text will flow and display on the page.

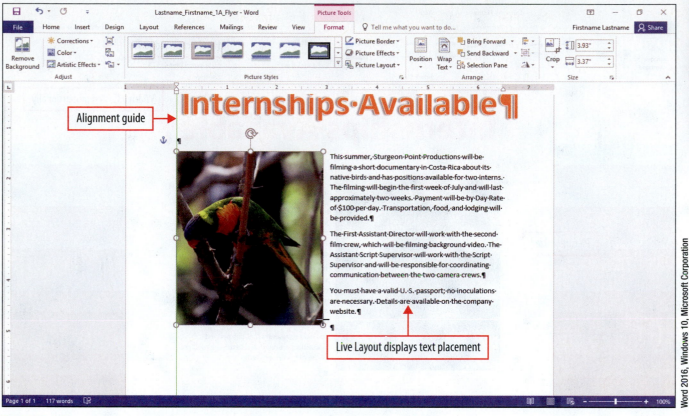

Internships·Available¶

Alignment guide

This·summer,·Sturgeon·Point·Productions·will·be·filming·a·short·documentary·in·Costa·Rica·about·its·native·birds·and·has·positions·available·for·two·interns.·The·filming·will·begin·the·first·week·of·July·and·will·last·approximately·two·weeks.·Payment·will·be·by·Day·Rate·of·$100·per·day.·Transportation,·food,·and·lodging·will·be·provided.¶

The·First·Assistant·Director·will·work·with·the·second·film·crew,·which·will·be·filming·background·video.·The·Assistant·Script·Supervisor·will·work·with·the·Script·Supervisor·and·will·be·responsible·for·coordinating·communication·between·the·two·camera·crews.¶

You·must·have·a·valid·U.·S.·passport;·no·inoculations·are·necessary.·Details·are·available·on·the·company·website.¶

Live Layout displays text placement

Word 2016, Windows 10, Microsoft Corporation

FIGURE 1.9

2 Continue to drag up and to the left until the bottom of the graphic is aligned at approximately **4 inches on the vertical ruler**. Notice that the graphic is proportionally resized.

3 On the **Quick Access Toolbar**, click **Undo** ↺ to restore the picture to its original size.

ANOTHER WAY   On the Format tab, in the Adjust group, click Reset Picture.

4 On the ribbon, under **Picture Tools**, on the **Format tab**, in the **Size group**, click in the **Shape Height** box ↕ 0.29". Type **3.8** and then press Enter. If necessary, scroll down to view the entire picture on your screen, and then compare your screen with Figure 1.10.

When you use the Shape Height and Shape Width boxes to change the size of a graphic, the graphic will always resize proportionally; that is, the width adjusts as you change the height and vice versa.

ANOTHER WAY   A *spin box* is a small box with an upward- and downward-pointing arrow that lets you move rapidly through a set of values by clicking. You can change the height or width of a picture object by clicking the Shape Height or Shape width spin box arrows.

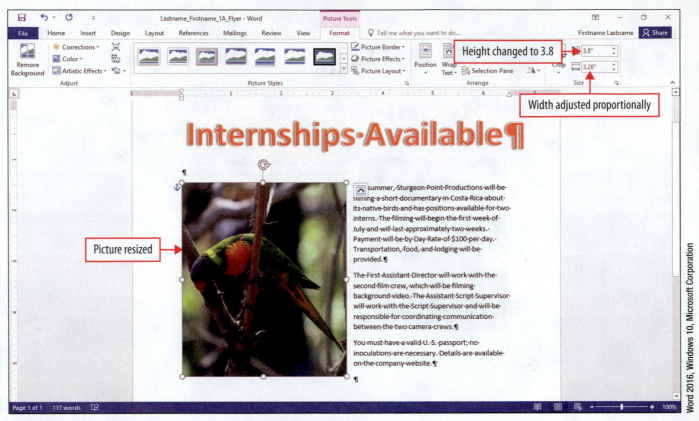

FIGURE 1.10

5 **Save** 🖫 your document.

Activity 1.07 | Positioning a Picture

5.2.7

There are two ways to move a picture in a document. You can point to the picture and then drag it to a new position. You can also change the picture settings in a dialog box, which gives you more precise control over the picture location.

1 Be sure the picture is selected. On the ribbon, click the **Format tab**. In the **Arrange group**, click **Position**, and then click **More Layout Options**.

2 In the **Layout** dialog box, be sure the **Position tab** is selected. Under **Horizontal**, click the **Alignment** option button. To the right of **Alignment**, click the **arrow**, and then click **Right**. To the right of **relative to**, click the **arrow**, and then click **Margin**.

3 Under **Vertical**, click the **Alignment** option button. Change the **Alignment** options to **Top relative to Line**. Compare your screen with Figure 1.11.

With these alignment settings, the picture will move to the right margin of the page and the top edge will align with the top of the first line of the paragraph to which it is anchored.

Layout dialog box

Relative to Margin selected

Right Alignment selected

Vertical Alignment set to Top relative to Line

FIGURE 1.11

4 At the bottom of the **Layout** dialog box, click **OK**, and then on the **Quick Access Toolbar**, click **Save** 🖫. Notice that the picture moves to the right margin, and the text wraps on the left side of the picture. Compare your screen with Figure 1.12.

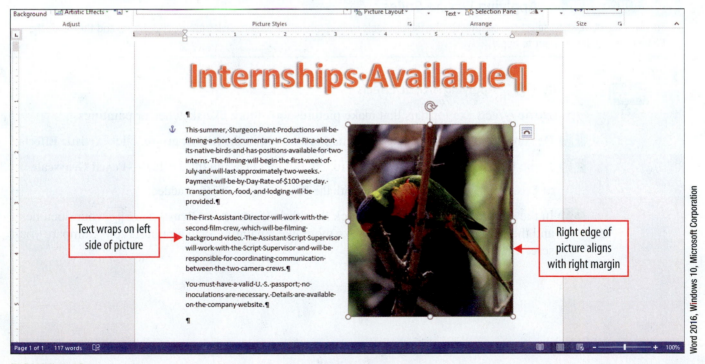

Text wraps on left side of picture

Right edge of picture aligns with right margin

FIGURE 1.12

MOS
5.2.2

Activity 1.08 │ **Applying Picture Effects**

Picture styles include shapes, shadows, frames, borders, and other special effects with which you can stylize an image. *Picture Effects* enhance a picture with effects such as a shadow, glow, reflection, or 3-D rotation.

1 Be sure the picture is selected. On the **Format tab**, in the **Picture Styles group**, click **Picture Effects**.

2 Point to **Soft Edges**, and then click **5 Point**.

The Soft Edges feature fades the edges of the picture. The number of points you choose determines how far the fade goes inward from the edges of the picture.

3 Compare your screen with Figure 1.13, and then **Save** 🖫 your document.

Soft Edges picture effect applied to picture

FIGURE 1.13

More Knowledge | **Applying Picture Styles**

To apply a picture style, select the picture. On the Picture Tools Format tab, in the Picture Styles group, click More, and then click the Picture Style that you want to apply.

5.2.1

Activity 1.09 | **Applying Artistic Effects**

Artistic effects are formats that make pictures look more like sketches or paintings.

1 Be sure the picture is selected. On the **Format tab**, in the **Adjust group**, click **Artistic Effects**.

2 In the first row of the gallery, point to, but do not click, the third effect—**Pencil Grayscale**.

Live Preview displays the picture with the *Pencil Grayscale* effect added.

3 In the second row of the gallery, click the third effect—**Paint Brush**. **Save** 🖫 your document, and then notice that the picture looks more like a painting than a photograph. Compare your screen with Figure 1.14.

Paint Brush artistic effect applied to picture

FIGURE 1.14

Activity 1.10 │ Adding a Page Border

Page borders frame a page and help to focus the information on the page.

1 Click anywhere outside the picture to deselect it. On the **Design tab**, in the **Page Background group**, click **Page Borders**.

2 In the **Borders and Shading** dialog box, on the **Page Border tab**, under **Setting**, click **Box**. Under **Style**, scroll the list and click the seventh style—double lines.

3 Click the **Color arrow**, and then in the sixth column, click the first color—**Orange, Accent 2**.

4 Under **Apply to**, be sure *Whole document* is selected, and then compare your screen with Figure 1.15.

Borders and Shading dialog box

Box setting

Double line style

Border color

FIGURE 1.15

5 At the bottom of the **Borders and Shading** dialog box, click **OK**.

6 Press [Ctrl] + [Home] to move to the top of the document, click **Save** 🖫, and then compare your screen with Figure 1.16.

Page border applied to document

FIGURE 1.16

Objective 3 | Insert and Modify Text Boxes and Shapes

GO! Learn How
Video W1-3

Word has predefined *shapes* and *text boxes* that you can add to your documents. A shape is an object such as a line, arrow, box, callout, or banner. A text box is a movable, resizable container for text or graphics. Use these objects to add visual interest to your document.

MOS
5.1.1, 5.2.7

Activity 1.11 | Inserting, Sizing, and Positioning a Shape

1 Press ↓ one time to move to the blank paragraph below the title. Press Enter four times to create additional space for a text box, and notice that the picture anchored to the paragraph moves with the text.

2 Press Ctrl + End to move to the bottom of the document, and notice that your insertion point is positioned in the empty paragraph at the end of the document. Press Delete to remove the blank paragraph.

3 Click the **Insert tab**, and then in the **Illustrations group**, click **Shapes** to display the gallery. Compare your screen with Figure 1.17.

Shapes button

Shapes gallery

Rounded Rectangle shape

FIGURE 1.17

4 Under **Rectangles**, click the second shape—**Rounded Rectangle**, and then move your pointer. Notice that the ⊞ pointer displays.

5 Position the ⊞ pointer near the left margin at approximately **8 inches on the vertical ruler**. Click one time to insert a 1-inch by 1-inch rounded rectangle. The exact location is not important.

A blue rectangle with rounded edges displays.

6 To the right of the rectangle object, click **Layout Options** , and then at the bottom of the gallery, click **See more** to display the Layout dialog box.

🔄 **ANOTHER WAY**   On the Format tab, in the Arrange group, click Position, and then click More Layout Options.

7 In the **Layout** dialog box, under **Horizontal**, click **Alignment**. To the right of **Alignment**, click the **arrow**, and then click **Centered**. To the right of **relative to**, click the **arrow**, and then click **Page**. Under **Vertical**, select the existing number in the **Absolute position** box, and then type **1** To the right of **below**, be sure that **Paragraph** displays. Click **OK**.

> This action centers the rectangle on the page and positions the rectangle one inch below the last paragraph.

8 On the **Format tab**, click in the **Shape Height box** 📏 0.29" ↕ to select the existing text. Type **1.5** and then click in the **Shape Width box** 🔲 1.07" ↕. Type **4.5** and then press Enter.

9 Compare your screen with Figure 1.18, and then **Save** 💾 your document.

provided. ¶

The·First·Assistant·Director·will·work·with·the·
second·film·crew,·which·will·be·filming·
background·video.·The·Assistant·Script·Supervisor·
will·work·with·the·Script·Supervisor·and·will·be·
responsible·for·coordinating·communication·
between·the·two·camera·crews.¶

⬇ You·must·have·a·valid·U.·S.·passport;·no·
inoculations·are·necessary.·Details·are·available·
on·the·company·website.¶

Inserted, sized, and positioned rounded rectangle

Word 2016, Windows 10, Microsoft Corporation

FIGURE 1.18

MOS
5.2.4

Activity 1.12 │ Typing Text in a Shape and Formatting a Shape

1 If necessary, select the rectangle shape. Type **To set up an interview, apply online at:** and then press Enter. Type **www.SturgeonPointProductions.com**

2 Press Ctrl + A to select the text you just typed. Right-click over the selected text to display the mini toolbar, and then click **Bold** B . With the text still selected, click **Increase Font Size** A˙ three times to increase the font size to **16 pt**.

> Use the keyboard shortcut Ctrl + A to select all of the text in a text box.

3 With the text still selected, on the mini toolbar, click the **Font Color button arrow**. Under **Theme Colors**, click **Black, Text 1**.

4 Click outside the shape to deselect the text. Click the border of the shape to select the shape but not the text. On the **Format tab**, in the **Shape Styles group**, click **Shape Fill**. In the sixth column, click the fourth color—**Orange, Accent 2, Lighter 40%**.

5 With the shape still selected, in the **Shape Styles group**, click **Shape Outline**. In the sixth column, click the first color—**Orange, Accent 2**. Compare your screen with Figure 1.19, and then **Save** 💾 your document.

The·First·Assistant·Director·will·work·with·the·second·film·crew,·which·will·be·filming·background·video.·The·Assistant·Script·Supervisor·will·work·with·the·Script·Supervisor·and·will·be·responsible·for·coordinating·communication·between·the·two·camera·crews.¶

You·must·have·a·valid·U.·S.·passport;·no·inoculations·are·necessary.·Details·are·available·on·the·company·website.¶

Text typed and formatted, shape fill and outline applied →

To·set·up·an·interview,·apply·online·at:¶

www.SturgeonPointProductions.com¶

FIGURE 1.19

 MOS 5.1.4

Activity 1.13 | Inserting a Text Box

A text box is useful to differentiate portions of text from other text on the page. Because it is a *floating object*—a graphic that can be moved independently of the surrounding text characters—you can place a text box anywhere on the page.

1 Press Ctrl + Home to move to the top of the document.

2 On the **Insert tab**, in the **Text group**, click **Text Box**. At the bottom of the gallery, click **Draw Text Box**.

3 Position the ⊞ pointer over the first blank paragraph—aligned with the left margin and at approximately 1 inch on the vertical ruler. Drag down and to the right to create a text box approximately **1.5 inches** high and **4 inches** wide—the exact size and location need not be precise.

4 With the insertion point blinking in the text box, type the following, pressing Enter after each of the first *two* lines to create a new paragraph:

> **Interviews will be held:**
> **Friday and Saturday, January 14 and 15**
> **In the Career Services Conference Room**

5 Compare your screen with Figure 1.20, and then **Save** 🖫 your document.

Internships·Available¶

Text box with text →

Interviews·will·be·held:¶

Friday·and·Saturday,·January·14·and·15¶

In·the·Career·Services·Conference·Room¶

¶

FIGURE 1.20

Activity 1.14 | **Sizing and Positioning a Text Box and Formatting a Text Box Using Shape Styles**

1 ▶ Point to the text box border to display the ⬚ pointer. In the space below the *Internships Available* title, by dragging, move the text box until a horizontal green alignment guide displays above the first blank paragraph mark and a vertical green alignment guide displays in the center of the page, as shown in Figure 1.21. If the alignment guides do not display, drag the text box to position it approximately as shown in the Figure.

Word 2016, Windows 10, Microsoft Corporation

FIGURE 1.21

2 ▶ To place the text box precisely, on the **Format tab**, in the **Arrange group**, click **Position**, and then click **More Layout Options**.

3 ▶ In the **Layout** dialog box, under **Horizontal**, click **Alignment**. To the right of **Alignment**, click the **arrow**, and then click **Centered**. To the right of **relative to**, click the **arrow**, and then click **Page**.

4 ▶ Under **Vertical**, click in the **Absolute position** box, select the existing number, and then type **1.25** To the right of **below**, click the **arrow**, and then click **Margin**.

5 ▶ In the **Layout** dialog box, click the **Size tab**. Under **Height**, select the number in the **Absolute** box. Type **1.25** and then under **Width**, select the number in the **Absolute** box. Type **4** and then click **OK**.

> The text box is sized correctly, centered horizontally, and the top edge is positioned 1.25 inches below the top margin of the document.

6 ▶ On the ribbon, under **Drawing Tools**, click the **Format tab**. In the **Shape Styles group**, click **More** ⊽, and then in the first row, click the third style—**Colored Outline – Orange, Accent 2**.

7 ▶ On the **Format tab**, in the **Shape Styles group**, click **Shape Effects**. Point to **Shadow**, and then under **Outer**, in the first row, click the first effect—**Offset Diagonal Bottom Right**.

8 ▶ Click in the text box, and then press Ctrl + A to select all of the text. Right-click over the selected text to display the mini toolbar, change the **Font Size** to **16** and apply **Bold** B. Press Ctrl + E to center the text.

> Ctrl + E is the keyboard shortcut to center text in a document or object.

9 ▶ Click anywhere in the document to deselect the text box. Compare your screen with Figure 1.22, and then **Save** 💾 your document.

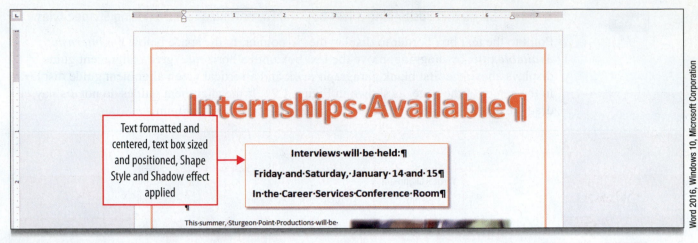

Text formatted and centered, text box sized and positioned, Shape Style and Shadow effect applied

Internships·Available¶

Interviews·will·be·held:¶

Friday·and·Saturday,·January·14·and·15¶

In·the·Career·Services·Conference·Room¶

This·summer,·Sturgeon·Point·Productions·will·be·

Word 2016, Windows 10, Microsoft Corporation

FIGURE 1.22

Objective 4   Preview and Print a Document

GO! Learn How
Video W1-4

While you are creating your document, it is useful to preview your document periodically to be sure that you are getting the result you want. Then, before printing, make a final preview to be sure the document layout is what you intended.

MOS
1.3.4

Activity 1.15 │ Adding a File Name to the Footer by Inserting a Field

Information in headers and footers helps to identify a document when it is printed or displayed electronically. Recall that a header is information that prints at the top of every page; a footer is information that prints at the bottom of every page. In this textbook, you will insert the file name in the footer of every Word document.

1▸ Click the **Insert tab**, and then in the **Header & Footer group**, click **Footer**.

2▸ At the bottom of the gallery, click **Edit Footer**.

The footer area displays with the insertion point blinking at the left edge, and on the ribbon, the Header & Footer Tools display.

↻ ANOTHER WAY   At the bottom edge of the page, right-click; from the shortcut menu, click Edit Footer.

3▸ On the ribbon, under the **Header & Footer Tools**, on the **Design tab**, in the **Insert group**, click **Document Info**, and then click **File Name**. Compare your screen with Figure 1.23.

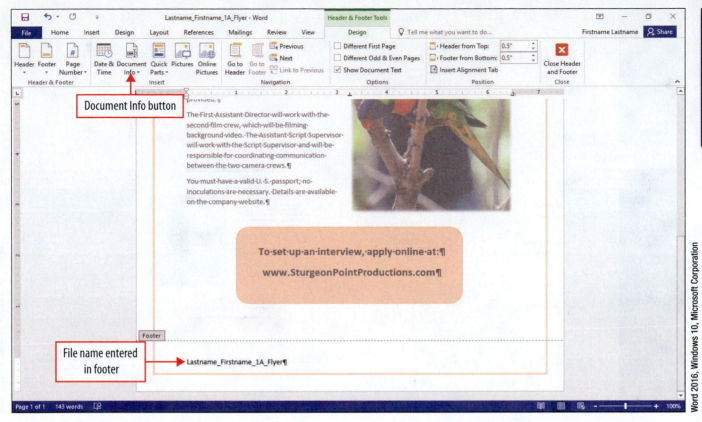

To·set·up·an·interview,·apply·online·at:¶

www.SturgeonPointProductions.com¶

Document Info button

File name entered in footer → Lastname_Firstname_1A_Flyer¶

Word 2016, Windows 10, Microsoft Corporation

FIGURE 1.23

4 On the **Design tab**, click **Close Header and Footer**, and then **Save** 💾 your document.

When the body of the document is active, the footer text is dimmed—it displays in gray. Conversely, when the footer area is active, the footer text is not dimmed; instead, the document text is dimmed.

🔄 **ANOTHER WAY**   Double-click in the document outside of the footer area to close the footer and return to the document.

MOS
1.4.5; 1.5.3

Activity 1.16 | Adding Document Properties and Previewing and Printing a Document

1 Press Ctrl + Home to move the insertion point to the top of the document. In the upper left corner of your screen, click the **File tab** to display **Backstage** view. On the right, at the bottom of the **Properties** list, click **Show All Properties**.

2 On the list of **Properties**, click to the right of **Tags** to display an empty box, and then type **internship, documentary**

3 Click to the right of **Subject** to display an empty box, and then type your course name and section number. Under **Related People**, be sure that your name displays as the author. If necessary, right-click the author name, click Edit Property, type your name, and click OK.

4 On the left, click **Print** to display the **Print Preview**. Compare your screen with Figure 1.24.

Here you can select any printer connected to your system and adjust the settings related to how you want to print. On the right, Print Preview displays your document exactly as it will print; the formatting marks do not display. At the bottom of the Print Preview area, in the center, the number of pages and arrows with which you can move among the pages in Print Preview displays. On the right, Zoom settings enable you to shrink or enlarge the Print Preview.

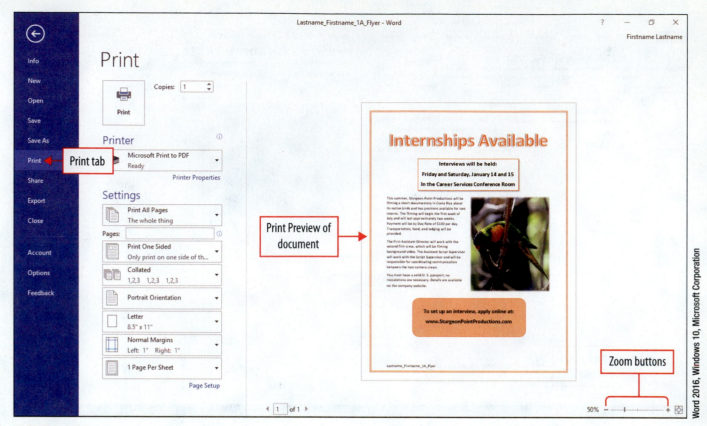

FIGURE 1.24

5 > In the lower right corner of the window, click **Zoom In** several times to view the document at a larger size, and notice that a larger preview is easier to read. Click **Zoom to Page** 🔲 to view the entire page.

6 > If you want to print your document on paper using the default printer on your system, in the upper left portion of the screen, click **Print**.

The document will print on your default printer; if you do not have a color printer, colors will print in shades of gray. Backstage view closes and your file redisplays in the Word window.

7 > **Save** 💾 your document. In the upper right corner of the Word window, click **Close** ⊠. If directed by your instructor to do so, submit your paper printout, your electronic image of your document that looks like a printed document, or your completed Word file.

> **END | You have completed Project 1A**

GO! With Google

Objective   Create a Flyer Using Google Docs

A L E R T !   **Working with Web-Based Applications and Services**

Computer programs and services on the web receive continuous updates and improvements, so the steps to complete this web-based activity may differ from the ones shown. You can often look at the screens and the information presented to determine how to complete the activity.

If you do not already have a Google account, you will need to create one before you begin this activity. Go to http://google.com and, in the upper right corner, click Sign In. On the Sign In screen, click Create Account. On the Create your Google Account page, complete the form, read and agree to the Terms of Service and Privacy Policy, and then click Next step. On the Welcome screen, click Get Started.

Activity │ Creating a Flyer

In this Activity, you will use Google Docs to create a flyer.

1 From the desktop, open your browser, navigate to http://google.com, and then sign in to your Google account. In the upper right corner of your screen, click **Google Apps** ⊞ and then click **Drive** ⬧.

2 To create a folder in which to store your web projects, click **NEW**, and then click **Folder**. In the **New folder** box, type **GO! Web Projects** and then click **Create** to create a folder on your Google drive. Double-click your **GO! Web Projects** folder to open it.

3 In the left pane, click **NEW**, and then click **Google Docs** to open a new tab in your browser and to start an Untitled document. At the top of the window, click **Untitled document** and then, using your own name as the file name, type **Lastname_Firstname_1A_Google_Doc** and then press Enter to change the file name.

4 To the right of the file name, point to the small file folder to display the ScreenTip **Move to folder**. Click the file folder and notice that your file is saved in the GO! Web Projects folder. Compare your screen with Figure A.

5 Click in your document to close the Move to folder dialog box and to position the insertion point at the top of the document. Type **Internships Available** and then press Enter two times. Type **Interviews will be held Friday and Saturday, January 14 and 15 in the Career Services Conference Room.**

6 Press Ctrl + A to select all of the text. Click the **Font size arrow** ▾, and then click **24**. With the text still selected, click **Center**.

7 Press Ctrl + End to move to the end of the document, and then press Enter. Click **Insert**, and then click **Image**. With **Upload** selected, click **Choose an image to upload**. Navigate to your student data files, click **w01A_Bird**, and then click **Open** to insert the picture.

8 Click the picture to select it, and then point to the square sizing handle at the upper left corner of the picture. Drag down and to the right until the sizing handle aligns with approximately **3 inches on the ruler**.

FIGURE A

(GO! With Google continues on the next page)

9 ▶ Click to the right of the picture and then press [Enter] twice. Type **Join our production crew in Costa Rica as we film a short documentary about its native birds. We are hiring two interns!**

10 ▶ Select the title **Internships Available** and then click **Text color** [A]. In the third column, click the sixth color—**dark orange 1**, and then apply **Bold** [B]. Your document will look similar to Figure B.

11 ▶ Your document will be saved automatically. Sign out of your Google account. Submit as instructed by your instructor.

Internships Available

Interviews will be held Friday and Saturday, January 14 and 15 in the Career Services Conference Room.

Join our production crew in Costa Rica as we film a short documentary about its native birds. We are hiring two interns!

FIGURE B

PROJECT ACTIVITIES

In Activities 1.17 through 1.29, you will format an information handout from Sturgeon Point Productions that describes internships available to students. Your completed document will look similar to Figure 1.25.

PROJECT FILES

If your instructor wants you to submit Project 1B in the MyITLab Grader system, log in to MyITLab, locate Grader Project 1B, and then download the files for this project.

For Project 1B, you will need the following file:
w01B_Programs

You will save your document as:
Lastname_Firstname_1B_Programs

PROJECT RESULTS

GO!
Walk Thru
Project 1B

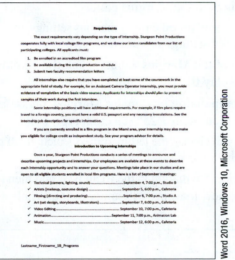

Word 2016, Windows 10, Microsoft Corporation

FIGURE 1.25 Project 1B Information Handout

GO! Learn How
Video W1-5

Document layout includes *margins*—the space between the text and the top, bottom, left, and right edges of the paper. Paragraph layout includes line spacing, indents, and tabs. In Word, the information about paragraph formats is stored in the paragraph mark at the end of a paragraph. When you press Enter, the new paragraph mark contains the formatting of the previous paragraph, unless you take steps to change it.

MOS
1.3.1

Activity 1.17 | Setting Margins

> **ALERT!** To submit as an autograded project, log into MyITLab and download the files for this project, and begin with those files instead of w01B_Programs.

1 Start Word, and then click **Open Other Documents**. Navigate to the student files that accompany this textbook, and then open the document **w01B_Programs**. On the **Home tab**, in the **Paragraph group**, be sure **Show/Hide** ¶ is active so that you can view the formatting marks.

2 Click the **File tab**, and then click **Save As**. Navigate to your **Word Chapter 1** folder, and then using your own name, **Save** the document as **Lastname_Firstname_1B_Programs**

3 Click the **Layout tab**. In the **Page Setup group**, click **Margins**, and then take a moment to study the settings in the Margins gallery.

> If you have recently used custom margins settings, they will display at the top of this gallery. Other commonly used settings also display.

4 At the bottom of the **Margins** gallery, click the command followed by an ellipsis—**Custom Margins** to display the **Page Setup** dialog box.

5 In the **Page Setup** dialog box, under **Margins**, press Tab as necessary to select the value in the **Left** box, and then, with *1.25"* selected, type **1**

> This action will change the left margin to 1 inch on all pages of the document. You do not need to type the inch (") mark.

6 Press Tab to select the margin in the **Right** box, and then type **1** At the bottom of the dialog box, notice that the new margins will apply to the **Whole document**. Compare your screen with Figure 1.26.

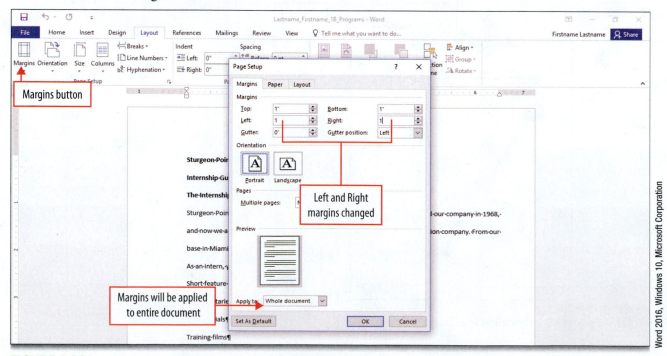

FIGURE 1.26

7 Click **OK** to apply the new margins and close the dialog box. If the ruler below the ribbon is not displayed, on the View tab, in the Show group, select the Ruler check box.

8 Scroll to position the bottom of **Page 1** and the top of **Page 2** on your screen. Notice that the page edges display, and the page number and total number of pages display on the left side of the status bar.

9 Near the bottom edge of **Page 1**, point anywhere in the bottom margin area, right-click, and then click **Edit Footer** to display the footer area.

10 On the ribbon, under the **Header & Footer Tools**, on the **Design tab**, in the **Insert group**, click **Document Info**, and then click **File Name**.

11 Double-click anywhere in the document to close the footer area, and then **Save** 🔲 your document.

Activity 1.18 | Aligning Paragraphs

Alignment refers to the placement of paragraph text relative to the left and right margins. Most paragraph text uses *left alignment*—aligned at the left margin, leaving the right margin uneven. Three other types of paragraph alignment are: *center alignment*—centered between the left and right margins; *right alignment*—aligned at the right margin with an uneven left margin; and *justified alignment*—text aligned evenly at both the left and right margins. The table in Figure 1.27 shows examples of these alignment types.

TYPES OF PARAGRAPH ALIGNMENT		
ALIGNMENT	**BUTTON**	**DESCRIPTION AND EXAMPLE**
Align Left	📄	Align Left is the default paragraph alignment in Word. Text in the paragraph aligns at the left margin, and the right margin is uneven.
Center	📄	Center alignment aligns text in the paragraph so that it is centered between the left and right margins.
Align Right	📄	Align Right aligns text at the right margin. Using Align Right, the left margin, which is normally even, is uneven.
Justify	📄	The Justify alignment option adds additional space between words so that both the left and right margins are even. Justify is often used when formatting newspaper-style columns.

Word 2016, Windows 10, Microsoft Corporation

FIGURE 1.27

1 Scroll to position the middle of **Page 2** on your screen, look at the left and right margins, and notice that the text is justified—both the right and left margins of multiple-line paragraphs are aligned evenly at the margins. On the **Home tab**, in the **Paragraph group**, notice that **Justify** 📄 is active.

> To achieve a justified right margin, Word adjusts the size of spaces between words, which can result in unattractive spacing in a document that spans the width of a page. Many individuals find such spacing difficult to read.

2 Press Ctrl + A to select all of the text in the document, and then on the **Home tab**, in the **Paragraph group**, click **Align Left** 📄.

🔄 ANOTHER WAY   On the Home tab, in the Editing group, click Select, and then click Select All.

3 Press Ctrl + Home to move to the beginning of the document. In the left margin area, point to the left of the first paragraph—*Sturgeon Point Productions*—until the 𝄃 pointer displays, and then click one time to select the paragraph.

> Use this technique to select entire lines of text.

4 On the mini toolbar, in the **Font Size** box, select the existing number, type **40** and then press Enter.

Use this technique to change the font size to a size that is not available on the Font Size list.

5 Select the second paragraph—*Internship Guide*—and then on the mini toolbar, change the **Font Size** to **26 pt**. Point to the left of the first paragraph—*Sturgeon Point Productions*—to display the pointer again, and then drag down to select the first two paragraphs, which form the title and subtitle of the document.

6 On the **Home tab**, in the **Paragraph group**, click **Center** ≡ to center the title and subtitle between the left and right margins, and then compare your screen with Figure 1.28.

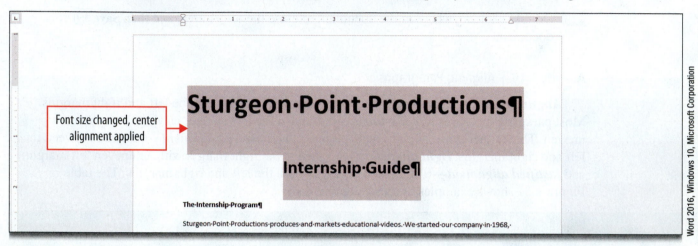

Font size changed, center alignment applied

Sturgeon·Point·Productions¶

Internship·Guide¶

The·Internship·Program¶

Sturgeon·Point·Productions·produces·and·markets·educational·videos.·We·started·our·company·in·1968,·

Word 2016, Windows 10, Microsoft Corporation

FIGURE 1.28

7 Near the top of **Page 1**, locate the first bold subheading—*The Internship Program*. Point to the left of the paragraph to display the pointer, and then click one time to select the text.

8 With *The Internship Program* selected, use your mouse wheel or the vertical scroll bar to bring the bottom portion of **Page 1** into view. Locate the subheading *Requirements*. Move the pointer to the left of the paragraph to display the pointer, hold down Ctrl, and then click one time. Release Ctrl, and then scroll to the middle of **Page 2**. Use the same technique to select the third subheading—*Introduction to Upcoming Internships*.

Three subheadings are selected; in Windows-based programs, you can hold down Ctrl to select multiple items.

9 Click **Center** ≡ to center all three subheadings, and then click **Save** 🖫.

MOS
2.2.3

Activity 1.19 | Setting Line Spacing

Line spacing is the distance between lines of text in a paragraph. Three of the most commonly used line spacing options are shown in the table in Figure 1.29.

LINE SPACING OPTIONS	
ALIGNMENT	**DESCRIPTION, EXAMPLE, AND INFORMATION**
Single spacing	**This text in this example uses single spacing**. Single spacing was once the most commonly used spacing in business documents. Now, because so many documents are read on a computer screen rather than on paper, single spacing is becoming less popular.
Multiple 1.08 spacing	**This text in this example uses multiple 1.08 spacing**. The default line spacing in Microsoft Word 2016 is 1.08, which is slightly more than single spacing to make the text easier to read on a computer screen. Many individuals now prefer this spacing, even on paper, because the lines of text appear less crowded.
Double spacing	**This text in this example uses double spacing**. College research papers and draft documents that need space for notes are commonly double-spaced; there is space for a full line of text between each document line.

FIGURE 1.29

Word 2016, Windows 10, Microsoft Corporation

1 Press Ctrl + Home to move to the beginning of the document. Press Ctrl + A to select all of the text in the document.

2 With all of the text in the document selected, on the **Home tab**, in the **Paragraph group**, click **Line and Paragraph Spacing** ⌄, and notice that the text in the document is double-spaced—**2.0** is checked. Compare your screen with Figure 1.30.

🔄 BY TOUCH   Tap the ribbon commands.

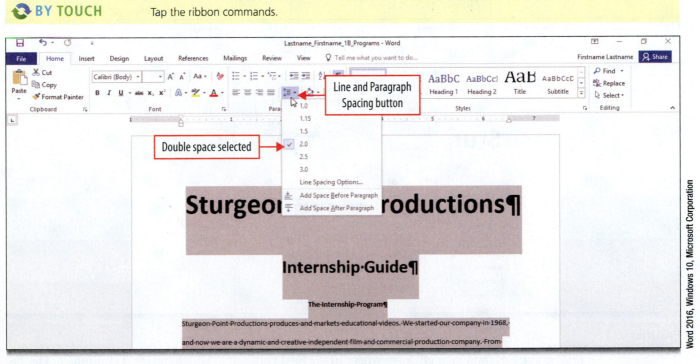

FIGURE 1.30

Word 2016, Windows 10, Microsoft Corporation

3 On the **Line Spacing** menu, click the *third* setting—**1.5**—and then click anywhere in the document to deselect the text. Compare your screen with Figure 1.31, and then **Save** 🖫 your document.

FIGURE 1.31

2.2.3

Activity 1.20 | Indenting Text

Indenting the first line of each paragraph is a common technique to distinguish paragraphs.

1 Below the title and subtitle of the document, click anywhere in the paragraph that begins *Sturgeon Point Productions produces*.

2 On the **Home tab**, in the **Paragraph group**, click the **Dialog Box Launcher** ⌐.

3 In the **Paragraph** dialog box, on the **Indents and Spacing tab**, under **Indentation**, click the **Special arrow**, and then click **First line** to indent the first line by 0.5", which is the default indent setting. Compare your screen with Figure 1.32.

FIGURE 1.32

4 Click **OK**, and then click anywhere in the next paragraph, which begins *As an intern*. On the ruler under the ribbon, drag the **First Line Indent** marker ▽ to **0.5 inches on the horizontal ruler**, and then compare your screen with Figure 1.33.

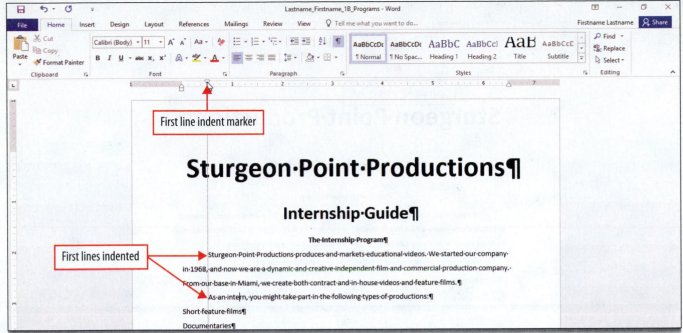

FIGURE 1.33

Word 2016, Windows 10, Microsoft Corporation

5 By using either of the techniques you just practiced, or by using the Format Painter, apply a first line indent of **0.5"** to the paragraph that begins *Here is a partial* to match the indent of the remaining paragraphs in the document.

6 **Save** 💾 your document.

MOS
1.2.3

Activity 1.21 | Setting Space Before and After Paragraphs

Adding space after each paragraph is another technique to differentiate paragraphs.

1 Press Ctrl + A to select all of the text in the document. Click the **Layout tab**, and then in the **Paragraph group**, under **Spacing**, click the **After spin box up arrow** one time to change the value to **6 pt**.

To change the value in the box, you can also select the existing number, type a new number, and then press Enter. This document will use 6 pt spacing after paragraphs to add space.

🔄 **ANOTHER WAY** On either the Home tab or the Layout tab, display the Paragraph dialog box from the Paragraph group, and then under Spacing, click the spin box arrows as necessary.

2 Press Ctrl + Home, and then compare your screen with Figure 1.34.

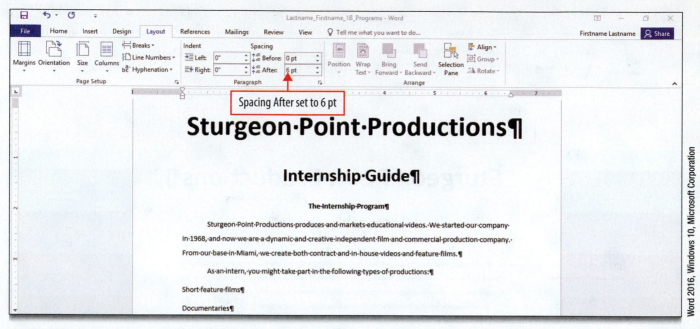

Spacing After set to 6 pt

FIGURE 1.34

3 Near the top of **Page 1**, select the subheading **The Internship Program**, including the paragraph mark following it. Scroll down using the vertical scroll bar, hold down [Ctrl], and then select the **Requirements** and **Introduction to Upcoming Internships** subheadings.

> **ALERT!** **Did your screen zoom when you were selecting?**
>
> Holding down [Ctrl] and using the mouse wheel at the same time will zoom your screen.

4 With all three subheadings selected, in the **Paragraph group**, under **Spacing**, click the **Before up spin box arrow** two times to set the **Spacing Before** to **12 pt**. Compare your screen with Figure 1.35, and then **Save** 🖫 your document.

This action increases the amount of space above each of the subheadings, which will make them easy to distinguish in the document. The formatting is applied only to the selected paragraphs.

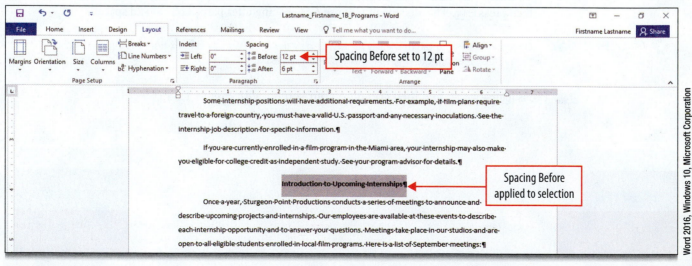

Spacing Before set to 12 pt

Spacing Before applied to selection

FIGURE 1.35

GO! Learn How
Video W1-6

To display a list of information, you can choose a **bulleted list**, which uses **bullets**—text symbols such as small circles or check marks—to introduce each item in a list. You can also choose a **numbered list**, which uses consecutive numbers or letters to introduce each item in a list.

Use a bulleted list if the items in the list can be introduced in any order; use a numbered list for items that have definite steps, a sequence of actions, or are in chronological order.

3.3.1

Activity 1.22 | Creating a Bulleted List

1 In the upper portion of **Page 1**, locate the paragraph *Short feature films*, and then point to this paragraph from the left margin area to display the ⟋ pointer. Drag down to select this paragraph and the next five paragraphs—ending with the paragraph *Recordings of live concerts*.

2 On the **Home tab**, in the **Paragraph group**, click **Bullets** ⯬ to change the selected text to a bulleted list.

The 6 pt spacing between each of the bulleted points is removed and each bulleted item is automatically indented.

3 On the ruler, point to **First Line Indent** ▽ and read the ScreenTip, and then point to **Hanging Indent** ⌂. Compare your screen with Figure 1.36.

By default, Word formats bulleted items with a first line indent of 0.25" and adds a Hanging Indent at 0.5". The hanging indent maintains the alignment of text when a bulleted item is more than one line.

You can modify the list indentation by using Decrease Indent ⯠ or Increase Indent ⯡. Decrease Indent moves your paragraph closer to the margin. Increase Indent moves your paragraph farther away from the margin.

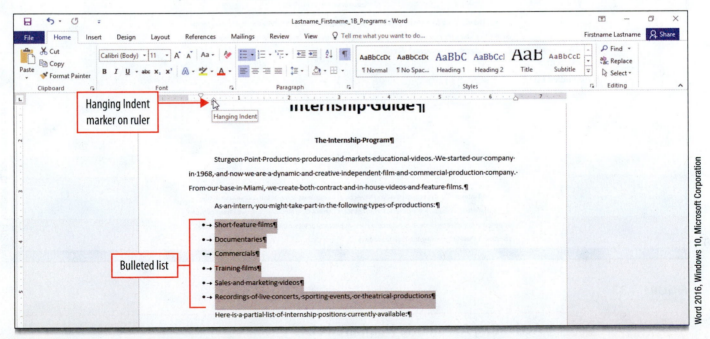

FIGURE 1.36

Word 2016, Windows 10, Microsoft Corporation

4 Scroll down slightly, and then by using the ⟋ pointer from the left margin area, select the five internship positions, beginning with *Production Assistant* and ending with *Assistant Set Designer*. In the **Paragraph group**, click **Bullets** ⯬.

5 ▸ Scroll down to view **Page 2**. Apply bullets to all of the paragraphs that indicate the September meetings and meeting dates, beginning with *Technical* and ending with *Music*.

6 ▸ **Save** 🔲 your document.

Activity 1.23 | Creating a Numbered List

3.3.1

1 ▸ Under the subheading *Requirements*, in the paragraph that begins *The exact requirements*, click to position the insertion point at the *end* of the paragraph, following the colon. Press Enter to create a blank paragraph. Notice that the paragraph is indented because the First Line Indent from the previous paragraph carried over to the new paragraph.

2 ▸ To change the indent formatting for this paragraph, on the ruler, drag the **First Line Indent** marker ▽ to the left so that it is positioned directly above the lower button.

3 ▸ Being sure to include the period, type **1.** and press Spacebar. Compare your screen with Figure 1.37.

Word determines that this paragraph is the first item in a numbered list and formats the new paragraph accordingly, indenting the list in the same manner as the bulleted list. The space after the number changes to a tab, and the AutoCorrect Options button displays to the left of the list item. The tab is indicated by a right arrow formatting mark.

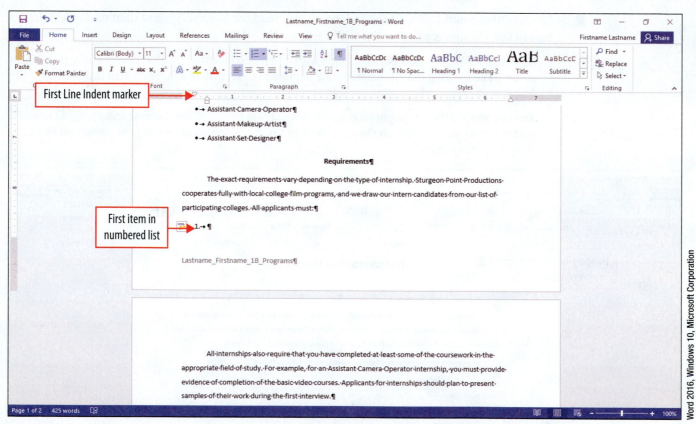

FIGURE 1.37

ALERT! **Activating Automatic Numbered Lists**

If a numbered list does not begin automatically, click the File tab, and then click the Options tab. On the left side of the Word Options dialog box, click Proofing. Under AutoCorrect options, click the AutoCorrect Options button. In the AutoCorrect dialog box, click the AutoFormat As You Type tab. Under *Apply as you type*, select the *Automatic numbered lists* check box, and then click OK two times to close both dialog boxes.

---

4 Click **AutoCorrect Options** ⚡, and then compare your screen with Figure 1.38.

From the displayed list, you can remove the automatic formatting here, or stop using the automatic numbered lists option in this document. You also have the option to open the AutoCorrect dialog box to *Control AutoFormat Options*.

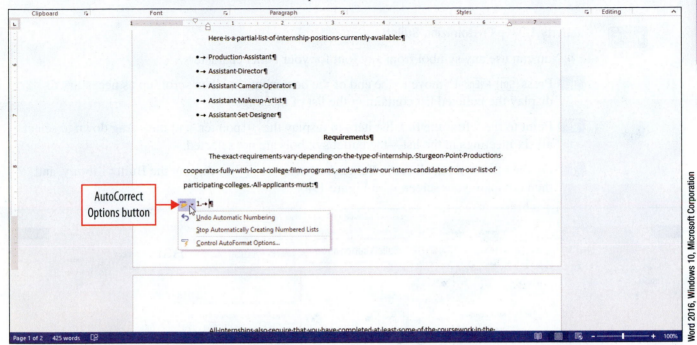

FIGURE 1.38

5 Click **AutoCorrect Options** ⚡ again to close the menu without selecting any of the commands. Type **Be enrolled in an accredited film program** and press Enter. Notice that the second number and a tab are added to the next line.

6 Type **Be available during the entire production schedule** and press Enter. Type **Submit two faculty recommendation letters** and then compare your screen with Figure 1.39. **Save** 💾 your document.

FIGURE 1.39

3.3.2

Activity 1.24 | Customizing Bullets

You can use any symbol from any font for your bullet characters.

1 Press [Ctrl] + [End] to move to the end of the document, and then scroll up as necessary to display the bulleted list containing the list of meetings.

2 Point to the left of the first list item to display the pointer, and then drag down to select all six meetings in the list—the bullet symbols are not selected.

3 On the mini toolbar, click the **Bullets button arrow** to display the Bullet Library, and then compare your screen with Figure 1.40.

FIGURE 1.40

4 Under **Bullet Library**, click the **check mark** symbol. If the check mark is not available, choose another bullet symbol.

5 With the bulleted list still selected, right-click over the list, and then on the mini toolbar, double-click **Format Painter** to activate it for multiple use.

ANOTHER WAY   On the Home tab, in the Clipboard group, double-click Format Painter.

6 Use the vertical scroll bar or your mouse wheel to scroll to view **Page 1**. Move the pointer to the left of the first item in the first bulleted list to display the ⇱ pointer, and then drag down to select all six items in the list and to apply the format of the third bulleted list—the check mark bullets—to this list. Repeat this procedure to change the bullets in the second list to check marks. Press (Esc) to turn off **Format Painter**, and then **Save** 🖫 your document. Compare your screen with Figure 1.41.

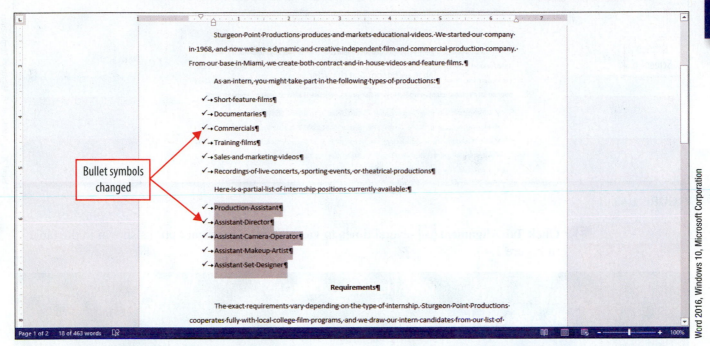

FIGURE 1.41

Objective 7   Set and Modify Tab Stops

Word 2016, Windows 10, Microsoft Corporation

GO! Learn How
Video W1-7

Tab stops mark specific locations on a line of text. Use tab stops to indent and align text, and use the (Tab) key to move to tab stops.

Activity 1.25 | Setting Tab Stops

1 Scroll to view the lower portion of **Page 2**, and then by using the ⇱ pointer at the left of the first item, select all of the items in the bulleted list. Notice that there is a tab mark between the name of the meeting and the date.

The arrow that indicates a tab is a nonprinting formatting mark.

2 To the left of the horizontal ruler, point to **Tab Alignment** 🔲 to display the *Left Tab* ScreenTip, and then compare your screen with Figure 1.42.

FIGURE 1.42

3 ▶ Click **Tab Alignment** 🔲 several times to view the tab alignment options shown in the table in Figure 1.43.

TAB ALIGNMENT OPTIONS

TYPE	TAB ALIGNMENT BUTTON DISPLAYS THIS MARKER	DESCRIPTION
Left	🔲	Text is left aligned at the tab stop and extends to the right.
Center	🔲	Text is centered around the tab stop.
Right	🔲	Text is right aligned at the tab stop and extends to the left.
Decimal	🔲	The decimal point aligns at the tab stop.
Bar	🔲	A vertical bar displays at the tab stop.
First Line Indent	▽	Text in the first line of a paragraph indents.
Hanging Indent	🔲	Text in all lines except the first line in the paragraph indents.

FIGURE 1.43

4 ▶ Display **Left Tab** 🔲. Along the lower edge of the horizontal ruler, point to and then click at **3.5 inches on the horizontal ruler**. Notice that all of the dates left align at the new tab stop location, and the right edge of the column is uneven.

5 ▶ Compare your screen with Figure 1.44, and then **Save** 🔲 your document.

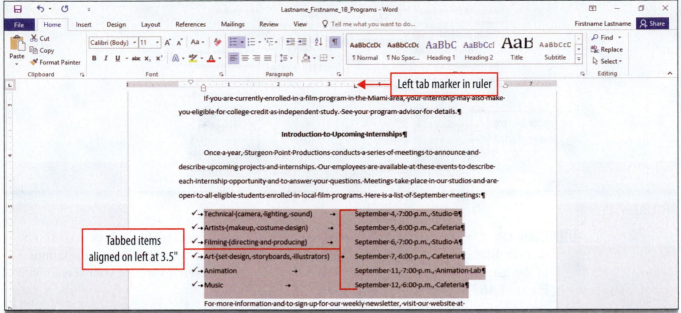

Word 2016, Windows 10, Microsoft Corporation

FIGURE 1.44

Activity 1.26 | Modifying Tab Stops

Tab stops are a form of paragraph formatting. Therefore, the information about tab stops is stored in the paragraph mark in the paragraphs to which they were applied.

1 With the bulleted list still selected, on the ruler, point to the new tab marker at *3.5 inches on the horizontal ruler*, and then when the *Left Tab* ScreenTip displays, drag the tab marker to **4 inches on the horizontal ruler**.

In all of the selected lines, the text at the tab stop left aligns at 4 inches.

2 On the ruler, point to the tab marker that you moved to display the *Left Tab* ScreenTip, and then double-click to display the **Tabs** dialog box.

ANOTHER WAY On the Home tab, in the Paragraph group, click the Dialog Box Launcher. At the bottom of the Paragraph dialog box, click the Tabs button.

3 In the **Tabs** dialog box, under **Tab stop position**, if necessary select *4"* and then type **6**

4 Under **Alignment**, click the **Right** option button. Under **Leader**, click the **2** option button. Near the bottom of the **Tabs** dialog box, click **Set**.

Because the Right tab will be used to align the items in the list, the tab stop at 4" is no longer necessary.

5 In the **Tabs** dialog box, in the **Tab stop position** box, click **4"** to select this tab stop, and then in the lower portion of the **Tabs** dialog box, click the **Clear** button to delete this tab stop, which is no longer necessary. Compare your screen with Figure 1.45.

FIGURE 1.45

> **6** ▸ Click **OK**. On the ruler, notice that the left tab marker at *4″* no longer displays, a right tab marker displays at *6″*, and a series of dots—a ***dot leader***—displays between the columns of the list. Notice also that the right edge of the column is even. Compare your screen with Figure 1.46.

> A ***leader character*** creates a solid, dotted, or dashed line that fills the space to the left of a tab character and draws the reader's eyes across the page from one item to the next. When the character used for the leader is a dot, it is commonly referred to as a dot leader.

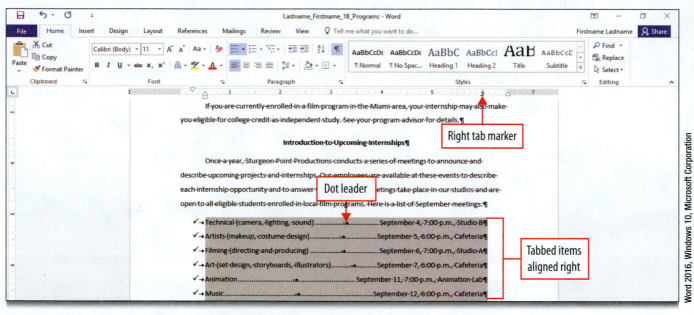

FIGURE 1.46

> **7** ▸ In the bulleted list that uses dot leaders, locate the *Art* meeting, and then click to position the insertion point at the end of that line, after the word *Cafeteria*. Press Enter to create a new blank bullet item.

> **8** ▸ Type **Video Editing** and press Tab. Notice that a dot leader fills the space to the tab marker location.

> **9** ▸ Type **September 10, 7:00 p.m., Cafeteria** and notice that the text moves to the left to maintain the right alignment of the tab stop.

> **10** ▸ **Save** 🖫 your document.

GO! Learn How
Video W1-8

SmartArt graphics are designer-quality visual representations of information, and Word provides many different layouts from which you can choose. You can also insert a link to an online video from a variety of online sources, thus enabling the reader to view the video when connected to the Internet. SmartArt graphics and videos can communicate your messages or ideas more effectively than plain text, and these objects add visual interest to a document or web page.

5.3.1

Activity 1.27 | Inserting a SmartArt Graphic

1 Press Ctrl + Home to move to the top of the document, and then click to the right of the subtitle *Internship Guide*.

2 Click the **Insert tab**, and then in the **Illustrations group**, point to **SmartArt** to display its ScreenTip. Read the ScreenTip, and then click **SmartArt**.

3 In the center portion of the **Choose a SmartArt Graphic** dialog box, scroll down and examine the numerous types of SmartArt graphics available.

4 On the left, click **Process**, and then by using the ScreenTips, locate and click **Basic Chevron Process**. Compare your screen with Figure 1.47.

At the right of the dialog box, a preview and description of the SmartArt displays.

FIGURE 1.47

5 Click **OK** to insert the SmartArt graphic.

To the left of the inserted SmartArt graphic, the text pane may display. The text pane provides one method for entering text into your SmartArt graphic. If you choose not to use the text pane to enter text, you can close it.

6 On the ribbon, under **SmartArt Tools**, on the **Design tab**, in the **Create Graphic group**, notice the **Text Pane** button. If the text pane button is selected, click Text Pane to close the pane.

7 In the SmartArt graphic, in the first blue arrow, click **[Text]**, and notice that *[Text]* is replaced by a blinking insertion point.

The word *[Text]* is called ***placeholder text***, which is nonprinting text that indicates where you can type.

8 Type **Apply Online**

9 Click the placeholder text in the middle arrow. Type **Interview** and then click the placeholder text in the third arrow. Type **Train on the Job** and then compare your screen with Figure 1.48.

Word 2016, Windows 10, Microsoft Corporation

FIGURE 1.48

10 Save 🖫 your document.

Activity 1.28 | Sizing and Formatting a SmartArt Graphic

5.3.2

1 Click the **SmartArt solid graphic border** to select it. Be sure that none of the arrows have sizing handles around their border, which would indicate the arrow was selected, not the entire graphic.

2 Click the **Format tab**, and then in the **Size group**, if necessary click Size to display the Shape Height and Shape Width boxes.

3 Set the **Height** to **1.75"** and the **Width** to **6.5"**, and then compare your screen with Figure 1.49.

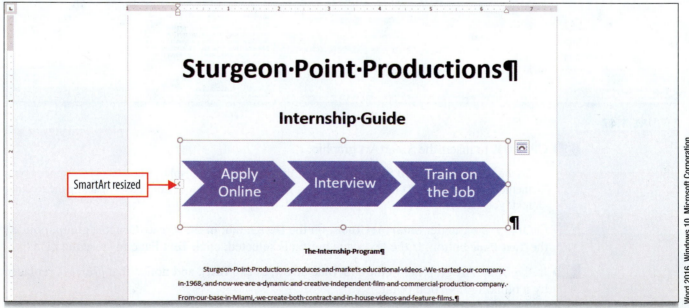

Word 2016, Windows 10, Microsoft Corporation

FIGURE 1.49

4 With the SmartArt graphic still selected, click the **SmartArt Tools Design tab**, and then in the **SmartArt Styles group**, click **Change Colors**. Under **Colorful**, click the fourth style—**Colorful Range - Accent Colors 4 to 5**.

5 On the **SmartArt Tools Design tab**, in the **SmartArt Styles group**, click **More**. Under **3-D**, click the second style—**Inset**. Click **Save**, and then compare your screen with Figure 1.50.

Word 2016, Windows 10, Microsoft Corporation

FIGURE 1.50

Activity 1.29 | Inserting an Online Video

Microsoft's research indicates that two-thirds of people who open Word documents never edit them; they only read them. So with more and more documents being read online—and not on paper—it makes sense that you may want to include videos in your Word documents.

1 Press Ctrl + End to move to the end of the document.

2 On the **Insert tab**, in the **Media group**, click **Online Video**.

Here you can search the web for an online video, search YouTube, or enter an *embed code* to insert a link to a video from a website. An embed code is a code that creates a link to a video, picture, or other type of *rich media* content. Rich media, also called *interactive media*, refers to computer interaction that responds to your actions; for example, by presenting text, graphics, animation, video, audio, or games.

3 In the **Bing Video Search** box, type **Go 1B Video** and then press Enter.

Several videos display based on the search term that you typed.

4 Point to several of the videos and notice that a ScreenTip displays a description of the video. Click one of the videos that includes the words *Go 1B Video* in the ScreenTip, and then click **Insert**. Compare your screen with Figure 1.51.

For·more·information·and·to·sign·up·for·our·weekly·newsletter,·visit·our·website·at·
www.sturgeonpointproductions.com.·Be·sure·to·view·the·following·video·to·learn·about·some·of·the·
important·skills·you·will·develop·as·an·intern·with·Sturgeon·Point·Productions.

Online Video embedded
in document.
Your video may differ.

The Arts
Costume Design

Word 2016, Windows 10, Microsoft Corporation

FIGURE 1.51

ALERT!	**Are you unable to locate or play the video?**

If you are unable to locate a video using the search words that you entered in Step 3, in the Bing Video Search box, type MyITLab and then insert the first video that displays. Depending upon your computer configuration, the video may not play.

5 On the **Picture Tools Format** tab, in the **Size** group, click in the **Height** box to select the value. Type **1.5** and then press Enter to change the size of the video.

6 Click **Save** 🖫, and then press Ctrl + Home to move to the top of your document.

7 Click the **File tab**, and then in the lower right portion of the screen, click **Show All Properties**. In the **Tags** box, type **internship** and in the **Subject** box, type your course name and section number. In the **Author** box, replace the existing text with your first and last name.

8 On the left, click **Print** to display **Print Preview**. At the bottom of the preview, click the **Next Page** ▶ and **Previous Page** ◀ buttons to move between pages. If necessary, return to the document and make any necessary changes.

9 **Save** 🖫 your document. In the upper right corner of the Word window, click **Close** ✕. If directed by your instructor to do so, submit your paper printout, your electronic image of your document that looks like a printed document, or your completed Word file.

END | You have completed Project 1B

GO! With Google

Objective Create an Information Handout

ALERT!   **Working with Web-Based Applications and Services**

Computer programs and services on the web receive continuous updates and improvements, so the steps to complete this web-based activity may differ from the ones shown. You can often look at the screens and the information presented to determine how to complete the activity.

If you do not already have a Google account, you will need to create one before you begin this activity. Go to http://google.com and, in the upper right corner, click Sign In. On the Sign In screen, click Create Account. On the Create your Google Account page, complete the form, read and agree to the Terms of Service and Privacy Policy, and then click Next step. On the Welcome screen, click Get Started.

Activity | Creating a Handout with Bulleted and Numbered Lists

In this Activity, you will use Google Docs to create an information handout.

1 From the desktop, open your browser, navigate to **http://google.com**, and then sign in to your Google account. In the upper right corner of your screen, click **Google Apps**, and then click **Drive**. Double-click your **GO! Web Projects** folder to open it. If you have not created this folder, refer to the instructions in the first Google Docs project in this chapter.

2 In the left pane, click **NEW**, and then click **Google Docs**. Click **File**, and then click **Open**. Click **Upload**, and then click **Select a file from your computer**. From your student data files, click **w01_1B_Web** and then click **Open** to open the file and upload it to your GO! Web Projects folder.

3 In the upper left corner of the Google Docs window, select **w01_1B_Web** and then type **Lastname_Firstname_1B_Google_Doc** and then press Enter to rename the file.

4 Press Ctrl + A to select all of the text. Click **Line spacing**, and then click **1.5**. Click **Left align**.

5 Select the six lines of text beginning with *Short feature films* and ending with *Recording of live concerts*, and then click **Bulleted list** to apply bullets to the selected text. Select the list of internship positions beginning with *Production Assistant* and ending with *Assistant Set Designer*, and then click **Bulleted list**. Compare your screen with Figure A.

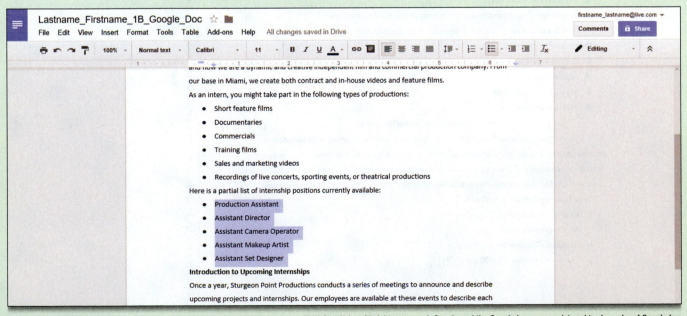

FIGURE A

(GO! With Google continues on the next page)

6 ▶ Select the last five lines of the document beginning with *Artists* and ending with *Music*. To create a numbered list from the selection, click **Numbered list** 📄.

7 ▶ Select the first three lines of text in the document, and then click **Center** 📄. Click in the *Introduction to Upcoming Internships* heading, and then click **Center** 📄.

8 ▶ Click at the beginning of the paragraph that begins *Sturgeon Point Production produces and markets*, and then press Tab. Look at the ruler and notice that the first line indent is applied.

9 ▶ With the insertion point in the same paragraph, double-click **Paint format** 📄. Then, click in the paragraphs that begin *As an intern*, *Here is a partial list*, and *Once a year* to apply the first line indent to each of the paragraphs. Click **Paint format** 📄 to turn it off. Compare your screen with Figure B.

10 ▶ Your document will be saved automatically. Sign out of your Google account, and then submit as instructed by your instructor.

Sturgeon Point Productions

Internship Guide

The Internship Program

Sturgeon Point Productions produces and markets educational videos. We started our company in 1968, and now we are a dynamic and creative independent film and commercial production company. From our base in Miami, we create both contract and in-house videos and feature films.

As an intern, you might take part in the following types of productions:

- Short feature films
- Documentaries
- Commercials
- Training films
- Sales and marketing videos
- Recordings of live concerts, sporting events, or theatrical productions

Here is a partial list of internship positions currently available:

- Production Assistant
- Assistant Director
- Assistant Camera Operator
- Assistant Makeup Artist
- Assistant Set Designer

Introduction to Upcoming Internships

Once a year, Sturgeon Point Productions conducts a series of meetings to announce and describe upcoming projects and internships. Our employees are available at these events to describe each internship opportunity and to answer your questions. Meetings take place in our studios and are open to all eligible students enrolled in local film programs. Here is a list of September meetings:

1. Artists—September 5, 6:00 p.m.
2. Filming—September 6, 7:00 p.m.
3. Art—September 7, 6:00 p.m.
4. Animation—September 11, 7:00 p.m.
5. Music—September 12, 6:00 p.m.

FIGURE B

GO! To Work

MICROSOFT OFFICE SPECIALIST (MOS) SKILLS IN THIS CHAPTER

PROJECT 1A	PROJECT 1B
1.1.1 Create a blank document	**1.3.1** Modify page setup
1.1.4 Insert text from a file or external source	**2.2.3** Set line and paragraph spacing and indentation
1.3.4 Insert headers and footers	**3.3.1** Create a numbered or bulleted list
1.4.5 Add document properties	**3.3.2** Change bullet characters or number formats for a list level
1.4.6 Show or hide formatting symbols	**5.3.1** Create a SmartArt graphic
1.5.3 Print all or part of a document	**5.3.2** Format a SmartArt graphic
5.1.1 Insert shapes	**5.3.3** Modify SmartArt graphic content
5.1.2 Insert pictures	
5.1.4 Insert text boxes	
5.2.1 Apply artistic effects	
5.2.2 Apply picture effects	
5.2.4 Format objects	
5.2.6 Wrap text around objects	
5.2.7 Position objects	

BUILD YOUR E-PORTFOLIO

An E-Portfolio is a collection of evidence, stored electronically, that showcases what you have accomplished while completing your education. Collecting and then sharing your work products with potential employers reflects your academic and career goals. Your completed documents from the following projects are good examples to show what you have learned: 1G, 1K, and 1L.

GO! FOR JOB SUCCESS

Video: Personal Branding

Your instructor may assign this video to your class, and then ask you to think about, or discuss with your classmates, these questions:

FotolEdhar / Fotolia

How do you suggest job seekers communicate their unique value—their personal brand—to potential employers online?

What are the best ways to network online and offline?

What are some of the biggest pitfalls in using social media to communicate a personal brand?

END OF CHAPTER

SUMMARY

In this chapter, you started Word and practiced navigating the Word window, and you entered, edited, and formatted text. You also inserted text from another Word file.

Graphics include pictures, shapes, and text boxes. In this chapter, you formatted objects by applying styles, effects, and text-wrapping options, and you sized and positioned objects on the page.

SmartArt graphics visually represent your ideas, and there are many SmartArt graphics from which to choose. You can also use online videos in your documents to provide visual information to the reader.

Word documents can be formatted to display your information attractively. You can add a page border, add bulleted and numbered lists, change margins and tabs, and modify paragraph and line spacing.

GO! LEARN IT ONLINE

Review the concepts, key terms, and MOS skills in this chapter by completing these online challenges, which you can find at **MyITLab**.

Matching and Multiple Choice: Answer matching and multiple choice questions to test what you learned in this chapter.

Lessons on the GO!: Learn how to use all the new apps and features as they are introduced by Microsoft.

MOS Prep Quiz: Answer questions to review the MOS skills that you practiced in this chapter.

GO! COLLABORATIVE TEAM PROJECT (Available in **MyITLab** and Instructor Resource Center)

If your instructor assigns this project to your class, you can expect to work with one or more of your classmates—either in person or by using Internet tools—to create work products similar to those that you created in this chapter. A team is a group of workers who work together to solve a problem, make a decision, or create a work product. Collaboration is when you work together with others as a team in an intellectual endeavor to complete a shared task or achieve a shared goal.

PROJECT GUIDE FOR WORD CHAPTER 1

Your instructor will assign Projects from this list to ensure your learning and assess your knowledge.

	Project Guide for Word Chapter 1		
Project	**Apply Skills from These Chapter Objectives**	**Project Type**	**Project Location**
1A *MyITLab*	Objectives 1-4 from Project 1A	**1A Instructional Project (Grader Project)** A guided review of the skills from Project.	In MyITLab and in text
1B *MyITLab*	Objectives 5-8 from Project 1B	**1B Instructional Project (Grader Project)** A guided review of the skills from Project.	In MyITLab and in text
1C	Objectives 1-4 from Project 1A	**1C Skills Review (Scorecard Grading)** A guided review of the skills from Project 2A.	In text
1D	Objectives 5-8 from Project 1B	**1D Skills Review (Scorecard Grading)** A guided review of the skills from Project 2B.	In text
1E *MyITLab*	Objectives 1-4 from Project 1A	**1E Mastery (Grader Project) Mastery and Transfer of Learning** A demonstration of your mastery of the skills in Project 2A with extensive decision making.	In MyITLab and in text
1F *MyITLab*	Objectives 5-8 from Project 1B	**1F Mastery (Grader Project) Mastery and Transfer of Learning** A demonstration of your mastery of the skills in Project 2B with extensive decision making.	In MyITLab and in text
1G *MyITLab*	Objectives 1-8 from Project 1A and 1B	**1G Mastery (Grader Project) Mastery and Transfer of Learning** A demonstration of your mastery of the skills in Projects 2A and 2B with extensive decision making.	In MyITLab and in text
1H	Combination of Objectives from Projects 1A and 1B	**1H GO! Fix It (Scorecard Grading) Critical Thinking** A demonstration of your mastery of the skills in Projects 1A and 1B by creating a correct result from a document that contains errors you must find.	Instructor Resource Center (IRC) and MyITLab
1I	Combination of Objectives from Projects 1A and 1B	**1I GO! Make It (Scorecard Grading) Critical Thinking** A demonstration of your mastery of the skills in Projects 1A and 1B by creating a result from a supplied picture.	IRC and MyITLab
1J	Combination of Objectives from Projects 1A and 1B	**1J GO! Solve It (Rubric Grading) Critical Thinking** A demonstration of your mastery of the skills in Projects 1A and 1B, your decision-making skills, and your critical thinking skills. A task-specific rubric helps you self-assess your result.	IRC and MyITLab
1K	Combination of Objectives from Projects 1A and 1B	**1K GO! Solve It (Rubric Grading) Critical Thinking** A demonstration of your mastery of the skills in Projects 1A and 1B, your decision-making skills, and your critical thinking skills. A task-specific rubric helps you self-assess your result.	In text
1L	Combination of Objectives from Projects 1A and 1B	**1L GO! Think (Rubric Grading) Critical Thinking** A demonstration of your understanding of the chapter concepts applied in a manner that you would outside of college. An analytic rubric helps you and your instructor grade the quality of your work by comparing it to the work an expert in the discipline would create.	In text
1M	Combination of Objectives from Projects 1A and 1B	**1M GO! Think (Rubric Grading) Critical Thinking** A demonstration of your understanding of the chapter concepts applied in a manner that you would outside of college. An analytic rubric helps you and your instructor grade the quality of your work by comparing it to the work an expert in the discipline would create.	IRC and MyITLab
1N	Combination of Objectives from Projects 1A and 1B	**1N You and GO! (Rubric Grading) Critical Thinking** A demonstration of your understanding of the chapter concepts applied in a manner that you would in a personal situation. An analytic rubric helps you and your instructor grade the quality of your work.	IRC and MyITLab
1O	Combination of Objectives from Projects 1A and 1B	**1O Collaborative Team Project for WORD Chapter 1 Critical Thinking** A demonstration of your understanding of concepts and your ability to work collaboratively in a group role-playing assessment, requiring both collaboration and self-management.	IRC and MyITLab

GLOSSARY

GLOSSARY OF CHAPTER KEY TERMS

Alignment The placement of paragraph text relative to the left and right margins.

Alignment guide A green vertical or horizontal line that displays when you are moving or sizing an object to assist you with object placement.

Artistic effects Formats applied to images that make pictures resemble sketches or paintings.

Bulleted list A list of items with each item introduced by a symbol such as a small circle or check mark, and which is useful when the items in the list can be displayed in any order.

Bullets Text symbols such as small circles or check marks that precede each item in a bulleted list.

Center alignment The alignment of text or objects that is centered horizontally between the left and right margin.

Dot leader A series of dots preceding a tab that guides the eye across the line.

Drawing objects Graphic objects, such as shapes, diagrams, lines, or circles.

Embed code A code that creates a link to a video, picture, or other type of rich media content.

Floating object A graphic that can be moved independently of the surrounding text characters.

Formatting marks Characters that display on the screen, but do not print, indicating where the Enter key, the Spacebar, and the Tab key were pressed; also called nonprinting characters.

Graphics Pictures, charts, or drawing objects.

Inline object An object or graphic inserted in a document that acts like a character in a sentence.

Interactive media Computer interaction that responds to your actions; for example, by presenting text, graphics, animation, video, audio, or games. Also referred to as rich media.

Justified alignment An arrangement of text in which the text aligns evenly on both the left and right margins.

Layout Options Picture formatting options that control the manner in which text wraps around a picture or other object.

Leader character Characters that form a solid, dotted, or dashed line that fills the space preceding a tab stop.

Left alignment An arrangement of text in which the text aligns at the left margin, leaving the right margin uneven.

Line spacing The distance between lines of text in a paragraph.

Live Layout A feature that reflows text as you move or size an object so that you can view the placement of surrounding text.

Margins The space between the text and the top, bottom, left, and right edges of the paper.

Nonprinting characters Characters that display on the screen, but do not print; also called formatting marks.

Numbered list A list that uses consecutive numbers or letters to introduce each item in a list.

Object anchor The symbol that indicates to which paragraph an object is attached.

Picture effects Effects that enhance a picture, such as a shadow, glow, reflection, or 3-D rotation.

Picture styles Frames, shapes, shadows, borders, and other special effects that can be added to an image to create an overall visual style for the image.

Placeholder text Nonprinting text that holds a place in a document where you can type.

Rich media Computer interaction that responds to your actions; for example, by presenting text, graphics, animation, video, audio, or games. Also referred to as interactive media.

Right alignment An arrangement of text in which the text aligns at the right margin, leaving the left margin uneven.

Rotation handle A symbol with which you can rotate a graphic to any angle; displays above the top center sizing handle.

Shapes Lines, arrows, stars, banners, ovals, rectangles, and other basic shapes with which you can illustrate an idea, a process, or a workflow.

SmartArt A designer-quality visual representation of your information that you can create by choosing from among many different layouts to effectively communicate your message or ideas.

Spin box A small box with an upward- and downward-pointing arrow that lets you move rapidly through a set of values by clicking.

Tab stop A specific location on a line of text, marked on the Word ruler, to which you can move the insertion point by pressing the Tab key, and which is used to align and indent text.

Template A preformatted document that you can use as a starting point and then change to suit your needs.

Text box A movable resizable container for text or graphics.

Text effects Decorative formats, such as shadowed or mirrored text, text glow, 3-D effects, and colors that make text stand out.

Text wrapping The manner in which text displays around an object.

Toggle button A button that can be turned on by clicking it once, and then turned off by clicking it again.

Wordwrap The feature that moves text from the right edge of a paragraph to the beginning of the next line as necessary to fit within the margins.

Skills Review Project 1C Photography

In the following Skills Review, you will create a flyer advertising a photography internship with Sturgeon Point Productions. Your completed document will look similar to Figure 1.52.

PROJECT FILES

For Project 1C, you will need the following files:

New blank Word document
w01C_Building
w01C_Photographer

You will save your document as:

Lastname_Firstname_1C_Photography

Build from Scratch

PROJECT RESULTS

Internship Available for
Still Photographer

This position requires skill in the use of:

Professional full-frame DSLR cameras

Tilt-shift lenses for tall buildings

This fall, Sturgeon Point Productions will film a documentary on the historic architecture in and around Milwaukee, Wisconsin.

The filming will take place during the last two weeks of September. If the weather is not conducive to outdoor shooting, it is possible that filming will continue into the first week of October.

The still photographer will accompany the director during the first two weeks of September to scout locations and take photographs for the purpose of planning the filming schedule. The photographer will also accompany the film crew throughout filming.

Photographs taken during pre-production and filming will be used for advertising and marketing and published in an upcoming book on the history of the city of Milwaukee.

Submit Your Application by June 30!

Lastname_Firstname_1C_Photography

Word 2016, Windows 10, Microsoft Corporation

FIGURE 1.52

(Project 1C Photography continues on the next page)

1 ▶ Start Word and then click **Blank document**. On the **Home tab**, in the **Paragraph group**, if necessary, click Show/Hide to display the formatting marks. If the rulers do not display, click the View tab, and then in the Show group, select the Ruler check box.

a. Type **Internship Available for Still Photographer** and then press Enter two times. Type the following text: **This fall, Sturgeon Point Productions will film a documentary on the historic architecture in and around Milwaukee, Wisconsin.** Press Enter.

b. On the ribbon, click the **Insert tab**. In the **Text group**, click the **Object button arrow**, and then click **Text from File**. In the **Insert File** dialog box, navigate to the student files that accompany this chapter, locate and select **w01C_Photographer**, and then click **Insert**. Delete the blank paragraph at the end of the document.

c. Including the paragraph mark, select the first paragraph of text—*Internship Available for Still Photographer*. On the **Home tab**, in the **Font group**, click **Text Effects and Typography**. In the **Text Effects and Typography** gallery, in the first row, click the fourth effect—**Fill – White, Outline – Accent 5, Shadow**.

d. With the text still selected, in the **Font group**, click in the **Font Size** box to select the existing font size. Type **44** and then press Enter. In the **Font group**, click the **Font Color button arrow**. Under **Theme Colors**, in the fourth column, click the first color—**Blue-Gray, Text 2**.

e. With the text still selected, in the **Font group**, click **Text Effects and Typography**. Point to **Shadow**, and then under **Outer**, in the second row, click the third style—**Offset Left**. In the **Paragraph group**, click **Center**.

f. On the **Quick Access Toolbar**, click **Save**. Under **Save As**, click **Browse**. Navigate to your **Word Chapter 1** folder. In the **File name** box, replace the existing text with **Lastname_Firstname_1C_Photography** and then click **Save**.

2 ▶ In the paragraph that begins *The filming*, click to position the insertion point at the beginning of the paragraph. On the **Insert tab**, in the **Illustrations group**, click **Pictures**. In the **Insert Picture** dialog box, navigate to your student data files, locate and click **w01C_Building**, and then click **Insert**.

a. To the right of the selected picture, click the **Layout Options** button, and then under **With Text Wrapping**, click the first option—**Square**. **Close** the Layout Options.

b. On the **Format tab**, in the **Size group**, click in the **Shape Height** box to select the value, type **2.7** and then press Enter.

c. With the picture selected, on the **Format tab**, in the **Arrange group**, click **Position**, and then click **More Layout Options**. In the **Layout** dialog box, on the **Position tab**, in the middle of the dialog box under **Vertical**, click the **Alignment** option button. To the right of **Alignment**, click the arrow, and then click **Top**. To the right of **relative to**, click the arrow, and then click **Line**. Click **OK**.

d. On the **Format tab**, in the **Picture Styles group**, click **Picture Effects**. Point to **Soft Edges**, and then click **5 Point**. On the **Format tab**, in the **Adjust group**, click **Artistic Effects**. In the fourth row, click the third effect—**Crisscross Etching**.

e. Click anywhere outside the picture to deselect it. On the **Design tab**, in the **Page Background group**, click **Page Borders**. In the **Borders and Shading** dialog box, on the **Page Border tab**, under **Setting**, click **Box**. Under **Style**, scroll the list and then click the third style from the bottom—a black line that fades to gray.

f. Click the **Color arrow**, and then in the next to last column, click the first color—**Blue, Accent 5**. Under **Apply to**, be sure **Whole document** is selected, and then click **OK**. Click **Save**.

3 ▶ Click the **Insert tab**, and then in the **Illustrations group**, click **Shapes** to display the gallery. Under **Basic Shapes**, in the second row, click the fifth shape—**Frame**.

a. Position the ✛ pointer anywhere in the blank area at the bottom of the document. Click one time to insert a 1" by 1" frame. The exact location need not be precise. To the right of the shape, click the **Layout Options** button, and at the bottom click **See more**.

b. In the **Layout** dialog box, under **Horizontal**, click the **Alignment** option button. To the right of **Alignment**, click the arrow, and then click **Centered**. To the right of **relative to**, click the arrow, and then click **Page**. Under **Vertical**, click the **Absolute**

(Project 1C Photography continues on the next page)

position option button. In the **Absolute position** box, select the existing number, and then type **1** To the right of **below**, click the arrow, and then click **Paragraph**. Click **OK**.

c. On the **Format tab**, click in the **Shape Height** box. Type **1.5** and then click in the **Shape Width** box. Type **5.5** and then press Enter.

d. If necessary, select the frame shape. On the **Format tab**, in the **Shape Styles group**, click **More** ▾. In the **Shape Styles** gallery, in the first row, click the sixth style—**Colored Outline - Blue, Accent 5**. Type **Submit Your Application by June 30!** Select the text you just typed, and then on the mini toolbar, change the **Font Size** to **22**.

4 Click outside of the frame to deselect it, and then press Ctrl + Home to move to the top of the document. Press ↓ two times to move to the blank paragraph below the title. Press Enter four times to make space for a text box.

a. On the **Insert tab**, in the **Text group**, click **Text Box**. At the bottom of the gallery, click **Draw Text Box**. Position the ✛ pointer over the first blank paragraph at the left margin. Drag down and to the right to create a text box approximately 1.5 inches high and 4 inches wide—the exact size and location need not be precise.

b. With the insertion point blinking in the text box, type the following, pressing Enter after the first two lines to create a new paragraph:

This position requires skill in the use of:
Professional full-frame DSLR cameras
Tilt-shift lenses for tall buildings

c. To precisely place the text box, on the **Format tab**, in the **Arrange group**, click **Position**, and then click **More Layout Options**. In the **Layout** dialog box, under **Horizontal**, click the **Alignment** button. To the right of **Alignment**, click the arrow, and then click **Centered**. To the right of **relative to**, click the arrow, and then click **Page**.

d. Under **Vertical**, click the **Absolute position** button. In the **Absolute position** box, select the existing number. Type **2** To the right of **below**, click the arrow, and then click **Margin**.

e. In the **Layout** dialog box, click the **Size tab**. Under **Height**, select the number in the **Absolute** box. Type **1** and then under **Width**, select the number in the **Absolute** box. Type **3.75** and then click **OK**.

f. In the text box, select all of the text. If necessary, right-click over the selected text to display the mini toolbar. Change the **Font Size** to **12**, apply **Bold**, and then press Ctrl + E to **Center** the text.

g. On the **Format tab**, in the **Shape Styles group**, click **Shape Effects**. Point to **Shadow**, and then under **Outer**, in the first row, click the first style—**Offset Diagonal Bottom Right**.

h. In the **Shape Styles group**, click **Shape Outline**. In the fifth column, click the first color—**Blue, Accent 1** to change the color of the text box border. Click **Shape Fill**, and then in the fifth column, click the second color—**Blue, Accent 1, Lighter 80%**. Click **Save**.

5 Click the **Insert tab**, and then in the **Header & Footer group**, click **Footer**. At the bottom of the menu, click **Edit Footer**. On the **Header & Footer Tools Design tab**, in the **Insert group**, click **Document Info**, and then click **File Name**. Double-click in the document outside of the footer area to close the footer and return to the document.

a. Press Ctrl + Home to move the insertion point to the top of the document. In the upper left corner of your screen, click the **File tab** to display **Backstage** view. On the right, at the bottom of the **Properties list**, click **Show All Properties**.

b. On the list of Properties, click to the right of **Tags** to display an empty box, and then type **internship, documentary** Click to the right of **Subject** to display an empty box, and then type your course name and section #. Under **Related People**, be sure that your name displays as the author. If necessary, right-click the author name, click Edit Property, type your name, and click OK.

c. **Save** your document. In the upper right corner of the Word window, click **Close**. If directed by your instructor to do so, submit your paper printout, your electronic image of your document that looks like a printed document, or your completed Word file.

END | You have completed Project 1C

Skills Review Project 1D Internship

In the following Skills Review, you will edit an information handout regarding production and development internships with Sturgeon Point Productions. Your completed document will look similar to Figure 1.53.

PROJECT FILES

For Project 1D, you will need the following file:

w01D_Internship

You will save your document as:

Lastname_Firstname_1D_Internship

PROJECT RESULTS

STURGEON POINT PRODUCTIONS

Sturgeon Point Productions is a full service film and video production facility located in Miami, Florida. Celebrating over 45 years of producing top quality commercial and independent film, our projects range from award winning documentaries and live action short features, to live concert and sporting events, to popular educational and training series of videos for schools, businesses, trade shows and multi-media presentations. We currently offer internships to film students in participating local colleges and universities, in both our development and production departments.

In-House Office Internships

Sturgeon Point Productions is looking for story analysts, research, post production and production assistants to work in our offices. We offer college credit as independent study at participating schools for one semester, which can be repeated for up to one year from the start date of the internship. To receive credit, interns must:

1. Be enrolled as a film major at a participating local college or university
2. Maintain a 3.0 GPA
3. Receive satisfactory monthly progress reports from their direct supervisor

Lastname_Firstname_1D_Internship

Following is a list of departments in our Miami office, currently seeking development and production interns:

✓ Development Department.. Researcher
✓ Development Department..Asst. to Producer
✓ Development Department...Writer's Assistant
✓ Post Production...Asst. Editor
✓ Post Production...Asst. Sound Editor
✓ Production...Asst. Office Manager

Additional Information

For more information and to sign up for our weekly newsletter, visit our website at www.sturgeonpointproductions.com. Be sure to view the following video to learn about some of the important skills you will develop as an intern with Sturgeon Point Productions.

The Arts Costume Design

Lastname_Firstname_1D_Internship

FIGURE 1.53

Word 2016, Windows 10, Microsoft Corporation

(Project 1D Internship continues on the next page)

1 Start Word, click **Open Other Documents**, and then click **Browse**. Navigate to your student files, and then open **w01D_Internship**. On the **Home tab**, in the **Paragraph group**, be sure **Show/Hide** is active. Click the **File tab**, and then click **Save As**. Navigate to your **Word Chapter 1** folder, and then **Save** the document as **Lastname_Firstname_1D_Internship**

a. Click the **Layout tab**. In the **Page Setup group**, click **Margins**, and then click **Custom Margins**. In the **Page Setup** dialog box, press Tab as necessary to select the value in the **Left** box. Type **1** and then press Tab to select the value in the **Right** box. Type **1** and then click **OK**.

b. Scroll down to view the bottom of **Page 1**, point anywhere in the bottom margin area, right-click, and then click **Edit Footer** to display the footer area. On the **Header & Footer Tools Design tab**, in the **Insert group**, click **Document Info**, and then click **File Name**. Double-click anywhere in the document to close the footer area.

c. Press Ctrl + A to select all of the text in the document, and then on the **Home tab**, in the **Paragraph group**, click **Align Left**.

d. Press Ctrl + Home. Select the document title, and then on the **Home tab**, in the **Paragraph group**, click **Center**.

e. Locate the first bold subheading—*In-House Office Internships*. Point to the left of the paragraph to display the pointer, and then click one time to select the text. With *In-House Office Internships* selected, locate the subheading *Additional Information*. Move the pointer to the left of the paragraph to display the pointer, hold down Ctrl, and then click one time to select both paragraphs. In the **Paragraph group**, click **Center**.

f. Press Ctrl + A to select all of the text in the document. On the **Home tab**, in the **Paragraph group**, click **Line and Paragraph Spacing**, and then click **1.5**.

2 Below the title of the document, click anywhere in the paragraph that begins *Sturgeon Point Productions is a full service*. On the **Home tab**, in the **Paragraph group**, click the **Dialog Box Launcher**.

a. In the **Paragraph** dialog box, on the **Indents and Spacing tab**, under **Indentation**, click the **Special**

arrow, and then click **First line** to indent the first line by 0.5". Click **OK**, and then click anywhere in the paragraph that begins *Sturgeon Point Productions is looking for*. On the ruler under the ribbon, drag the **First Line Indent** marker to **0.5 inches on the horizontal ruler**.

b. Press Ctrl + A to select all of the text in the document. Click the **Layout tab**, and then in the **Paragraph group**, under **Spacing**, click the **After spin box up arrow** one time to change the value to **6 pt**.

c. Select the subheading **In-House Office Internships**, including the paragraph mark following it. Scroll down, hold down Ctrl, and then select the subheading **Additional Information**. With both subheadings selected, in the **Paragraph group**, under **Spacing**, click the **Before up spin box arrow** two times to set the **Spacing Before** to **12 pt**. **Save** your document.

3 Locate the first paragraph that begins *Development Department*, and then point to this paragraph from the left margin area to display the pointer. Drag down to select this paragraph and the next five paragraphs so that six paragraphs are selected. On the **Home tab**, in the **Paragraph group**, click **Bullets** to change the selected text to a bulleted list.

a. Under the subheading *In-House Office Internships*, in the paragraph that begins *Sturgeon Point Productions is looking*, click to position the insertion point at the *end* of the paragraph, following the colon. Press Enter to create a blank paragraph. On the ruler, drag the **First Line Indent** marker to the left so that it is positioned directly above the lower button. Being sure to include the period, type **1.** and then press Spacebar to create the first item in a numbered list.

b. Type **Be enrolled as a film major at a participating local college or university** and then press Enter. Type **Maintain a 3.0 GPA** and then press Enter. Type **Receive satisfactory monthly progress reports from their direct supervisor**

c. Scroll down to view the bulleted list of departments, and then select all six bulleted items in the list. On the mini toolbar, click the **Bullets button arrow**, and then under **Bullet Library**, click the **check mark** symbol. If the check mark is not available, choose another bullet symbol.

(Project 1D Internship continues on the next page)

4 With the list selected, move the pointer to the horizontal ruler, and then point to and click at **3.5 inches on the horizontal ruler** to align the job titles at the tab mark.

a. With the bulleted list still selected, on the ruler, point to the new tab marker at **3.5 inches on the horizontal ruler**, and then when the *Left Tab* ScreenTip displays, drag the tab marker to **4 inches on the horizontal ruler**.

b. On the ruler, point to the tab marker that you moved to display the *Left Tab* ScreenTip, and then double-click to display the **Tabs** dialog box.

c. In the **Tabs** dialog box, under **Tab stop position**, if necessary select *4"*, and then type **6** Under **Alignment**, click the **Right** option button. Under **Leader**, click the **2** option button. Near the bottom of the **Tabs** dialog box, click **Set**.

d. Under **Tab stop position**, select **4"**, and then click **Clear** to delete the tab stop. Click **OK**. **Save** your document.

5 Press Ctrl + Home to move to the top of the document, and then in the title, click to the right of the *S* in *PRODUCTIONS*.

a. Click the **Insert tab**, and then in the **Illustrations group**, click **SmartArt**. On the left, click **Relationship**, and then scroll the list to the bottom. Locate and then click **Basic Venn**. Click **OK** to insert the SmartArt graphic. If necessary, close the Text Pane.

b. In the SmartArt graphic, click **[Text]** in the top circle shape. Type **Film** and then in the lower left shape, click the placeholder **[Text]**. Type **Video** and then in the third circle, type **Internet**

c. Click the SmartArt graphic border to select it. Click the **Format tab**, and then in the **Size group**, if necessary click **Size** to display the **Shape Height** and **Shape Width** boxes. Set the **Height** to **3"** and the **Width** to **6.5"**.

d. With the SmartArt graphic still selected, on the ribbon, under **SmartArt Tools**, click the **Design tab**, and then in the **SmartArt Styles group**, click **Change Colors**. Under **Colorful**, click the third style—**Colorful Range - Accent Colors 3 to 4**. On the **Design tab**, in the **SmartArt Styles group**, click **More** ▾. Under **3-D**, in the first row, click the third style—**Cartoon**.

6 Hold down Ctrl and then press End to move to the end of the document. On the **Insert tab**, in the **Media group**, click **Online Video**. Click in the **Bing Video Search** box. Including the quotation marks, type **"Go 2013 1B video"** and then press Enter. In the first row, click the first video, and then click **Insert**.

a. On the **Format tab**, in the **Size group**, change the **Height** to **2.0**

b. Click the **File tab**, and then on the right, click **Show All Properties**. In the **Tags** box, type **internship** and in the **Subject** box type your course name and section number. If necessary, in the **Author** box, replace the existing text with your first and last name. Click **Save**.

c. Click the **File tab**, and then click **Print** to display **Print Preview**. At the bottom of the preview, click the **Next Page** and **Previous Page** buttons to move between pages. If necessary, return to the document and make any necessary changes.

d. **Save** your document. In the upper right corner of the Word window, click **Close**. If directed by your instructor to do so, submit your paper printout, your electronic image of your document that looks like a printed document, or your completed Word file.

END | You have completed Project 1D

Mastering Word **Project 1E Documentary**

In the following Mastery project, you will create a flyer announcing a special event being hosted by Sturgeon Point Productions. Your printed results will look similar to those in Figure 1.54.

Apply 1A skills from these Objectives:

1 Create a New Document and Insert Text

2 Insert and Format Graphics

3 Insert and Modify Text Boxes and Shapes

4 Preview and Print a Document

PROJECT FILES

For Project 1E, you will need the following files:

New blank Word document
w01E_Antarctica
w01E_Filmmaker

You will save your document as:

Lastname_Firstname_1E_Documentary

PROJECT RESULTS

Build from
Scratch

FIGURE 1.54

(Project 1E Documentary continues on the next page)

Mastering Word   Project 1E Documentary (continued)

1 Start Word and display a **Blank document** with the ruler and formatting marks displayed.

2 Type **Sturgeon Point Productions Presents Aria Pacheco** and then press Enter. From your student data files, insert the text file **w01E_Filmmaker**. Using your own name, **Save** the document in your **Word Chapter 1** folder as **Lastname_Firstname_1E_Documentary**

3 To the document title, apply the **Fill – White, Outline – Accent 1, Glow – Accent 1** text effect, and then change the **Font Size** to **36**.

4 Change the title **Font Color** to **Blue-Gray, Text 2**—in the fourth column, the first color. Apply an **Outer Shadow** using **Offset Left**—in the second row, the third style. **Center** the title.

5 Position the insertion point at the beginning of the paragraph that begins with *This year*, and then from your student data files, insert the picture **w01E_Antarctica**.

6 Change the **Layout Options** to **Square** and then change the **Height** of the picture to **2.25** Using the **Position** command, display the **Layout** dialog box, and then change the **Horizontal Alignment** to **Right relative to** the **Margin**.

7 Apply a **10 Point Soft Edges** picture effect to the image, and then display the **Artistic Effects** gallery. In the third row, apply the fourth effect—**Mosaic Bubbles**.

8 Deselect the picture. Apply a **Page Border** to the document using the **Shadow** setting. Select the first style, and change the **Color** to **Blue-Gray, Text 2**. Change the **Width** to **3 pt**.

9 Below the last paragraph, draw a **Text Box** and then change the **Height** to **1.5** and the **Width** to **4.5**

10 To precisely place the text box, display the **Layout** dialog box. Change the **Horizontal Alignment** to **Centered**, **relative to** the **Page**, and then change the **Vertical Absolute position** to **0.5** below the **Paragraph**.

11 In the text box, type the following text:

> **Date: April 5**
>
> **Time: 8 p.m.**
>
> **Place: Studio G Screening Room**

12 In the text box, change the font size of all the text to **18**. Apply **Bold** and **Center**. Apply a **Shape Style** to the text box—under **Theme Styles**, in the last row, select the second style—**Intense Effect – Blue, Accent 1**. Change the **Shape Outline** to **Black, Text 1**.

13 Insert the **File Name** in the footer, and then display the document properties. As the **Tags** type **documentary, interview** and as the **Subject** type your course and section number. Be sure your name is indicated as the **Author**. **Save** your file.

14 Display the **Print Preview** and, if necessary, return to the document and make any necessary changes. **Save** your document and **Close** Word. If directed by your instructor to do so, submit your paper printout, your electronic image of your document that looks like a printed document, or your completed Word file.

END | You have completed Project 1E

Mastering Word **Project 1F Pitch Festival**

In the following Mastery project, you will edit a document with information regarding an event that Sturgeon Point Productions is holding for college students. Your printed results will look similar to those in Figure 1.55.

Apply 1B skills from these Objectives:

5 Change Document and Paragraph Layout

6 Create and Modify Lists

7 Set and Modify Tab Stops

8 Insert a SmartArt Graphic and an Online Video

PROJECT FILES

For Project 1F, you will need the following file:

w01F_Pitch_Festival

You will save your document as:

Lastname_Firstname_1F_Pitch_Festival

Build from Scratch

PROJECT RESULTS

Pitch Festival!

Do you have a story that must be told? Pitch us your project during the Sturgeon Point Productions annual Pitch Festival! We're setting up several days of conference video calls for college students that are currently enrolled in an accredited film production program anywhere in the United States. If your idea is selected, you will be flown to our studios in Miami, Florida to pitch your idea to our staff of producers and development executives. The following video provides additional information:

Sturgeon Point Productions is one of the leading independent film and video companies in the Miami area. We are currently looking for new, fresh, exciting ideas for short and full-length feature films and documentaries. We like character driven stories that can be shot on an independent budget within one or two locations, preferably either in our studios or in the Miami area. We are currently looking for scripts, ideas, and concepts that are in one of the following categories:

1. Human interest or educational
2. Political or journalistic
3. Biographical or documentary

The Pitch Festival will take place at our secure website on the following dates and times. There are no entry fees to pitch; this unique opportunity to pitch to our staff of professional filmmakers is absolutely free for college film students. Sign up now at www.sturgeonpointproductions.com/pitchfest for one of the following pitch sessions:

- September 12, 11 a.m...Short and Feature Film Pitches
- September 13, 8 p.m. ....Biographical and Documentary Film Pitches
- September 14, 7 p.m. .... Educational Series Pitches

Lastname_Firstname_1F_Pitch_Festival

Word 2016, Windows 10, Microsoft Corporation

FIGURE 1.55

(Project 1F Pitch Festival continues on the next page)

Mastering Word   Project 1F Pitch Festival (continued)

1 Start Word, and then from your student files, open **w01F_Pitch_Festival**. Display formatting marks, and then **Save** the file in your **Word Chapter 1** folder as **Lastname_Firstname_1F_Pitch_Festival**

2 Insert the **File Name** in the footer, and then change the **Line Spacing** for the entire document to **1.5**. **Center** the document title, and then change the title font size to **24**. Change the **Top** and **Bottom** margins to **0.5**

3 Select the three paragraphs below the title, and then apply a **First line** indent of **0.5"**.

4 Select the entire document, and then change the **Spacing Before** to **6 pt** and the **Spacing After** to **6 pt**.

5 Select the last three paragraphs containing the dates, and then apply filled square bullets. If the bullets are not available, choose another bullet style. With the bulleted list selected, set a **Right** tab with **dot leaders** at **6"**.

6 Locate the paragraph that begins *Sturgeon Point Productions*, and then click at the end of the paragraph, after the colon. Press Enter and remove the first line indent from the new paragraph.

7 In the blank line you inserted, create a numbered list with the following three numbered items:

Human interest or educational

Political or journalistic

Biographical or documentary

8 Position the insertion point at the end of the document after the word *Pitches*. Do *not* insert a blank line. Insert a **SmartArt** graphic from the **Process**

category. Toward the bottom of the gallery, select and insert the **Equation** SmartArt. Select the outside border of the SmartArt, and then change the **Height** of the SmartArt to **1** and the **Width** to **6.5**

9 With the SmartArt selected, change the layout to **Square**, and change the **Horizontal Alignment** to **Centered relative to** the **Page**. Change the **Vertical Alignment** to **Bottom relative to** the **Margin**.

10 In the first circle type **Your Ideas** and in the second circle type **Our Experts** In the third circle type **Pitch Festival!**

11 Change the SmartArt color to **Colorful Range – Accent Colors 4 to 5**. Apply the **3-D Polished** style.

12 Click at the end of the first paragraph below the title. Press Enter, remove the first line indent, and then center the blank line. Insert an **Online Video**. In the **Bing Video Search** box, type **Go 1F Video** and then insert the video that displays a blue SmartArt. Change the height of the video to **1.5** and then **Save**.

13 Display the document properties. In the **Tags** box, type **pitch festival** and in the **Subject** box, type your course name and section number. In the **Author** box, replace the existing text with your first and last name. **Save** the file.

14 Display the **Print Preview** and if necessary, return to the document and make any necessary changes. **Save** your document and **Close** Word. If directed by your instructor to do so, submit your paper printout, your electronic image of your document that looks like a printed document, or your completed Word file.

END | You have completed Project 1F

Mastering Word Project 1G Educational Website

Apply **1A** and **1B** skills from these Objectives:

1 Create a New Document and Insert Text

2 Insert and Format Graphics

3 Insert and Modify Text Boxes and Shapes

4 Preview and Print a Document

5 Change Document and Paragraph Layout

6 Create and Modify Lists

7 Set and Modify Tab Stops

8 Insert a SmartArt Graphic and an Online Video

Build from Scratch

In the following Mastery project, you will create a flyer that details a new educational website that Sturgeon Point Productions has developed for instructors. Your printed results will look similar to those in Figure 1.56.

PROJECT FILES

For Project 1G, you will need the following files:

New blank Word document
w01G_Education
w01G_Media

You will save your document as:

Lastname_Firstname_1G_Educational_Website

PROJECT RESULTS

Word 2016, Windows 10, Microsoft Corporation

FIGURE 1.56

(Project 1G Educational Website continues on the next page)

Mastering Word | Project 1G Educational Website (continued)

1 Start Word and display a blank document. Display formatting marks and the ruler. **Save** the document in your **Word Chapter 1** folder as **Lastname_Firstname_1G_Educational_Website**

2 Type **Educational Websites** and then press Enter. Type **Sturgeon Point Productions is offering website tie-ins with every educational video title in our catalog, at no additional cost.** Press Spacebar, and then with the insertion point positioned at the end of the sentence that you typed, insert the text from your student data file **w01G_Education**.

3 Change the **Line Spacing** for the entire document to **1.5** and the spacing **After** to **6 pt**. To each of the four paragraphs that begin *Sturgeon Point Productions*, *As educators*, *When submitting*, and *The video*, apply a **First Line** indent of **0.5"**.

4 Change the **font size** of the title to **50** and the **Line Spacing** to **1.0**. **Center** the title. With the title selected, display the **Text Effects and Typography** gallery. In the first row, apply the second effect—**Fill – Blue, Accent 1, Shadow**.

5 Click at the beginning of the paragraph below the title, and then from your student data files, insert the picture **w01G_Media**. Change the picture **Height** to **2** and the **Layout Options** to **Square**. Format the picture with **Soft Edges** in **10 Point**.

6 Use the **Position** command to display the **Layout** dialog box. Change the picture position so that the **Horizontal Alignment** is **Right relative to** the **Margin**. Change the **Vertical Alignment** to **Top relative to** the **Line**.

7 Select the five paragraphs beginning with *Historic interactive timelines* and ending with *Quizzes and essay exams*, and then apply check mark bullets.

8 In the paragraph below the bulleted list, click after the colon. Press Enter and remove the first line indent. Type a numbered list with the following three numbered items:

    The title in which you are interested
    The name of the class and subject
    Online tools you would like to see created

9 With the insertion point located at the end of the numbered list, insert a **SmartArt** graphic. In the **Process** category, locate and select the **Basic Chevron Process**. In the first shape type **View** In the second shape type **Interact** and in the third shape type **Assess**

10 Change the SmartArt color to **Colorful Range – Accent Colors 4 to 5**, and then apply the **3-D Flat Scene** style. Change the **Height** of the SmartArt to **1** and the **Width** to **6.5** Change the **Layout Options** to **Square**, the **Horizontal Alignment** to **Centered relative to** the **Page**, and the **Vertical Alignment** to **Bottom relative to** the **Margin**.

11 Select the days and times at the end of the document, and then set a **Right** tab with **dot leaders** at **6"**.

12 Click in the blank line below the tabbed list, and **Center** the line. Insert an **Online Video**. In the **Bing Video Search** box, type **Pearson Higher Education Learning** and then insert the first video that displays. Change the video **Height** to **1.5**

13 Below the video, insert a **Rounded Rectangle** shape. The exact location need not be precise. Change the **Shape Height** to **1.5** and the **Shape Width** to **6.5** Display the **Shape Styles** gallery, and then in the fourth row, apply the second style—**Subtle Effect - Blue, Accent 1**.

14 Use the **Position** command to display the **Layout** dialog box, and then change the position so that both the **Horizontal** and **Vertical Alignment** are **Centered relative to** the **Margin**. In the rectangle, type **Sturgeon Point Productions** and then press Enter. Type **Partnering with Educators to Produce Rich Media Content** and then change the font size of all of the text in the text box to **16**.

15 Move to the top of the document and insert a **Text Box** above the title. The exact location need not be precise. Change the **Height** of the text box to **0.5** and the width to **3.7** Type **Sturgeon Point Productions** and then change the font size to **22 Center** the text.

16 Use the **Position** command to display the **Layout** dialog box, and then position the text box so that the **Horizontal Alignment** is **Centered relative to the Page** and the **Vertical Absolute position** is **0.5 below** the **Page**.

17 With the text box selected, display the **Shape Fill** gallery, and then in the next to last column, select the second color—**Blue, Accent 5, Lighter 80%**. Change

(Project 1G Educational Website continues on the next page)

Mastering Word **Project 1G Educational Website** (continued)

the **Shape Outline** to the same color—**Blue, Accent 5, Lighter 80%**.

18 Deselect the text box. Apply a **Page Border** to the document. Use the **Box** setting, and choose the first style. Change the **Color** to **Blue, Accent 5**.

19 Change the **Top** margin to **1.25** and insert the **File Name** in the footer.

20 Display the document properties. As the **Tags** type **website** and as the **Subject** type your course and section number. Be sure your name displays in the **Author** box. **Save** your document and **Close** Word. If directed by your instructor to do so, submit your paper printout, your electronic image of your document that looks like a printed document, or your completed Word file.

END | You have completed Project 1G

Apply a combination of the 1A and 1B skills.

Build From Scratch

| GO! Fix It | Project 1H Casting Call | MyITLab |

| GO! Make It | Project 1I Development Team | MyITLab |

| GO! Solve It | Project 1J Softball | MyITLab |

| GO! Solve It | Project 1K Production |

PROJECT FILES

For Project 1K, you will need the following files:

w01K_Production
w01K_Studio

You will save your document as:

Lastname_Firstname_1K_Production

From the student files that accompany this textbook, locate and open the file w01K_Production. Format the document using techniques you learned in this chapter to create an appropriate flyer aimed at filmmakers. From your student data files, insert the picture w01K_Studio, and then format the picture with an artistic effect. Insert a SmartArt graphic that illustrates two or three important points about the company. Use text effects and text wrapping so that the flyer is easy to read and understand and has an attractive design. Save the file in your Word Chapter 1 folder as **Lastname_Firstname_1K_Production** and submit it as directed.

Performance Level

Performance Criteria		Exemplary: You consistently applied the relevant skills	Proficient: You sometimes, but not always, applied the relevant skills	Developing: You rarely or never applied the relevant skills
	Use text effects	Text effects applied to text in an attractive and appropriate manner.	Text effects are applied but do not appropriately display text.	Text effects not used.
	Insert and format a picture	The picture is inserted and text wrapping and an artistic effect are applied.	The picture is inserted but not formatted properly.	No picture is inserted in the document.
	Insert and format SmartArt	The SmartArt is inserted and appropriately formatted.	The SmartArt is inserted but no formatting is applied.	No SmartArt is inserted in the document.

END | You have completed Project 1K

OUTCOMES-BASED ASSESSMENTS (CRITICAL THINKING)

RUBRIC

The following outcomes-based assessments are *open-ended assessments*. That is, there is no specific correct result; your result will depend on your approach to the information provided. Make *Professional Quality* your goal. Use the following scoring rubric to guide you in *how* to approach the problem and then to evaluate *how well* your approach solves the problem.

The *criteria*—Software Mastery, Content, Format and Layout, and Process—represent the knowledge and skills you have gained that you can apply to solving the problem. The *levels of performance*—Professional Quality, Approaching Professional Quality, or Needs Quality Improvements—help you and your instructor evaluate your result.

	Your completed project is of Professional Quality if you:	Your completed project is Approaching Professional Quality if you:	Your completed project Needs Quality Improvements if you:
1-Software Mastery	Choose and apply the most appropriate skills, tools, and features and identify efficient methods to solve the problem.	Choose and apply some appropriate skills, tools, and features, but not in the most efficient manner.	Choose inappropriate skills, tools, or features, or are inefficient in solving the problem.
2-Content	Construct a solution that is clear and well organized, contains content that is accurate, appropriate to the audience and purpose, and is complete. Provide a solution that contains no errors of spelling, grammar, or style.	Construct a solution in which some components are unclear, poorly organized, inconsistent, or incomplete. Misjudge the needs of the audience. Have some errors in spelling, grammar, or style, but the errors do not detract from comprehension.	Construct a solution that is unclear, incomplete, or poorly organized, contains some inaccurate or inappropriate content, and contains many errors of spelling, grammar, or style. Do not solve the problem.
3-Format and Layout	Format and arrange all elements to communicate information and ideas, clarify function, illustrate relationships, and indicate relative importance.	Apply appropriate format and layout features to some elements, but not others. Overuse features, causing minor distraction.	Apply format and layout that does not communicate information or ideas clearly. Do not use format and layout features to clarify function, illustrate relationships, or indicate relative importance. Use available features excessively, causing distraction.
4-Process	Use an organized approach that integrates planning, development, self-assessment, revision, and reflection.	Demonstrate an organized approach in some areas, but not others; or, use an insufficient process of organization throughout.	Do not use an organized approach to solve the problem.

Apply a combination of the 1A and 1B skills.

Build from Scratch

GO! Think **Project 1L Classes**

PROJECT FILES

For Project 1L, you will need the following file:

New blank Word document

You will save your document as:

Lastname_Firstname_1L_Classes

The Human Resources director at Sturgeon Point Productions needs to create a flyer to inform full-time employees of educational opportunities beginning in September. The courses are taught each year by industry professionals and are designed to improve skills in motion picture and television development and production. Employees who have been with Sturgeon Point Productions for at least two years are eligible to take the courses free of cost. The classes provide employees with opportunities to advance their careers, gain valuable skills, and achieve technical certification. All courses take place in Studio G. Interested employees should contact Elana Springs in Human Resources to sign up. Information meetings are being held at 5:30 according to the following schedule: television development on June 15; motion picture production on June 17; and recording services on June 21.

Create a flyer with basic information about the courses and information meetings. Be sure the flyer is easy to read and understand and has an attractive design. Save the document as **Lastname_Firstname_1L_Classes** and submit it as directed.

END | You have completed Project 1L

Build from Scratch

GO! Think **Project 1M Store**   MyITLab

Build from Scratch

You and GO! **Project 1N Family Flyer**   MyITLab

Build from Scratch

GO! Collaborative Team Project **Project 1O Bell Orchid Hotels**   MyITLab

Introducing Microsoft Excel 2016

Excel 2016

Georgejmclittle/Fotolia

Excel 2016: Introduction

Quantitative information! Defined as a type of information that can be counted or that communicates the quantity of something, quantitative information can be either easy or hard to understand—depending on how it is presented. According to Stephen Few, in his book *Show Me the Numbers*: "Quantitative information forms the core of what businesses must know to operate effectively."

Excel 2016 is a tool to communicate quantitative business information effectively. Sometimes you need to communicate quantitative relationships. For example, the number of units sold per geographic region shows a relationship of sales to geography. Sometimes you need to summarize numbers. A list of every student enrolled at your college with his or her major indicated is not as informative as a summary of the total number of students in each major. In business, the most common quantitative information is some measure of money—costs, sales, payroll, expenses—and so on.

Rather than just a tool for making calculations, Excel is now a tool for you to communicate and collaborate with others. When you want to communicate visually with tables and graphs, Excel 2016 has many features to help you do so. If you engage in Business Intelligence activities, you will find rich tools for forecasting and analysis. Excel is the world's most widely used and familiar data analysis tool.

Creating a Worksheet and Charting Data

PROJECT 1A

OUTCOMES
Create a sales report with an embedded column chart and sparklines.

OBJECTIVES

1. Create, Save, and Navigate an Excel Workbook
2. Enter Data in a Worksheet
3. Construct and Copy Formulas and Use the SUM Function
4. Format Cells with Merge & Center, Cell Styles, and Themes
5. Chart Data to Create a Column Chart and Insert Sparklines
6. Print a Worksheet, Display Formulas, and Close Excel

PROJECT 1B

OUTCOMES
Calculate the value of an inventory.

OBJECTIVES

7. Check Spelling in a Worksheet
8. Enter Data by Range
9. Construct Formulas for Mathematical Operations
10. Edit Values in a Worksheet
11. Format a Worksheet

Lee Torrens/Shutterstock

In This Chapter 🖥 GO! to Work with Excel

In this chapter, you will use Microsoft Excel 2016 to create and analyze data organized into columns and rows. After entering data in a worksheet, you can perform complex calculations, analyze the data to make logical decisions, and create attractive charts that help readers visualize your data in a way they can understand and that is meaningful. In this chapter, you will create and modify Excel workbooks. You will practice the basics of worksheet design, create a footer, enter and edit data in a worksheet, and chart data. You will save, preview, and print workbooks, and you will construct formulas for mathematical operations.

The projects in this chapter relate to **Pro Fit Marietta**, a distributor of fitness equipment and apparel to private gyms, personal trainers, health clubs, corporate wellness centers, hotels, college athletic facilities, physical therapy practices, and multi-unit residential properties. The company's mission is to find, test, and distribute the highest-quality fitness products in the world to its customers for the benefit of consumers. Their popular blog provides useful tips on how to use the latest workout and fitness equipment. The company is located in Marietta, Georgia, which is metropolitan Atlanta's largest suburb.

Sales Report with Embedded Column Chart and Sparklines

MyITLab
Project 1A Training
Project 1A Grader

PROJECT ACTIVITIES

In Activities 1.01 through 1.17, you will create an Excel worksheet for Michelle Barry, the President of Pro Fit Marietta. The worksheet displays the second quarter sales of cardio equipment for the current year and includes a chart to visually represent the data. Your completed worksheet will look similar to Figure 1.1.

PROJECT FILES

MyITLab
grader

If your instructor wants you to submit Project 1A in the MyITLab Grader system, log in to MyITLab, locate Grader Project 1A, and then download the files for this project.

For Project 1A, you will need the following file:

New blank Excel workbook

You will save your workbook as:

Lastname_Firstname_1A_Quarterly_Sales

Lastname_Firstname_1A_Quarterly_Sales_formulas (if your instructor requires)

PROJECT RESULTS

Build From
Scratch

GO!
Walk Thru
Project 1A

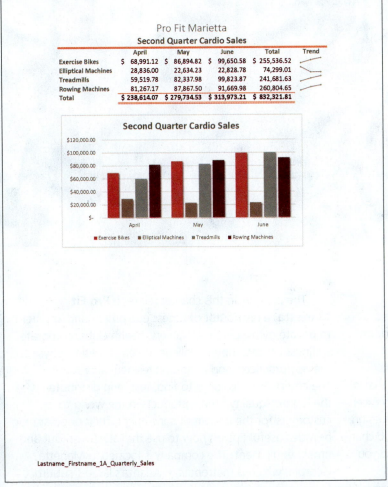

Excel 2016, Windows 10, Microsoft Corporation

FIGURE 1.1 Project 1A Quarterly Sales

Objective 1 Create, Save, and Navigate an Excel Workbook

GO! Learn How
Video E1-1

On startup, Excel displays a new blank *workbook*—the Excel document that stores your data—which contains one or more pages called a *worksheet*. A worksheet—or *spreadsheet*—is stored in a workbook, and is formatted as a pattern of uniformly spaced horizontal rows and vertical columns. The intersection of a column and a row forms a box referred to as a *cell*.

MOS
1.1.1

Activity 1.01 | Starting Excel, Navigating Excel, and Naming and Saving a Workbook

> **ALERT!** To submit as an autograded project, log into MyITLab, download the files for this project, and begin with those files instead of a new blank workbook.

1 Start Excel, and on the opening screen, click **Blank workbook**. In the lower right corner of the window, on the status bar, if necessary, click the Normal button ⊞, and then to the right, locate the zoom—magnification—level.

Your zoom level should be 100%, although some figures in this textbook may be shown at a higher zoom level. The *Normal view* maximizes the number of cells visible on your screen and keeps the column letters and row numbers closer to the cells.

> **BY TOUCH** On Excel's opening screen, tap Blank workbook.

2 On the ribbon, click the **File tab**, on the left click **Save As**, under **Save As**, click **Browse** to display the **Save As** dialog box, and then navigate to the location where you will store your workbooks for this chapter.

3 In your storage location, create a new folder named **Excel Chapter 1** and then open the new folder to display its folder window. In the **File name** box, notice that *Book1* displays as the default file name.

4 In the **File name** box, click **Book1** to select it, and then using your own name, type **Lastname_Firstname_1A_Quarterly_Sales** being sure to include the underscore (_) instead of spaces between words.

5 Click **Save**. Compare your screen with Figure 1.2, and then take a moment to study the parts of the Excel window described in the table in Figure 1.3.

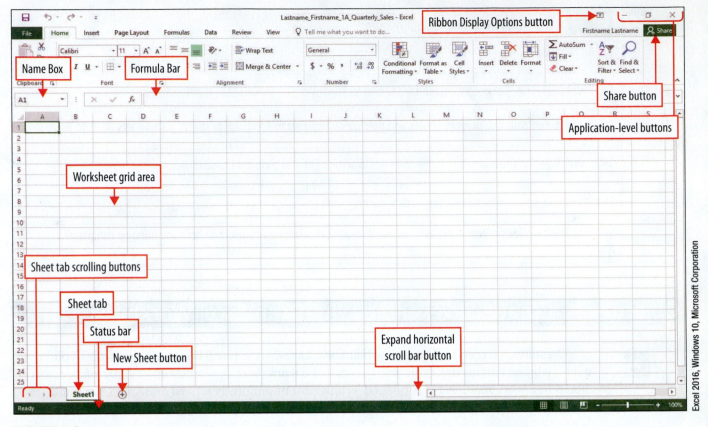

FIGURE 1.2

PARTS OF THE EXCEL WINDOW	
SCREEN PART	**DESCRIPTION**
Horizontal scroll bar button	Increases or decreases the width of the horizontal scroll bar by sliding left or right.
Formula Bar	Displays the value or formula contained in the active cell; also permits entry or editing.
Sheet tab	Identifies the worksheet in the workbook.
New sheet button	Inserts an additional worksheet.
Name Box	Displays the name of the selected cell, table, chart, or object.
Share button	Opens the Share pane from which you can save your file to the cloud—your OneDrive—and then share it with others so you can collaborate.
Sheet tab scrolling buttons	Display sheet tabs that are not in view when there are numerous sheet tabs.
Status bar	Displays the current cell mode, page number, worksheet information, view and zoom buttons, and for numerical data, common calculations such as Sum and Average.
Application-level buttons	Minimize, close, or restore the previous size of the displayed workbook window.
Ribbon Display Options button	Displays various ways you can display the ribbon—the default is Show Tabs and Commands.
Worksheet grid area	Displays the columns and rows that intersect to form the worksheet's cells.

FIGURE 1.3

6 ▸ Take a moment to study Figure 1.4 and the table in Figure 1.5 to become familiar with the Excel worksheet window.

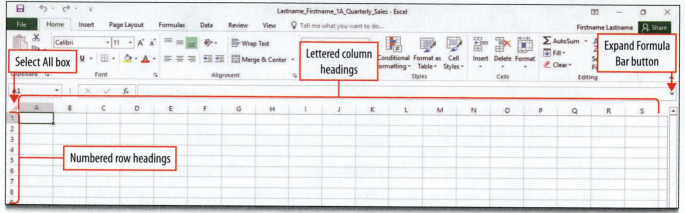

FIGURE 1.4

Excel 2016, Windows 10, Microsoft Corporation

PARTS OF THE EXCEL WORKSHEET WINDOW	
WORKBOOK WINDOW ELEMENT	**DESCRIPTION**
Excel pointer	Displays the location of the pointer.
Expand Formula Bar button	Increases the height of the Formula Bar to display lengthy cell content.
Lettered column headings	Indicate the column letter.
Numbered row headings	Indicate the row number.
Select All box	Selects all the cells in a worksheet.

Excel 2016, Windows 10, Microsoft Corporation

FIGURE 1.5

7 In the lower right corner of the screen, in the horizontal scroll bar, click the **right scroll arrow** one time to shift **column A** out of view.

A *column* is a vertical group of cells in a worksheet. Beginning with the first letter of the alphabet, *A*, a unique letter identifies each column—this is called the *column heading*. Clicking one of the horizontal scroll bar arrows shifts the window either left or right one column at a time.

8 Point to the **right scroll arrow**, and then hold down the left mouse button until the columns begin to scroll rapidly to the right; release the mouse button when you begin to see pairs of letters as the column headings.

BY TOUCH Anywhere on the worksheet, slide your finger to the left to view columns to the right.

9 Slowly drag the horizontal scroll box to the left, and notice that just above the scroll box, ScreenTips with the column letters display as you drag. Drag the horizontal scroll box left or right—or click the left or right scroll arrow—as necessary to position **column Z** near the center of your screen.

Column headings after column Z use two letters starting with AA, AB, and so on through ZZ. After that, columns begin with three letters beginning with AAA. This pattern provides 16,384 columns. The last column is XFD.

10 In the vertical scroll bar, click the **down scroll arrow** one time to move **Row 1** out of view.

A *row* is a horizontal group of cells. Beginning with number 1, a unique number identifies each row—this is the *row heading*, located at the left side of the worksheet. A single worksheet can have 1,048,576 rows of data.

11 Use the skills you just practiced to scroll horizontally to display **column A**, and if necessary, **row 1**.

12 Click **Save** 🖫.

GO! Learn How
Video E1-2

Cell content, which is anything you type in a cell, can be one of two things: either a *constant value*—referred to simply as a *value*—or a *formula*. A formula is an equation that performs mathematical calculations on values in your worksheet. The most commonly used values are *text values* and *number values*, but a value can also include a date or a time of day. A text value is also referred to as a *label*.

Activity 1.02 │ Entering Text, Using AutoComplete, and Using the Name Box to Select a Cell

A text value usually provides information about number values in other worksheet cells. For example, a title such as Second Quarter Cardio Sales gives the reader an indication that the data in the worksheet relates to information about sales of cardio equipment during the three-month period April through June.

1 Point to and then click the cell at the intersection of **column A** and **row 1** to make it the *active cell*—the cell is outlined and ready to accept data.

The intersecting column letter and row number form the *cell reference*—also called the *cell address*. When a cell is active, its column letter and row number are highlighted. The cell reference of the selected cell, *A1*, displays in the Name Box.

2 With cell **A1** as the active cell, type the worksheet title **Pro Fit Marietta** and then press Enter. Compare your screen with Figure 1.6.

Text or numbers in a cell are referred to as *data*. You must confirm the data you type in a cell by pressing Enter or by some other keyboard movement, such as pressing Tab or an arrow key. Pressing Enter moves the active cell to the cell below.

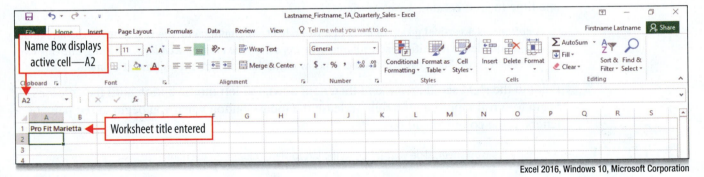

Excel 2016, Windows 10, Microsoft Corporation

FIGURE 1.6

3 In cell **A1**, notice that the text does not fit; the text extends into cell **B1** to the right.

If text is too long for a cell and cells to the right are empty, the text will display. If the cells to the right contain other data, only the text that will fit in the cell displays.

4 In cell **A2**, type the worksheet subtitle **Second Quarter Cardio Sales** and then press Enter. Compare your screen with Figure 1.7.

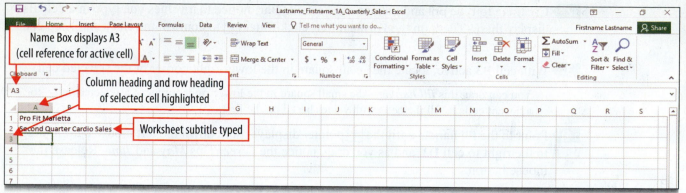

FIGURE 1.7

Excel 2016, Windows 10, Microsoft Corporation

5 ▸ Above **column A**, click in the **Name Box** to select the cell reference *A3*. Type **a4** and then press Enter to make cell **A4** the active cell. In cell **A4**, type **Exercise Bikes** to form the first row title, and then press Enter.

> The text characters that you typed align at the left edge of the cell—referred to as *left alignment*—and cell A5 becomes the active cell. Left alignment is the default for text values. You can type a cell address in the Name Box and press Enter to move to a specific cell quickly.

6 ▸ In cell **A5**, type **E** and notice the text from the previous cell displays.

> If the first characters you type in a cell match an existing entry in the column, Excel fills in the remaining characters for you. This feature, called *AutoComplete*, assists only with alphabetic values.

7 ▸ Continue typing the remainder of the row title **lliptical Machines** and press Enter.

> The AutoComplete suggestion is removed when the entry you are typing differs from the previous value.

8 ▸ In cell **A6**, type **Treadmills** and press Enter. In cell **A7**, type **Rowing Machines** and press Enter. In cell **A8**, type **Total** and press Enter. On the Quick Access Toolbar, click **Save** 🖫.

> **↻ ANOTHER WAY**   Use the keyboard shortcut Ctrl + S to save changes to your workbook.

Activity 1.03 | Using Auto Fill and Keyboard Shortcuts

MOS
2.1.4

1 ▸ Click cell **B3**. Type **A** and notice that when you begin to type in a cell, on the **Formula Bar**, the **Cancel** and **Enter** buttons become active, as shown in Figure 1.8.

FIGURE 1.8

Excel 2016, Windows 10, Microsoft Corporation

2 Continue to type **pril** and then on the **Formula Bar**, notice that values you type in a cell also display there. Then, on the **Formula Bar**, click **Enter** ☑ to confirm the entry and keep cell **B3** active.

3 With cell **B3** active, locate the small square in the lower right corner of the selected cell.

You can drag this *fill handle*—the small square in the lower right corner of a selected cell—to adjacent cells to fill the cells with values based on the first cell.

4 Point to the **fill handle** until the ⊞ pointer displays, hold down the left mouse button, drag to the right to cell **D3**, and as you drag, notice the ScreenTips *May* and *June*. Release the mouse button.

5 Under the text that you just filled, click the **Auto Fill Options** button ⊞ that displays, and then compare your screen with Figure 1.9.

Auto Fill generates and extends a *series* of values into adjacent cells based on the value of other cells. A series is a group of things that come one after another in succession; for example, *April*, *May*, *June*.

The Auto Fill Options button displays options to fill the data; options vary depending on the content and program from which you are filling, and the format of the data you are filling.

Fill Series is selected, indicating the action that was taken. Because the options are related to the current task, the button is referred to as being ***context sensitive***.

Excel 2016, Windows 10, Microsoft Corporation

FIGURE 1.9

6 Click in any cell to cancel the display of the list.

The list no longer displays; the button will display until you perform some other screen action.

7 Press Ctrl + Home, which is the keyboard shortcut to make cell **A1** active.

8 On the Quick Access Toolbar, click **Save** 🖫 to save the changes you have made to your workbook.

9 Take a moment to study the table in Figure 1.10 to become familiar with keyboard shortcuts with which you can navigate the Excel worksheet.

KEYBOARD SHORTCUTS TO NAVIGATE THE EXCEL WORKSHEET	
TO MOVE THE LOCATION OF THE ACTIVE CELL:	**PRESS:**
Up, down, right, or left one cell	↑, ↓, →, ←
Down one cell	Enter
Up one cell	Shift + Enter
Up one full screen	PageUp
Down one full screen	PageDown
To column A of the current row	Home
To the last cell in the last column of the active area (the rectangle formed by all the rows and columns in a worksheet that contain entries)	Ctrl + End
To cell A1	Ctrl + Home
Right one cell	Tab
Left one cell	Shift + Tab
To the cell one worksheet window to the right	Alt + PageDown
To the cell one worksheet window to the left	Alt + PageUp
To the cell containing specific content that you enter in the Find and Replace dialog box	Shift + F5
To the cell that corresponds with the cell reference you enter in the Go To dialog box	F5

FIGURE 1.10

Excel 2016, Windows 10, Microsoft Corporation

Activity 1.04 | Aligning Text and Adjusting the Size of Columns

MOS
5.1.4

1 In the **column heading area**, point to the vertical line between **column A** and **column B** to display the ⊞ pointer, press and hold down the left mouse button, and then compare your screen with Figure 1.11.

A ScreenTip displays information about the width of the column. The default width of a column is 64 *pixels*. A pixel, short for *picture element*, is a point of light measured in dots per square inch. Sixty-four pixels equal 8.43 characters, which is the average number of characters that will fit in a cell using the default font. The default font in Excel is Calibri and the default font size is 11.

FIGURE 1.11

Excel 2016, Windows 10, Microsoft Corporation

2 Drag to the right, and when the number of pixels indicated in the ScreenTip reaches **120 pixels**, release the mouse button. If you are not satisfied with your result, click Undo ↺ on the Quick Access Toolbar and begin again.

This width accommodates the longest row title in cells A4 through A8—*Elliptical Machines*. The worksheet subtitle in cell A2 spans more than one column and still does not fit in column A.

3 Point to cell **B3** and then drag across to select cells **B3**, **C3**, and **D3**. Compare your screen with Figure 1.12; if you are not satisfied with your result, click anywhere and begin again.

The three cells, B3 through D3, are selected and form a *range*—two or more cells on a worksheet that are adjacent (next to each other) or nonadjacent (not next to each other). This range of cells is referred to as *B3:D3*. When you see a colon (:) between two cell references, the range includes all the cells between the two cell references.

A range of cells you select this way is indicated by a dark border, and Excel treats the range as a single unit so you can make the same changes to more than one cell at a time. The selected cells in the range are highlighted except for the first cell in the range, which displays in the Name Box.

When you select a range of data, the *Quick Analysis tool* displays in the lower right corner of the selected range, with which you can analyze your data by using Excel tools such as charts, color-coding, and formulas.

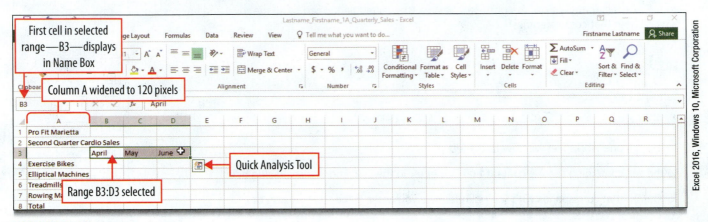

FIGURE 1.12

BY TOUCH To select a range, tap a cell to display a circular gripper in the upper left and lower right corners of the cell, and then drag one of the grippers as necessary to select the desired range.

4 With the range **B3:D3** selected, point anywhere over the selected range, right-click, and then on the mini toolbar, click **Center** ☰. On the Quick Access Toolbar, click **Save** 🖫.

The column titles *April*, *May*, *June* align in the center of each cell.

Activity 1.05 | Entering Numbers

To type number values, use either the number keys across the top of your keyboard or the numeric keypad if you have one—laptop computers might not have a numeric keypad.

1 Under *April*, click cell **B4**, type **68991.12** and then on the **Formula Bar**, click **Enter** ✓ to maintain cell **B4** as the active cell. Compare your screen with Figure 1.13.

By default, *number* values align at the right edge of the cell. The default *number format*—a specific way in which Excel displays numbers—is the *general format*. In the default general format, whatever you type in the cell will display, with the exception of trailing zeros to the right of a decimal point. For example, in the number 237.50 the *0* following the *5* is a trailing zero and would not display.

Data that displays in a cell is the *displayed value*. Data that displays in the Formula Bar is the *underlying value*. The number of digits or characters that display in a cell—the displayed value—depends on the width of the column. Calculations on numbers will always be based on the underlying value, not the displayed value.

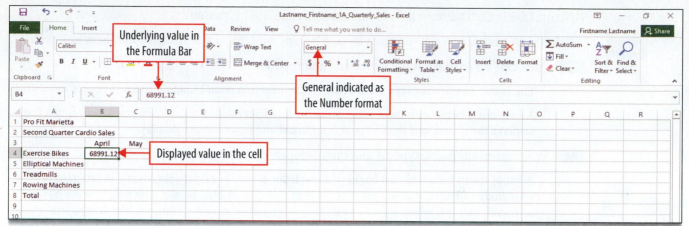

FIGURE 1.13

Excel 2016, Windows 10, Microsoft Corporation

2 Press Tab to make cell **C4** active. Type **86894.82** and then press Tab to move to cell **D4**. Type **99650.58** and then press Enter to move to cell **B5** in the next row. Then, by using the same technique, enter the remaining sales numbers as shown:

	APRIL	MAY	JUNE
Elliptical Machines	28836	22634.23	22828.78
Treadmills	59519.78	82337.98	99823.87
Rowing Machines	81267.17	87867.50	91669.98

3 Compare the numbers you entered with Figure 1.14, and then **Save** 💾 your workbook.

In the default General format, trailing zeros to the right of a decimal point will not display. For example, when you type *87867.50*, the cell displays 87867.5 instead.

FIGURE 1.14

Excel 2016, Windows 10, Microsoft Corporation

Objective 3 | Construct and Copy Formulas and Use the SUM Function

GO! Learn How
Video E1-3

A cell contains either a constant value (text or numbers) or a formula. A formula is an equation that performs mathematical calculations on values in other cells, and then places the result in the cell containing the formula. You can create formulas or use a ***function***—a prewritten formula that looks at one or more values, performs an operation, and then returns a value.

Activity 1.06 │ Constructing a Formula and Using the SUM Function

4.1.2

In this Activity, you will practice three different ways to sum a group of numbers in Excel.

1 Click cell **B8** to make it the active cell and type **=**

The equal sign (=) displays in the cell with the insertion point blinking, ready to accept more data.

All formulas begin with the = sign, which signals Excel to begin a calculation. The Formula Bar displays the = sign, and the Formula Bar Cancel and Enter buttons display.

2 At the insertion point, type **b4** and then compare your screen with Figure 1.15.

A list of Excel functions that begin with the letter *B* may briefly display—as you progress in your study of Excel, you will use functions of this type. A blue border with small corner boxes surrounds cell B4, which indicates that the cell is part of an active formula. The color used in the box matches the color of the cell reference in the formula.

FIGURE 1.15

Excel 2016, Windows 10, Microsoft Corporation

3 At the insertion point, type **+** and then type **b5**

A border of another color surrounds cell B5, and the color matches the color of the cell reference in the active formula. When typing cell references, it is not necessary to use uppercase letters.

4 At the insertion point, type **+b6+b7** and then press [Enter].

The result of the formula calculation—*238614.1*—displays in the cell. Recall that in the default General format, trailing zeros do not display.

5 Click cell **B8** again, look at the **Formula Bar**, and then compare your screen with Figure 1.16.

The formula adds the values in cells B4 through B7, and the result displays in cell B8. In this manner, you can construct a formula by typing. Although cell B8 displays the *result* of the formula, the formula itself displays in the Formula Bar. This is referred to as the ***underlying formula***.

Always view the Formula Bar to be sure of the exact content of a cell—*a displayed number may actually be a formula*.

FIGURE 1.16

Excel 2016, Windows 10, Microsoft Corporation

6 Click cell **C8** and type **=** to signal the beginning of a formula. Then, point to cell **C4** and click one time.

> The reference to the cell C4 is added to the active formula. A moving border surrounds the referenced cell, and the border color and the color of the cell reference in the formula are color coded to match.

7 At the insertion point, type **+** and then click cell **C5**. Repeat this process to complete the formula to add cells **C6** and **C7**, and then press [Enter].

> The result of the formula calculation—*279734.5*—displays in the cell. This method of constructing a formula is the ***point and click method***.

8 Click cell **D8**. On the **Home tab**, in the **Editing group**, click **AutoSum**, and then compare your screen with Figure 1.17.

> SUM is an Excel function—a prewritten formula. A moving border surrounds the range D4:D7 and =*SUM(D4:D7)* displays in cell D8.

> The **=** sign signals the beginning of a formula, *SUM* indicates the type of calculation that will take place (addition), and *(D4:D7)* indicates the range of cells on which the sum calculation will be performed. A ScreenTip provides additional information about the action.

FIGURE 1.17

↻ ANOTHER WAY   Use the keyboard shortcut [Alt] + [=]; or, on the Formulas tab, in the Function Library group, click the AutoSum button.

---

9 Look at the **Formula Bar**, and notice that the formula also displays there. Then, look again at the cells surrounded by the moving border.

> When you activate the ***Sum function***, Excel first looks *above* the active cell for a range of cells to sum. If no range is above the active cell, Excel will look to the *left* for a range of cells to sum. If the proposed range is not what you want to calculate, you can select a different group of cells.

10 Press [Enter] to construct a formula by using the prewritten SUM function.

> Your total is *313973.2*. Because the Sum function is frequently used, it has its own button in the Editing group on the Home tab of the ribbon. A larger version of the button also displays on the Formulas tab in the Function Library group. This button is also referred to as ***AutoSum***.

11 Notice that the totals in the range **B8:D8** display only one decimal place. Click **Save** [💾].

> Number values that are too long to fit in the cell do *not* spill over into the unoccupied cell to the right in the same manner as text values. Rather, Excel rounds the number to fit the space.

> ***Rounding*** is a procedure that determines which digit at the right of the number will be the last digit displayed and then increases it by one if the next digit to its right is 5, 6, 7, 8, or 9.

Activity 1.07 | Copying a Formula by Using the Fill Handle

You have practiced three ways to create a formula—by typing, by using the point-and-click technique, and by using a Function button from the ribbon. You can also copy formulas. When you copy a formula from one cell to another, Excel adjusts the cell references to fit the new location of the formula.

1 Click cell **E3**, type **Total** and then press Enter.

The text in cell E3 is centered because the centered format continues from the adjacent cell.

2 With cell **E4** as the active cell, hold down Alt, and then press =. Compare your screen with Figure 1.18.

Alt + = is the keyboard shortcut for the SUM function. Recall that Excel first looks above the selected cell for a proposed range of cells to sum, and if no data is detected, Excel looks to the left and proposes a range of cells to sum.

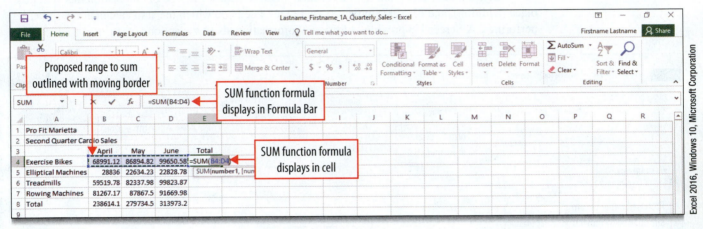

FIGURE 1.18

3 On the **Formula Bar**, click **Enter** ✓ to display the result and keep cell **E4** active.

The total dollar amount of *Exercise Bikes* sold in the quarter is *255536.5*. In cells E5:E8, you can see that you need a formula similar to the one in E4, but formulas that refer to the cells in row 5, row 6, and so on.

4 With cell **E4** active, point to the fill handle in the lower right corner of the cell until the + pointer displays. Then, drag down through cell **E8**; if you are not satisfied with your result, on the Quick Access Toolbar, click Undo ↻ and begin again. Compare your screen with Figure 1.19.

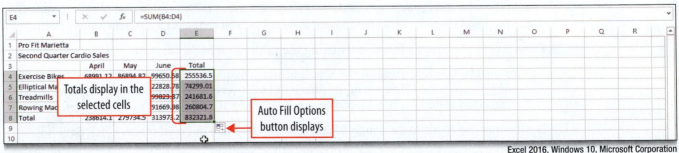

FIGURE 1.19

5 Click cell **E5**, look at the **Formula Bar**, and notice the formula =*SUM(B5:D5)*. Click cell **E6**, look at the **Formula Bar**, and then notice the formula =*SUM(B6:D6)*.

In each row, Excel copied the formula but adjusted the cell references *relative to* the row number. This is called a *relative cell reference*—a cell reference based on the relative position of the cell that contains the formula and the cells referred to in the formula.

The calculation is the same, but it is performed on the cells in that particular row. Use this method to insert numerous formulas into spreadsheets quickly.

6 Click cell **F3**, type **Trend** and then press Enter. **Save** 🔲 your workbook.

Objective 4 | Format Cells with Merge & Center, Cell Styles, and Themes

GO! Learn How
Video E1-4

Format—change the appearance of—cells to make your worksheet attractive and easy to read.

Activity 1.08 | Using Merge & Center and Applying Cell Styles

MOS
2.2.1, 2.2.7

1 Select the range **A1:F1**, and then in the **Alignment group**, click **Merge & Center**. Then, select the range **A2:F2** and click **Merge & Center**.

The *Merge & Center* command joins selected cells into one larger cell and centers the contents in the merged cell; individual cells in the range B1:F1 and B2:F2 can no longer be selected—they are merged into cell A1 and A2, respectively.

🔄 **ANOTHER WAY**   Select the range, right-click over the selection, and then on the mini toolbar, click the Merge & Center command.

2 Click cell **A1**. In the **Styles group**, click **Cell Styles**, and then compare your screen with Figure 1.20.

A *cell style* is a defined set of formatting characteristics, such as font, font size, font color, cell borders, and cell shading.

FIGURE 1.20

3 ▶ In the displayed gallery, under **Titles and Headings**, click **Title** and notice that the row height adjusts to accommodate the larger font size.

4 ▶ Click cell **A2**, display the **Cell Styles** gallery, and then under **Titles and Headings**, click **Heading 1**.

Use cell styles to maintain a consistent look in a worksheet and across worksheets in a workbook.

5 ▶ Select the horizontal range **B3:F3**, hold down Ctrl, and then select the vertical range **A4:A8** to select the column titles and the row titles. Release Ctrl.

Use this technique to select two or more ranges that are nonadjacent—not next to each other.

6 ▶ With the two ranges selected, display the **Cell Styles** gallery, click **Heading 4** to apply this cell style to the column titles and row titles, and then **Save** 🔲 your workbook.

Activity 1.09 | Formatting Financial Numbers

2.2.5

1 ▶ Select the range **B4:E4**, hold down Ctrl, and then select the range **B8:E8**. Release Ctrl.

This range is referred to as *b4:e4,b8:e8* with a comma separating the references to the two nonadjacent ranges.

 ANOTHER WAY In the Name Box type b4:e4,b8:e8 and then press Enter.

2 ▶ With the two ranges selected, on the **Home tab**, in the **Number group**, click **Accounting Number Format** $ ▾. Compare your screen with Figure 1.21.

The ***Accounting Number Format*** applies a thousand comma separator where appropriate, inserts a fixed U.S. dollar sign aligned at the left edge of the cell, applies two decimal places, and leaves a small amount of space at the right edge of the cell to accommodate a parenthesis when negative numbers are present. Excel widens the columns to accommodate the formatted numbers.

At the bottom of your screen, in the status bar, Excel displays the results for some common calculations that might be made on the range; for example, the Average of the numbers selected and the Count—the number of items selected.

FIGURE 1.21

 ANOTHER WAY Display the Cell Styles gallery, and under Number Format, click Currency.

3 Select the range **B5:E7**, and then in the **Number group**, click **Comma Style** ⟨,⟩.

The **Comma Style** inserts a thousand comma separator where appropriate and applies two decimal places. Comma Style also leaves space at the right to accommodate a parenthesis when negative numbers are present.

When preparing worksheets with financial information, the first row of dollar amounts and the total row of dollar amounts are formatted in the **Accounting Number Format**; that is, with thousand comma separators, dollar signs, two decimal places, and space at the right to accommodate a parenthesis for negative numbers, if any. Rows that are *not* the first row or the total row should be formatted with the Comma Style.

4 Select the range **B8:E8**. In the **Styles group**, display the **Cell Styles** gallery, and then under **Titles and Headings**, click **Total**. Click any blank cell to cancel the selection, and then compare your screen with Figure 1.22.

This is a common way to apply borders to financial information. The single border indicates that calculations were performed on the numbers above, and the double border indicates that the information is complete. Sometimes financial documents do not display values with cents; rather, the values are rounded up. You can do this by selecting the cells, and then clicking the Decrease Decimal button two times.

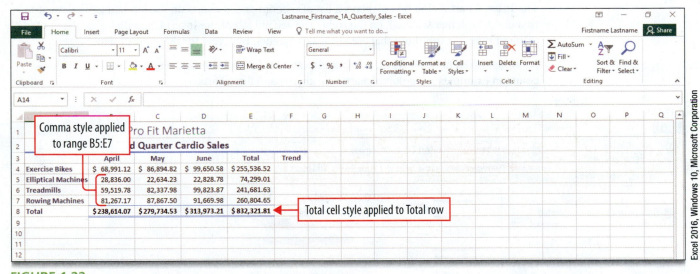

FIGURE 1.22

Activity 1.10 | Changing the Workbook Theme

MOS
1.3.6

A *theme* is a predefined set of colors, fonts, lines, and fill effects that coordinate for an attractive look.

1 Click the **Page Layout tab**, and then in the **Themes group**, click **Themes**.

2 Click the **Retrospect** theme, and notice that the cell styles change to match the new theme. Click **Save** ⊞.

More Knowledge | **Formatting a Cell's Font, Style, Size, or Color with Individual Commands**

Instead of using Cell Styles, you could use a combination of individual commands to format a cell. For example, on the Home tab, in the Font group, you can change a cell's font by clicking the Font arrow and selecting a different font. You can change the font size by clicking the Font Size arrow and selecting a size. From the same group, you can apply various styles to the cell—such as Bold or Italic or Underline. To change a cell's font color, in the Font Group, click the Font Color arrow and select a different color.

Objective 5 | Chart Data to Create a Column Chart and Insert Sparklines

GO! Learn How
Video E1-5

A *chart* is a graphic representation of data in a worksheet. Data in a chart is easier to understand than a table of numbers. *Sparklines* are tiny charts embedded in a cell that give a visual trend summary alongside your data. A sparkline makes a pattern more obvious to the eye.

Activity 1.11 | Charting Data and Using Recommended Charts to Select and Insert a Column Chart

5.1.1, 5.1.3

Recommended Charts is an Excel feature that displays a customized set of charts that, according to Excel's calculations, will best fit your data based on the range of data that you select. In this Activity, you will create a *column chart* showing the monthly sales of cardio equipment by category during the second quarter. A column chart is useful for illustrating comparisons among related numbers. The chart will enable the company president, Michelle Barry, to see a pattern of overall monthly sales.

1 Select the range **A3:D7**.

When charting data, typically you should *not* include totals—include only the data you want to compare.

2 With the data that you want to compare selected, click the **Insert tab**, and then in the **Charts group**, click **Recommended Charts**. Compare your screen with Figure 1.23.

The Insert Chart dialog box displays a list of recommended charts on the left and a preview of the first chart, which is selected, on the right. The second tab of the Insert Chart dialog box includes all chart types—even those that are not recommended by Excel for this type of data.

By using different *chart types*, you can display data in a way that is meaningful to the reader—common examples are column charts, pie charts, and line charts.

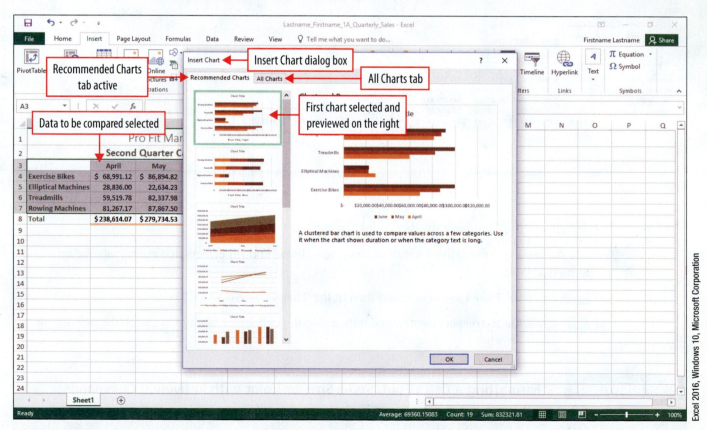

FIGURE 1.23

3 In the **Insert Chart** dialog box, use the scroll bar to scroll down about one-third of the way, and then click the second Clustered Column chart. Compare your screen with Figure 1.24.

Here, *each type of cardio equipment* displays its *sales for each month*. A clustered column chart is useful to compare values across a few categories, especially if the order of categories is not important.

FIGURE 1.24

Excel 2016, Windows 10, Microsoft Corporation

4 In the **Insert Chart** dialog box, click the chart directly above the selected chart—the first clustered column chart. Compare your screen with Figure 1.25.

In this clustered column chart, *each month* displays its *sales for each type of cardio equipment*. When constructing a chart, you can switch the row and column data in this manner to display the data in a way that is most useful to the reader. Here, the president of Pro Fit Marietta wants to compare sales of each type of equipment by month to detect patterns.

The comparison of data—either by month or by type of equipment—depends on the type of analysis you want to perform. You can select either chart, or, after your chart is complete, you can use the *Switch/Row Column* command on the ribbon to swap the data over the axis; that is, data being charted on the vertical axis will move to the horizontal axis and vice versa.

FIGURE 1.25

5 In the lower right corner of the **Insert Chart** dialog box, click **OK** to insert the selected chart into the worksheet. Compare your screen with Figure 1.26.

Your selected column chart displays in the worksheet, and the charted data is bordered by colored lines. Because the chart object is selected—surrounded by a border and displaying sizing handles—contextual tools named *Chart Tools* display and add contextual tabs next to the standard tabs on the ribbon.

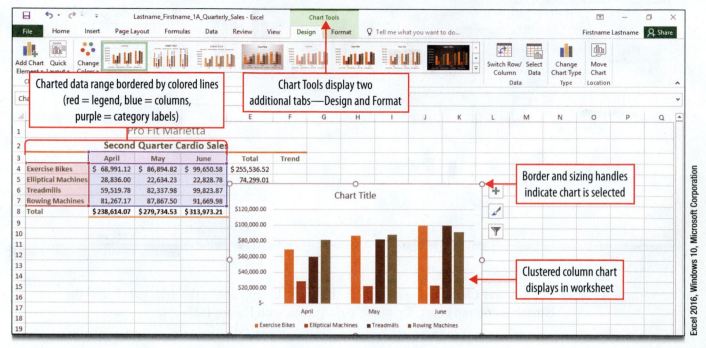

FIGURE 1.26

Activity 1.12 | Using the Chart Tools to Apply Chart Styles

1 On the ribbon, locate the contextual tabs under **Chart Tools—Design** and **Format**.

When a chart is selected, Chart Tools become available and these two tabs provide commands for working with the chart.

Based on the data you selected in your worksheet and the chart you selected in the Insert Chart dialog box, Excel constructs a column chart and adds *category labels*—the labels that display along the bottom of the chart to identify the category of data. This area is referred to as the *category axis* or the *x-axis*.

Depending on which arrangement of row and column data you select in the Insert Chart dialog box, Excel arranges either the row titles or the column titles as the category names. Here, based on your selection, the column titles that form the category labels are bordered in purple, indicating the cells that contain the category names.

On the left side of the chart, Excel includes a numerical scale on which the charted data is based; this is the *value axis* or the *y-axis*. Along the lower edge of the chart, a *legend*, which is a chart element that identifies the patterns or colors that are assigned to the categories in the chart, displays. Here, the row titles are bordered in red, indicating the cells containing the legend text.

2 To the right of the chart, notice the three buttons, and then point to each button to display its ScreenTip, as shown in Figure 1.27.

The *Chart Elements button* enables you to add, remove, or change chart elements such as the title, legend, gridlines, and data labels.

The *Chart Styles button* enables you to set a style and color scheme for your chart.

The *Chart Filters button* enables you to change which data displays in the chart—for example, to see only the data for *May* and *June* or only the data for *Treadmills* and *Rowing Machines*.

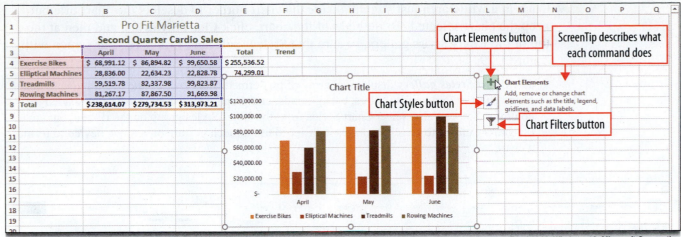

FIGURE 1.27

3 In the worksheet data, locate the group of cells bordered in blue.

Each of the twelve cells bordered in blue is referred to as a ***data point***—a value that originates in a worksheet cell. Each data point is represented in the chart by a ***data marker***—a column, bar, area, dot, pie slice, or other symbol in a chart that represents a single data point.

Related data points form a ***data series***; for example, there is a data series for *April*, for *May*, and for *June*. Each data series has a unique color or pattern represented in the chart legend.

4 On the **Design tab**, in the **Chart Layouts group**, click **Quick Layout**, and then compare your screen with Figure 1.28.

In the Quick Layout gallery, you can change the overall layout of the chart by selecting a predesigned ***chart layout***—a combination of chart elements, which can include a title, legend, labels for the columns, and the table of charted cells.

FIGURE 1.28

5 *Point* to several different layouts to see how Live Preview displays the effect on your chart, and then click the **Quick Layout** button again without changing the layout.

6 In the chart, click anywhere in the text *Chart Title* to select the title box, watch the **Formula Bar** as you begin to type **Second** and notice that AutoComplete fills in the subtitle for you. Press Enter at any point to insert the worksheet subtitle as the chart title.

7 Click in a white area just slightly *inside* the chart border to deselect the chart title but keep the chart selected. To the right of the chart, click **Chart Styles** ✎, and then at the top of the **Chart Styles** gallery, be sure that **Style** is selected. Compare your screen with Figure 1.29.

The *Chart Styles gallery* displays an array of predefined *chart styles*—the overall visual look of the chart in terms of its colors, backgrounds, and graphic effects such as flat or shaded columns. You can also select Chart Styles from the Chart Styles group on the ribbon, but having the gallery closer to the chart makes it easier to use a touch gesture on a touch device to format a chart.

FIGURE 1.29

8 On the right side of the **Style** gallery, scroll down about halfway, and then by using the ScreenTips as your guide, locate and click **Style 6**.

This style uses a white background, formats the columns with theme colors, and applies a slight shadowed effect to the columns. With this clear visual representation of the data, the president can see the sales of all product categories in each month, and can see that the sale of exercise bikes and treadmills has risen markedly during the quarter.

9 At the top of the gallery, click **Color**. Under **Colorful**, point to the third row of colors to display the ScreenTip *Color 3*, and then click to apply the **Color 3** variation of the theme colors.

10 Point to the top border of the chart to display the ⇱ pointer, and then drag the upper left corner of the chart just inside the upper left corner of cell **A10**, approximately as shown in Figure 1.30.

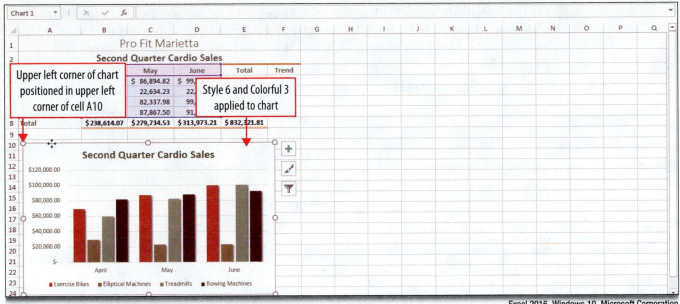

Excel 2016, Windows 10, Microsoft Corporation

FIGURE 1.30

11 Click any cell to deselect the chart, and notice that the chart buttons no longer display to the right of the chart and the Chart Tools no longer display on the ribbon. Click **Save** 💾.

> Contextual tabs display when an object is selected and then are removed from view when the object is deselected.

Activity 1.13 │ Creating and Formatting Sparklines

By creating sparklines, you provide a context for your numbers. Your readers will be able to see the relationship between a sparkline and its underlying data quickly.

1 Select the range **B4:D7**, which represents the monthly sales figures for each product and for each month. Click the **Insert tab**, and then in the **Sparklines group**, click **Line**. In the displayed **Create Sparklines** dialog box, notice that the selected range *B4:D7* displays.

2 With the insertion point blinking in the **Location Range** box, type **f4:f7** which is the range of cells where you want the sparklines to display. Compare your screen with Figure 1.31.

Excel 2016, Windows 10, Microsoft Corporation

FIGURE 1.31

🔄 **ANOTHER WAY** In the worksheet, select the range F4:F7 to insert it into the Location Range box.

3 Click **OK** to insert the sparklines in the range **F4:F7**, and then on the **Design tab**, in the **Show group**, click the **Markers** check box to select it.

> Alongside each row of data, the sparkline provides a quick visual trend summary for sales of each cardio item over the three-month period. For example, you can see instantly that of the four items, only Elliptical Machines had declining sales for the period.

4 ▶ On the **Design tab**, in the **Style group**, click **More** ⊟. In the second row, click the fourth style—**Sparkline Style Accent 4, Darker 25%**. Press Ctrl + Home to deselect the range and make cell **A1** the active range. Click **Save** 🖫, and then compare your screen with Figure 1.32.

Use markers, colors, and styles in this manner to further enhance your sparklines.

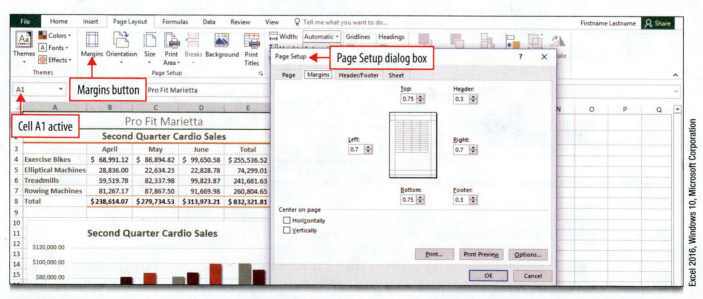

FIGURE 1.32

Excel 2016, Windows 10, Microsoft Corporation

Objective 6 · Print a Worksheet, Display Formulas, and Close Excel

GO! Learn How
Video E1-6

Use the **Show Formulas** command to display the formula in each cell instead of the resulting value. Use the commands on the Page Layout tab to prepare for printing.

Activity 1.14 | Creating a Footer and Centering a Worksheet

1.3.8, 1.3.4

For each Excel project in this textbook, you will create a footer containing the file name, which includes your name and the project name. You will also center the data horizontally on the page to create an attractive result if your worksheet is printed.

1 ▶ If necessary, click cell **A1** to deselect the chart. Click the **Page Layout tab**, and then in the **Page Setup group**, click **Margins**. At the bottom of the **Margins** gallery, click **Custom Margins**, to display the **Page Setup** dialog box. Compare your screen with Figure 1.33.

Excel 2016, Windows 10, Microsoft Corporation

FIGURE 1.33

2 On the **Margins tab**, under **Center on page**, select the **Horizontally** check box.

This action will center the data and chart horizontally on the page, as shown in the Preview area.

3 In the **Page Setup** dialog box, click the **Header/Footer tab**, and then in the center of the dialog box, click **Custom Footer**. In the **Footer** dialog box, with your insertion point blinking in the **Left section**, on the row of buttons, click **Insert File Name**. Compare your screen with Figure 1.34.

&[File] displays in the Left section. Here you can type or insert information from the row of buttons into the left, middle, or right section of the footer. The Custom Header button displays a similar screen to enter information in the header of the worksheet.

FIGURE 1.34

4 Click **OK** two times.

The vertical dotted line between columns indicates that as currently arranged, only the columns to the left of the dotted line will print on the first page. The exact position of the vertical line may depend on your default printer setting.

ANOTHER WAY Deselect the chart. On the Insert tab, in the Text group, click Header & Footer to display Page Layout view. Click in the left section of the displayed footer, and then in the Header & Footer Elements group, click File Name. Click any cell in the workbook to deselect the footer area, and then on the status bar, click the Normal button to return to Normal view.

Activity 1.15 | Adding Document Properties and Printing a Workbook

1.4.6, 1.5.3

1 In the upper left corner of your screen, click the **File tab** to display **Backstage** view. In the lower right corner, click **Show All Properties**.

2 As the **Tags**, type **cardio sales** In the **Subject** box, type your course name and section number. Be sure your name displays in the **Author** box and edit if necessary.

3 On the left, click **Print** to view the **Print Preview**. Compare your screen with Figure 1.35.

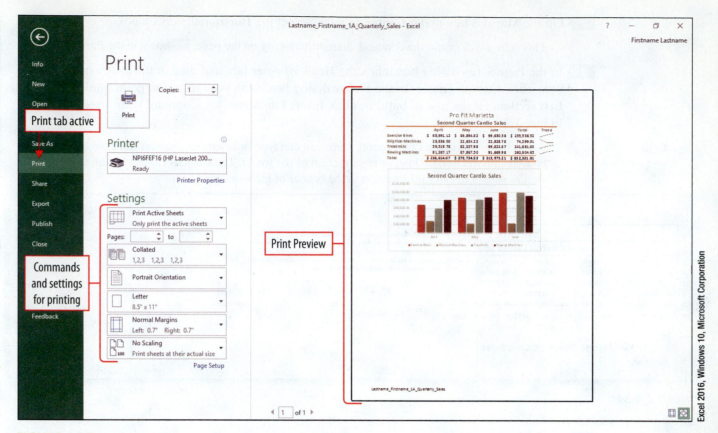

FIGURE 1.35

> 4 ▸ Note any adjustments that need to be made, and then on the left, click **Save** to save and return to the workbook.

> **NOTE** | **What Does Your Instructor Require for Submission? A Paper Printout, an Image That Looks Like a Printed Document, or Your Excel File?**
>
> You can produce a paper printout of your worksheet or an electronic image of your worksheet that looks like a printed document. Or, your instructor may want only your completed Excel file.

> 5 ▸ If you are directed to print on paper, be sure that a printer is available to your system. Press Ctrl + F2, which is the keyboard shortcut to display the **Print Preview**, and then under **Print**, click the **Print** button.

> 6 ▸ If you are directed to create an electronic image of your worksheet that looks like a printed document, click the **File tab**, on the left click **Export**, and then on the right, click **Create PDF/XPS**. In the **Publish as PDF or XPS** dialog box, navigate to your storage location, in the **Save as type** box, be sure **PDF** is indicated, and then click **Publish** to create the PDF file.

Activity 1.16 | Printing a Section of the Worksheet

1.5.1

From Backstage view, you can print only the portion of the worksheet that you select, and there are times you might want to do this.

> 1 ▸ Select the range **A2:F5** to select only the subtitle and the data for *Exercise Bikes* and *Elliptical Machines* and the column titles

2 Press `Ctrl` + `F2`, which is the keyboard shortcut to display **Print Preview**, and then under **Settings**, click the first arrow, which currently displays *Print Active Sheets*. On the list that displays, click **Print Selection**, and then compare your screen with Figure 1.36.

Excel 2016, Windows 10, Microsoft Corporation

FIGURE 1.36

3 If directed by your instructor, print the selection on paper; otherwise, in the upper left corner, click **Back** ⊖ to return to your workbook.

4 Press `Ctrl` + `Home`, and then click **Save** 🔒.

Activity 1.17 | Changing Page Orientation and Displaying, Printing, and Hiding Formulas

1.4.8, 1.5.4

When you type a formula in a cell, the cell displays the *results* of the formula calculation. Recall that this value is called the displayed value. You can view and print the underlying formulas in the cells. When you do so, a formula often takes more horizontal space to display than the result of the calculation.

1 If necessary, redisplay your worksheet. Because you will make some temporary changes to your workbook, on the Quick Access Toolbar, click **Save** 🔒 to be sure your work is saved up to this point.

2 On the **Formulas tab**, in the **Formula Auditing group**, click **Show Formulas**.

> 🔄 **ANOTHER WAY**   Hold down `Ctrl`, and then press `~` (usually located below `Esc`).

3 In the **column heading area**, point to the **column A** heading to display the ⬇ pointer, hold down the left mouse button, and then drag to the right to select columns **A:F**. Compare your screen with Figure 1.37.

FIGURE 1.37

> **NOTE** **Turning the Display of Formulas On and Off**
>
> The Show Formulas button is a toggle button. Clicking it once turns the display of formulas on—the button will be shaded. Clicking the button again turns the display of formulas off.

---

4 ▶ Point to the column heading boundary between any two of the selected columns to display the ⊞ pointer, and then double-click to AutoFit the selected columns.

AutoFit adjusts the width of a column to fit the cell content of the *widest* cell in the column.

> 🔄 **ANOTHER WAY** With the columns selected, on the Home tab, in the Cells group, click Format, and then click AutoFit Column Width.

5 ▶ On the **Page Layout tab**, in the **Page Setup group**, click **Orientation**, and then click **Landscape**. In the **Scale to Fit** group, click the **Width arrow**, and then click **1 page** to scale the data to fit onto one page.

Scaling shrinks the width or height of the printed worksheet to fit a maximum number of pages and is convenient for printing formulas. Although it is not always the case, formulas frequently take up more space than the actual data.

> 🔄 **ANOTHER WAY** In the Scale to Fit group, click the Dialog Box Launcher button to display the Page tab of the Page Setup dialog box. Then, under Scaling, click the Fit to option button.

6 ▶ In the **Page Setup group**, click **Margins**, click **Custom Margins**, and then on the **Margins tab**, under **Center on page**, be sure the **Horizontally** check box is selected—select it if necessary.

7 ▶ Click **OK** to close the dialog box. Check to be sure your chart is centered below the data and the left and right edges are slightly inside column A and column F—use the 🔾 pointer to drag a chart edge and then deselect the chart if necessary.

8 Click any cell so that the chart is not selected, and then press [Ctrl] + [F2] to display the **Print Preview**. Under **Settings**, if necessary switch back to the option to **Print Active Sheets**. If directed to do so by your instructor, print on paper; or, to save the workbook in this format, click Save As and name the worksheet **Lastname_Firstname_1A_Quarterly_Sales_formulas**

> If you save the workbook with this new name, your original workbook is automatically saved and closed.

9 If you did not save your formulas worksheet, on the left, click **Close**, and when prompted, click **Don't Save** so that you do *not* save the changes you made—displaying formulas, changing column widths and orientation, and scaling—to print your formulas.

10 In the upper right corner of your screen, click **Close** [X] to close Excel.

END | You have completed Project 1A

GO! With Google

Objective	**Create** a Sales Report with an Embedded Column Chart Using Google Sheets

> **ALERT!** | **Working with Web-Based Applications and Services**
>
> Computer programs and services on the web receive continuous updates and improvements, so the steps to complete this web-based Activity may differ from the ones shown. You can often look at the screens and the information presented to determine how to complete the Activity.
>
> If you do not already have a Google account, you will need to create one before you begin this activity. Go to http://google.com and in the upper right corner, click Sign In. On the Sign In screen, click Create Account. On the Create your Google Account page, complete the form, read and agree to the Terms of Service and Privacy Policy, and then click Next step. On the Welcome screen, click Get Started.

Activity | Creating a Sales Report with an Embedded Column Chart Using Google Sheets

In this Activity, you will use Google Sheets to create a sales report and chart similar to the one you created in Project 1A.

1 From the desktop, open your browser, (use a browser other than Edge), navigate to **http://google.com** and then click the **Google Apps** menu ⊞. Click **Drive**, and then if necessary, sign in to your Google account.

2 Open your **GO! Web Projects** folder—or click NEW to create and then open this folder if necessary.

3 In the left pane, click **NEW**, and then click **Google Sheets**. From your Windows taskbar, open **File Explorer**, navigate to your Student Data Files for this chapter, and then in the **File List**, double-click to open **e01_1A_Web**.

4 In the displayed Excel worksheet, select the range **A1:E8**, right-click over the selection, click **Copy**, and then **Close** Excel. **Close** the **File Explorer** window.

5 In your blank Google Sheet, with cell **A1** active, point to cell **A1**, right-click, and then click **Paste**; by copying and pasting the data, you can create this project more quickly without having to do extra typing. In the column heading area, point to the border between **column A** and **column B** to display the ↔ pointer, and then widen **column A** slightly so that all of the data in rows 4–8 displays.

6 Select the range **A1:E1**. On the toolbar, click **Merge cells** ⊞. On the toolbar, click the **Align arrow** ▾, and then click **Center** ☰. Repeat for the range **A2:E2**, and then apply **Bold** **B** to cells **A1** and **A2**.

7 Select the range with the month names, center them, and apply **Bold** **B**. Apply **Bold** **B** to the totals in the range **B8:E8**.

8 Select the range **A3:D7** (the data without the totals and without the titles). On the menu bar, click **Insert**, and

then click **Chart**. In the **Chart Editor** dialog box, notice the three tabs.

9 In the **Chart Editor** window, with the first chart type selected, click the **Chart types tab**, and then select the **Switch rows/columns** check box.

10 Click the **Customization tab**. In the **Title** box, replace the existing text with **Second Quarter Cardio Sales**

11 Click the **Legend arrow**, and then click **None**. Click the **Background arrow**, and then in the fourth column, click the third color—**light yellow 3**.

12 In the lower left corner, click **Insert**. Point anywhere inside the selected chart, hold down the left mouse button to display the 🖑 pointer, and then drag the chart slightly below the data. Then using the corner sizing handles resize and reposition the chart attractively below the data.

13 At the top of the worksheet, click the text *Untitled spreadsheet*, and then using your own name, type **Lastname_Firstname_EX_1A_Web** and press ENTER.

14 If you are instructed to submit your file to your instructor, you can either share the file through Google Drive, or create a PDF or Excel file. Click the File menu, point to Download as, and click the format you want. The file will download to your default download folder as determined by your browser settings. Ask your instructor in what format he or she would like to receive your file.

15 **Close** the browser tab—a new Google Sheet always opens in a new window in your browser; your work is automatically saved. Notice that your new Google Sheet displays in the file list on your Google Drive. Sign out of your Google account.

Inventory Valuation

PROJECT ACTIVITIES

In Activities 1.18 through 1.27 you will create a workbook for Josh Feingold, Operations Manager, which calculates the retail value of an inventory of plyometric training products. Your completed worksheet will look similar to Figure 1.38.

PROJECT FILES

If your instructor wants you to submit Project 1B in the MyITLab Grader system, log in to MyITLab, locate Grader Project 1B, and then download the files for this project.

For Project 1B, you will need the following file:

New blank Excel workbook

You will save your workbook as:

Lastname_Firstname_1B_Plyo_Products

PROJECT RESULTS

Pro Fit Marietta
Plyometric Products Inventory Valuation

		As of September 30			
	Warehouse Location	Quantity in Stock	Retail Price	Total Retail Value	Percent of Total Retail Value
Power Hurdle	Atlanta	125	$ 32.95	$ 4,118.75	1.41%
Speed Hurdle	Atlanta	995	59.95	59,650.25	20.37%
Stackable Steps	Marietta	450	251.59	113,215.50	38.65%
Pro Jump Rope	Marietta	1,105	49.95	55,194.75	18.84%
Plyometric Box Set	Marietta	255	158.05	40,302.75	13.76%
Plyometric Mat	Atlanta	215	94.99	20,422.85	6.97%
Total Retail Value for All Products				$ 292,904.85	

Lastname_Firstname_1B_Plyo_Products

Excel 2016, Windows 10, Microsoft Corporation

FIGURE 1.38 Project 1B Plyo Products

GO! Learn How
Video E1-7

In Excel, the spelling checker performs similarly to the other Microsoft Office programs.

Activity 1.18 | **Checking Spelling in a Worksheet**

> **ALERT!** To submit as an autograded project, log into MyITLab, download the files for this project, and begin with those files instead of a new blank workbook.

1 Start Excel and display a new blank workbook. In cell **A1**, type **Pro Fit Marietta** and press Enter. In cell **A2**, type **Plyometric Products Inventory** and press Enter.

2 Click the **File tab**, on the left click **Save As**, under **Save As**, click **Browse** to display the **Save As** dialog box, and then navigate to your **Excel Chapter 1** folder. As the **File name**, using your own name, type **Lastname_Firstname_1B_Plyo_Products** and then click **Save**.

3 Press Tab to move to cell **B3**, type **Quantity** and press Tab. In cell **C3**, type **Average Cost** and press Tab. In cell **D3**, type **Retail Price** and press Tab.

4 Click cell **C3**, and then look at the **Formula Bar**. Notice that in the cell, the displayed value is cut off; however, in the **Formula Bar**, the entire text value—the underlying value—displays. Compare your screen with Figure 1.39.

> Text that is too long to fit in a cell extends into cells on the right only if they are empty. If the cell to the right contains data, the text in the cell to the left is truncated—cut off. The entire value continues to exist, but it is not completely visible.

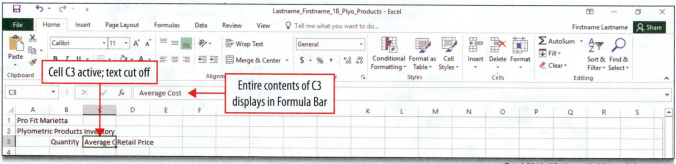

FIGURE 1.39

Excel 2016, Windows 10, Microsoft Corporation

5 Click cell **E3**, type **Total Retail Value** and press Tab. In cell **F3**, type **Percent of Total Retail Value** and press Enter.

6 Click cell **A4**. *Without* correcting the spelling error, type **Powr Hurdle** Press Enter. In the range **A5:A10**, type the remaining row titles shown below. Then compare your screen with Figure 1.40.

Speed Hurdle

Stackable Steps

Pro Jump Rope

Plyometric Box Set

Plyometric Mat

Total Retail Value for All Products

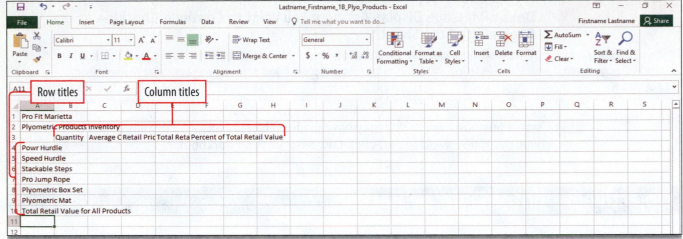

FIGURE 1.40

Excel 2016, Windows 10, Microsoft Corporation

7 In the **column heading area**, point to the right boundary of **column A** to display the ➕ pointer, and then drag to the right to widen **column A** to **215** pixels.

8 Select the range **A1:F1**, **Merge & Center** the text, and then from the **Cell Styles** gallery, apply the **Title** style.

9 Select the range **A2:F2**, **Merge & Center** the text, and then from the **Cell Styles** gallery, apply the **Heading 1** style. Press Ctrl + Home to move to the top of your worksheet.

10 With cell **A1** as the active cell, click the **Review tab**, and then in the **Proofing group**, click **Spelling**. Compare your screen with Figure 1.41.

FIGURE 1.41

Excel 2016, Windows 10, Microsoft Corporation

🔄 **ANOTHER WAY**   Press F7, which is the keyboard shortcut for the Spelling command.

11 In the **Spelling** dialog box, under **Not in Dictionary**, notice the word *Powr*.

The spelling tool does not have this word in its dictionary. Under *Suggestions*, Excel provides a list of suggested spellings.

12 Under **Suggestions**, click **Power**, and then click **Change**.

Powr, a typing error, is changed to *Power*. A message box displays *The spelling check is complete for the entire sheet*—unless you have additional unrecognized words. Because the spelling check begins its checking process starting with the currently selected cell, it is good practice to return to cell A1 before starting the Spelling command.

13 Correct any other errors you may have made. When the message displays, *Spell check complete. You're good to go!*, click **OK**. **Save** 🖫 your workbook.

Objective 8   Enter Data by Range

GO! Learn How
Video E1-8

You can enter data by first selecting a range of cells. This is a time-saving technique, especially if you use the numeric keypad to enter the numbers.

Activity 1.19 | Entering Data by Range

1 Select the range **B4:D9**, type **125** and then press Enter.

The value displays in cell B4, and cell B5 becomes the active cell.

2 With cell **B5** active in the range, and pressing Enter after each entry, type the following, and then compare your screen with Figure 1.42:

1125
450
1105
255
215

After you enter the last value and press Enter, the active cell moves to the top of the next column within the selected range. Although it is not required to enter data in this manner, you can see that selecting the range before you enter data saves time because it confines the movement of the active cell to the selected range. When you select a range of data, the Quick Analysis button displays.

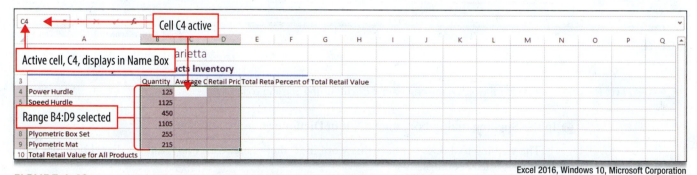

FIGURE 1.42

Excel 2016, Windows 10, Microsoft Corporation

3 With the selected range still active, from the following table, beginning in cell **C4** and pressing Enter after each entry, enter the data for the **Average Cost** column and then the **Retail Price** column. If you prefer, deselect the range to enter the values—typing in a selected range is optional.

AVERAGE COST	RETAIL PRICE
15.50	32.95
29.55	59.95
125.95	251.59
18.75	49.95
85.25	159.05
49.95	94.99

Recall that the default number format for cells is the *General* number format, in which numbers display exactly as you type them and trailing zeros do not display, even if you type them.

4 Click any blank cell, and then compare your screen with Figure 1.43. Correct any errors you may have made while entering data, and then click **Save** 🖫.

	A	B	C	D	E	F	G	H
1	Pro Fit Marietta							
2	**Plyometric Products Inventory**							
3		Quantity	Average C	Retail Pric	Total Reta	Percent of Total Retail Value		
4	Power Hurdle	125	15.5	32.95				
5	Speed Hurdle	1125	29.55	59.95				
6	Stackable Steps	450	125.95	251.59				
7	Pro Jump Rope	1105	18.75	49.95				
8	Plyometric Box Set	255	85.25	159.05				
9	Plyometric Mat	215	49.95	94.99				
10	Total Retail Value for All Products							
11								

Data entered

Excel 2016, Windows 10, Microsoft Corporation

FIGURE 1.43

Objective 9 | Construct Formulas for Mathematical Operations

GO! Learn How
Video E1-9

Operators are symbols with which you can specify the type of calculation you want to perform in a formula.

Activity 1.20 | Using Arithmetic Operators

1 Click cell **E4**, type **=b4*d4** and notice that the two cells are outlined as part of an active formula. Then press Enter.

The *Total Retail Value* of all *Power Hurdle* items in inventory—*4118.75*—equals the *Quantity* (125) times the *Retail Price* (selling price) of 32.95. In Excel, the asterisk (*) indicates multiplication.

2 Take a moment to study the symbols you will use to perform basic mathematical operations in Excel as shown in the table in Figure 1.44, which are referred to as *arithmetic operators*.

SYMBOLS USED IN EXCEL FOR ARITHMETIC OPERATORS	
OPERATOR SYMBOL	**OPERATION**
+	Addition
–	Subtraction (also negation)
*	Multiplication
/	Division
%	Percent
^	Exponentiation

Excel 2016, Windows 10, Microsoft Corporation

FIGURE 1.44

3 Click cell **E4**.

> You can see that in cells E5:E9 you need a formula similar to the one in E4, but one that refers to the cells in row 5, row 6, and so forth. Recall that you can copy formulas and the cell references will change *relative to* the row number.

4 With cell **E4** selected, position your pointer over the fill handle in the lower right corner of the cell until the + pointer displays. Then, drag down through cell **E9** to copy the formula.

5 Select the range **B4:B9**, and then on the **Home tab**, in the **Number group**, click **Comma Style**. In the **Number group**, click **Decrease Decimal** two times to remove the decimal places from these values.

> Comma Style formats a number with two decimal places; because these are whole numbers referring to quantities, no decimal places are necessary.

 ANOTHER WAY   Select the range, display the Cell Styles gallery, and then under Number Format, click Comma [0].

6 Select the range **E4:E9**, and then at the bottom of your screen, in the status bar, notice the displayed values for **Average**, **Count**, and **Sum**—*50158.89167, 6* and *300953.35*.

> When you select a range of numerical data, Excel's *AutoCalculate* feature displays three calculations in the status bar by default—Average, Count, and Sum. Here, Excel indicates that if you averaged the selected values, the result would be *50158.89167*, there are *6* cells in the selection that contain values, and that if you added the values the result would be *300953.35*.

> You can display three additional calculations to this area by right-clicking the status bar and selecting them—Numerical Count, Minimum, and Maximum.

Activity 1.21 | Using the Quick Analysis Tool

MOS
5.1.4

Recall that the Quick Analysis button displays when you select a range of data. Quick Analysis is convenient because it keeps common commands close to your mouse pointer and also displays commands in a format that is easy to touch with your finger if you are using a touchscreen device.

1 Be sure the range **E4:E9** is still selected. In the lower right corner of the selected range, click **Quick Analysis**, and then in the displayed gallery, click **Totals**. *Point to*, but do not click, the first **Sum** button, which shows blue cells at the bottom. Compare your screen with Figure 1.45.

> Here, the shaded cells on the button indicate what will be summed and where the result will display, and a preview of the result displays in the cell bordered with a gray shadow.

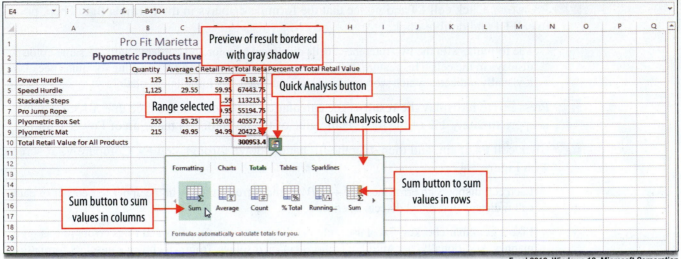

FIGURE 1.45

Excel 2016, Windows 10, Microsoft Corporation

2 Click the first **Sum** button to display the column total *300953.4* formatted in Bold.

Sums calculated using the Quick Analysis tool are formatted in Bold.

3 Select the range **C5:E9** and apply the **Comma Style** $\boxed{,}$; notice that Excel widens the columns to accommodate the data.

4 Select the range **C4:E4**, hold down Ctrl, and then click cell **E10**. Release Ctrl, and then apply the **Accounting Number Format** $\boxed{\$ \cdot}$. Notice that Excel widens the columns as necessary.

5 Click cell **E10**, and then from the **Cell Styles** gallery, apply the **Total** style. Click any blank cell, **Save** $\boxed{\;}$ your workbook, and then compare your screen with Figure 1.46.

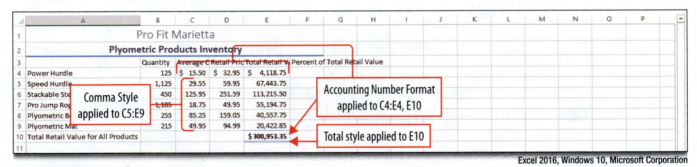

FIGURE 1.46

Excel 2016, Windows 10, Microsoft Corporation

Activity 1.22 | Copying Formulas Containing Absolute Cell References

4.1.1

In a formula, a relative cell reference refers to a cell by its position *relative to* the cell that contains the formula. An **absolute cell reference**, on the other hand, refers to a cell by its *fixed* position in the worksheet, for example, the total in cell E10.

A relative cell reference automatically adjusts when a formula is copied. In some calculations, you do *not* want the cell reference to adjust; rather, you want the cell reference to remain the same when the formula is copied.

1 Click cell **F4**, type = and then click cell **E4**. Type **/** and then click cell **E10**.

The formula *=E4/E10* indicates that the value in cell E4 will be *divided* by the value in cell E10. Why? Because Mr. Feingold wants to know the percentage by which each product's Total Retail Value makes up the Total Retail Value for All Products.

Arithmetically, the percentage is computed by dividing the *Total Retail Value* for each product by the *Total Retail Value for All Products*. The result will be a percentage expressed as a decimal.

2 Press [Enter]. Click cell **F4** and notice that the formula displays in the **Formula Bar**. Then, point to cell **F4** and double-click.

The formula, with the two referenced cells displayed in color and bordered with the same color, displays in the cell. This feature, called the *range finder*, is useful for verifying formulas because it visually indicates which workbook cells are included in a formula calculation.

3 Press [Enter] to redisplay the result of the calculation in the cell, and notice that .013686, which is approximately 1% of the total retail value of the inventory, is made up of Power Hurdles.

4 Click cell **F4** again, and then drag the fill handle down through cell **F9**. Compare your screen with Figure 1.47.

Each cell displays an error message—*#DIV/0!* and a green triangle in the upper left corner of each cell indicates that Excel detects an error.

Like a grammar checker, Excel uses rules to check for formula errors and flags errors in this manner. Additionally, the Auto Fill Options button displays, from which you can select formatting options for the copied cells.

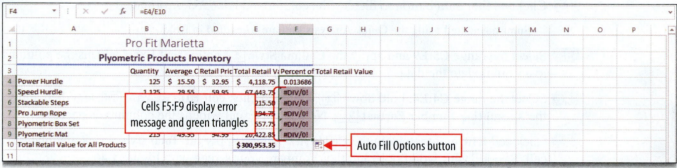

FIGURE 1.47

Excel 2016, Windows 10, Microsoft Corporation

5 Click cell **F5**, and then to the left of the cell, point to the **Error Checking** button ⊘ to display its ScreenTip—*The formula or function used is dividing by zero or empty cells.*

In this manner, Excel suggests the cause of an error.

6 Look at the **Formula Bar** and examine the formula.

The formula is =E5/E11. The cell reference to E5 is correct, but the cell reference following the division operator (/) is *E11*, and E11 is an *empty* cell.

7 Click cell **F6**, point to the **Error Checking** button ⊘, and in the **Formula Bar** examine the formula.

Because the cell references are relative, Excel builds the formulas by increasing the row number for each equation. But in this calculation, the divisor must always be the value in cell E10—the *Total Retail Value for All Products*.

8 Point to cell **F4**, and then double-click to place the insertion point within the cell.

9 Within the cell, use the arrow keys as necessary to position the insertion point to the left of *E10*, and then press [F4]. Compare your screen with Figure 1.48.

Dollar signs ($) display, which changes the reference to cell E10 to an absolute cell reference. The use of the dollar sign to denote an absolute reference is not related in any way to whether or not the values you are working with are currency values. It is simply the symbol that Excel uses to denote an absolute cell reference.

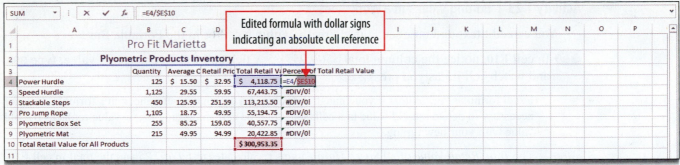

Excel 2016, Windows 10, Microsoft Corporation

FIGURE 1.48

🔄 **ANOTHER WAY**   Edit the formula so that it indicates *=E4/E10*.

10 ▸ On the **Formula Bar**, click **Enter** ✓ so that **F4** remains the active cell. Then, drag the fill handle to copy the new formula down through cell **F9**. Compare your screen with Figure 1.49.

Excel 2016, Windows 10, Microsoft Corporation

FIGURE 1.49

11 ▸ Click cell **F5**, examine the formula in the **Formula Bar**, and then examine the formulas for cells **F6**, **F7**, **F8**, and **F9**.

For each formula, the cell reference for the *Total Retail Value* of each product changed relative to its row; however, the value used as the divisor—*Total Retail Value for All Products* in cell E10—remained absolute. You can see that by using either relative or absolute cell references, it is easy to duplicate formulas without typing them.

12 ▸ Save 💾 your workbook.

More **Knowledge**   **Calculate a Percentage if You Know the Total and the Amount**

Using the equation *amount/total = percentage*, you can calculate the percentage by which a part makes up a total—with the percentage formatted as a decimal. For example, if on a test you score 42 points correctly out of 50, your percentage of correct answers is 42/50 = 0.84 or 84%.

Objective 10   Edit Values in a Worksheet

GO! Learn How
Video E1-10

Excel performs calculations on numbers; that is why you use Excel. If you make changes to the numbers, Excel automatically *re*-calculates the results. This is one of the most powerful and valuable features of Excel.

Activity 1.23 | Editing Values in a Worksheet

You can edit text and number values directly within a cell or in the Formula Bar.

1 In cell **E10**, notice the column total *$300,953.35*. Click cell **B5**. To change its value, type **995** and watch cell E5 as you press [Enter].

Excel formulas *recalculate* if you change the value in a cell that is referenced in a formula. It is not necessary to delete the old value in a cell; selecting the cell and typing a new value replaces the old value with your new typing.

The *Total Retail Value* of all *Speed Hurdle* items recalculates to *59,650.25* and the total in cell E10 recalculates to *$293,159.85*. Additionally, all of the percentages in column F recalculate.

2 Point to cell **D8**, and then double-click to place the insertion point within the cell. Use the arrow keys to move the insertion point to the left or right of *9*, and use either [Del] or [Backspace] to delete *9* and then type **8** so that the new Retail Price is *158.05*.

3 Watch cell **E8** and **E10** as you press [Enter], and then notice the recalculation of the formulas in those two cells.

Excel recalculates the value in cell E8 to *40,302.75* and the value in cell E10 to *$292,904.85*. Additionally, all of the percentages in column F recalculate because the *Total Retail Value for All Products* recalculated.

4 Point to cell **A2** so that the [✛] pointer is positioned slightly to the right of the word *Inventory*, and then double-click to place the insertion point in the cell. Edit the text to add the word **Valuation** pressing [Spacebar] as necessary, and then press [Enter].

5 Click cell **B3**, and then in the **Formula Bar**, click to place the insertion point after the letter *y*. Press [Spacebar] one time, type **in Stock** and then on the **Formula Bar**, click **Enter** [✓]. Click **Save** [💾], and then compare your screen with Figure 1.50.

Recall that if text is too long to fit in the cell and the cell to the right contains data, the text is truncated—cut off—but the entire value still exists as the underlying value.

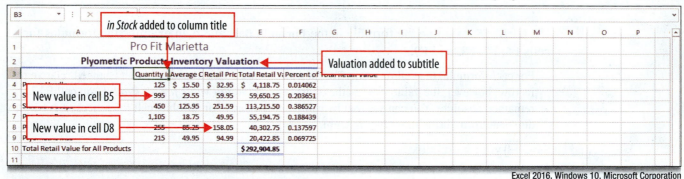

Excel 2016, Windows 10, Microsoft Corporation

FIGURE 1.50

Activity 1.24 | Formatting Cells with the Percent Style

2.2.5

A percentage is part of a whole expressed in hundredths. For example, 75 cents is the same as 75 percent of one dollar. The Percent Style button formats the selected cell as a percentage rounded to the nearest hundredth.

1 Click cell **F4**, and then in the **Number group**, click **Percent Style** [%].

Your result is 1%, which is *0.014062* rounded to the nearest hundredth and expressed as a percentage. Percent Style displays the value of a cell as a percentage.

2 Select the range **F4:F9**, right-click over the selection, and then on the mini toolbar, click **Percent Style** [%], click **Increase Decimal** [🔢] two times, and then click **Center** [≡].

Percent Style may not offer a percentage precise enough to analyze important financial information—adding additional decimal places to a percentage makes data more precise.

3 ▶ Click any cell to cancel the selection, **Save** 🖫 your workbook, and then compare your screen with Figure 1.51.

FIGURE 1.51

Excel 2016, Windows 10, Microsoft Corporation

Objective 11 Format a Worksheet

GO! Learn How
Video E1-11

Formatting refers to the process of specifying the appearance of cells and the overall layout of your worksheet. Formatting is accomplished through various commands on the ribbon, for example, applying Cell Styles, and also from commands on shortcut menus, using keyboard shortcuts, and in the Format Cells dialog box.

Activity 1.25 │ Inserting and Deleting Rows and Columns

MOS
1.3.5

1 ▶ In the **row heading area** on the left side of your screen, point to the row heading for **row 3** to display the ➡ pointer, and then right-click to simultaneously select the row and display a shortcut menu.

2 ▶ On the shortcut menu, click **Insert** to insert a new **row 3** above the selected row.

The rows below the new row 3 move down one row, and the Insert Options button displays. By default, the new row uses the formatting of the row *above*.

🔄 **ANOTHER WAY**   Select the row, on the Home tab, in the Cells group, click the Insert button arrow, and then click Insert Sheet Rows. Or, select the row and click the Insert button—the default setting of the button inserts a new sheet row above the selected row.

3 ▶ Click cell **E11**. On the **Formula Bar**, notice that the range changed to sum the new range **E5:E10**. Compare your screen with Figure 1.52.

If you move formulas by inserting additional rows or columns in your worksheet, Excel automatically adjusts the formulas. Excel adjusted all of the formulas in the worksheet that were affected by inserting this new row.

FIGURE 1.52

Excel 2016, Windows 10, Microsoft Corporation

4 ▶ Click cell **A3**, type **As of September 30** and then on the **Formula Bar**, click **Enter** ☑ to maintain **A3** as the active cell. **Merge & Center** the text across the range **A3:F3**, and then apply the **Heading 2** cell style.

5 ▶ In the **column heading area**, point to **column B** to display the ⬇ pointer, right-click, and then click **Insert**.

A column is inserted to the left of column B. By default, the new column uses the formatting of the column to the *left*.

🔄 **ANOTHER WAY** Select the column, on the Home tab, in the Cells group, click the Insert button arrow, and then click Insert Sheet Columns. Or, select the column and click the Insert button—the default setting of the button inserts a new sheet column to the right of the selected column.

---

6 ▶ Click cell **B4**, type **Warehouse Location** and then press Enter.

7 ▶ In cell **B5**, type **Atlanta** and then type **Atlanta** again in cells **B6** and **B10**. Use AutoComplete to speed your typing by pressing Enter as soon as the AutoComplete suggestion displays. In cells **B7**, **B8**, and **B9**, type **Marietta**

8 ▶ In the **column heading area**, point to **column D**, right-click, and then click **Delete**.

The remaining columns shift to the left, and Excel adjusts all the formulas in the worksheet accordingly. You can use a similar technique to delete a row in a worksheet.

9 ▶ Compare your screen with Figure 1.53, and then **Save** 💾 your workbook.

FIGURE 1.53

Excel 2016, Windows 10, Microsoft Corporation

Activity 1.26 │ Adjusting Column Widths and Wrapping Text

[MOS]
1.3.7, 2.2.4

Use the Wrap Text command to display the contents of a cell on multiple lines.

1 ▶ In the **column heading area**, point to the **column B** heading to display the ⬇ pointer, and then drag to the right to select **columns B:F**.

2 ▶ With the columns selected, in the **column heading area**, point to the right boundary of any of the selected columns to display the ➕ pointer, and then drag to set the width to **95 pixels**.

Use this technique to format multiple columns or rows simultaneously.

3 ▶ Select the range **B4:F4** that comprises the column headings, and then on the **Home tab**, in the **Alignment group**, click **Wrap Text** 📑. Notice that the row height adjusts to display the titles on multiple lines.

4 ▶ With the range **B4:F4** still selected, in the **Alignment group**, click **Center** ≡ and **Middle Align** ≡. With the range **B4:F4** still selected, apply the **Heading 4** cell style.

The Middle Align command aligns text so that it is centered between the top and bottom of the cell.

5 Select the range **B5:B10**, right-click, and then on the mini toolbar, click **Center** ☰. Click cell **A11**, and then from the **Cell Styles** gallery, under **Themed Cell Styles**, click **40% - Accent1**. **Save** 🖫 your workbook.

Activity 1.27 | Changing Theme Colors

You can change only the theme *colors* of a workbook—without changing the theme fonts or effects.

1 On the **Page Layout tab**, in the **Themes group**, click **Colors**, and then click **Green** to change the Theme Color. Click any blank cell, and then compare your screen with Figure 1.54.

	A	C	D	E	F	G	H	I	J	K	L	M	N
1	Theme colors changed to Green / Pro Fit Marietta												
2	Plyometric Products Inventory Valuation												
3	As of September 30												
4		Warehouse Location	Quantity in Stock	Retail Price	Total Retail Value	Percent of Total Retail Value							
5	Power Hurdle	Atlanta	125	$ 32.95	$ 4,118.75	1.41%							
6	Speed Hurdle	Atlanta	995	59.95	59,650.25	20.37%							
7	Stackable Steps	Marietta	450	251.59	113,215.50	38.65%							
8	Pro Jump Rope	Marietta	1,105	49.95	55,194.75	18.84%							
9	Plyometric Box Set	Marietta	255	158.05	40,302.75	13.76%							
10	Plyometric Mat	Atlanta	215	94.99	20,422.85	6.97%							
11	Total Retail Value for All Products				$ 292,904.85								
12													

FIGURE 1.54

2 On the **Page Layout tab**, in the **Page Setup group**, click **Margins**, and then click **Custom Margins**.

3 In the **Page Setup** dialog box, on the **Margins tab**, under **Center on page**, select the **Horizontally** check box.

This action will center the data horizontally on the page, as shown in the Preview area.

4 Click the **Header/Footer tab**, and then in the center of the dialog box, click **Custom Footer**. In the **Footer** dialog box, with your insertion point blinking in the **Left section**, on the row of buttons, click **Insert File Name** 🗎.

&[File] displays in the Left section. Here you can type or insert information from the row of buttons into the left, middle, or right section of the footer. The Custom Header button displays a similar screen to enter information in the header of the worksheet.

5 Click **OK** two times.

6 Click the **File tab** to display Backstage view, and then in the lower right corner, click **Show All Properties**.

7 As the **Tags**, type **plyo products, inventory** and as the **Subject**, type your course name and section number. Be sure your name displays in the **Author** box, or edit it if necessary.

8 On the left, click **Print** to view the **Print Preview**. At the bottom of the **Print Preview**, click **Next Page** ▶, and notice that as currently formatted, the worksheet occupies two pages.

9 Under **Settings**, click **Portrait Orientation**, and then click **Landscape Orientation**. Compare your screen with Figure 1.55.

You can change the orientation on the Page Layout tab, or here, in Print Preview. Because it is in the Print Preview that you will often see adjustments that need to be made, commonly used settings display on the Print tab in Backstage view.

Excel 2016, Windows 10, Microsoft Corporation

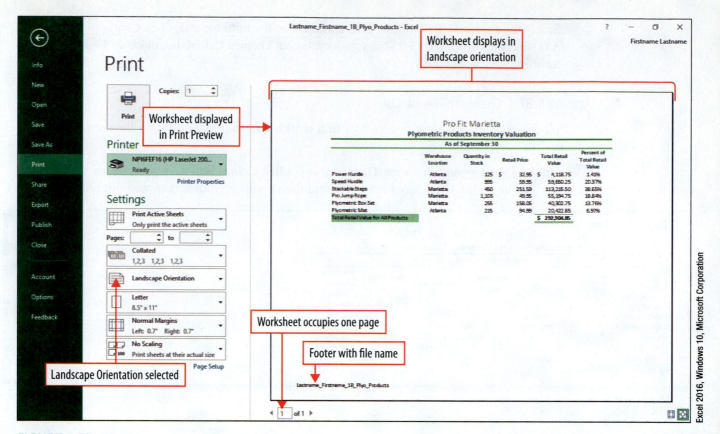

FIGURE 1.55

10 ▶ On the left, click **Save**. By using the techniques you practiced in Project 1A and as directed by your instructor, print, create a PDF image that looks like a printed document, or submit your completed Excel file. If required by your instructor, print or create an electronic version of your worksheet with formulas displayed.

11 ▶ In **Backstage** view, click **Close** to close your workbook, and then **Close** ☒ Excel.

END | You have completed Project 1B

GO! With Google

Objective   Creating an Inventory Valuation Report

> **ALERT!**   **Working with Web-Based Applications and Services**
>
> Computer programs and services on the web receive continuous updates and improvements, so the steps to complete this web-based Activity may differ from the ones shown. You can often look at the screens and the information presented to determine how to complete the Activity.
>
> If you do not already have a Google account, you will need to create one before you begin this activity. Go to http://google.com and in the upper right corner, click Sign In. On the Sign In screen, click Create Account. On the Create your Google Account page, complete the form, read and agree to the Terms of Service and Privacy Policy, and then click Next step. On the Welcome screen, click Get Started.

Activity | Creating an Inventory Valuation Report Using Google Sheets

In this Activity, you will use Google Sheets to create an inventory valuation report similar to the one you created in Project 1B.

1 From the desktop, open your browser (a browser other than Edge), navigate to **http://google.com** and then click the **Google Apps** menu ⚏. Click **Drive**, and then if necessary, sign in to your Google account.

2 Open your **GO! Web Projects** folder—or click New to create and then open this folder if necessary.

3 In the left pane, click **NEW**, and then click **Google Sheets**. From your Windows taskbar, open **File Explorer**, navigate to your Student Data Files for this chapter, and then in the **File List**, double-click the Word document **e01_1B_Web**; to complete this project quickly and eliminate extra typing, you will copy the data from a Word document.

4 In the displayed Word document, click anywhere in the text, and then in the upper left corner, click to select the **Table Select** ⊞ to select the entire Word table. Right-click anywhere over the selection, and then click **Copy**. **Close** Word. **Close** the **File Explorer** window.

5 In your blank Google Sheet, with cell **A1** active, point to cell **A1**, right-click, and then click **Paste**. In the column heading area, point to the border between **column A** and **column B** to display the ↔ pointer, and then widen **column A** slightly so that all of the data in rows 4–10 displays.

6 Select the range **A1:E1**. On the toolbar, click **Merge cells** ⊞. On the toolbar, click the **Align arrow** ▾, and then click **Center** ≡. Repeat for the range **A2:E2**, and then apply **Bold** **B** to cells **A1** and **A2**.

7 Select the range **B3:E3**, on the menu bar click **Format**, point to **Text wrapping**, and then click **Wrap**. **Center** these column titles and apply **Bold** **B**.

8 Select the range **C4:C9**, on the menu bar click **Format**, point to **Number**, on the fly-out menu click **Number**, and then if necessary, on the toolbar, click **Decrease decimal places** ◂ two times.

9 Click cell **E4**, type **=** and then click cell **C4**. Type ***** and then click cell **D4**. Press ⏎. Click cell **E4**, point to the fill handle in the lower right corner of the cell, and then drag down to cell **E9**.

10 Select the range **E4:E9**. On the toolbar, click **Functions** **Σ ▾**, click **SUM**, and then press ⏎.

11 Select the range **D4:E4**, hold down ⎈Ctrl, and then select cell **E10**. On the menu bar, click **Format**, point to **Number**, and then in the fly-out menu click **Currency**.

12 Select cell **A10**, hold down ⎈Ctrl, and then click cell **E10**. Apply **Bold** **B**.

13 Click cell **A1**, hold down ⎈Ctrl, and then click cell **A2**, cell **A10**, and cell **E10**. With the four cells selected, on the toolbar, click **Fill color** 🖌▾, and then in the fourth column, click the third color—**light yellow 3**.

14 At the top of the worksheet, click the text *Untitled spreadsheet*, and then using your own name, type **Lastname_Firstname_EX_1B_Web** and press ENTER.

(GO! With Google continues on the next page)

GO! With Google

Lastname_Firstname_EX_1B_Web

File Edit View Insert Format Data Tools Add-ons Help

	A	B	C	D	E
1	Pro Fit Marietta				
2	Plyometric Products Inventory Valuation				
3		Warehouse Location	Quantity In Stock	Retail Price	Total Retail Value
4	Power Hurdle	Atlanta	125	$32.95	$4,118.75
5	Speed Hurdle	Atlanta	995	59.95	59650.25
6	Stackable Steps	Marietta	450	251.59	113215.5
7	Pro Jump Rope	Marietta	1,105	49.95	55194.75
8	Plyometric Box Set	Marietta	255	158.05	40302.75
9	Plyometric Mat	Atlanta	215	94.99	20422.85
10	Total Retail Value for All Products				$292,904.85
11					

FIGURE A

GO! To Work

MICROSOFT OFFICE SPECIALIST (MOS) SKILLS IN THIS CHAPTER

PROJECT 1A	PROJECT 1B
1.1.1 Create a workbook	**1.3.5** Insert and delete columns or rows
1.3.4 Modify page setup	**1.3.7** Adjust row height and column width
1.3.6 Change workbook themes	**2.2.5** Apply number formats
1.3.8 Insert headers and footers	**2.2.6** Apply cell formats
1.4.6 Modify document properties	**4.1.1** Insert references
1.4.8 Display formulas	**5.1.4** Analyze data by using Quick Analysis
1.5.1 Set a print area	
1.5.3 Print all or part of a workbook	
1.5.4 Set print scaling	
2.1.4 Fill cells by using Auto Fill	
2.2.1 Merge cells	
2.2.5 Apply number formats	
2.2.7 Apply cell styles	
2.3.1 Insert sparklines	
5.1.1 Create a new chart	
5.1.3 Switch between rows and columns in source data	
5.2.2 Add and modify chart elements	
5.2.3 Apply chart layouts and styles	

BUILD YOUR E-PORTFOLIO

An E-Portfolio is a collection of evidence, stored electronically, that showcases what you have accomplished while completing your education. Collecting and then sharing your work products with potential employers reflects your academic and career goals. Your completed documents from the following projects are good examples to show what you have learned: 1G, 1K, and 1L.

GO! FOR JOB SUCCESS

Video: Customer Service

Your instructor may assign this video to your class, and then ask you to think about, or discuss with your classmates, these questions:

FotolEdhar / Fotolia

If you were interviewing people for your company, what would you look for in terms of their dress and personal presentation?

What might you want to change about your personal dress for work or for an interview?

Do you feel that it's right to "judge a book by its cover"? Why or why not?

END OF CHAPTER

SUMMARY

In Excel, you work with worksheets that are contained in a workbook. A worksheet is formatted as a pattern of uniformly spaced horizontal rows and vertical columns, the intersection of which forms a cell.

A cell can contain a constant value— referred to as a value—or a formula, which is an equation that performs mathematical calculations on the values in your worksheet. Common values are text and numbers.

You can insert sparklines in an Excel worksheet, which are tiny charts embedded in a cell that give a visual trend summary alongside your data. A sparkline makes a pattern more obvious to the eye.

Charts provide a graphic representation of data in a worksheet. Use the Recommended Charts feature to display customized charts that, according to Excel's calculations, will best represent your data.

GO! LEARN IT ONLINE

Review the concepts, key terms, and MOS skills in this chapter by completing these online challenges, which you can find at **MyITLab**.

Matching and Multiple Choice: Answer matching and multiple choice questions to test what you learned in this chapter.

Lessons on the GO!: Learn how to use all the new apps and features as they are introduced by Microsoft.

MOS Prep Quiz: Answer questions to review the MOS skills that you practiced in this chapter.

GO! COLLABORATIVE TEAM PROJECT (Available in **MyITLab** and Instructor Resource Center)

If your instructor assigns this project to your class, you can expect to work with one or more of your classmates—either in person or by using Internet tools—to create work products similar to those that you created in this chapter. A team is a group of workers who work together to solve a problem, make a decision, or create a work product. Collaboration is when you work together with others as a team in an intellectual endeavor to complete a shared task or achieve a shared goal.

PROJECT GUIDE FOR EXCEL CHAPTER 1

Your instructor will assign Projects from this list to ensure your learning and assess your knowledge.

	PROJECT GUIDE FOR EXCEL CHAPTER 1		
Project	**Apply Skills from These Chapter Objectives**	**Project Type**	**Project Location**
1A **MyITLab**	Objectives 1–6 from Project 1A	**1A Instructional Project (Grader Project)** Guided instruction to learn the skills in Project 1A.	In text
1B **MyITLab**	Objectives 7–11 from Project 1B	**1B Instructional Project (Grader Project)** Guided instruction to learn the skills in Project 1B.	In text
1C	Objectives 1–6 from Project 1A	**1C Skills Review (Scorecard Grading)** A guided review of the skills from Project 1A.	In text
1D	Objectives 7–11 from Project 1B	**1D Skills Review (Scorecard Grading)** A guided review of the skills from Project 1B.	In text
1E **MyITLab**	Objectives 1–6 from Project 1A	**1E Mastery (Grader Project)** **Mastery and Transfer of Learning** A demonstration of your mastery of the skills in Project 1A with extensive decision making.	In text
1F **MyITLab**	Objectives 7–11 from Project 1B	**1F Mastery (Grader Project)** **Mastery and Transfer of Learning** A demonstration of your mastery of the skills in Project 1B with extensive decision making.	In text
1G **MyITLab**	Objectives 1–11 from Projects 1A and 1B	**1G Mastery (Grader Project)** **Mastery and Transfer of Learning** A demonstration of your mastery of the skills in Projects 1A and 1B with extensive decision making.	In text
1H	Combination of Objectives from Projects 1A and 1B	**1H GO! Fix It (Scorecard Grading)** **Critical Thinking** A demonstration of your mastery of the skills in Projects 1A and 1B by creating a correct result from a document that contains errors you must find.	Instructor Resource Center (IRC)
1I	Combination of Objectives from Projects 1A and 1B	**1I GO! Make It (Scorecard Grading)** **Critical Thinking** A demonstration of your mastery of the skills in Projects 1A and 1B by creating a result from a supplied picture.	IRC
1J	Combination of Objectives from Projects 1A and 1B	**1J GO! Solve It (Rubric Grading)** **Critical Thinking** A demonstration of your mastery of the skills in Projects 1A and 1B, your decision-making skills, and your critical-thinking skills. A task-specific rubric helps you self-assess your result.	IRC
1K	Combination of Objectives from Projects 1A and 1B	**1K GO! Solve It (Rubric Grading)** **Critical Thinking** A demonstration of your mastery of the skills in Projects 1A and 1B, your decision-making skills, and your critical-thinking skills. A task-specific rubric helps you self-assess your result.	In text
1L	Combination of Objectives from Projects 1A and 1B	**1L GO! Think (Rubric Grading)** **Critical Thinking** A demonstration of your understanding of the chapter concepts applied in a manner that you would outside of college. An analytic rubric helps you and your instructor grade the quality of your work by comparing it to the work an expert in the discipline would create.	In text
1M	Combination of Objectives from Projects 1A and 1B	**1M GO! Think (Rubric Grading)** **Critical Thinking** A demonstration of your understanding of the chapter concepts applied in a manner that you would outside of college. An analytic rubric helps you and your instructor grade the quality of your work by comparing it to the work an expert in the discipline would create.	IRC
1N	Combination of Objectives from Projects 1A and 1B	**1N You and GO! (Rubric Grading)** **Critical Thinking** A demonstration of your understanding of the chapter concepts applied in a manner that you would in a personal situation. An analytic rubric helps you and your instructor grade the quality of your work.	IRC
1O	Combination of Objectives from Projects 1A and 1B	**1O Cumulative Group Project for Excel Chapter 1** A demonstration of your understanding of concepts and your ability to work collaboratively in a group role-playing assessment, requiring both collaboration and self-management.	IRC

GLOSSARY

GLOSSARY OF CHAPTER KEY TERMS

Absolute cell reference A cell reference that refers to cells by their fixed position in a worksheet; an absolute cell reference remains the same when the formula is copied.

Accounting Number Format The Excel number format that applies a thousand comma separator where appropriate, inserts a fixed U.S. dollar sign aligned at the left edge of the cell, applies two decimal places, and leaves a small amount of space at the right edge of the cell to accommodate a parenthesis for negative numbers.

Active cell The cell, surrounded by a border, ready to receive data or be affected by the next Excel command.

Arithmetic operators The symbols +, −, *, /, %, and ^ used to denote addition, subtraction (or negation), multiplication, division, percentage, and exponentiation in an Excel formula.

Auto Fill An Excel feature that generates and extends values into adjacent cells based on the values of selected cells.

AutoCalculate A feature that displays three calculations in the status bar by default—Average, Count, and Sum—when you select a range of numerical data.

AutoComplete A feature that speeds your typing and lessens the likelihood of errors; if the first few characters you type in a cell match an existing entry in the column, Excel fills in the remaining characters for you.

AutoFit An Excel feature that adjusts the width of a column to fit the cell content of the widest cell in the column.

AutoSum A button that provides quick access to the SUM function.

Category axis The area along the bottom of a chart that identifies the categories of data; also referred to as the x-axis.

Category labels The labels that display along the bottom of a chart to identify the categories of data; Excel uses the row titles as the category names.

Cell The intersection of a column and a row.

Cell address Another name for a cell reference.

Cell content Anything typed into a cell.

Cell reference The identification of a specific cell by its intersecting column letter and row number.

Cell style A defined set of formatting characteristics, such as font, font size, font color, cell borders, and cell shading.

Chart The graphic representation of data in a worksheet; data presented as a chart is usually easier to understand than a table of numbers.

Chart Elements button A button that enables you to add, remove, or change chart elements such as the title, legend, gridlines, and data labels.

Chart Filters button A button that enables you to change which data displays in the chart.

Chart layout The combination of chart elements that can be displayed in a chart such as a title, legend, labels for the columns, and the table of charted cells.

Chart style The overall visual look of a chart in terms of its graphic effects, colors, and backgrounds; for example, you can have flat or beveled columns, colors that are solid or transparent, and backgrounds that are dark or light.

Chart Styles button A button that enables you to set a style and color scheme for your chart.

Chart Styles gallery A group of predesigned chart styles that you can apply to an Excel chart.

Chart types Various chart formats used in a way that is meaningful to the reader; common examples are column charts, pie charts, and line charts.

Column A vertical group of cells in a worksheet.

Column chart A chart in which the data is arranged in columns and that is useful for showing data changes over a period of time or for illustrating comparisons among items.

Column heading The letter that displays at the top of a vertical group of cells in a worksheet; beginning with the first letter of the alphabet, a unique letter or combination of letters identifies each column.

Comma Style The Excel number format that inserts thousand comma separators where appropriate and applies two decimal places; Comma Style also leaves space at the right to accommodate a parenthesis when negative numbers are present.

Constant value Numbers, text, dates, or times of day that you type into a cell.

Context sensitive A command associated with the currently selected or active object; often activated by right-clicking a screen item.

Data Text or numbers in a cell.

Data marker A column, bar, area, dot, pie slice, or other symbol in a chart that represents a single data point; related data points form a data series.

Data point A value that originates in a worksheet cell and that is represented in a chart by a data marker.

Data series Related data points represented by data markers; each data series has a unique color or pattern represented in the chart legend.

Displayed value The data that displays in a cell.

Excel pointer An Excel window element with which you can display the location of the pointer.

Expand Formula Bar button An Excel window element with which you can increase the height of the Formula Bar to display lengthy cell content.

Expand horizontal scroll bar button An Excel window element with which you can increase the width of the horizontal scroll bar.

Fill handle The small square in the lower right corner of a selected cell.

Format Changing the appearance of cells and worksheet elements to make a worksheet attractive and easy to read.

Formula An equation that performs mathematical calculations on values in a worksheet.

Formula Bar An element in the Excel window that displays the value or formula contained in the active cell; here you can also enter or edit values or formulas.

Function A predefined formula—a formula that Excel has already built for you—that performs calculations by using specific values in a particular order.

General format The default format that Excel applies to numbers; this format has no specific characteristics—whatever you type in the cell will display, with the exception that trailing zeros to the right of a decimal point will not display.

Label Another name for a text value, and which usually provides information about number values.

Left alignment The cell format in which characters align at the left edge of the cell; this is the default for text entries and is an example of formatting information stored in a cell.

Legend A chart element that identifies the patterns or colors that are assigned to the categories in the chart.

Lettered column headings The area along the top edge of a worksheet that identifies each column with a unique letter or combination of letters.

Merge & Center A command that joins selected cells in an Excel worksheet into one larger cell and centers the contents in the merged cell.

Name Box An element of the Excel window that displays the name of the selected cell, table, chart, or object.

Normal view A screen view that maximizes the number of cells visible on your screen and keeps the column letters and row numbers close to the columns and rows.

Number format A specific way in which Excel displays numbers in a cell.

Number values Constant values consisting of only numbers.

Numbered row headings The area along the left edge of a worksheet that identifies each row with a unique number.

Operators The symbols with which you can specify the type of calculation you want to perform in an Excel formula.

Picture element A point of light measured in dots per square inch on a screen; 64 pixels equals 8.43 characters, which is the average number of characters that will fit in a cell in an Excel worksheet using the default font.

Pixel The abbreviated name for a picture element.

Point and click method The technique of constructing a formula by pointing to and then clicking cells; this method

is convenient when the referenced cells are not adjacent to one another.

Quick Analysis Tool A tool that displays in the lower right corner of a selected range, with which you can analyze your data by using Excel tools such as charts, color-coding, and formulas.

Range Two or more selected cells on a worksheet that are adjacent or nonadjacent; because the range is treated as a single unit, you can make the same changes or combination of changes to more than one cell at a time.

Range finder An Excel feature that outlines cells in color to indicate which cells are used in a formula; useful for verifying which cells are referenced in a formula.

Recommended Charts An Excel feature that displays a customized set of charts that, according to Excel's calculations, will best fit your data based on the range of data that you select.

Relative cell reference In a formula, the address of a cell based on the relative positions of the cell that contains the formula and the cell referred to in the formula.

Rounding A procedure in which you determine which digit at the right of the number will be the last digit displayed and then increase it by one if the next digit to its right is 5, 6, 7, 8, or 9.

Row A horizontal group of cells in a worksheet.

Row heading The numbers along the left side of an Excel worksheet that designate the row numbers.

Scaling The process of shrinking the width and/or height of printed output to fit a maximum number of pages.

Select All box A box in the upper left corner of the worksheet grid that, when clicked, selects all the cells in a worksheet.

Series A group of things that come one after another in succession; for example, January, February, March, and so on.

Sheet tab scrolling buttons Buttons to the left of the sheet tabs used to display Excel sheet tabs that are not in view; used when there are more sheet tabs than will display in the space provided.

Sheet tabs The labels along the lower border of the Excel window that identify each worksheet.

Show Formulas A command that displays the formula in each cell instead of the resulting value.

Sparkline A tiny chart in the background of a cell that gives a visual trend summary alongside your data; makes a pattern more obvious.

Spreadsheet Another name for a worksheet.

Status bar The area along the lower edge of the Excel window that displays, on the left side, the current cell mode, page number, and worksheet information; on the right side, when numerical data is selected, common calculations such as Sum and Average display.

SUM function A predefined formula that adds all the numbers in a selected range of cells.

Switch Row/Column A charting command to swap the data over the axis—data being charted on the vertical axis will move to the horizontal axis and vice versa.

Text values Constant values consisting of only text, and which usually provide information about number values; also referred to as labels.

Theme A predefined set of colors, fonts, lines, and fill effects that coordinate with each other.

Underlying formula The formula entered in a cell and visible only on the Formula Bar.

Underlying value The data that displays in the Formula Bar.

Value Another name for a constant value.

Value axis A numerical scale on the left side of a chart that shows the range of numbers for the data points; also referred to as the Y-axis.

Workbook An Excel file that contains one or more worksheets.

Worksheet The primary document that you use in Excel to work with and store data, and which is formatted as a pattern of uniformly spaced horizontal and vertical lines.

Worksheet grid area A part of the Excel window that displays the columns and rows that intersect to form the worksheet's cells.

X-axis Another name for the horizontal (category) axis.

Y-axis Another name for the vertical (value) axis.

Skills Review Project 1C Step Sales

In the following Skills Review, you will create a new Excel worksheet with a chart that summarizes the first quarter sales of fitness equipment for step training. Your completed worksheet will look similar to Figure 1.56.

PROJECT FILES

For Project 1C, you will need the following file:

New blank Excel workbook

You will save your workbook as:

Lastname_Firstname_1C_Step_Sales

PROJECT RESULTS

Build From
Scratch

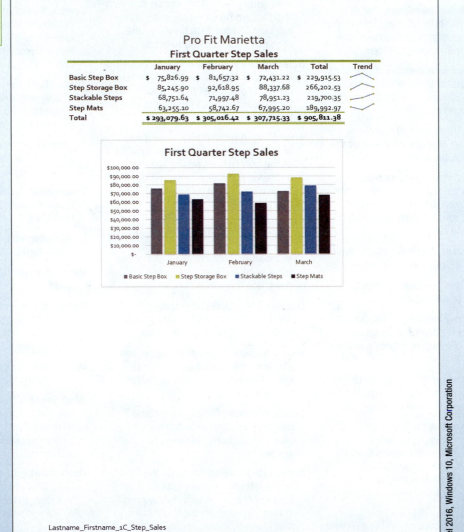

FIGURE 1.56

(Project 1C Step Sales continues on the next page)

Skills Review   Project 1C Step Sales (continued)

1 ▶ Start Excel and open a new blank workbook. Click the **File tab** to display **Backstage** view, click **Save As**, and then navigate to your **Excel Chapter 1** folder. In the **File name** box, using your own name, type **Lastname_Firstname_1C_Step_Sales** and then press Enter.

a. With cell **A1** as the active cell, type the worksheet title **Pro Fit Marietta** and then press Enter. In cell **A2**, type the worksheet subtitle **First Quarter Step Sales** and then press Enter.

b. Click in cell **A4**, type **Basic Step Box** and then press Enter. In cell **A5**, type **Step Storage Box** and then press Enter. In cell **A6**, type **Stackable Steps** and then press Enter. In cell **A7**, type **Step Mats** and then press Enter. In cell **A8**, type **Total** and then press Enter.

c. Click cell **B3**. Type **January** and then in the **Formula Bar**, click **Enter** to keep cell **B3** the active cell. With **B3** as the active cell, point to the fill handle in the lower right corner of the selected cell, drag to the right to cell **D3**, and then release the mouse button to enter the text *February* and *March*.

d. Press Ctrl + Home to make cell **A1** the active cell. In the **column heading area**, point to the vertical line between **column A** and **column B** to display the ⬌ pointer, hold down the left mouse button, and drag to the right to increase the column width to **130 pixels**.

e. Point to cell **B3**, and then drag across to select cells **B3** and **C3** and **D3**. With the range **B3:D3** selected, point anywhere over the selected range, right-click, and then on the mini toolbar, click **Center**.

f. Click cell **B4**, type **75826.99** and press Tab to make cell **C4** active. Enter the remaining values, as shown in **Table 1**, pressing Tab to move across the rows and Enter to move down the columns.

TABLE 1

	January	February	March
Basic Step Box	75826.99	81657.32	72431.22
Step Storage Box	85245.90	92618.95	88337.68
Stackable Steps	68751.64	71997.48	78951.23
Step Mats	63255.10	58742.67	67995.20

2 ▶ Click cell **B8** to make it the active cell and type =

a. At the insertion point, type **b4** and then type + Type **b5** and then type **+b6+b7** Press Enter. Your result is *293079.6*.

b. Click in cell **C8**. Type = and then click cell **C4**. Type + and then click cell **C5**. Repeat this process to complete the formula to add cells **C6** and **C7** to the formula, and then press Enter. Your result is *305016.4*.

c. Click cell **D8**. On the **Home tab**, in the **Editing group**, click **AutoSum**, and then press Enter to construct a formula by using the SUM function. Your result is *307715.3*.

d. In cell **E3** type **Total** and press Enter. With cell **E4** as the active cell, hold down Alt, and then press =. On the **Formula Bar**, click **Enter** to display the result and keep cell **E4** active.

e. With cell **E4** active, point to the fill handle in the lower right corner of the cell. Drag down through cell **E8**, and then release the mouse button to copy the formula with relative cell references down to sum each row.

3 ▶ Click cell **F3**. Type **Trend** and then press Enter.

a. Select the range **A1:F1**, and then on the **Home tab**, in the **Alignment group**, click **Merge & Center**. Select the range **A2:F2** and **Merge & Center** the selection.

b. Click cell **A1**. In the **Styles group**, click **Cell Styles**. Under **Titles and Headings**, click **Title**. Click cell **A2**, display the **Cell Styles** gallery, and then click **Heading 1**.

c. Select the range **B3:F3**, hold down Ctrl, and then select the range **A4:A8**. From the **Cell Styles** gallery, click **Heading 4** to apply this cell style to the column and row titles.

d. Select the range **B4:E4**, hold down Ctrl, and then select the range **B8:E8**. On the **Home tab**, in the **Number group**, click **Accounting Number Format**. Select the range **B5:E7**, and then in the **Number group**, click **Comma Style**. Select the range **B8:E8**. From the **Styles group**, display the **Cell Styles** gallery, and then under **Titles and Headings**, click **Total**.

e. On the ribbon, click the **Page Layout tab**, and then in the **Themes group**, click **Themes** to display the **Themes** gallery. Click the **Basis** theme. (This theme widens the columns slightly). On the Quick Access Toolbar, click **Save**.

(Project 1C Step Sales continues on the next page)

4 Select the range **A3:D7**, which includes the row titles, the column titles, and the data without the totals. Click the **Insert tab**, and then in the **Charts group**, click **Recommended Charts**. In the **Insert Chart** dialog box, scroll down and click the fifth recommended chart—a **Clustered Column** chart in which *each month* displays its *sales for each type of step training equipment*. Click **OK**.

a. In the chart, click anywhere in the text *Chart Title* to select the text box. Watch the **Formula Bar** as you type **First** and then let AutoComplete complete the title by pressing [Enter].

b. Click in a white area just slightly *inside* the chart border to deselect the chart title but keep the chart selected. To the right of the chart, click the second button—the **Chart Styles** button 🖌.

   Be sure the **Style** tab is selected. Use the scroll bar to scroll down, and then by using the ScreenTips, locate and click **Style 6**.

c. At the top of the gallery, click **COLOR**. Under **Colorful**, point to the fourth row of colors to display the ScreenTip *Color 4*, and then click to apply the **Color 4** variation of the theme colors.

d. Point to the top border of the chart to display the 🔭 pointer, and then drag the upper left corner of the chart just to the center of cell **A10** to visually center it below the data.

5 Select the range **B4:D7**. Click the **Insert tab**, and then in the **Sparklines group**, click **Line**. In the **Create Sparklines** dialog box, in the **Location Range** box, type **f4:f7** and then click **OK** to insert the sparklines.

a. On the **Design tab**, in the **Show group**, select the **Markers** check box to display markers in the sparklines.

b. On the **Design tab**, in the **Style group**, click **More** ⊟ and then in the second row, click the fourth style—**Sparkline Style Accent 4, Darker 25%**.

6 Click cell **A1** to deselect the chart. Click the **Page Layout tab**, and then in the **Page Setup group**, click **Margins**. Click **Custom Margins**. In the **Page Setup** dialog box, on the **Margins tab**, under **Center on page**, select the **Horizontally** check box.

a. Click the **Header/Footer tab**, and then click **Custom Footer**. With your insertion point in the **Left section**, click **Insert File Name**. Click **OK** two times.

b. Click the **File tab** to display **Backstage** view. In the lower right corner, click **Show All Properties**. As the **Tags**, type **step sales, 1st quarter** In the **Subject** box, type your course name and section number. Be sure your name displays as the author—edit if necessary.

c. On the left, click **Save**.

d. By using the techniques you practiced in Project 1A and as directed by your instructor, print, create a PDF image that looks like a printed document, or submit your completed Excel file. If required by your instructor, print or create an electronic version of your worksheet with formulas displayed. In the upper right corner of your Excel window, click Close.

END | You have completed Project 1C

Apply 1B skills from these Objectives:

7 Check Spelling in a Worksheet

8 Enter Data by Range

9 Construct Formulas for Mathematical Operations

10 Edit Values in a Worksheet

11 Format a Worksheet

In the following Skills Review, you will create a worksheet that summarizes the inventory of band and tubing exercise equipment. Your completed worksheet will look similar to Figure 1.57.

PROJECT FILES

For Project 1D, you will need the following file:

New blank Excel workbook

You will save your workbook as:

Lastname_Firstname_1D_Band_Inventory

Build From Scratch

PROJECT RESULTS

Pro Fit Marietta
Band and Tubing Inventory

	Material	Quantity in Stock	Retail Price	Total Retail Value	Percent of Total Retail Value
As of June 30					
Super Strength Bands	Latex	225	$ 48.98	$ 11,020.50	25.16%
Medium Tubing	Rubber	198	27.95	5,534.10	12.64%
Resistance Band, Average	Latex	165	42.95	7,086.75	16.18%
Mini Bands, Medium	Latex	245	25.95	6,357.75	14.52%
Mini Bands, Heavy	Rubber	175	32.95	5,766.25	13.17%
Heavy Tubing	Latex	187	42.95	8,031.65	18.34%
Total Retail Value for All Products				$ 43,797.00	

Lastname_Firstname_1D_Band_Inventory

Excel 2016, Windows 10, Microsoft Corporation

FIGURE 1.57

(Project 1D Band and Tubing Inventory continues on the next page)

1 ▶ Start Excel and display a new blank workbook. **Save** the workbook in your **Excel Chapter 1** folder as **Lastname_Firstname_1D_Band_Inventory** In cell **A1** type **Pro Fit Marietta** and in cell **A2** type **Band and Tubing Inventory**

a. Click cell **B3**, type **Quantity in Stock** and press Tab. In cell **C3** type **Average Cost** and press Tab. In cell **D3**, type **Retail Price** and press Tab. In cell **E3**, type **Total Retail Value** and press Tab. In cell **F3** type **Percent of Total Retail Value** and press Enter.

b. Click cell **A4**, type **Super Strength Bands** and press Enter. In the range **A5:A10**, type the remaining row titles as shown below, including any misspelled words.

   Medium Tubing

   Resistnce Band, Average

   Mini Bands, Medium

   Mini Bands, Heavy

   Heavy Tubing

   Total Retail Value for All Products

c. Press Ctrl + Home to move to the top of your worksheet. On the **Review tab**, in the **Proofing group**, click **Spelling**. Correct *Resistnce* to **Resistance** and any other spelling errors you may have made, and then when the message displays, *Spell check complete. You're good to go!* click **OK**.

d. In the **column heading area**, point to the right boundary of **column A** to display the ⊞ pointer, and then drag to the right to widen **column A** to **225** pixels.

e. In the **column heading area**, point to the **column B** heading to display the ⬇ pointer, and then drag to the right to select **columns B:F**. With the columns selected, in the **column heading area**, point to the right boundary of any of the selected columns, and then drag to the right to set the width to **100 pixels**.

f. Select the range **A1:F1**. On the **Home tab**, in the **Alignment group**, click **Merge & Center**, and then in the **Cell Styles** gallery, apply the **Title** style. Select the range **A2:F2**. **Merge & Center** the text across the selection, and then in the **Cell Styles** gallery, apply the **Heading 1** style.

2 ▶ On the **Page Layout tab**, in the **Themes group**, change the **Colors** to **Blue Green**. Select the empty range

B4:D9. With cell **B4** active in the range, type **225** and then press Enter.

a. With cell **B5** active in the range, and pressing Enter after each entry, type the following data in the *Quantity in Stock* column:

   198
   265
   245
   175
   187

b. With the selected range still active, from the following table, beginning in cell **C4** and pressing Enter after each entry, enter the following data for the **Average Cost** column and then the **Retail Price** column. If you prefer, type without selecting the range first; recall that this is optional.

Average Cost	Retail Price
22.75	48.98
15.95	27.95
26.90	42.95
12.95	25.95
18.75	32.95
26.90	42.95

3 ▶ In cell **E4**, type **=b4*d4** and then press Enter to construct a formula that calculates the *Total Retail Value* of the *Super Strength Bands* (Quantity in Stock X Retail Price).

a. Click cell **E4**, position your pointer over the fill handle, and then drag down through cell **E9** to copy the formula with relative cell references.

b. Select the range **B4:B9**, and then on the **Home tab**, in the **Number group**, click **Comma Style**. Then, in the **Number group**, click **Decrease Decimal** two times to remove the decimal places from these non-currency values.

c. To calculate the *Total Retail Value for All Products*, select the range **E4:E9**, and then in the lower right corner of the selected range, click the **Quick Analysis** button 📧.

(Project 1D Band and Tubing Inventory continues on the next page)

d. In the gallery, click **Totals**, and then click the *first* **Sum** button, which visually indicates that the column will be summed with a result at the bottom of the column.

e. Select the range **C5:E9** and apply the **Comma Style**. Select the range **C4:E4**, hold down Ctrl, and then click cell **E10**. With the nonadjacent cells selected, apply the **Accounting Number Format**. Click cell **E10**, and then from the **Cell Styles** gallery, apply the **Total** style.

f. Click cell **F4**, type = and then click cell **E4**. Type / and then click cell **E10**. Press F4 to make the reference to cell *E10* absolute, and then on the **Formula Bar**, click **Enter** so that cell **F4** remains the active cell. Drag the fill handle to copy the formula down through cell **F9**.

g. Point to cell **B6**, and then double-click to place the insertion point within the cell. Use the arrow keys to move the insertion point to the left or right of *2*, and use either Delete or Backspace to delete *2*, and then type **1** and press Enter so that the new *Quantity in Stock* is *165*. Notice the recalculations in the worksheet.

4 Select the range **F4:F9**, right-click over the selection, and then on the mini toolbar, click **Percent Style**. Click **Increase Decimal** two times, and then **Center** the selection.

a. In the **row heading area** on the left side of your screen, point to **row 3** to display the ➡ pointer, and then right-click to simultaneously select the row and display a shortcut menu. On the shortcut menu, click **Insert** to insert a new **row 3**.

b. Click cell **A3**, type **As of June 30** and then on the **Formula Bar**, click **Enter** to keep cell **A3** as the active cell. **Merge & Center** the text across the range **A3:F3**, and then apply the **Heading 2** cell style.

5 In the **column heading area**, point to **column B**. When the ⬇ pointer displays, right-click, and then click **Insert** to insert a new column.

a. Click cell **B4**, type **Material** and then press Enter. In cell **B5**, type **Latex** and then press Enter. In cell **B6**, type **Rubber** and then press Enter.

b. Using AutoComplete to speed your typing by pressing Enter as soon as the AutoComplete suggestion displays, in cells **B7**, **B8**, and **B10** type **Latex** and in cell **B9** type **Rubber**

c. In the **column heading area**, point to the right boundary of **column B**, and then drag to the left and set the width to **90 pixels**. In the **column heading area**, point to **column D**, right-click, and then click **Delete**.

d. Select the column titles in the range **B4:F4**, and then on the **Home tab**, in the **Alignment group**, click **Wrap Text**, **Center**, and **Middle Align**. With the range still selected, apply the **Heading 4** cell style.

e. Click cell **A11**, and then in the **Cell Styles** gallery, under **Themed Cell Styles**, click **40% - Accent1**.

6 Click the **Page Layout tab**, and then in the **Page Setup group**, click **Margins**. Click **Custom Margins**. In the **Page Setup** dialog box, on the **Margins tab**, under **Center on page**, select the **Horizontally** check box.

a. Click the **Header/Footer tab**, and then click **Custom Footer**. With your insertion point in the **Left section**, click **Insert File Name**. Click **OK** two times.

b. In the **Page Setup group**, click **Orientation**, and then click **Landscape**.

c. Click the **File tab** to display **Backstage** view. In the lower right corner, click **Show All Properties**. As the **Tags**, type **bands, tubing, inventory** In the **Subject** box, type your course name and section number. Be sure your name displays as the author—edit if necessary.

d. On the left, click **Save**.

e. By using the techniques you practiced in Project 1A and as directed by your instructor, print, create a PDF image that looks like a printed document, or submit your completed Excel file. If required by your instructor, print or create an electronic version of your worksheet with formulas displayed. In the upper right corner of your Excel window, click Close.

End | You have completed Project 1D

Mastering Excel Project 1E Gym Sales

In the following Mastering Excel project, you will create a worksheet comparing the sales of different types of home gym equipment sold in the second quarter. Your completed worksheet will look similar to Figure 1.58.

PROJECT FILES

For Project 1E, you will need the following file:

e01_1E_Gym_Sales

You will save your workbook as:

Lastname_Firstname_1E_Gym_Sales

PROJECT RESULTS

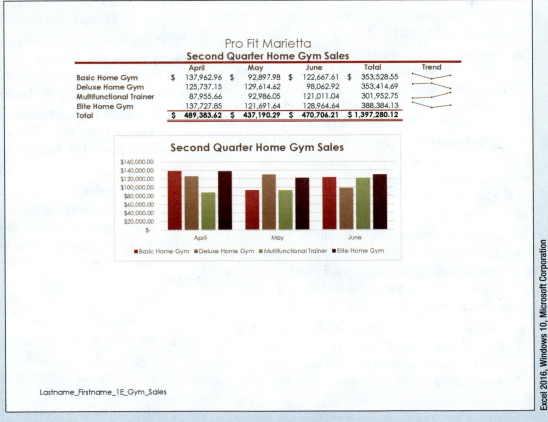

FIGURE 1.58

(Project 1E Gym Sales continues on the next page)

Mastering Excel Project 1E Gym Sales (continued)

1 Start Excel, and then on the opening screen, in the lower left, click **Open Other Workbooks**. Click **Browse**, and then navigate to your student data files for this chapter. Open the file **e01_1E_Gym_Sales**. Click the **File tab**, on the left click **Save As**, and then click **Browse**. In the **Save As** dialog box, navigate to your **Excel Chapter 1** folder, and then using your own name, save the file as **Lastname_Firstname_1E_Gym_Sales**

2 Change the theme to **Wisp**.

3 In cell **B3**, use the fill handle to fill the months *May* and *June* in the range **C3:D3**.

4 **Merge & Center** the title across the range **A1:F1**, and then apply the **Title** cell style. **Merge & Center** the subtitle across the range **A2:F2**, and then apply the **Heading 1** cell style. **Center** the column titles in the range **B3:F3**.

5 Widen **column A** to **180 pixels**, and then widen columns **B:F** to **115 pixels**. In the range **B7:D7**, enter the monthly sales figures for the Elite Home Gym as shown in the table below:

	April	May	June
Elite Home Gym	137727.85	121691.64	128964.64

6 In cell **B8**, on the **Home tab**, use the **AutoSum** command to sum the April sales. Copy the resulting formula across to cells **C8:D8** to sum the May monthly sales and the June monthly sales. In cell **E4**, use the **AutoSum** button to sum the *Basic Home Gym* sales. Copy the formula down to cells **E4:E8**.

7 Apply the **Heading 4** cell style to the row titles and the column titles. Apply the **Total** cell style to the totals in the range **B8:E8**.

8 Apply the **Accounting Number Format** to the first row of sales figures and to the total row. Apply the **Comma Style** to the remaining sales figures.

9 To compare the monthly sales of each product visually, select the range that represents the sales figures for the three months, including the month names and the product names—do not include any totals in the range. With this data selected, use the **Recommended Charts** command to insert a **Clustered Column** chart with the month names displayed on the category axis and the product names displayed in the legend.

10 Move the chart so that its upper left corner is positioned in the center of cell **A10**. Then drag the center right sizing handle to the right until the right edge of the chart aligns with the right edge of **column E**; this will display the legend on one row and, after you add the sparklines, center the chart below the data.

11 Apply **Chart Style 6** and **Color 2** under **Colorful**. Change the **Chart Title** to **Second Quarter Home Gym Sales**

12 In the range **F4:F7**, insert **Line** sparklines that compare the monthly data. Do not include the totals. Show the sparkline **Markers** and apply **Sparkline Style Accent 2, Darker 50%** in the first row, the second style.

13 Center the worksheet **Horizontally** on the page, and then insert a **Footer** with the **File Name** in the **left section**.

14 Change the **Orientation** to **Landscape**. Display the document properties, and then as the **Tags** type **home gym, sales** As the **Subject**, type your course name and section number. Be sure your name displays as the **Author**. Check your worksheet by previewing it in **Print Preview**, and then make any necessary corrections.

15 **Save** your workbook. By using the techniques you practiced in Project 1A and as directed by your instructor, print, create a PDF image that looks like a printed document, or submit your completed Excel file. If required by your instructor, print or create an electronic version of your worksheet with formulas displayed. In the upper right corner of your Excel window, click **Close**.

END | You have completed Project 1E

Mastering Excel   Project 1F Balance Sales

In the following Mastering Excel project, you will create a worksheet that summarizes the sales of balance and stabilization equipment that Pro Fit Marietta is marketing. Your completed worksheet will look similar to Figure 1.59.

PROJECT FILES

For Project 1F, you will need the following file:

e01_1F_Balance_Sales

You will save your workbook as:

Lastname_Firstname_1F_Balance_Sales

PROJECT RESULTS

Pro Fit Marietta
Balance and Stabilization Sales
Month Ending March 31

	Quantity Sold	Retail Price	Total Sales	Percent of Total Sales
Balance Pillow	275	$ 22.95	$ 6,311.25	5.43%
Slide Board	382	75.50	28,841.00	24.82%
Foam Roller	251	39.50	9,914.50	8.53%
Rebounder	162	139.95	22,671.90	19.51%
Stability Ball	380	51.50	19,570.00	16.84%
Balance Board	206	84.95	17,499.70	15.06%
Balance Pad	150	75.99	11,398.50	9.81%
Total Sales for All Products			$ 116,206.85	

Lastname_Firstname_1F_Balance_Sales

Excel 2016, Windows 10, Microsoft Corporation

FIGURE 1.59

(Project 1F Balance Sales continues on the next page)

Mastering Excel   Project 1F Balance Sales (continued)

1 Start Excel, and then on the opening screen, in the lower left, click **Open Other Workbooks**. Click **Browse**, and then navigate to your student data files for this chapter. Open the file **e01_1F_Balance_Sales**. Click the **File tab**, on the left click **Save As**, and then click **Browse**. In the **Save As** dialog box, navigate to your **Excel Chapter 1** folder, and then using your own name, save the file as **Lastname_Firstname_1F_Balance_Sales**

2 **Merge & Center** the title and the subtitle across **columns A:F**. Apply the **Title** and **Heading 1** cell styles respectively.

3 Make cell **A1** the active cell, and then check spelling in your worksheet. Correct *Silde* to **Slide**. Widen **column A** to **180 pixels** and **columns B:F** to **95 pixels**.

4 In cell **E4**, construct a formula to calculate the *Total Sales* of the *Balance Pillow* by multiplying the *Quantity Sold* times the *Retail Price*. Copy the formula down for the remaining products.

5 Select the range **E4:E10**, and then use the **Quick Analysis** tool to **Sum** the *Total Sales for All Products*, which will be formatted in Bold. To the total in cell **E11**, apply the **Total** cell style.

6 Using absolute cell references as necessary so that you can copy the formula, in cell **F4**, construct a formula to calculate the *Percent of Total Sales* for the first product. Copy the formula down for the remaining products.

7 To the computed percentages, apply **Percent Style** with two decimal places, and then **Center** the percentages.

8 Apply the **Comma Style** with no decimal places to the *Quantity Sold* figures. To cells **D4**, **E4**, and **E11** apply the **Accounting Number Format**.

9 To the range **D5:E10**, apply the **Comma Style**.

10 Change the *Retail Price* of the *Slide Board* to **75.50** and the *Quantity Sold* of the *Balance Pad* to **150**

11 Delete **column B**.

12 Insert a new **row 3**. In cell **A3**, type **Month Ending March 31** and then **Merge & Center** the text across the range **A3:E3**. Apply the **Heading 2** cell style.

13 To cell **A12**, apply the **20%-Accent1** cell style.

14 Select the four column titles, apply **Wrap Text**, **Middle Align**, and **Center** formatting, and then apply the **Heading 3** cell style.

15 Center the worksheet **Horizontally** on the page, and then insert a **Footer** with the **File Name** in the **left section**.

16 Display the document properties, and then as the **Tags**, type **balance, stability, sales** In the **Subject** box, add your course name and section number. Be sure your name displays as the Author.

17 **Save** your workbook. By using the techniques you practiced in Project 1A and as directed by your instructor, print, create a PDF image that looks like a printed document, or submit your completed Excel file. If required by your instructor, print or create an electronic version of your worksheet with formulas displayed. In the upper right corner of your Excel Window, click **Close**.

END | You have completed Project 1F

Mastering Excel Project 1G Regional Sales

In the following Mastering Excel project, you will create a new worksheet that compares annual sales by region. Your completed worksheet will look similar to Figure 1.60.

PROJECT FILES

For Project 1G, you will need the following file:

e01_1G_Regional_Sales

You will save your workbook as

Lastname_Firstname_1G_Regional_Sales

PROJECT RESULTS

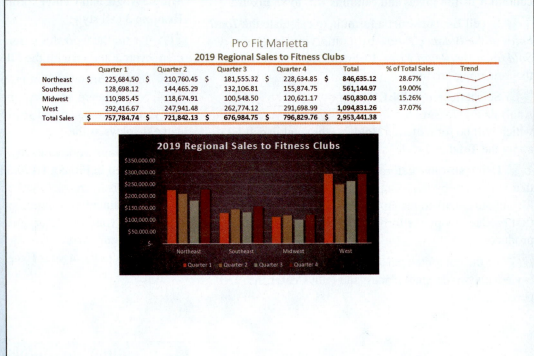

FIGURE 1.60

(Project 1G Regional Sales continues on the next page)

Mastering Excel   Project 1G Regional Sales Project 1G (continued)

1 Start Excel, and then on the opening screen, in the lower left, click **Open Other Workbooks**. Click **Browse**, and then navigate to your student data files for this chapter. Open the file **e01_1G_Regional_Sales**. Click the **File tab**, on the left click **Save As**, and then click **Browse**. In the **Save As** dialog box, navigate to your **Excel Chapter 1** folder, and then using your own name, save the file as **Lastname_Firstname_1G_Regional_Sales**

2 Change the **Theme** to **Retrospect**. Set the width of **column A** to **80 pixels** and the width of columns **B:H** to **110 pixels**.

3 **Merge & Center** the title across the range **A1:H1**, and then apply the **Title** cell style. **Merge & Center** the subtitle across the range **A2:H2**, and then apply the **Heading 1** cell style.

4 Select the seven column titles, apply **Center** formatting, and then apply the **Heading 4** cell style.

5 By using the **Quick Analysis** tool, **Sum** the *Quarter 1* sales, and then copy the formula across for the remaining Quarters; the Quick Analysis tool formats totals in Bold.

6 Select the *Northeast* sales for the four quarters, and then display the **Quick Analysis** gallery for **Totals**. Click the second **Sum** option—the sixth item in the gallery—which displays the column selection in yellow. Copy the formula down through cell **F7**; recall that the Quick Analysis tool formats sums in Bold.

7 Apply the **Accounting Number Format** to the first row of sales figures and to the total row. Apply the **Comma Style** to the remaining sales figures. Format the totals in **row 7** with the **Total** cell style.

8 **Insert** a new **row 6** with the row title **Midwest** and the following sales figures for each quarter: **110985.45** and **118674.91** and **100548.50** and **120621.17** Copy the formula in cell **F5** down to cell **F6** to sum the new row.

9 Using absolute cell references as necessary so that you can copy the formula, in cell **G4** construct a formula to calculate the *Percent of Total Sales* for the first region. Copy the formula down for the remaining regions.

10 To the computed percentages, apply **Percent Style** with two decimal places, and then **Center** the percentages.

11 Insert **Line** sparklines in the range **H4:H7** that compare the quarterly data. Do not include the totals. Show the sparkline **Markers** and apply the second style in the second row—**Sparkline Style Accent 2, Darker 25%**.

12 **Save** your workbook. To compare the quarterly sales of each region visually, select the range that represents the sales figures for the four quarters, including the quarter names and each region—do not include any totals in the range. With this data selected, by using the **Recommended Charts** command, insert a **Clustered Column** with the regions as the category axis and the Quarters as the legend.

13 Apply **Chart Style 8** and **Color 3** under **Colorful**. Position the chart so that its upper right corner aligns with the upper right corner of cell **F10**.

14 Change the **Chart Title** to **2019 Regional Sales to Fitness Clubs**

15 Deselect the chart. Change the page **Orientation** to **Landscape**, center the worksheet **Horizontally** on the page, and then insert a footer with the file name in the left section.

16 Show the document properties. As the **Tags**, type **fitness clubs, sales** In the **Subject** box, type your course name and section number. Be sure your name displays as the Author.

17 **Save** your workbook. By using the techniques you practiced in Project 1A and as directed by your instructor, print, create a PDF image that looks like a printed document, or submit your completed Excel file. If required by your instructor, print or create an electronic version of your worksheet with formulas displayed. In the upper right corner of your Excel Window, click **Close**.

END | You have completed Project 1G

Apply a combination of the **1A** and **1B** skills.

Build From Scratch

GO! Fix It	Project 1H Team Sales	MyITLab
GO! Make It	Project 1I Agility Sales	MyITLab
GO! Solve It	Project 1J Kettlebell Sales	MyITLab
GO! Solve It	Project 1K Commission	

PROJECT FILES

For Project 1K, you will need the following file:

e01K_Commission

You will save your workbook as:

Lastname_Firstname_1K_Commission

Open the file e01K_Commission and save it as **Lastname_Firstname_1K_Commission** Complete the worksheet by using Auto Fill to complete the month headings, and then calculating the Total Commission for each month and for each region. Insert and format appropriate sparklines in the Trend column. Format the worksheet attractively with a title and subtitle, check spelling, adjust column width, and apply appropriate financial formatting. Insert a chart that compares the total sales commission for each region with the months displaying as the categories, and format the chart attractively. Include the file name in the footer, add appropriate properties, and submit as directed.

Performance Level

Performance Criteria	Exemplary: You consistently applied the relevant skills	Proficient: You sometimes, but not always, applied the relevant skills	Developing: You rarely or never applied the relevant skills
Create formulas	All formulas are correct and are efficiently constructed.	Formulas are correct but not always constructed in the most efficient manner.	One or more formulas are missing or incorrect; or only numbers were entered.
Create a chart	Chart created properly.	Chart was created but incorrect data was selected.	No chart was created.
Insert and format sparklines	Sparklines inserted and formatted properly.	Sparklines were inserted but incorrect data was selected or sparklines were not formatted.	No sparklines were inserted.
Format attractively and appropriately	Formatting is attractive and appropriate.	Adequately formatted but difficult to read or unattractive.	Inadequate or no formatting.

END | You have completed Project 1K

OUTCOMES-BASED ASSESSMENTS (CRITICAL THINKING)

RUBRIC

The following outcomes-based assessments are *open-ended assessments*. That is, there is no specific correct result; your result will depend on your approach to the information provided. Make *Professional Quality* your goal. Use the following scoring rubric to guide you in *how* to approach the problem and then to evaluate *how well* your approach solves the problem.

The *criteria*—Software Mastery, Content, Format and Layout, and Process—represent the knowledge and skills you have gained that you can apply to solving the problem. The *levels of performance*—Professional Quality, Approaching Professional Quality, or Needs Quality Improvements—help you and your instructor evaluate your result.

	Your completed project is of Professional Quality if you:	Your completed project is Approaching Professional Quality if you:	Your completed project Needs Quality Improvements if you:
1-Software Mastery	Choose and apply the most appropriate skills, tools, and features and identify efficient methods to solve the problem.	Choose and apply some appropriate skills, tools, and features, but not in the most efficient manner.	Choose inappropriate skills, tools, or features, or are inefficient in solving the problem.
2-Content	Construct a solution that is clear and well organized, contains content that is accurate, appropriate to the audience and purpose, and is complete. Provide a solution that contains no errors of spelling, grammar, or style.	Construct a solution in which some components are unclear, poorly organized, inconsistent, or incomplete. Misjudge the needs of the audience. Have some errors in spelling, grammar, or style, but the errors do not detract from comprehension.	Construct a solution that is unclear, incomplete, or poorly organized, contains some inaccurate or inappropriate content, and contains many errors of spelling, grammar, or style. Do not solve the problem.
3-Format and Layout	Format and arrange all elements to communicate information and ideas, clarify function, illustrate relationships, and indicate relative importance.	Apply appropriate format and layout features to some elements, but not others. Overuse features, causing minor distraction.	Apply format and layout that does not communicate information or ideas clearly. Do not use format and layout features to clarify function, illustrate relationships, or indicate relative importance. Use available features excessively, causing distraction.
4-Process	Use an organized approach that integrates planning, development, self-assessment, revision, and reflection.	Demonstrate an organized approach in some areas, but not others; or, use an insufficient process of organization throughout.	Do not use an organized approach to solve the problem.

Apply a combination of the **1A** and **1B** skills.

GO! Think   Project 1L Video Sales

PROJECT FILES

For Project 1L, you will need the following file:

New blank Excel workbook

You will save your workbook as:

Lastname_Firstname_1L_Video_Sales

Michelle Barry, President of Pro Fit Marietta, needs a worksheet that summarizes the following data regarding the first quarter sales of training videos. Michelle would like the worksheet to include a calculation of the total sales for each type of video and a total of the sales of all of the videos. She would also like to know each type of video's percentage of total sales.

	Number Sold	Price
Pilates	156	29.99
Step	392	14.99
Weight Training	147	54.99
Kickboxing	282	29.99
Yoga	165	34.99

Create a worksheet that provides Michelle with the information needed. Include appropriate worksheet, column, and row titles. Using the formatting skills that you practiced in this chapter, format the worksheet in a manner that is professional and easy to read and understand. Insert a footer with the file name and add appropriate document properties. Save the file as **Lastname_Firstname_1L_Video_Sales** and print or submit as directed by your instructor.

END | You have completed Project 1L

GO! Think   Project 1M Expenses   **MyITLab**

You and GO!   Project 1N Personal Expenses   **MyITLab**

GO! Collaborative Team Project   Project 1O Bell Orchid Hotels   **MyITLab**

Introduction to Microsoft Access 2016

Bigpa/Fotolia

Introduction to Access 2016

Microsoft Access 2016 provides a convenient way to organize data that makes it easy for you to utilize and present information. Access uses tables to store the data; like Excel spreadsheets, data is stored in rows and columns in a table. So why use a database rather than an Excel spreadsheet? By using a database, you can manipulate and work with data in a more robust manner. For example, if you have thousands of records about patients in a hospital, you can easily find all of the records that pertain to the patients who received a specific type of medicine on a particular day. Information from one table can be used to retrieve information from another table. For example, by knowing a patient's ID number, you can

view immunization records or view insurance information or view hospitalization records. Having information stored in an Access database enables you to make bulk changes to data at one time even when it is stored in different tables.

It's easy to get started with Access by using one of the many prebuilt database templates. For example, a nonprofit organization can track events, donors, members, and donations for a nonprofit organization. A small business can use a prebuilt database to track inventory, create invoices, monitor projects, manage pricing, track competitors, and manage quotes.

Getting Started with Microsoft Access 2016

PROJECT 1A

OUTCOMES
Create a new database.

OBJECTIVES

1. Identify Good Database Design
2. Create a Table and Define Fields in a Blank Desktop Database
3. Change the Structure of Tables and Add a Second Table
4. Create a Query, Form, and Report
5. Close a Database and Close Access

PROJECT 1B

OUTCOMES
Create a database from a template.

OBJECTIVES

6. Use a Template to Create a Database
7. Organize Objects in the Navigation Pane
8. Create a New Table in a Database Created with a Template
9. Print a Report and a Table

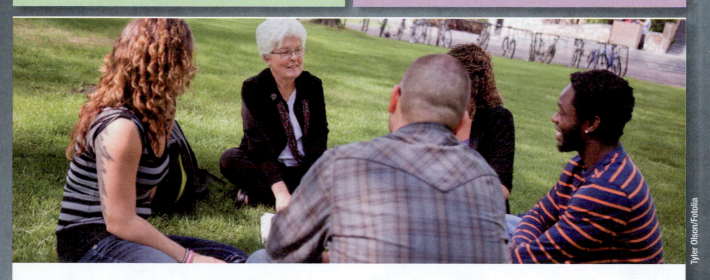

Tyler Olson/Fotolia

In This Chapter 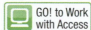 GO! to Work with Access

In this chapter, you will use Microsoft Access 2016 to organize a collection of related information. You will create new databases, create tables, and enter data into the tables. You will create a query, a form, and a report—all of which are Access objects that make a database useful for locating and analyzing information. You will also create a complete database from a template that you can use as provided, or that you can modify to meet your needs. In this chapter, you will also learn how to apply good database design principles to your Access database and to define the structure of a database.

The projects in this chapter relate to **Texas Lakes Community College**, which is located in the Austin, Texas, area. Its four campuses serve over 30,000 students and offer more than 140 certificate programs and degrees. The college has a highly acclaimed Distance Education program and an extensive Workforce Development program. The college makes positive contributions to the community through cultural and athletic programs and has significant partnerships with businesses and nonprofit organizations. Popular fields of study include nursing and health care, solar technology, computer technology, and graphic design.

PROJECT **1A**

Student Advising Database
with Two Tables

MyITLab
Project 1A Training
Project 1A Grader

PROJECT ACTIVITIES

In Activities 1.01 through 1.17, you will assist Dr. Daniel Martinez, Vice President of Student Services at Texas Lakes Community College, in creating a new database for tracking students and their faculty advisors. Your completed database objects will look similar to Figure 1.1.

 PROJECT FILES   **MyITLab** grader   If your instructor wants you to submit Project 1A in the MyITLab grader system, log in to MyITLab, locate grader Project1A, and then download the files for this project.

For Project 1A, you will need the following files:

Blank desktop database
a01A_Students (Excel workbook)
a01A_Faculty_Advisors (Excel workbook)

You will save your database as:

Lastname_Firstname_1A_Advising

 PROJECT RESULTS

Build From
Scratch

GO!
Walk Thru
Project 1A

Access 2016, Windows 10, Microsoft Corporation

FIGURE 1.1 Project 1A Advising

PROJECT RESULTS

In this project, using your own name, you will create the following database and objects. Your instructor may ask for printouts or PDF electronic images:

Lastname_Firstname_1A_Advising	Database file
Lastname Firstname 1A Students	Table
Lastname Firstname 1A Faculty Advisors	Table
Lastname Firstname 1A All Students Query	Query
Lastname Firstname 1A Student Form	Form
Lastname Firstname 1A Faculty Advisors Report	Report

Objective 1 Identify Good Database Design

GO! Learn How
Video A1-1

A *database* is an organized collection of *data*—facts about people, events, things, or ideas—related to a specific topic or purpose. *Information* is data that is accurate, timely, and organized in a useful manner. Your contact list is a type of database, because it is a collection of data about one topic—the people with whom you communicate. A simple database of this type is called a *flat database* because it is not related or linked to any other collection of data. Another example of a simple database is your music collection. You do not keep information about your music collection in your contact list because the data is not related to the people in your contact list.

A more sophisticated type of database is a *relational database*, because multiple collections of data in the database are related to one another—for example, data about the students, the courses, and the faculty members at a college. Microsoft Access 2016 is a relational *database management system*—also referred to as a *DBMS*—which is software that controls how related collections of data are stored, organized, retrieved, and secured.

Activity 1.01 │ Using Good Design Techniques to Plan a Database

ALERT! **To submit as an autograded project, log into MyITLab and download the files for this project, and begin with those files instead of a new, blank database. For Project 1A using Grader, read Activities 1.01 and 1.02 carefully. Begin working with the database in Activity 1.03. For Grader to award points accurately, when saving an object, do not include your Lastname Firstname at the beginning of the object name.**

Before creating a new database, the first step is to determine the information you want to keep track of by asking yourself, *What questions should this database be able to answer?* The purpose of a database is to store the data in a manner that makes it easy to find the information you need by asking questions. For example, in a student database for Texas Lakes Community College, the questions to be answered might include:

- How many students are enrolled at the college?
- How many students have not yet been assigned a faculty advisor?
- Which students live in Austin, Texas?
- Which students owe money for tuition?
- Which students are majoring in Information Systems Technology?

Tables are the foundation of an Access database because all of the data is stored in one or more tables. A table is similar in structure to an Excel worksheet because data is organized into rows and columns. Each table row is a *record*—all of the categories of data pertaining to one person, place, event, thing, or idea. Each table column is a *field*—a single piece of information for every record. For example, in a table storing student contact information, each row forms a record for only one student. Each column forms a field for every record—for example, the student ID number or the student last name.

When organizing the fields of information in your table, break each piece of information into its smallest, most useful part. For example, create three fields for the name of a student—one field for the last name, one field for the first name, and one field for the middle name or initial.

The *first principle of good database design* is to organize data in the tables so that *redundant*—duplicate—data does not occur. For example, record the student contact information in only *one* table, so that if a student's address changes, you can change the information in just one place. This conserves space, reduces the likelihood of errors when inputting new data, and does not require remembering all of the places where a student's address is stored.

The *second principle of good database design* is to use techniques that ensure the accuracy and consistency of data as it is entered into the table. Proofreading data is critical to maintaining accuracy in a database. Typically, many different people enter data into a database—think of all the people who enter data about students at your college. When entering a state in a student contacts table, one person might enter the state as *Texas*, while another might enter the state as *TX*. Use design techniques to help those who enter data into a database to enter the data more accurately and consistently.

Normalization is the process of applying design rules and principles to ensure that your database performs as expected. Taking the time to plan and create a database that is well designed will ensure that you can retrieve meaningful information from the database.

The tables of information in a relational database are linked or joined to one another by a *common field*—a field in two or more tables that stores the same data. For example, a Students table includes the Student ID, name, and full address of every student. The Student Activities table includes the club name and the Student ID of members, but not the name or address, of each student in the club. Because the two tables share a common field—Student ID—you can use the data together to create a list of names and addresses of all of the students in a particular club. The names and addresses are stored in the Students table, and the Student IDs of the club members are stored in the Student Activities table.

GO! Learn How
Video A1-2

Three methods are used to create a new Access database. One method is to create a new database using a **database template**—a preformatted database designed for a specific purpose. A second method is to create a new database from a **blank desktop database**. A blank desktop database is stored on your computer or other storage device. Initially, it has no data and has no database tools; you create the data and the tools as you need them. A third method is to create a **custom web app** database from scratch or by using a template that you can publish and share with others over the Internet.

Regardless of the method you use, you must name and save the database before you can create any **objects** in it. Objects are the basic parts of a database; you create objects to store your data, to work with your data, and to display your data. The most common database objects are tables, queries, forms, and reports. Think of an Access database as a container for the objects that you create.

1.1.1

Activity 1.02 | Starting with a Blank Desktop Database

1 Start Microsoft Access 2016. Take a moment to compare your screen with Figure 1.2 and study the parts of the Microsoft Access opening screen described in the table in Figure 1.3.

From this Access opening screen, you can open an existing database, create a custom web app, create a blank desktop database, or create a new database from a template.

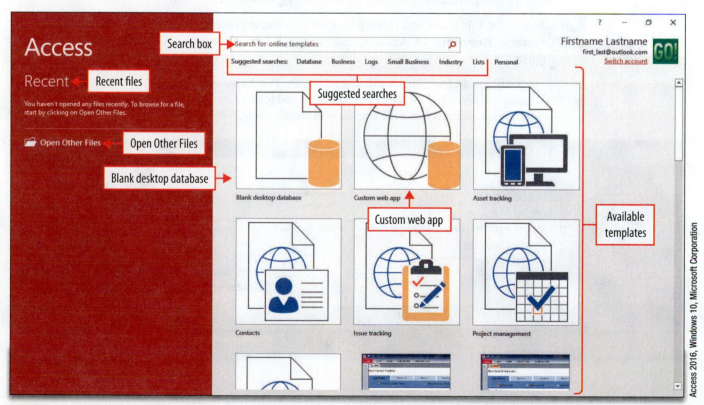

FIGURE 1.2

MICROSOFT ACCESS OPENING SCREEN ELEMENTS	
SCREEN ELEMENT	**DESCRIPTION**
Available templates	Starts a database for a specific purpose that includes built-in objects and tools ready for use.
Blank desktop database	Starts a blank database that is stored on your computer or on a portable storage device.
Custom web app	Starts a web app database that can be published and shared on the Internet.
Open Other Files	Enables you to open a database file from your computer, a shared location, or other location that you have designated.
Recent files	Displays a list of database files that have been recently opened.
Search box	Enables you to search the Microsoft Office website for templates.
Suggested searches	Enables you to click a category to start an online search for a template.

FIGURE 1.3

2 In the Access opening screen, click **Blank desktop database**. In the **Blank desktop database** dialog box, to the right of the **File Name** box, click **Browse** ▭. In the **File New Database** dialog box, navigate to the location where you are saving your databases for this chapter, create a **New folder** named **Access Chapter 1** and then press ⏎.

3 In the **File name** box, notice that *Database1* displays as the default file name—the number at the end of your file name might differ if you have saved a database previously with the default name. In the **Save as type** box, notice that the default database type is *Microsoft Access 2007 – 2016 Databases*, which means that you can open a database created in Access 2016 by using Access 2007, Access 2010, or Access 2013.

4 Click in the **File name** box. Using your own name, replace the existing text with **Lastname_Firstname_1A_Advising** and then click **OK** or press ⏎. Compare your screen with Figure 1.4.

In the Blank desktop database dialog box, in the File Name box, the name of your database displays. Under the File Name box, the drive and folder where the database will be stored displays. An Access database has a file extension of *.accdb*.

FIGURE 1.4

5 In the **Blank desktop database** dialog box, click **Create**. Compare your screen with Figure 1.5, and then take a moment to study the screen elements described in the table in Figure 1.6.

Access creates the new database and opens *Table1*. Recall that a table is an Access object that stores data in columns and rows, similar to the format of an Excel worksheet. Table objects are the foundation of a database because tables store data that is used by other database objects.

FIGURE 1.5

MICROSOFT ACCESS DATABASE WINDOW ELEMENTS	
ACCESS WINDOW ELEMENT	**DESCRIPTION**
Navigation Pane	Displays the database objects that can be opened in the object window.
Object tab	Identifies the open object.
Object window	Displays the active or open object(s), including tables, queries, or other objects.
Close button for object	Closes the active object.
Ribbon	Displays commands grouped by related tasks and stored on different tabs.
Status bar	Indicates the active view and the status of action occurring within the database on the left; provides buttons on the right to switch between Datasheet view and Design view.
Table Tools	Provides tools on two tabs for working with the active table object, these are contextual tabs—only available when a table object is active.
Close button for application (Access)	Closes the active database and Access.

FIGURE 1.6

2.1.1, 2.4.1

Activity 1.03 | Assigning the Data Type and Name to Fields

After you have named and saved your database, the next step is to consult your database design plan and then create the tables for your data. Limit the data in each table to *one* subject. For example, in this project, your database will have two tables—one for student information and one for faculty advisor information.

Recall that each column in a table is a field; field names display at the top of each column of the table. Recall also that each row in a table is a record—all of the data pertaining to one person, place, thing, event, or idea. Each record is broken up into its smallest usable parts—the fields. Use meaningful names for fields; for example, *Last Name*.

1 Notice the new blank table that displays in Datasheet view, and then take a moment to study the elements of the table's object window. Compare your screen with Figure 1.7.

The table displays in ***Datasheet view***, which displays the data in columns and rows similar to the format of an Excel worksheet. Another way to view a table is in ***Design view***, which displays the underlying design—the ***structure***—of the table's fields. The ***object window*** displays the open object—in this instance, the table object.

In a new blank database, there is only one object—a new blank table. Because you have not yet named this table, the object tab displays a default name of *Table1*. Access creates the first field and names it *ID*. In the ID field, Access assigns a unique sequential number—each number incremented by one—to each record as it is entered into the table.

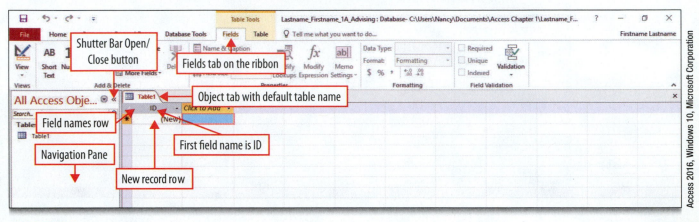

FIGURE 1.7

2 In the **Navigation Pane**, click **Shutter Bar Open/Close** « to collapse the **Navigation Pane** to a narrow bar on the left.

The ***Navigation Pane*** displays and organizes the names of the objects in a database. From the Navigation Pane, you can open objects. Collapse or close the Navigation Pane to display more of the object—in this case, the table.

ANOTHER WAY   Press F11 to close or open the Navigation Pane.

3 In the field names row, click anywhere in the text *Click to Add* to display a list of data types. Compare your screen with Figure 1.8.

A ***data type*** classifies the kind of data that you can store in a field, such as numbers, text, or dates. A field in a table can have only one data type. The data type of each field should be included in your database design. After selecting the data type, you can name the field.

ANOTHER WAY   To the right of *Click to Add*, click the arrow.

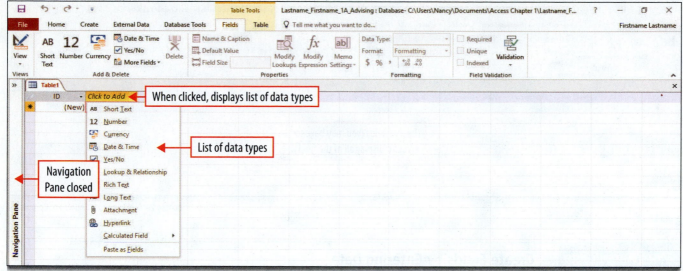

FIGURE 1.8

Access 2016, Windows 10, Microsoft Corporation

4 In the list of data types, click **Short Text**, and notice that in the second column, *Click to Add* changes to *Field1*, which is selected. Type **Last Name** and then press ⏎.

The second column displays *Last Name* as the field name, and, in the third column, the data types list displays. The **Short Text data type** describes text, a combination of text and numbers, or numbers that do not represent a quantity or are not used in calculations, such as the Postal Code. This data type enables you to enter up to 255 characters in the field.

ANOTHER WAY   With the list of data types displayed, type the character that is underscored to select the data type. For example, type *t* to select Short Text or type *u* to select Currency.

5 In the third field name box, type **t** to select *Short Text*, type **First Name** and then press ⏎.

6 In the fourth field name box, click **Short Text**, type **Middle Initial** and then press ⏎.

7 Create the remaining fields from the table below by first selecting the data type, typing the field name, and then pressing ⏎. The field names in the table will display on one line—do not be concerned if the field names do not completely display in the column; you will adjust the column widths later.

Data Type		Short Text	Short Text	Short Text	Short Text	Short Text	Short Text	Short Text	Short Text	Short Text	Short Text	Currency
Field Name	ID	Last Name	First Name	Middle Initial	Address	City	State	Postal Code	Phone	Email	Faculty Advisor ID	Amount Owed

The Postal Code and Phone fields are assigned a data type of Short Text because the numbers are never used in calculations. The Amount Owed field is assigned the **Currency data type**, which describes monetary values and numeric data that can be used in calculations and that have one to four decimal places. A U.S. dollar sign ($) and two decimal places are automatically included for all of the numbers in a field with the Currency data type.

8 If necessary, scroll to bring the first column—ID—into view, and then compare your screen with Figure 1.9.

Access automatically created the ID field, and you created 11 additional fields in the table.

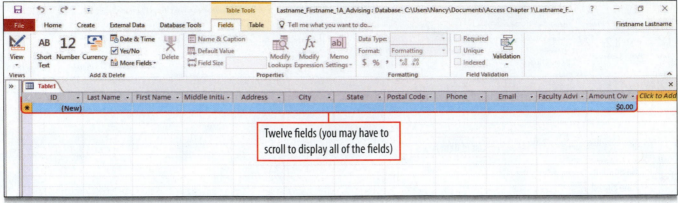

FIGURE 1.9

Access 2016, Windows 10, Microsoft Corporation

More Knowledge   **Create Fields by Entering Data**

You can create a new field in Datasheet view by typing the data in a new column. Access automatically assigns a data type based on the data you enter. For example, if you enter a date, Access assigns the Date & Time data type. If you enter a monetary amount, Access assigns the Currency data type. If Access cannot determine the data type based on the data entered, the Short Text data type is assigned. You can always change the data type if an incorrect data type is assigned. If you use this method to create fields, you must check the assigned data types to be sure they are correct. You must also rename the fields because Access assigns the names as *Field1*, *Field2*, and so on.

2.4.3, 2.4.6

Activity 1.04 | **Renaming Fields and Changing Data Types in a Table**

1 ▶ In the first column, click anywhere in the text *ID*. On the ribbon, under **Table Tools**, on the **Fields tab**, in the **Properties group**, click **Name & Caption**. In the **Enter Field Properties** dialog box, in the **Name** box, change *ID* to **Student ID**

The field name *Student ID* is a more precise description of the data contained in this field. In the Enter Field Properties dialog box, you have the option to use the **Caption** property to display a name for a field different from the one that displays in the Name box. Many database designers do not use spaces in field names; instead, they might name a field *LastName* or *LName* and then create a caption for the field so it displays as *Last Name* in tables, forms, or reports. In the Enter Field Properties dialog box, you can also provide a description for the field.

↻ ANOTHER WAY   Right-click the field name to display the shortcut menu, and then click Rename Field; or, double-click the field name to select the existing text, and then type the new field name.

2 ▶ Click **OK** to close the **Enter Field Properties** dialog box. On the ribbon, in the **Formatting group**, notice that the **Data Type** for the **Student ID** field is *AutoNumber*. Click the **Data Type arrow**, click **Short Text**, and then compare your screen with Figure 1.10.

In the new record row, the Student ID field is selected. By default, Access creates an ID field for all new tables and sets the data type for the field to AutoNumber. The **AutoNumber data type** describes a unique sequential or random number assigned by Access as each record is entered. Changing the data type of this field to Short Text enables you to enter a custom student ID number.

When records in a database have *no* unique value, such as a book ISBN or a license plate number, the AutoNumber data type is a useful way to automatically create a unique number. In this manner, you are sure that every record is different from the others.

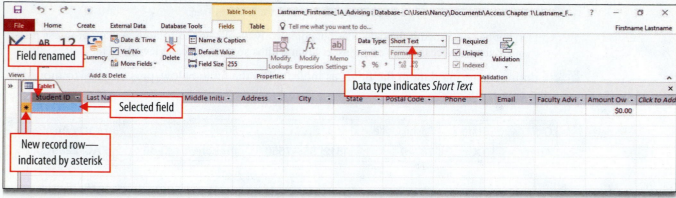

FIGURE 1.10

Access 2016, Windows 10, Microsoft Corporation

2.3.2, 2.2.4

Activity 1.05 | Adding a Record to a Table

A new contact list is not useful until you fill it with names and phone numbers. Likewise, a new database is not useful until you **populate** it by filling one or more tables with data. You can populate a table with records by typing data directly into the table.

1 ▶ In the new record row, click in the **Student ID** field to display the insertion point, type **1023045** and then press Enter. Compare your screen with Figure 1.11.

The pencil icon 🖉 in the **record selector box** indicates that a record is being entered or edited. The record selector box is the small box at the left of a record in Datasheet view. When clicked, the entire record is selected.

🔄 **ANOTHER WAY**   Press Tab to move the insertion point to the next field.

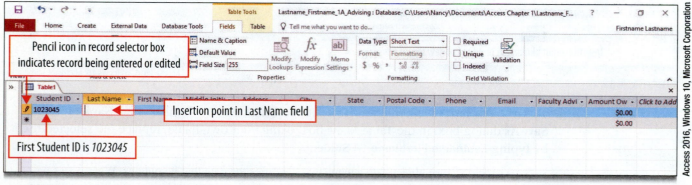

FIGURE 1.11

Access 2016, Windows 10, Microsoft Corporation

2 ▶ With the insertion point positioned in the **Last Name** field, type **Fresch** and then press Enter.

> ### NOTE   Correcting Typing Errors
>
> Correct any typing errors you make by using the techniques you have practiced in other Office applications. For example, use Backspace to remove characters to the left of the insertion point. Use Del to remove characters to the right of the insertion point. Or select the text you want to replace and type the correct information. Press Esc to exit out of a record that has not been completely entered.

3 ▶ In the **First Name** field, type **Jenna** and then press Enter.

4 ▶ In the **Middle Initial** field, type **A** and then press Enter.

5 ▸ In the **Address** field, type **7550 Douglas Ln** and then press Enter.

> Do not be concerned if the data does not completely display in the column. As you progress in your study of Access, you will adjust column widths so that you can view all of the data.

6 ▸ Continue entering data in the fields as indicated in the table below, pressing Enter to move to the next field.

City	State	Postal Code	Phone	Email	Faculty Advisor ID
Austin	**TX**	**78749**	**(512) 555-7550**	**jfresch@tlcc.edu**	**FAC-2289**

> **NOTE**   Format for Typing Telephone Numbers in Access
>
> Access does not require a specific format for typing telephone numbers in a record. The examples in this textbook use the format of Microsoft Outlook. Using such a format facilitates easy transfer of Outlook information to and from Access.

7 ▸ In the **Amount Owed** field, type **250** and then press Enter. Compare your screen with Figure 1.12.

> Pressing Enter or Tab in the last field moves the insertion point to the next row to begin a new record. Access automatically saves the record as soon as you move to the next row; you do not have to take any specific action to save a record.

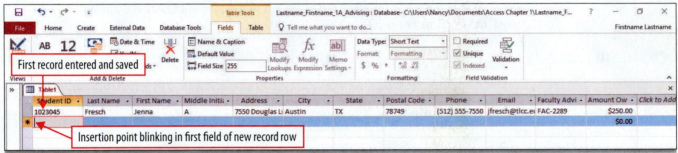

FIGURE 1.12

Access 2016, Windows 10, Microsoft Corporation

8 ▸ To give your table a meaningful name, on the Quick Access Toolbar, click **Save** 🖫. In the **Save As** dialog box, in the **Table Name** box, using your own name, replace the selected text by typing **Lastname Firstname 1A Students**

> Save each database object with a name that identifies the data that it contains. When you save objects within a database, it is not necessary to use underscores in place of the spaces between words. Your name is included as part of the object name so that you and your instructor can identify your printouts or electronic files easily.

9 ▸ In the **Save As** dialog box, click **OK**. Notice that the object tab—located directly above the *Student ID* field name—displays the new table name that you just entered.

> **More Knowledge**   Renaming or Deleting a Table
>
> To change the name of a table, close the table, display the Navigation Pane, right-click the table name, and then click Rename. Type the new name or edit as you would any selected text. To delete a table, close the table, display the Navigation Pane, right-click the table name, and then click Delete.

2.3.2

Activity 1.06 | Adding Additional Records to a Table

1 ▸ In the new record row, click in the **Student ID** field, and then enter the data for two additional students as shown in the table below. Press Enter or Tab to move from field to field. The data in each field will display on one line in the table.

Student ID	Last Name	First Name	Middle Initial	Address	City	State	Postal Code	Phone	Email	Faculty Advisor ID	Amount Owed
2345677	Ingram	Joseph	S	621 Hilltop Dr	Leander	TX	78646	(512) 555-0717	jingram@tlcc.edu	FAC-2377	378.5
3456689	Snyder	Amanda	J	4786 Bluff St	Buda	TX	78610	(512) 555-9120	asnyder@tlcc.edu	FAC-9005	0

2 ▶ Press **Enter**, and compare your screen with Figure 1.13

FIGURE 1.13

Access 2016, Windows 10, Microsoft Corporation

Activity 1.07 | Importing Data from an Excel Workbook into an Existing Access Table

2.3.4

You can type records directly into a table. You can also *import* data from a variety of sources. Importing is the process of copying data from one source or application to another application. For example, you can import data from a Word table or an Excel spreadsheet into an Access database because the data is arranged in columns and rows, similar to a table in Datasheet view.

In this Activity, you will *append*—add on—data from an Excel spreadsheet to your *1A Students* table. To append data, the table must already be created, and it must be closed.

1 ▶ In the upper right corner of the table, below the ribbon, click **Object Close** ☒ to close your **1A Students** table. Notice that no objects are open.

2 ▶ On the ribbon, click the **External Data tab**. In the **Import & Link group**, click **Excel**. In the **Get External Data – Excel Spreadsheet** dialog box, click **Browse**.

3 ▶ In the **File Open** dialog box, navigate to the student data files that accompany this chapter, double-click the Excel file **a01A_Students**, and then compare your screen with Figure 1.14.

The path to the *source file*—the file being imported—displays in the File name box. There are three options for importing data from an Excel spreadsheet: import the data into a *new* table in the current database, append a copy of the records to an existing table, or link the data from the spreadsheet to a linked table in the database. A *link* is a connection to data in another file. When linking, Access creates a table that maintains a link to the source data, so that changes to the data in one file are automatically made in the other—linked—file.

ANOTHER WAY Click the file name, and then in the File Open dialog box, click Open.

Path to file being imported (yours may vary)

Import option

Append option

Link option

FIGURE 1.14

4 ▸ Click the **Append a copy of the records to the table** option button, and then, in the box to the right, click the **arrow**.

Currently, your database has only one table, so no other tables display on the list. However, when a database has multiple tables, click the arrow to select the table to which you want to append records. The table into which you import or append data is referred to as the *destination table*.

5 ▸ Press Esc to cancel the list, and in the dialog box, click **OK**. If a security message displays, click Open. Compare your screen with Figure 1.15.

The first screen of the Import Spreadsheet Wizard displays. A *wizard* is a feature in a Microsoft Office program that walks you step by step through a process. The presence of scroll bars in the window indicates that records and fields are out of view. To append records from an Excel workbook to an existing database table, the column headings in the Excel worksheet or spreadsheet must be identical to the field names in the table. The wizard identified the first row of the spreadsheet as column headings, which are equivalent to field names.

FIGURE 1.15

6 In the lower right corner of the wizard, click **Next**. Notice that the name of your table displays under **Import to Table**. In the lower right corner of the wizard, click **Finish**.

7 In the **Get External Data – Excel Spreadsheet** dialog box, click **Close**. Open ⟩⟩ the **Navigation Pane**.

8 Point to the right edge of the **Navigation Pane** to display the ⟷ pointer. Drag to the right to increase the width of the **Navigation Pane** so that the entire table name displays, and then compare your screen with Figure 1.16.

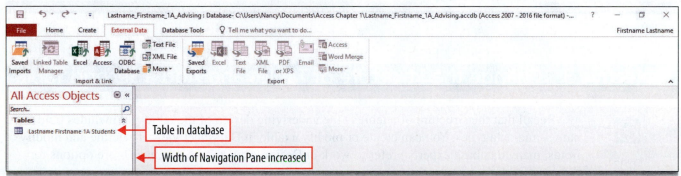

FIGURE 1.16

9 In the **Navigation Pane**, double-click your **1A Students** table to open the table in Datasheet view, and then **Close** ⟨⟨ the **Navigation Pane**.

🔄 **ANOTHER WAY**   To open an object from the Navigation Pane, right-click the object name, and then click Open.

10 ▶ In the lower left corner of your screen, locate the navigation area, and notice that there are a total of **25** records in the table—you entered three records and imported 22 additional records. Compare your screen with Figure 1.17.

The records that you entered and the records you imported from the Excel spreadsheet display in your table; the first record in the table is selected. The ***navigation area*** indicates the number of records in the table and has controls in the form of arrows that you click to move through the records.

FIGURE 1.17

GO! Learn How
Video A1-3

Recall that the structure of a table is the underlying design of the table and includes field names and data types. You can create or modify a table in Datasheet view. To define and modify fields, many database experts prefer to work in Design view, where you have more options for defining fields in a table.

2.4.9, 1.3.5

Activity 1.08 | Deleting a Table Field in Design View

In this Activity, you will delete the *Middle Initial* field from the table.

1 ▶ Click the **Home tab**, and then in the **Views group**, click the **View arrow** to display a list of views.

There are two views for tables: Datasheet view and Design view. Other objects have different views. On the list, Design view is represented by a picture of a pencil, a ruler, and an angle. Datasheet view is represented by a picture of a table arranged in columns and rows. In the Views group, if the top of the View button displays the pencil, ruler, and angle, clicking View will switch your view to Design view. Likewise, clicking the top of the View button that displays as a datasheet will switch your view to Datasheet view.

2 On the list, click **Design View**, and then compare your screen with Figure 1.18.

Design view displays the underlying design—the structure—of the table and its fields. In Design view, the records in the table do not display. You can only view the information about each field's attributes. Each field name is listed, along with its data type. You can add explanatory information about a field in the Description column, but it is not required.

You can decide how each field should look and behave in the Field Properties area. For example, you can set a specific field size in the Field Properties area. In the lower right corner, information displays about the active selection—in this case, the Field Name.

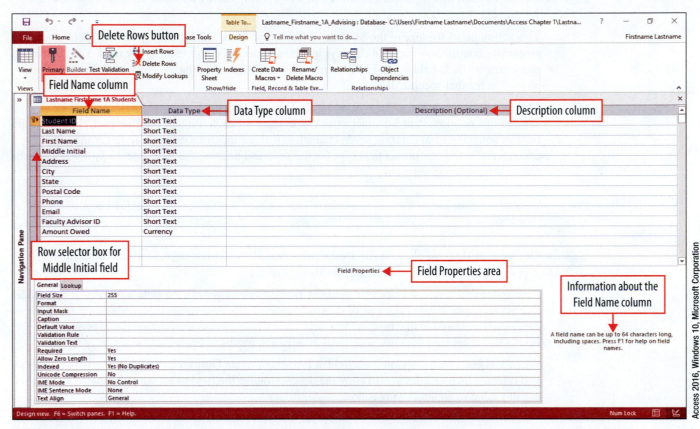

FIGURE 1.18

3 In the **Field Name** column, to the left of **Middle Initial**, point to the row selector box to display the ➡ pointer, and then click one time to select the entire row.

4 On the **Design tab**, in the **Tools group**, click **Delete Rows**. Read the warning in the message box, and then click **Yes**.

Deleting a field deletes both the field and its data. After you save the changes, you cannot undo this action, so Access prompts you to be sure you want to proceed. If you change your mind after deleting a field and saving the changes, you must add the field back into the table and then reenter the data for that field for every record.

↻ ANOTHER WAY   In Design view, right-click the selected row, and then click Delete Rows; or, in Datasheet view, select the field—column—and on the Home tab, in the Records group, click Delete.

2.4.4, 2.2.3

Activity 1.09 | Changing a Field Size and Adding a Description

Typically, many different individuals have the ability to enter data into a table. For example, at your college, many Registration Assistants enter and modify student and course information daily. Two ways to help reduce errors are to restrict what can be typed in a field and to add descriptive information to help the individuals when entering the data.

1 With your table still displayed in **Design** view, in the **Field Name** column, click anywhere in the **Student ID** field name.

2 In the lower area of the screen, under **Field Properties**, click **Field Size** to select the text **255**, and then type **7**

> This action limits the size of the Student ID field to no more than seven characters. *Field properties* control how the field displays and how data can be entered into the field. You can define properties for each field in the Field Properties area by first clicking the field name to display the properties for that specific data type.

> The default field size for a Short Text field is 255. Limiting the Field Size property to seven ensures that no more than 7 characters can be entered for each Student ID. However, this does not prevent someone from entering seven characters that are incorrect or entering fewer than seven characters. Setting the proper data type for the field and limiting the field size are two ways to help reduce errors during data entry.

 ANOTHER WAY　In Datasheet view, click in the field. Under Table Tools, on the Fields tab, in the Properties group, click in the Field Size box, and then type the number that represents the maximum number of characters for that field.

3 In the **Student ID** row, click in the **Description** box, type **Seven-digit Student ID number** and then press **Enter**. Compare your screen with Figure 1.19.

> Descriptions for fields in a table are optional. Include a description if the field name does not provide an obvious explanation of the type of data to be entered. If a description is provided for a field, when data is being entered in that field in Datasheet view, the text in the Description displays on the left side of the status bar to provide additional information for the individuals who are entering the data.

> When you enter a description for a field, a Property Update Options button displays below the text you typed, which enables you to copy the description for the field to all other database objects that use this table as an underlying source.

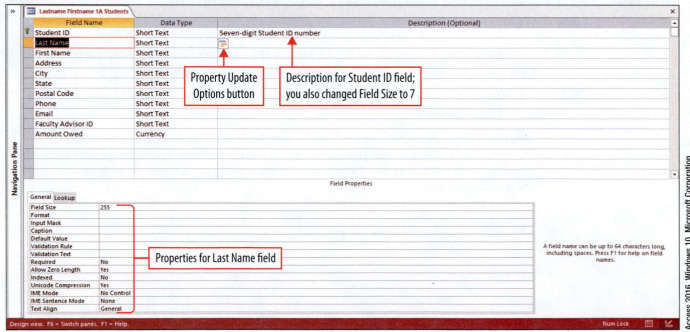

FIGURE 1.19

Access 2016, Windows 10, Microsoft Corporation

4 Click in the **State** field name box. In the **Field Properties** area, change the **Field Size** to **2** and in the **Description** box for this field, type **Two-character state abbreviation** and then press (Enter).

5 Click in the **Faculty Advisor ID** field name box. In the **Field Properties** area, change the **Field Size** to **8** and in the **Description** box for this field, type **Eight-character ID of the instructor assigned as advisor** and then press (Enter).

6 On the Quick Access Toolbar, click **Save** 🖫 to save the design changes to your table, and then notice the message.

> The message indicates that the field size property of one or more fields has changed to a shorter size. If more characters are currently present in the Student ID, State, or Faculty Advisor ID fields than you have allowed, the data will be *truncated*—cut off or shortened—because the fields were not previously restricted to these specific number of characters.

7 In the message box, click **Yes**.

More Knowledge   **Add a Table Description**

You can create a description to provide more information to users regarding the entire table. With the table displayed in Design view, click the Design tab. In the Show/Hide group, click Property Sheet. Click in the Description box, type the table description, and then press Enter. Close the Property Sheet.

MOS
1.3.5

Activity 1.10 | Viewing the Primary Key in Design View

Primary key refers to the required field in the table that uniquely identifies a record. For example, in a college registration database, your Student ID number identifies you as a unique individual—every student has a student number and no other student at the college has your exact student number. In the 1A Students table, the Student ID uniquely identifies each student.

When you create a table using the blank desktop database template, Access designates the first field as the primary key field and names the field ID. It is good database design practice to establish a primary key for every table, because doing so ensures that you do not enter the same record more than once. You can imagine the confusion if another student at your college had the same Student ID number as you do.

1 With your table still displayed in **Design** view, in the **Field Name** column, click in the **Student ID** box. To the left of the box, notice the small icon of a key, as shown in Figure 1.20.

> Access automatically designates the first field as the primary key field, but you can set any field as the primary key by clicking the field name, and then in the Tools group, clicking Primary Key.

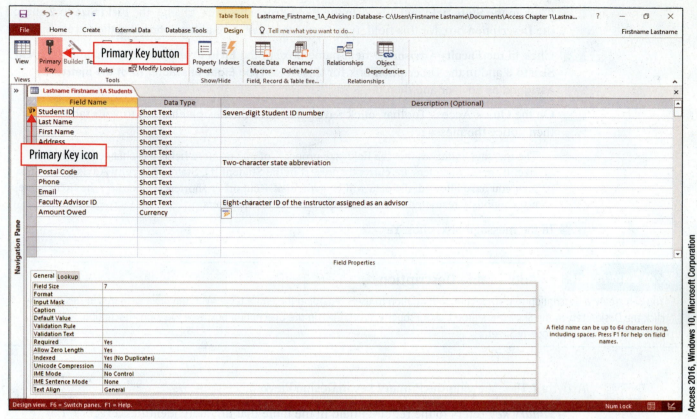

FIGURE 1.20

> **2** On the **Design tab**, in the **Views group**, notice that the View button displays a picture of a datasheet, indicating that clicking View will switch the view to Datasheet view. Click the top of the **View** button.

> If you make design changes to a table and switch views without first saving the table, Access will prompt you to save the table before changing views.

2.1.2

Activity 1.11 | Adding a Second Table to a Database by Importing an Excel Spreadsheet

Many Microsoft Office users track data in an Excel spreadsheet. The sorting and filtering capabilities of Excel are useful for a simple database where all of the information resides in one large Excel spreadsheet. However, Excel is limited as a database management tool because it cannot *relate* the information in multiple spreadsheets in a way that you can ask a question and get a meaningful result. Because data in an Excel spreadsheet is arranged in columns and rows, the spreadsheet can easily convert to an Access table by importing the spreadsheet.

> **1** On the ribbon, click the **External Data tab**, and then in the **Import & Link group**, click **Excel**. In the **Get External Data – Excel Spreadsheet** dialog box, to the right of the **File name** box, click **Browse**.

> **2** In the **File Open** dialog box, navigate to the location where your student data files are stored, and then double-click **a01A_Faculty_Advisors**. Compare your screen with Figure 1.21.

Get External Data – Excel Spreadsheet dialog box

Path to Excel file (yours may vary)

Browse button

Import option button selected

FIGURE 1.21

Access 2016, Windows 10, Microsoft Corporation

3 ▶ Be sure that the **Import the source data into a new table in the current database** option button is selected, click **OK**. If a security message displays, click Open.

The Import Spreadsheet Wizard displays the spreadsheet data.

4 ▶ In the upper left corner of the wizard, select the **First Row Contains Column Headings** check box.

The Excel data is framed, indicating that the first row of Excel column titles will become the Access table field names, and the remaining rows will become the individual records in the new Access table.

5 ▶ Click **Next**. Notice that the first column—*Faculty ID*—is selected, and in the upper area of the wizard, the **Field Name** and the **Data Type** display. Compare your screen with Figure 1.22.

In this step, under Field Options, you can review and change the name or the data type of each selected field. You can also identify fields in the spreadsheet that you do not want to import into the Access table by selecting the Do not import field (Skip) check box.

FIGURE 1.22

6 ▶ Click **Next**. In the upper area of the wizard, click the **Choose my own primary key** option button, and then be sure that **Faculty ID** displays.

> In the new table, Faculty ID will be the primary key. Every faculty member has a Faculty ID and no two faculty members have the same Faculty ID. By default, Access selects the first field as the primary key, but you can click the arrow and select a different field.

7 ▶ Click **Next**. In the **Import to Table** box, using your own name, type **Lastname Firstname 1A Faculty Advisors** and then click **Finish**.

8 ▶ In the **Get External Data – Excel Spreadsheet** dialog box, click **Close**. **Open** ⟩⟩ the **Navigation Pane**.

9 ▶ In the **Navigation Pane**, double-click your **1A Faculty Advisors** table to open it in Datasheet view, and then **Close** ⟨⟨ the **Navigation Pane**.

> Two tables that are identified by their object tabs are open in the object window. Your 1A Faculty Advisors table is the active table and displays the 29 records that you imported from the Excel spreadsheet.

10 ▶ In your **1A Faculty Advisors** table, click in the **Postal Code** field in the first record. On the ribbon, under **Table Tools**, click the **Fields tab**. In the **Formatting group**, click the **Data Type arrow**, and then click **Short Text**. Compare your screen with Figure 1.23.

> When you import data from an Excel spreadsheet, check the data types of all fields to ensure they are correct. Recall that if a field, such as the Postal Code, contains numbers that do not represent a quantity or are not used in calculations, the data type should be set to Short Text. To change the data type of a field, click in the field in any record.

FIGURE 1.23

Access 2016, Windows 10, Microsoft Corporation

Activity 1.12 | Adjusting Column Widths

You can adjust the column widths in a table displayed in Datasheet view by using techniques similar to those you use for Excel spreadsheets.

1 In the object window, click the *object tab* for your **1A Students** table to make it the active object and to display it in the object window.

Clicking an object tab along the top of the object window enables you to display the open object and make it active so that you can work with it. All of the columns in the datasheet are the same width, regardless of the length of the data in the field, the length of the field name, or the field size that was set. If you print the table as currently displayed, some of the data or field names will not print completely, so you will want to adjust the column widths.

2 In the column headings row, point to the right edge of the **Address** field to display the ⊞ pointer, and then compare your screen with Figure 1.24.

FIGURE 1.24

Access 2016, Windows 10, Microsoft Corporation

3 With the ⊞ pointer positioned as shown in Figure 1.24, double-click the right edge of the **Address** field.

The column width of the Address field widens to display the longest entry in the field fully. In this manner, the width of a column can be increased or decreased to fit its contents in the same manner as a column in an Excel spreadsheet. In Access, adjusting the column width to fit the contents is referred to as *Best Fit*.

4 Point to the **City** field name to display the ⬇ pointer, right-click to select the entire column and display the shortcut menu. Click **Field Width**, and then in the **Column Width** dialog box, click **Best Fit**.

This is a second way to adjust column widths.

5 If necessary, scroll to the right to view the last three fields. Point to the **Email** field name to display the ⬇ pointer, hold down the left mouse button, and then drag to the right to select this column, the **Faculty Advisor ID** column, and the **Amount Owed** column. Point to the right edge of any of the selected columns to display the ➕ pointer, and then double-click to apply **Best Fit** to all three columns.

> You can select multiple columns and adjust the widths of all of them at one time by using this technique or by right-clicking any of the selected columns, clicking Field Width, and clicking Best Fit in the Column Width dialog box.

6 If necessary, scroll to the left to view the **Student ID** field. To the left of the **Student ID** field name, click **Select All** ⬜. Notice that all of the fields are selected.

7 On the ribbon, click the **Home tab**. In the **Records group**, click **More**, and then click **Field Width**. In the **Column Width** dialog box, click **Best Fit**. Click anywhere in the **Student ID** field, and then compare your screen with Figure 1.25.

> Using the More command is a third way to adjust column widths. By using Select All, you can adjust the widths of all of the columns at one time. Adjusting the width of columns does not change the data in the table's records; it only changes the *display* of the data.

FIGURE 1.25

NOTE Adjusting Column Widths

After adjusting column widths, scroll horizontally and vertically to be sure that all of the data displays in all of the fields. Access adjusts column widths to fit the screen size based on the displayed data. If data is not displayed on the screen when you adjust column widths—even if you use Select All—the column width may not be adjusted adequately to display all of the data in the field. After adjusting column widths, click in any field to remove the selection of the column or columns, and then save the table before performing other tasks.

---

8 On the Quick Access Toolbar, click **Save** 🖫 to save the table design changes—changing the column widths.

> If you do not save the table after making design changes, Access prompts you to save it when you close the table.

MOS
1.5.2

Activity 1.13 | Printing a Table

There are times when you will want to print a table, even though a report may look more professional. For example, you may need a quick reference, or you may want to proofread the data that has been entered.

1 On the ribbon, click the **File tab**, click **Print**, and then click **Print Preview**. Compare your screen with Figure 1.26.

The table displays in Print Preview with the default zoom setting of One Page, a view that enables you to see how your table will print on the page. It is a good idea to view any object in Print Preview before printing so that you can make changes to the object if needed before actually printing it. In the navigation area, the Next Page button is darker (available), an indication that more than one page will print.

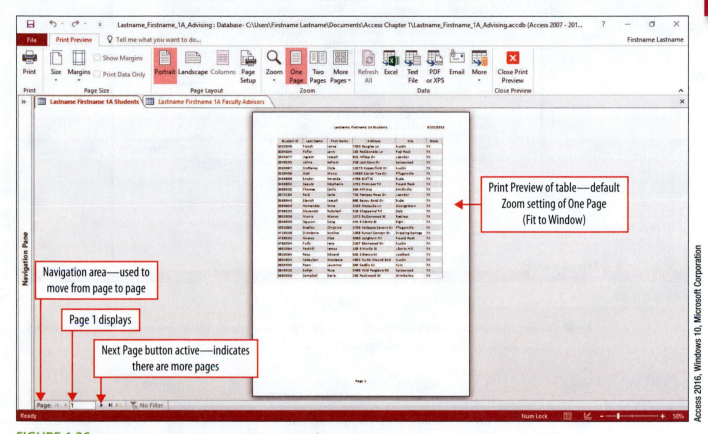

Print Preview of table—default Zoom setting of One Page (Fit to Window)

Navigation area—used to move from page to page

Page 1 displays

Next Page button active—indicates there are more pages

Access 2016, Windows 10, Microsoft Corporation

FIGURE 1.26

2 In the navigation area, click **Next Page** ▶ to display Page 2. Point to the top of the page to display the 🔍 pointer, click one time to zoom in, and then compare your screen with Figure 1.27.

The Print Preview display enlarges, and the Zoom Out pointer displays. The second page of the table displays the last five fields. The Next Page button is dimmed, indicating that the button is unavailable because there are no more pages after Page 2. The Previous Page button is available, indicating that a page exists before this page.

FIGURE 1.27

3 On the ribbon, on the **Print Preview tab**, in the **Zoom group**, click **Zoom** to change the zoom setting back to the default setting of One Page.

🔄 **ANOTHER WAY**   With the 🔍 pointer displayed on the page, click to zoom back to the One Page setting.

4 In the **Page Layout group**, click **Landscape**, and notice that there are only three fields on Page 2. In the navigation area, click **Previous Page** ◄ to display Page 1, and then compare your screen with Figure 1.28.

The orientation of the page to be printed changes. The header on the page includes the table name and current date, and the footer displays the page number. The change in orientation from portrait to landscape is not saved with the table. Each time you print, you must check the page orientation, the margins, and any other print parameters so that the object prints as you intend.

FIGURE 1.28

5 On the **Print Preview tab**, in the **Print group**, click **Print**. In the **Print** dialog box, under **Print Range**, verify that **All** is selected. Under **Copies**, verify that the **Number of Copies** is **1**. Compare your screen with Figure 1.29.

FIGURE 1.29

6 Determine if your instructor wants you to submit the individual database objects that you create within this Project, or if you will submit only your completed database file. Then, if you are creating and submitting the individual database objects—this is the first of five in this Project—determine if you are submitting the objects as a paper printout or as an electronic image that looks like a printed document.

7 To print on paper, in the **Print** dialog box, click **OK**, and then on the ribbon, in the **Close Preview group**, click **Close Print Preview**. If you are required to create and submit an electronic image of your document that looks like a printed document, in the Print dialog box, click Cancel, and then follow the steps in the following Note—or follow the specific directions provided by your instructor.

NOTE — Creating a PDF Electronic Image of Your Database Object That Looks Like a Printed Document

Display the object (table, query, form, report, and so on) in Print Preview and adjust margins and orientation as needed. On the Print Preview tab, in the Data group, click PDF or XPS. In the Publish as PDF or XPS dialog box, navigate to your chapter folder. Use the default file name, or follow your instructor's directions to name the object. If you wish to view the PDF file, in the dialog box, select the Open file after publishing check box. In the Publish as PDF or XPS dialog box, click Publish. If necessary, close any windows that try to display your PDF—Adobe Reader, Adobe Acrobat, or the Microsoft Edge browser, and then close the Export – PDF dialog box. On the ribbon, click Close Print Preview; your electronic image is saved. Close the Save Export Steps dialog box.

---

8 In the upper right corner of the object window, click **Close Object** ☒ to close your **1A Students** table. Notice that the **1A Faculty Advisors** table is the active object in the object window.

🔄 **ANOTHER WAY**   In the object window, right-click the 1A Students object tab, and then click Close.

---

9 In your **1A Faculty Advisors** table, to the left of the **Faculty ID** field name, click **Select All** ▦ to select all of the columns. On the **Home tab**, in the **Records group**, click **More**, and then click **Field Width**. In the **Column Width** dialog box, click **Best Fit** to adjust the widths of all of the columns so that all of the data displays. Click in any field in the table to cancel the selection. Scroll horizontally and vertically to be sure that all of the data displays in each field; if necessary, use the techniques you practiced to apply Best Fit to individual columns. **Save** 🖫 the changes you made to the table's column widths, and then click in any record to cancel the selection, if necessary

10 On the ribbon, click the **File tab**, click **Print**, and then click **Print Preview**. On the **Print Preview tab**, in the **Page Layout group**, click **Landscape**. Notice that the table will print on more than one page. In the **Page Size group**, click **Margins**, click **Normal**, and then notice that one more column moved to the first page—your results may differ depending on your printer's capabilities.

In addition to changing the page orientation to Landscape, you can change the margins to Normal to see if all of the fields will print on one page. In this instance, there are still too many fields to print on one page, although the Postal Code field moved from Page 2 to Page 1.

11 If directed to do so by your instructor, create a paper printout or a PDF electronic image of your **1A Faculty Advisors** table, and then click **Close Print Preview**. This is the second of five objects printed in this project.

12 In the object window, **Close** ☒ your **1A Faculty Advisors** table.

All of your database objects—your *1A Students* table and your *1A Faculty Advisors* table—are closed; the object window is empty.

Objective 4 · Create a Query, Form, and Report

GO! Learn How
Video A1-4

Recall that tables are the foundation of an Access database because all of the data is stored in one or more tables. You can use the data stored in tables in other database objects such as queries, forms, and reports.

MOS
3.1.1

Activity 1.14 │ Creating a Query by Using the Simple Query Wizard

A *query* is a database object that retrieves specific data from one or more database objects—either tables or other queries—and then, in a single datasheet, displays only the data that you specify when you design the query. Because the word *query* means *to ask a question*, think of a query as a question formed in a manner that Access can answer.

A *select query* is one type of Access query. A select query, also called a *simple select query*, retrieves (selects) data from one or more tables or queries and then displays the selected data in a datasheet. A select query creates a subset of the data to answer specific questions; for example, *Which students live in Austin, TX?*

The objects from which a query selects the data are referred to as the query's *data source*. In this Activity, you will create a simple query using a wizard that walks you step by step through the process. The process involves selecting the data source and indicating the fields that you want to include in the query results. The query—the question you want to ask—is *What is the name, email address, phone number, and Student ID of every student?*

> **1** ▶ On the ribbon, click the **Create tab**, and then in the **Queries group**, click **Query Wizard**. In the **New Query** dialog box, be sure **Simple Query Wizard** is selected, and then click **OK**. If a security message displays, click Open. Compare your screen with Figure 1.30.

In the wizard, the displayed table or query name is the object that was last selected on the Navigation Pane. The last object you worked with was your 1A Faculty Advisors table, so that object name displayed in the wizard.

FIGURE 1.30

> **2** ▶ In the wizard, click the **Tables/Queries arrow**, and then click your **Table: Lastname Firstname 1A Students**.

To create a query, first select the data source—the object from which the query is to select the data. The information you need to answer the question is stored in your 1A Students table, so this table is your data source.

3 Under **Available Fields**, click **Last Name**, and then click **Add Field** `>` to move the field to the **Selected Fields** list on the right. Double-click the **First Name** field to add the field to the **Selected Fields** list.

Use either method to add fields to the Selected Fields list—you can add fields in any order.

4 By using **Add Field** `>` or by double-clicking the field name, add the following fields to the **Selected Fields** list in the order specified: **Email**, **Phone**, and **Student ID**. Compare your screen with Figure 1.31.

Selecting these five fields will answer the question, *What is the name, email address, phone number, and Student ID of every student?*

FIGURE 1.31

5 In the wizard, click **Next**. Click in the **What title do you want for your query?** box. Using your own name, edit as necessary so that the query name is **Lastname Firstname 1A All Students Query** and then compare your screen with Figure 1.32.

FIGURE 1.32

6 In the wizard, click **Finish**. Select all of the columns, apply **Best Fit**, and then **Save** 🖫 the query. In the first record, click in the **Last Name** field to cancel the selection. Compare your screen with Figure 1.33.

Access *runs* the query—performs the actions indicated in your query design—by searching the records in the specified data source, and then finds the records that match specified criteria. The records that match the criteria display in a datasheet. A select query *selects*—pulls out and displays—*only* the information from the data source that you request, including the specified fields.

In the object window, Access displays every student from your 1A Students table—the data source—but displays *only* the five fields that you moved to the Selected Fields list in the Simple Query Wizard.

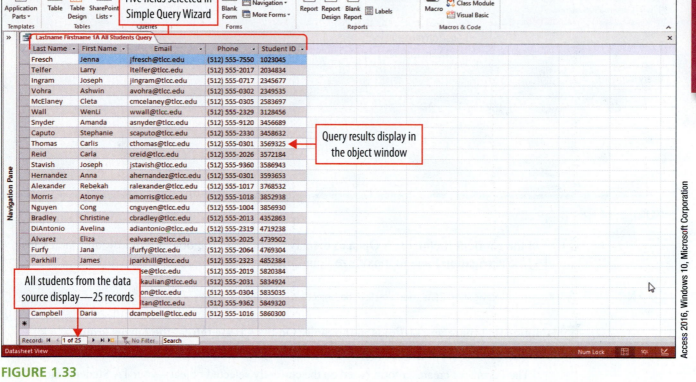

Five fields selected in Simple Query Wizard

Query results display in the object window

All students from the data source display—25 records

Access 2016, Windows 10, Microsoft Corporation

FIGURE 1.33

7 On the ribbon, click the **File tab**, click **Print**, and then click **Print Preview**. Notice that the query results will print on one page. As directed by your instructor, create a paper printout or PDF electronic image. Click **Close Print Preview**. This is the third of five objects printed in this project.

8 In the object window, **Close** ☒ the query.

4.1.1, 4.1.3

Activity 1.15 | Creating and Printing a Form

A *form* is an Access object with which you can enter data, edit data, or display data from a table or query. In a form, the fields are laid out in an attractive format on the screen, which makes working with the database easier for those who must enter and look up data.

One type of form displays only one record at a time. Such a form is useful not only to the individual who performs the data entry—typing in the records—but also to anyone who has the job of viewing information in the database. For example, when you visit the Records office at your college to obtain a transcript, someone displays your record on the screen. For the viewer, it is much easier to look at one record at a time using a form than to look at all of the student records in the database table.

1 **Open** ≫ the **Navigation Pane**. Drag the right edge of the **Navigation Pane** to the right to increase the width of the pane so that all object names display fully. Notice that a table name displays with a datasheet icon, and a query name displays an icon of two overlapping datasheets. Right-click your **1A Students** table, and then compare your screen with Figure 1.34.

FIGURE 1.34

2 On the shortcut menu, click **Open** to display the table in the object window, and then **Close** ⟪ the **Navigation Pane** to maximize your object window space.

⟳ ANOTHER WAY   In the Navigation Pane, double-click the object name to open it.

3 Notice that there are 11 fields in the table. On the **Create tab**, in the **Forms group**, click **Form**. Compare your screen with Figure 1.35.

The Form tool creates a form based on the currently selected object—your 1A Students table. The form displays all of the fields from the underlying data source—one record at a time—in a simple top-to-bottom format with all 11 fields in a single column. You can use this form as it displays, or you can modify it. Records that you create or edit in a form are automatically added to or updated in the underlying table or data source.

The new form displays in *Layout view*—the Access view in which you can make changes to elements of an object while it is open and displaying the data from the data source. Each field in the form displayed in Figure 1.35 displays the data for the first student record—*Jenna Fresch*—in your 1A Students table.

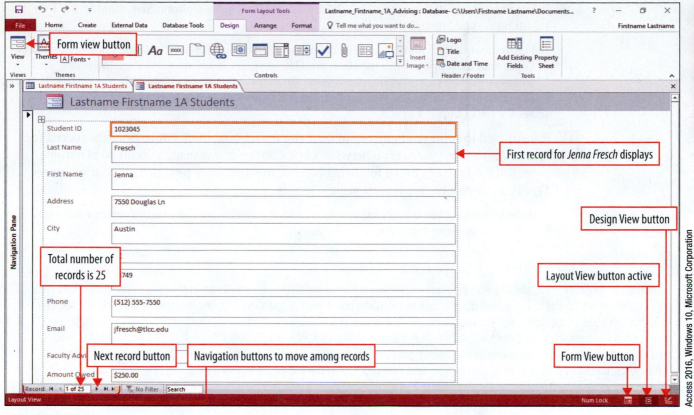

FIGURE 1.35

4 At the right side of the status bar, notice the three buttons. Point to each button to display its ScreenTip, and notice that **Layout View** 📑 is active, indicating that the form is displayed in Layout view.

5 In the status bar, click **Form View** 📑.

In *Form view*, you can view the records, create a new record, edit a record, and delete a record. You cannot change the layout or design of the form. Form view is useful for individuals who *access records* in your database. Layout view is useful for individuals who *design* the form.

🔄 **ANOTHER WAY**   On the Design tab, or on the Home tab, in the Views group, click View when the button displays an icon of a form.

6 In the navigation area, click **Next record** ▶ two times to display the third record—the record for *Joseph Ingram.*

Use the navigation buttons to scroll among the records and to display any single record.

7 Using your own name, **Save** 💾 the form as **Lastname Firstname 1A Student Form**

8 On the ribbon, click the **File tab**, click **Print**, and then on the right, click **Print**—do *not* click Print Preview because you are going to print a *single* record—not all of the records.

9 In the **Print** dialog box, under **Print Range**, click the **Selected Record(s)** option button, and then click **Setup**.

10 In the **Page Setup** dialog box, click the **Columns tab**. Under **Column Size**, double-click in the **Width** box, type **7.5** and then click **OK**.

> Forms are usually not printed, so the default width for a form created with the Form command is larger than most printers can handle to print on one page. If you do not change the width, the form will print on two pages because the column flows over the margins allowed by the printer. If, after changing the Width to 7.5, your form still prints on two pages, try entering a different value for Width; for example, 7 or 6.5.

11 If instructed to print your objects, in the **Print** dialog box, click **OK** to print the record for *Joseph Ingram* on one page; otherwise, click Cancel. If instructed to print an electronic copy, follow the steps in the following Note or the directions provided by your instructor. This is the fourth of five objects printed in this project.

> After printing, along the left edge of the record, the narrow bar—the *record selector bar*—displays in black, indicating that the record is selected.

NOTE   Printing a Single Form in PDF

On the File tab, click Print, and then on the right, click Print. In the Print dialog box, click Setup. In the Page Setup dialog box, click the Columns tab. Under Column Size, double-click in the Width box, type **7.5** and then click OK. In the Print dialog box, click Cancel. On the left edge of the form, click the record selector bar so that it is black—selected.

On the ribbon, click the External Data tab. In the Export group, click PDF or XPS. In the Publish as PDF or XPS dialog box, navigate to your chapter folder, and at the lower right corner of the dialog box, click Options. In the Options dialog box, under Range, click the Selected records option button, and then click OK. In the Publish as PDF or XPS dialog box, click Publish. If necessary, close Adobe Reader, Adobe Acrobat, or the Microsoft Edge browser.

---

12 **Close** ☒ the form object; leave your **1A Students** table open.

Activity 1.16 | Creating, Modifying, and Printing a Report

5.1.1, 1.5.1

A ***report*** is a database object that displays the fields and records from a table or query in an easy-to-read format suitable for printing. Create professional-looking reports to summarize database information.

1 **Open** ≫ the **Navigation Pane**, and then open your **1A Faculty Advisors** table by double-clicking the table name or by right-clicking the table name and clicking Open. **Close** ≪ the **Navigation Pane**.

2 On the **Create tab**, in the **Reports group**, click **Report**.

> The Report tool creates a report in Layout view and includes all of the fields and all of the records in the data source—your 1A Faculty Advisors table. Dotted lines indicate how the report would break across pages if you print it now. In Layout view, you can make quick changes to the report layout while viewing the data from the table.

3 Click the **Faculty ID** field name, and then on the ribbon, under **Report Layout Tools**, click the **Arrange tab**. In the **Rows & Columns group**, click **Select Column**, and then press Del. Using the same technique, delete the **Rank** field.

> The Faculty ID and Rank fields, along with the data, are deleted from the report. The fields readjust by moving to the left. Deleting the fields from the report does *not* delete the fields and data from the data source—your 1A Faculty Advisors table.

🔄 **ANOTHER WAY**   Right-click the field name, click Select Entire Column, and then press Del.

---

4 Click the **Address** field name, and then by using the scroll bar at the bottom of the screen, scroll to the right to display the **Cell Phone** field; be careful not to click in the report.

5 ▶ Hold down (Shift), and then click the **Cell Phone** field name to select all of the fields from *Address* through *Cell Phone*. With the field names selected—surrounded by a colored border—in the **Rows & Columns group**, click **Select Column**, and then press (Del).

Use this method to select and delete multiple columns in Layout view.

6 ▶ Scroll to the left, and notice that the four remaining fields display within the dotted lines— they are within the margins of the report. Click the **Campus** field name. Hold down (Shift), and then click the **First Name** field name to select the first three fields. In the **Rows & Columns group**, click **Select Column** to select all three fields.

7 ▶ On the ribbon, click the **Design tab**, and then in the **Tools group**, click **Property Sheet**.

The *Property Sheet* for the selected columns displays on the right side of the screen. Every object and every item in an object has an associated Property Sheet where you can make precise changes to the properties—characteristics—of selected items.

8 ▶ In the **Property Sheet**, if necessary, click the **Format tab**. Click **Width**, type **1.5** and then press (Enter). Compare your screen with Figure 1.36.

The width of the three selected fields changes to 1.5", and the fields readjust by moving to the left. You can change the Width property if you need to move columns within the margins of a report. In this report, the fields already displayed within the margins, but some reports may need this minor adjustment to print on one page.

⟳ ANOTHER WAY Select the column, and then drag the right edge of the column to the left to decrease the width of the field, or drag to the right to increase the width of the field.

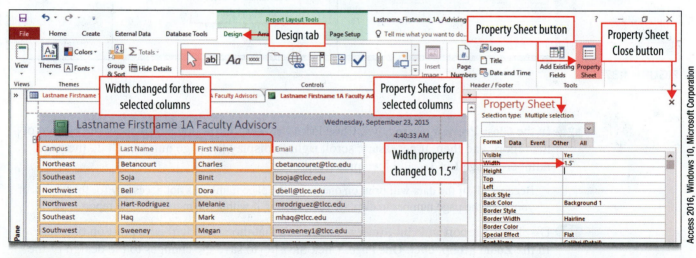

FIGURE 1.36

9 ▶ Close ⊠ the **Property Sheet**. Click the **Last Name** field name. On the ribbon, click the **Home tab**, and then in the **Sort & Filter group**, click **Ascending**.

Access sorts the report in ascending alphabetical order by the Last Name field. By default, tables are sorted in ascending order by the primary key field—in this instance, the Faculty ID field. Changing the sort order in the report does *not* change the sort order in the underlying table.

10 ▶ At the top of the report, to the right of the green report icon, click anywhere in the title of the report to select the title placeholder. On the **Home tab**, in the **Text Formatting group**, click the **Font Size arrow**, and then click **14**. Save 🖫 the report. In the **Save As** dialog box, in the **Report Name** box, add **Report** to the end of *Lastname Firstname 1A Faculty Advisors*, and then click **OK**.

11 On the **File tab**, click **Print**, and then click **Print Preview**. On the **Print Preview tab**, in the **Zoom group**, click **Two Pages**, and then compare your screen with Figure 1.37.

As currently formatted, the report will print on two pages, because the page number at the bottom of the report is positioned beyond the right margin of the report.

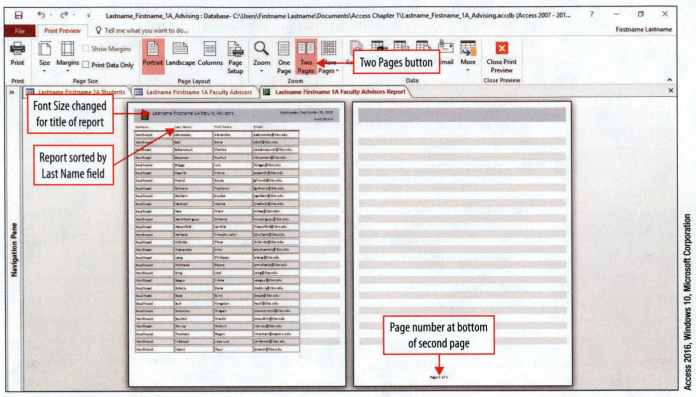

FIGURE 1.37

12 In the **Close Preview group**, click **Close Print Preview**. Scroll down to display the bottom of the report, and then, if necessary, scroll right to display the page number. Click the page number—**Page 1 of 1**—and then press Del.

Because all of the data will print on one page, the page number is not necessary for this report. If you want the page number to display, you can drag it within the margins of the report.

13 Display the report in **Print Preview**, and notice that the report will now print on one page. In the **Zoom group**, click **One Page**. Click **Save** 💾 to save the changes to the design of the report, and then create a paper printout or PDF electronic image as directed. Click **Close Print Preview**. This is the fifth or last object printed in this project.

When you create a report by using the Report tool, the default margins are 0.25 inch. Some printers require a greater margin, so your printed report may result in two pages. As you progress in your study of Access, you will practice making these adjustments. Also, if a printer is not installed on your system, the electronic PDF printout might result in a two-page report.

14 In the object window, right-click any **object tab**, and then click **Close All** to close all of the open objects. Notice that the object window is empty.

Objective 5 | Close a Database and Close Access

GO! Learn How
Video A1-5

When you close a table, any changes made to the records are saved automatically. If you made changes to the structure or adjusted column widths, you will be prompted to save the table when you close the table or when you switch views. Likewise, you will be prompted to save queries, forms, and reports if you make changes to the layout or design. If the Navigation Pane is open when you close Access, it will display when you reopen the database. When you are finished using your database, close the database, and then close Access.

Activity 1.17 | Closing a Database and Closing Access

1 **Open** » the **Navigation Pane**. If necessary, increase the width of the Navigation Pane so that all object names display fully. Notice that your report object displays with a green report icon. Compare your screen with Figure 1.38.

FIGURE 1.38

Access 2016, Windows 10, Microsoft Corporation

2 On the **File tab**, click **Close** to close the database but leave Access open. This action enables you to continue working in Access with another database if you want to do so. In the Access application window, in the upper right corner, click **Close** ☒ to close Access. As directed by your instructor, submit your database and the paper printouts or PDF electronic images of the five objects—two tables, one query, one form, and one report—that are the results of this project.

END | You have completed Project 1A

GO! With Google

Objective	Export an Access Table to an Excel Spreadsheet, Open as a Google Sheet, Edit a Record, and Save to Your Computer

Access web apps are designed to work with Microsoft's **SharePoint**, a service for setting up websites to share and manage documents. Your college may not have SharePoint installed, so you will use other tools to share objects from your database so that you can work collaboratively with others. Recall that Google Drive is Google's free, web-based word processor, spreadsheet, slide show, form, and data storage and sharing service. For Access, you can *export* a database object to an Excel worksheet, a PDF file, or a text file, and then save the file to Google Drive.

ALERT!   **Working with Web-Based Applications and Services**

Computer programs and services on the web receive continuous updates and improvements. Therefore, the steps to complete this web-based Activity may differ from the ones shown. You can often look at the screens and the information presented to determine how to complete the activity.

If you do not already have a Google account, you will need to create one before you begin this activity. Go to http://google.com and, in the upper right corner, click Sign In. On the Sign In screen, click Create Account. On the Create your Google Account page, complete the form, read and agree to the Terms of Service and Privacy Policy, and then click Next step. On the Welcome screen, click Get Started.

Activity | Exporting an Access Table to an Excel Spreadsheet, Saving the Spreadsheet to Google Drive, Editing a Record in Google Drive, and Saving to Your Computer

In this Activity, you will export your 1A Faculty Advisors table to an Excel spreadsheet, upload your Excel file to Google Drive as a Google Sheet, edit a record in the Google Sheet, and then download a copy of the edited spreadsheet to your computer.

1 Start Access, navigate to your **Access Chapter 1** folder, and then **Open** your **1A_Advising** database file. If necessary, on the Message Bar, click **Enable Content**. In the **Navigation Pane**, click your **1A Faculty Advisors** table to select it—do not open it.

2 On the ribbon, click the **External Data tab**, and then in the **Export group**, click **Excel**. In the **Export – Excel Spreadsheet** dialog box, click **Browse**, and then navigate to your **Access Chapter 1** folder. In the **File Save** dialog box, click in the **File name** box, type **Lastname_Firstname_a1A_Web** and then click **Save**.

3 In the **Export – Excel Spreadsheet** dialog box, under **Specify export options**, select the first two check boxes—**Export data with formatting and layout** and **Open the destination file after the export operation is complete**—and then click **OK**. Take a moment to examine the data in the file, and then **Close** Excel. In the **Export – Excel Spreadsheet** dialog box, click **Close**, and then **Close** Access. **Close** Excel.

4 Open your browser software, navigate to **http://drive.google.com**, and sign in to your Google account.

On the right side of the screen, click **Settings** ⚙▾ , and then click **Settings**. In the **Settings** dialog box, to the right of *Convert uploads*, if necessary, select the **Convert uploaded files to Google Docs editor format** check box. In the upper right, click **Done**.

It is necessary to select this setting; otherwise, your document will upload as a pdf file and cannot be edited without further action.

5 Open your **GO! Web Projects** folder—or create and then open this folder by clicking **NEW** and then **Folder**. On the left, click **NEW**, and then click **File upload**. In the **Open** dialog box, navigate to your **Access Chapter 1** folder, and then double-click your **a1A_Web** Excel file to upload it to Google Drive. When the message *Uploads completed* displays, **Close** the message box.

6 Double-click your **Lastname_Firstname_a1A_Web** file to display the file, and then compare your screen with Figure A.

The worksheet displays column letters, row numbers, and data.

(GO! With Google continues on the next page)

GO! With Google

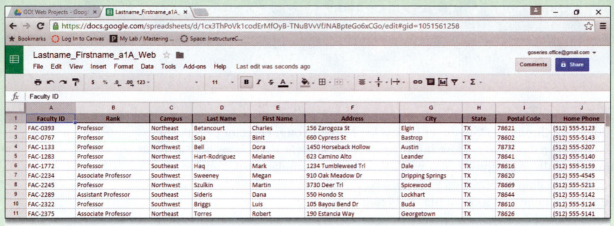

FIGURE A

7 Click in cell **C2**, and replace the current Campus with **Southwest** Click in cell **D2** and replace Betancourt with your last name. Press Tab and then replace Charles with your first name.

8 Above row **1** and to the left of column **A**, click **Select All** ____. On the menu bar, click **Format**, and then click **Clear formatting** so that the font is the same for all data; the cell borders are removed, and the formatting of the field names is removed.

9 In the column headings row, click **I** to select the entire column. On the menu bar, click **Format**, point to **Number**, and then click **Plain text** to format every number in the columns as text. Click in cell **A1** to deselect the column.

Recall that in Access, numbers that are not used in calculations should be formatted as Short Text. Because the formatting is cleared, you can enter new records into the spreadsheet in the same format as the existing records.

10 Click **File** to display the menu, point to **Download as**, and then click **Microsoft Excel (.xlsx)**. In the message box—usually displayed at the bottom of your screen—click the **Save arrow**, and then click **Save as**. In the **Save As** dialog box, navigate to your **Access Chapter 1** folder, click in the **File name** box, and type **Lastname_ Firstname_a1A_Web_Download** and then click **Save**. **Close** the message box.

> **NOTE** Saving the Downloaded File to the Access Chapter 1 Folder
>
> Depending on the browser you are using, you may need to open the file in Excel and then save the a1A_Web_Download worksheet to your Access Chapter 1 folder.

11 In Google Drive, at the upper right corner of your screen, click your user name, and then click **Sign out**. **Close** your browser window.

12 Start Excel. In the Excel opening screen, click **Open Other Workbooks**, and then click **Browse**. Navigate to your **Access Chapter 1** folder, and then double-click your **a1A_Web** Excel file. Notice that this file is the original file—the new record is not entered. If

you are required to print your documents, use one of the methods in the following Note. **Close** your Excel file; and, if prompted, save the changes to your worksheet. Then **Open** and print your a **1A_Web_Download** Excel file using one of the methods in the following Note. **Close** Excel; and, if prompted, save the changes to your worksheet. As directed by your instructor, submit your two workbooks and the two paper printouts or PDF electronic images that are the results of this project.

> **NOTE** Adding the File Name to the Footer and Printing or Creating a PDF Electronic Image of an Excel Spreadsheet on One Page
>
> Click the File tab, click Print, and then click Page Setup. In the Page Setup dialog box, on the Page tab, under Orientation, click Landscape. Under Scaling, click the Fit to option button. In the Page Setup dialog box, click the Header/Footer tab, and then click Custom Footer. With the insertion point blinking in the Left section box, click the Insert File Name button, and then click OK. In the Page Setup dialog box, click OK.
>
> To print on paper, click Print. To create a PDF electronic image, on the left side of your screen, click Export. Under Export, be sure Create PDF/XPS Document is selected, and then click Create PDF/XPS. Navigate to your Access Chapter 1 folder, and then click Publish to save the file with the default name and an extension of pdf.

Student Workshops Database

PROJECT ACTIVITIES

In Activities 1.18 through 1.25, you will assist Dr. Miriam Yong, Director of Student Activities, in creating a database to store information about student workshops held at Texas Lakes Community College campuses. You will use a database template that tracks event information, add workshop information to the database, and then print the results. Your completed report and table will look similar to Figure 1.39.

PROJECT FILES

MyITLab grader If your instructor wants you to submit Project 1B in the MyITLab Grader system, log in to MyITLab, locate Grader Project1B, and then download the files for this project.

For Project 1B, you will need the following file:

Desktop event management template a01B_Workshops (Excel workbook)

You will save your database as:

Lastname_Firstname_1B_Student_ Workshops

PROJECT RESULTS

Lastname Firstname 1B All Events   Tuesday, July 28, 2015   11:41:10 AM

Title	Start Time	End Time	Location
Your Online Reputation	3/9/2021 7:00:00 PM	3/9/2021 9:00:00 PM	Northeast Campus
Internet Safety			
Writing a Research Paper	3/10/2021 4:00:00 PM	3/10/2021 6:00:00 PM	Southwest Campus
Computer Skills			
Resume Writing	3/18/2021 2:00:00 PM	3/18/2021 4:00:00 PM	Northwest Campus
Job Skills			
Careers in the Legal Profession	3/19/2021 2:00:00 PM	3/19/2021 4:00:00 PM	Southeast Campus
Careers			
Transferring to a 4-Year University	4/8/2021 11:00:00 AM	4/8/2021 12:30:00 PM	Northeast Campus
Transfer			
Financial Aid	4/14/2021 7:00:00 PM	4/14/2021 8:30:00 PM	Southeast Campus
CC Info			
Sensitivity Training	4/15/2021 8:00:00 AM	4/15/2021 9:00:00 AM	Northwest Campus
Human Behavior			
Preparing for the Job Interview	4/15/2021 12:30:00 PM	4/15/2021 2:00:00 PM	Northwest Campus
Job Skills			
Class Note Taking	4/18/2021 12:30:00 PM	4/18/2021 1:30:00 PM	Southeast Campus
Study Skills			
Managing Time and Stress	4/18/2021 6:00:00 PM	4/18/2021 7:30:00 PM	Southwest Campus
Study Skills			
Work Smart at Your Computer	4/20/2021 10:00:00 AM	4/20/2021 11:00:00 AM	Northeast Campus
Computer Skills			
Preparing for Tests	4/20/2021 4:00:00 PM	4/20/2021 5:00:00 PM	Southeast Campus
Study Skills			

Page 1 of 1

Lastname Firstname 1B Workshop Locations   5/30/2015

Room ID	Campus/Location	Room	Seats	Room Arrangement	Equipment
NE-01	Northeast Campus	H265	150	Theater	Computer Projector, Surround Sound, Microphone
NE-02	Northeast Campus	B105	25	U-shaped	25 Computers, Projector
NW-01	Northwest Campus	C202	50	Lecture Classroom	Smart Board
SE-01	Southeast Campus	D148	20	U-shaped	White Board
SW-01	Southwest Campus	A15	35	Lecture Classroom	Computer Projector

Page 1

Access 2016, Windows 10, Microsoft Corporation

FIGURE 1.39 Project 1B Student Workshops

Objective 6   Use a Template to Create a Database

GO! Learn How
Video A1-6

A *database template* contains prebuilt tables, queries, forms, and reports that perform a specific task, such as tracking events. For example, your college may hold events such as athletic contests, plays, lectures, concerts, and club meetings. Using a predefined template, your college's Activities Director can quickly create a database to manage these events. The advantage of using a template to start a new database is that you do not have to create the objects—all you need to do is enter the data and modify the prebuilt objects to suit your needs.

The purpose of the database in this project is to track the student workshops that are held by Texas Lakes Community College. The questions to be answered might include:

- What workshops will be offered, and when will they be offered?
- In what rooms and on what campuses will the workshops be held?
- Which workshop locations have a computer projector for PowerPoint presentations?

MOS
1.1.2

Activity 1.18 | Using a Template to Create a Database

ALERT!   **To submit as an autograded project, log into MyITLab and download the files for this project, and begin with those files instead of the Desktop event managment template database. For Project 1B using Grader, read Activity 1.18 carefully. Begin working with the database in Activity 1.19. For Grader to award points accurately, when saving an object, do not include your Lastname Firstname at the beginning of the object name.**

There are two types of database templates—those that will be stored on your desktop and those that are designed to share with others over the Internet. In this Activity, you will use a desktop template to create your database.

1 Start Access. In the Access opening screen, scroll down to display a **Desktop vehicle maintenance** template and an **Asset tracking** template. Compare your screen with Figure 1.40.

These templates are included with the Access program. To store a database to manage vehicle maintenance on your desktop, select the *Desktop Vehicle maintenance* template. To publish a database to track assets and share it with others, select the *Asset tracking* template—the one that displays a globe image. The names of templates designed to create databases stored on your computer start with the word *Desktop*.

You can search the Microsoft Office website for more templates. You can also click a category under the search box, where templates will be suggested.

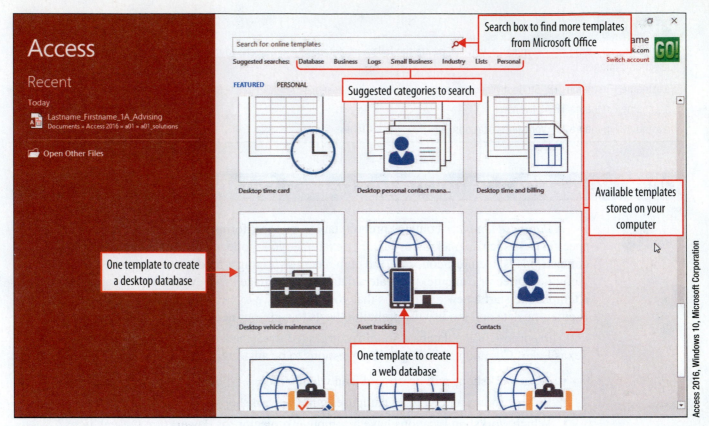

FIGURE 1.40

2 At the top of the window, click in the **Search for online templates** box, type **event** and then press Enter. Compare your screen with Figure 1.41.

> You must have an Internet connection to search for online templates. Access displays several templates, including the event management template.

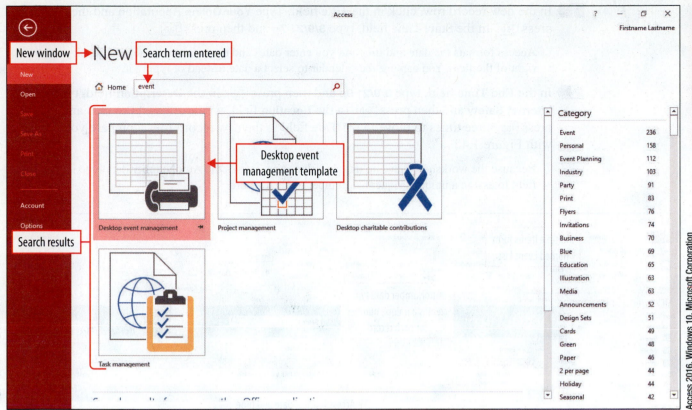

FIGURE 1.41

3 ▸ Click the **Desktop event management** template, and notice the description of the template. In the dialog box, to the right of the **File Name** box, click **Browse** 📁, and then navigate to your **Access Chapter 1** folder.

4 ▸ In the **File New Database** dialog box, click in the **File name** box to select the existing text. Using your own name, type **Lastname_Firstname_1B_Student_Workshops** and then press Enter.

5 ▸ In the **Desktop event management** dialog box, click **Create** to download the template and to save the database. If a welcome message box displays, click Get Started.

Access creates the *1B_Student_Workshops* database, and the database name displays in the title bar. A predesigned *form*—Event List—displays in the object window. Although you can enter events for any date, when you open the database in the future, the Event List form will display only those events for the current date and future dates.

6 ▸ Under the ribbon, on the **Message Bar**, a *SECURITY WARNING* may display. If it is, on the **Message Bar**, click **Enable Content**.

Databases provided by Microsoft are safe to use on your computer.

2.3.1

Activity 1.19 | Building a Table by Entering Records in a Multiple-Items Form and a Single-Record Form

One purpose of a form is to simplify the entry of data into a table—either for you or for others who enter data. In Project 1A, you created a simple form that enabled you to display or enter records in a table one record at a time. The Desktop Event management template creates a *multiple-items form* that enables you to display or enter *multiple* records in a table, but with an easier and simplified layout rather than typing directly into the table itself.

1 In the new record row, click in the **Title** field. Type **Your Online Reputation** and then press Tab. In the **Start Time** field, type **3/9/21 7p** and then press Tab.

> Access formats the date and time. As you enter dates and times, a small calendar displays to the right of the field. You can use the calendar to select a date instead of typing it.

2 In the **End Time** field, type **3/9/21 9p** and then press Tab. In the **Description** field, type **Internet Safety** and then press Tab. In the **Location** field, type **Northeast Campus** and then press Tab three times to move to the **Title** field in the new record row. Compare your screen with Figure 1.42.

> Because the workshops have no unique value, Access uses the AutoNumber data type in the ID field to assign a unique, sequential number to each record.

FIGURE 1.42

3 In the form, directly above the field names row, click **New Event**.

> A *single-record form* with the name *Event Details* displays, similar to the simple form you created in Project 1A. A single-record form enables you to display or enter one record at a time into a table.

4 Using Tab to move from field to field, enter the following record in the **Event Details** form—after entering the **End Time**, click in the **Description** field. Then compare your screen with Figure 1.43.

Title	Location	Start Time	End Time	Description
Writing a Research Paper	**Southwest Campus**	**3/10/21 4p**	**3/10/21 6p**	**Computer Skills**

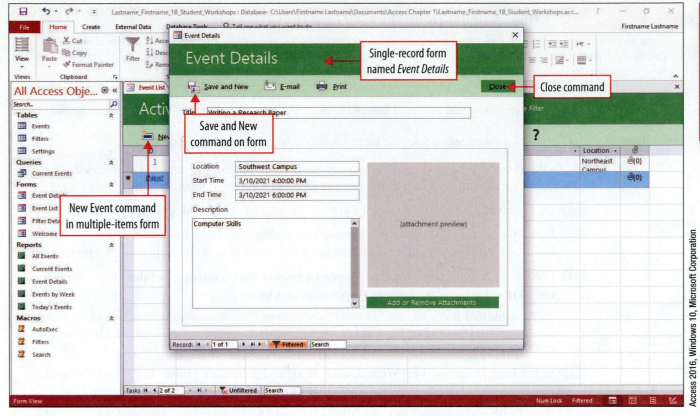

FIGURE 1.43

Access 2016, Windows 10, Microsoft Corporation

5 In the **Event Details** single-record form, in the upper right corner, click **Close**, and notice that the new record displays in the multiple-items form—*Event List*.

6 Enter the following records by using either the **Event List** form—the multiple-items form—or the **Event Details** form—the single-record form that is accessed by clicking the *New Event* command on the Event List form. Be sure the multiple-items form displays, and then compare your screen with Figure 1.44.

ID	Title	Start Time	End Time	Description	Location
3	**Resume Writing**	**3/18/21 2p**	**3/18/21 4p**	**Job Skills**	**Northwest Campus**
4	**Careers in the Legal Profession**	**3/19/21 2p**	**3/19/21 4p**	**Careers**	**Southeast Campus**

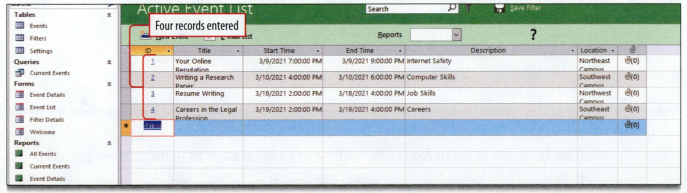

FIGURE 1.44

Access 2016, Windows 10, Microsoft Corporation

7 In the object window, click **Close** X to close the **Event List** form. Close « the Navigation Pane.

MOS
2.3.4

Activity 1.20 | Appending Records by Importing from an Excel Spreadsheet

In this Activity, you will append records to the table storing the data that displays in the Events List form. You will import the records from an Excel spreadsheet.

1 On the ribbon, click the **External Data tab**. In the **Import & Link group**, click **Excel**.

2 In the **Get External Data – Excel Spreadsheet** dialog box, click **Browse**. Navigate to the location where your student data files are stored, and then double-click **a01B_Workshops**.

3 Click the second option button—**Append a copy of the records to the table**—and then click **OK**. If a security message displays, click Open.

> The table that stores the data is named *Events*. Recall that other objects, such as forms, queries, and reports, display data from tables; so the Event Details form displays data that is stored in the Events table.

4 In the **Import Spreadsheet Wizard**, click **Next**, and then click **Finish**. In the **Get External Data – Excel Spreadsheet** dialog box, click **Close**.

5 **Open** » the **Navigation Pane**. Double-click **Event List** to open the form that displays data from the Events table, and then **Close** « the **Navigation Pane**. Compare your screen with Figure 1.45.

> A total of 12 records display; you entered four records, and you appended eight records from the a01B_Workshops Excel workbook. The data displays truncated in several fields because the columns are not wide enough to display all of the data.

FIGURE 1.45

6 To the left of the **ID** field name, click **Select All** ▢ to select all of the columns and rows.

7 In the field names row, point to the right edge of any of the selected columns to display the ✛ pointer, and then double-click to apply Best Fit to all of the columns. Click in any field to cancel the selection, and then **Save** 🖫 the form.

GO! Learn How
Video A1-7

MOS
1.3.4

Use the Navigation Pane to open objects, organize database objects, and perform common tasks, such as renaming an object or deleting an object.

Activity 1.21 | Grouping Database Objects in the Navigation Pane

The Navigation Pane groups and displays your database objects and can do so in predefined arrangements. In this Activity, you will group your database objects using the *Tables and Related Views* category, which groups objects by the table to which the objects are related. This grouping is useful because you can determine easily the table that is the data source of queries, forms, and reports.

1 **Open** » the **Navigation Pane**. At the top of the **Navigation Pane**, click **All Access Objects** arrow ⊙. On the list, under **Navigate To Category**, click **Tables and Related Views**. Compare your screen with Figure 1.46.

In the Navigation Pane, you can see the number of objects that are included in the Desktop Events Management template, including the table named *Events*. Other objects in the database that display data from the Events table include one query, two forms, and five reports. In the Navigation Pane, the Event List form is selected because it is open in the object window and is the active object.

Other objects might display on the Navigation Pane; for example, Filters and Unrelated Objects. These filters are objects created for use by the Desktop Event management template.

FIGURE 1.46

2 In the **Navigation Pane**, point to **Events: Table**, right-click, and then click **Open** to display the records in the underlying table.

The Events table is the active object in the object window. Use the Navigation Pane to open objects for use. The 12 records that display in the Event List multiple-items form are stored in this table. Recall that tables are the foundation of your database because your data must be stored in a table. You can enter records directly into a table or you can use a form to enter records.

↻ ANOTHER WAY   Double-click the table name to open it in the object window.

3 In the object window, click the **Event List tab** to display the form as the active object in the object window.

Recall that a form presents a more user-friendly screen for entering records into a table.

4 In the **Navigation Pane**, double-click the **Current Events** *report* (green icon) to open the report. Compare your screen with Figure 1.47.

> An advantage of using a template to create a database is that many objects, such as reports, are already designed for you.

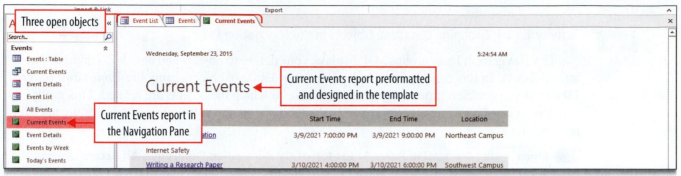

Access 2016, Windows 10, Microsoft Corporation

FIGURE 1.47

5 In the object window, **Close** ☒ the **Current Events** report.

6 By double-clicking or right-clicking, from the **Navigation Pane**, open the **Events by Week** report.

> In this predesigned report, the events are displayed by week. After entering records in the form or table, the preformatted reports are updated with the records from the table.

7 In the object window, right-click any one of the **object tabs**, and then click **Close All** to close all of the objects. **Close** ☒ the **Navigation Pane**.

Objective 8 | Create a New Table in a Database Created with a Template

GO! Learn How
Video A1-8

The Desktop Event management template included only one table—the *Events* table. It is easy to start a database with a template, and then you can add additional objects as needed.

Activity 1.22 | Using the Table Tool to Create a New Table

2.1.1, 2.1.5

Dr. Yong has information about the various locations where workshops are held. For example, on the Northeast Campus, she has information about the room, seating arrangements, number of seats, and multimedia equipment. In the Events table, workshops are scheduled in rooms at each of the four campuses. It would not make sense to store information about the campus rooms multiple times in the same table. It is *not* considered good database design to have duplicate information in a table.

When data becomes redundant, it is usually an indication that you need a new table to contain that information. In this Activity, you will create a table to track the workshop locations, the equipment, and the seating arrangements in each location.

1 On the ribbon, click the **Create tab**, and then in the **Tables group**, click **Table**.

2 In the field names row, click **Click to Add**, click **Short Text**, type **Campus/Location** and then press Enter.

3 In the third column, click **Short Text**, type **Room** and then press Enter. In the fourth column, click **Number**, type **Seats** and then press Enter.

> The *Number data type* describes numbers that represent a quantity and may be used in calculations. For the Seats field, you may need to determine how many seats remain after reservations are booked for a room. In the new record row, a *0* displays in the field.

4 In the fifth column, type **t** to select *Short Text*, type **Room Arrangement** and then press Enter. In the sixth column, type **t** and then type **Equipment** On your keyboard, press ↓.

> With the data type list displayed, you can select the data type by either clicking it or typing the letter that is underscored for the data type.

> This table has six fields. Access automatically creates the first field in the table—the ID field—to ensure that every record has a unique value. Before naming each field, you must define the data type for the field.

5 Right-click the **ID** field name, and then click **Rename Field**. Type **Room ID** and then press Enter. On the **Fields tab**, in the **Formatting group**, click the **Data Type arrow**, and then click **Short Text**. On the ribbon, in the **Field Validation group**, notice that **Unique** is selected.

> Recall that, by default, Access creates the ID field with the AutoNumber data type so that the field can be used as the primary key. Here, this field will store a unique room ID that is a combination of letters, symbols, and numbers; therefore, it is appropriate to change the data type to Short Text. In Datasheet view, the primary key field is identified by the selection of the Unique check box.

More Knowledge | **Create a Table from a Template with Application Parts**

To create a table using the Application Parts gallery, click the Create tab, and in the Templates group click Application Parts. Under Quick Start, click Comments. In the Create Relationship dialog box, specify a relationship between the Comments table and an associated table, and click Next to choose the lookup column, and then click Create to create the table. If you choose No relationship, click Create to create the table. The Comments table displays in the Navigation Pane.

2.3.2

Activity 1.23 | Entering Records Into a New Table

1 In the new record row, click in the **Room ID** field. Enter the following record, pressing Enter or Tab to move from one field to the next. Do not be concerned that all of your text does not display; you will adjust the column widths later. After entering the record, compare your screen with Figure 1.48.

> Recall that Access saves a record when you move to another row within the table. You can press either Enter or Tab to move between fields in a table.

Room ID	Campus/Location	Room	Seats	Room Arrangement	Equipment
NE-01	**Northeast Campus**	**H265**	**150**	**Theater**	**Computer Projector, Surround Sound, Microphone**

Access 2016, Windows 10, Microsoft Corporation

FIGURE 1.48

2 In the **Views group**, click the top of the **View** button to switch to **Design** view. In the **Save As** dialog box, in the **Table Name** box, using your own name, type **Lastname Firstname 1B Workshop Locations** and then click **OK**.

> Recall that when you switch views or when you close a table, Access prompts you to save the table if you have not previously saved it.

ANOTHER WAY   On the right side of the status bar, click Design View ⬚ to switch to Design view.

3 In the **Field Name** column, to the left of **Room ID**, notice the key icon.

In Design view, the key icon indicates that the field—Room ID—is the primary key field.

4 In the **Views group**, click the top of the **View** button to switch back to **Datasheet** view.

ANOTHER WAY   On the right side of the status bar, click Datasheet View ⬚ to switch to Datasheet view.

5 In the new record row, click in the **Room ID** field. Enter the following records, pressing [Enter] or [Tab] to move from one field to the next.

Room ID	Campus/Location	Room	Seats	Room Arrangement	Equipment
SW-01	Southwest Campus	A15	35	Lecture Classroom	Computer Projector
NW-01	Northwest Campus	C202	50	Lecture Classroom	Smart Board
SE-01	Southeast Campus	D148	20	U-shaped	White Board
NE-02	Northeast Campus	B105	25	U-shaped	25 Computers, Projector

6 To the left of the **Room ID** field name, click **Select All** ⬚ to select all of the columns and rows in the table. On the **Home tab**, in the **Records group,** click **More,** and then click **Field Width.** In the **Column Width** dialog box, click **Best Fit** to display all of the data in each column. Click in any field to cancel the selection, and then **Save** 🖫 the changes to the table. In the object window, **Close** ⨉ your **1B Workshop Locations** table.

7 **Open** » the **Navigation Pane,** and notice that your new table displays in its own group. Point to the right edge of the **Navigation Pane** to display the ⟷ pointer. Drag to the right to increase the width of the **Navigation Pane** so that your entire table name displays. Compare your screen with Figure 1.49.

Recall that organizing the Navigation Pane by Tables and Related Views groups the objects by each table and displays the related objects under each table name.

FIGURE 1.49

1.5.1

Recall that one advantage to starting a new database with a template, instead of from a blank database, is that many report objects are already created for you.

Activity 1.24 | Viewing Reports and Printing a Report

1 ▶ In the **Navigation Pane**, double-click the report (not the form) name **Event Details** to open it in the object window.

This prebuilt Event Details report displays in an attractively arranged format.

2 ▶ **Close** ☒ the **Event Details** report. Open the **All Events** report, and then **Close** ⟪ the **Navigation Pane**. On the **Home** tab, in the **Views group**, click the top of the **View** button to switch to **Layout** view.

Recall that Layout view enables you to make changes to an object while viewing the data in the fields. Each prebuilt report displays the records in the table in different useful formats.

> **↻ ANOTHER WAY** On the right side of the status bar, click Layout View 🔲 to switch to Layout view.

3 ▶ At the top of the report, click the title—*All Events*—to display a colored border around the title. Click to the left of the letter *A* to place the insertion point there. Using your own name, type **Lastname Firstname 1B** and then press [Spacebar]. Press [Enter], and then **Save** 🔲 the report.

Including your name in the title will help you and your instructor identify any submitted work.

4 ▶ On right side of the status bar, click **Print Preview** 🔲. In the navigation area, notice that the navigation arrows are unavailable, an indication that this report will print on one page.

> **↻ ANOTHER WAY** On the Home tab, in the Views group, click the View arrow, and then click Print Preview. Or, on the File tab, click Print, and then click Print Preview. Or, right-click the object tab, and then click Print Preview.

5 ▶ Create a paper printout or PDF electronic image as instructed. Click **Close Print Preview**, and then **Close** ☒ the report, saving any changes. This is the first of two objects printed in this project.

1.5.2

Activity 1.25 | Printing a Table

When printing a table, use the Print Preview command to determine if the table will print on one page or if you need to adjust column widths, margins, or page orientation. Recall that there will be occasions when you print a table for a quick reference or for proofreading. For a more professional-looking format, create and print a report.

1 ▶ **Open** ⟫ the **Navigation Pane**, double-click your **1B Workshop Locations** table to open it in the object window, and then **Close** ⟪ the **Navigation Pane**.

2 ▶ On the ribbon, click the **File tab**, click **Print**, and then click **Print Preview**.

The table displays how it will look when printed. Generally, tables are not printed, so there is no Print Preview option on the View button or on the status bar.

The navigation area displays *1* in the Pages box, and the navigation arrows to the right of the box are active, an indication that the table will print on more than one page.

3 ▶ In the navigation area, click **Next Page** ▶.

The second page of the table displays the last field. Whenever possible, try to print all of the fields horizontally on one page. Of course, if there are many records, more than one page may be needed to print all of the records and all of the fields.

4 On the **Print Preview tab**, in the **Page Layout group**, click **Landscape**, and then compare your screen with Figure 1.50. In landscape orientation, notice that the entire table will print on one page—all of the navigation buttons are unavailable.

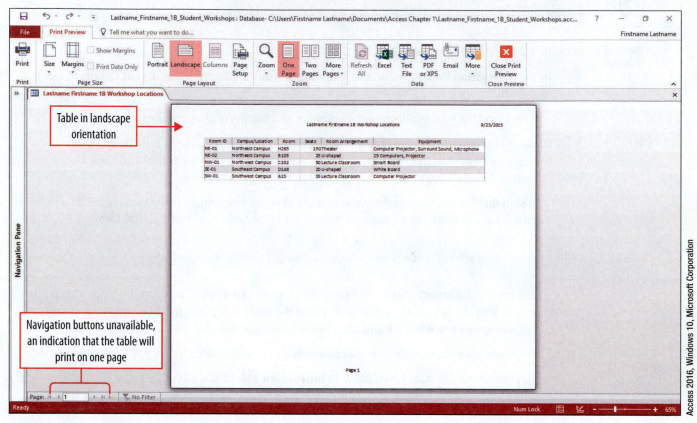

Table in landscape orientation

Navigation buttons unavailable, an indication that the table will print on one page

Access 2016, Windows 10, Microsoft Corporation

FIGURE 1.50

5 Create a paper printout or PDF electronic image as instructed, and then click **Close Print Preview**. This is the second or last object printed in this project.

6 **Close** ☒ your **1B Workshop Locations** table. For the convenience of the next individual opening the database, **Open** ⟫ the **Navigation Pane**.

7 On the right side of the title bar, click **Close** ☒ to close the database and to close Access. As directed by your instructor, submit your database and the paper printout or PDF electronic images of the two objects—one report and one table—that are the results of this project.

> **END | You have completed Project 1B**

GO! With Google

Objective	Export an Access Table to a Word Document, Save to Google Drive, Add a Record, and Save to Your Computer

Access web apps are designed to work with Microsoft's SharePoint, a service for setting up websites to share and manage documents. Your college may not have SharePoint installed, so you will use other tools to share objects from your database so that you can work collaboratively with others. Recall that Google Drive is Google's free, web-based word processor, spreadsheet, slide show, form, and data storage and sharing service. For Access, you can export a database object to an Excel worksheet, a PDF file, or a text file, and then save the file to Google Drive.

> **ALERT!** **Working with Web-Based Applications and Services**
>
> Computer programs and services on the web receive continuous updates and improvements. Therefore, the steps to complete this web-based activity may differ from the ones shown. You can often look at the screens and the information presented to determine how to complete the activity.
>
> If you do not already have a Google account, you will need to create one before you begin this activity. Go to http://google.com and, in the upper right corner, click Sign In. On the Sign In screen, click Create Account. On the Create your Google Account page, complete the form, read and agree to the Terms of Service and Privacy Policy, and then click Next step. On the Welcome screen, click Get Started.

Activity | Exporting an Access Table to a Word Document, Saving the Document to Google Drive, Adding a Record in Google Drive, and Saving to Your Computer

In this Activity, you will export your 1B Workshop Locations table to a Word document, upload your Word file to Google Drive as a Google Doc, add a record in Google Drive, and then download a copy of the edited document to your computer.

1 Start Access, navigate to your **Access Chapter 1** folder, and then **Open** your **1B_Student_Workshops** database file. If necessary, on the Message Bar, click **Enable Content**, and then **Close** the **Event List** form. In the **Navigation Pane**, click your **1B Workshop Locations** table to select it—do not open it.

2 On the ribbon, click the **External Data tab**. In the **Export group**, click **More**, and then click **Word**. In the **Export – RTF File** dialog box, click **Browse**, and then navigate to your **Access Chapter 1** folder. In the **File Save** dialog box, click in the **File name** box, using your own name, type **Lastname_Firstname_a1B_Web** and then click **Save**.

3 In the **Export – RTF File** dialog box, under **Specify export options**, select the second check box—**Open the destination file after the export operation is complete**—and then click **OK**. Take a moment to examine the data in the file, and then **Close** Word. In the **Export – RTF File** dialog box, click **Close**, and then **Close** Access.

Notice that the table is too wide to display fully with Portrait orientation

4 Open your browser software, navigate to **http://drive.google.com**, and sign in to your Google account. On the right side of the screen, click **Settings** ⚙, and then click **Settings**. In the **Settings** dialog box, to the right of *Convert uploads*, if necessary, select the **Convert uploaded files to Google Docs editor format** check box. In the upper right, click **Done**.

It is necessary to select this setting; otherwise, your document will upload as a pdf file and cannot be edited without further action.

5 Open your **GO! Web Projects** folder—or create and then open this folder by clicking **NEW** and then clicking **New folder**. On the left, click **NEW**, and then click **File upload**. In the **Choose File to Upload** dialog box, navigate to your **Access Chapter 1** folder, and then double-click your **a1B_Web** Word file to upload it to Google Drive. When the title bar of the message box indicates *Upload complete*, **Close** the message box.

6 Double-click your **a1B_Web** file to open the file in Google Docs. Notice that the table is not fully displayed on the page.

(GO! With Google continues on the next page)

GO! With Google

7 ▶ Click **File** to display a menu, and then click **Page setup**. In the **Page setup** dialog box, under **Orientation**, click **Landscape**. Click **OK**.

The table displays fully with Landscape orientation.

8 ▶ Click in the last cell in the table, and press ⌨Tab. Add the following record, and compare with Figure A

Field	Room ID	Campus/Location	Room	Seats	Room Arrangement	Equipment
	SE-02	**Southeast Campus**	**D120**	**20**	**Testing Lab**	**20 Computers**

FIGURE A

9 ▶ On the menu, click **File**, point to **Download as**, and then click **Microsoft Word (.docx)**. In the message box—usually displays at the bottom of your screen—click the **Save arrow**, and then click **Save as**. In the **Save As** dialog box, navigate to your **Access Chapter 1** folder, click in the **File name** box, and type **Lastname_Firstname_a1B_Web_Download** and then click **Save**. **Close** the message box.

10 ▶ In Google Drive, at the upper right corner of your screen, click your user name, and then click **Sign out**. **Close** your browser window.

11 ▶ Start Word. In the Word opening screen, click **Open**. Under **Open**, click **Browse**. Navigate to your **Access Chapter 1** folder, and then double-click your **a1B_Web** Word file. Notice that this file is the original

file—the new record is not entered. If you are required to print your documents, use one of the methods in the following Note. **Close** your Word file; and, if prompted, save the changes to your document. Then **Open** and print your **a1B_Web_Download** Word file using one of the methods in the following Note. **Close** Word; and, if prompted, save the changes to your document. As directed by your instructor, submit your two documents and the two paper printouts or PDF electronic images that are the results of this project.

NOTE Adding the File Name to the Footer and Printing or Creating a PDF Electronic Image

Click the Insert tab. In the Header & Footer group, click Footer, and then click Blank. With Type here selected, in the Insert group, click Document Info, and then click File Name. Close the Footer window. Click the Layout tab. In the Page Setup group, click Orientation, and then click Landscape.

To print on paper, click File, and then click Print. To create a pdf electronic image of your printout, click File, and then click Export. Under Export, be sure Create PDF/XPS Document is selected, and then click Create PDF/XPS. Navigate to your Access Chapter 1 folder, and then click Publish to save the file with the default name and an extension of pdf.

GO! To Work

MICROSOFT OFFICE SPECIALIST (MOS) SKILLS IN THIS CHAPTER	
PROJECT 1A	**PROJECT 1B**
1.1.1 Create a blank desktop database	**1.1.2** Create a database from a template
1.3.5 Change views of objects	**1.3.4** Display objects in the Navigation Pane
1.5.1 Print reports	**1.5.1** Print reports
1.5.2 Print records	**1.5.2** Print records
2.1.1 Create a table	**2.1.1** Create a table
2.1.2 Import data into tables	**2.1.5** Create a table from a template with application parts
2.2.3 Add table descriptions	**2.3.1** Update records
2.3.2 Add records	**2.3.4** Append records from external data
2.3.4 Append records from external data	
2.4.1 Add fields to tables	
2.4.3 Change field captions	
2.4.4 Change field sizes	
2.4.5 Change field data types	
2.4.6 Configure fields to auto-increment	
2.4.9 Delete fields	
3.1.1 Run a query	
4.1.1 Create a form	
4.1.3 Save a form	
5.1.1 Create a report based on a query or table	

BUILD YOUR E-PORTFOLIO

An E-Portfolio is a collection of evidence, stored electronically, that showcases what you have accomplished while completing your education. Collecting and then sharing your work products with potential employers reflects your academic and career goals. Your completed documents from the following projects are good examples to show what you have learned: 1G, 1K, and 1L.

GO! FOR JOB SUCCESS

Video: Goal Setting

Your instructor may assign this video to your class, and then ask you to think about, or discuss with your classmates, these questions:

FotoIEdhar / Fotolia

Is there anything you would change about Theo's behavior at his performance evaluation? Why or why not?

SMART goals are goals that are specific, measurable, achievable, realistic, and time-frame specific. Is Theo's first goal of beating his sales numbers by 10 percent next year a SMART goal?

How important do you think it is to set career development goals for yourself? Why?

END OF CHAPTER

SUMMARY

Principles of good database design, also known as normalization, help ensure that the data in your database is accurate and organized in a way that you can retrieve information that is useful.

You can create a database from scratch by using the blank desktop database template or a custom web app or by using a template that contains prebuilt tables, queries, forms, reports, and other objects.

Tables are the foundation of a database, but before entering records in a table, you must define the data type and name the field. Common data types are Short Text, Number, Currency, and Date/Time.

Use forms to enter data into a table or view the data in a table. Use queries to retrieve information from tables. Reports display information from tables in a professional-looking format.

GO! LEARN IT ONLINE

Review the concepts and key terms in this chapter by completing these online challenges, which you can find at **MyITLab**.

Matching and Multiple Choice: Answer matching and multiple-choice questions to test what you learned in this chapter.

Lessons on the GO!: Learn how to use all the new apps and features as they are introduced by Microsoft.

MOS Prep Quiz: Answer questions to review the MOS skills that you have practiced in this chapter.

GO! COLLABORATIVE TEAM PROJECT (Available in **MyITLab** and Instructor Resource Center)

If your instructor assigns this project to your class, you can expect to work with one or more of your classmates—either in person or by using Internet tools—to create work products similar to those that you created in this chapter. A team is a group of workers who work together to solve a problem, make a decision, or create a work product. Collaboration is when you work together with others as a team in an intellectual endeavor to complete a shared task or achieve a shared goal.

REVIEW AND ASSESSMENT GUIDE FOR ACCESS CHAPTER 1

Your instructor will assign Projects from this list to ensure your learning and assess your knowledge.

	REVIEW AND ASSESSMENT GUIDE FOR ACCESS CHAPTER 1		
Project	**Apply Skills from These Chapter Objectives**	**Project Type**	**Project Location**
1A **MyITLab**	Objectives 1–5 from Project 1A	**1A Instructional Project (Grader Project)** Guided instruction to learn the skills in Project A.	In MyITLab and in text
1B **MyITLab**	Objectives 6–9 from Project 1B	**1B Instructional Project (Grader Project)** Guided instruction to learn the skills in Project A.	In MyITLab and in text
1C	Objectives 1–5 from Project 1A	**1C Chapter Review (Scorecard Grading)** A guided review of the skills from Project 1A.	In text
1D	Objectives 6–9 from Project 1B	**1D Chapter Review (Scorecard Grading** A guided review of the skills from Project 1B.	In text
1E **MyITLab**	Objectives 1–5 from Project 1A	**1E Mastery (Grader Project)** **Mastery and Transfer of Learning** A demonstration of your mastery of the skills in Project 1A with extensive decision making.	In MyITLab and in text
1F **MyITLab**	Objectives 6–9 from Project 1B	**1F Mastery (Grader Project)** **Mastery and Transfer of Learning** A demonstration of your mastery of the skills in Project 1B with extensive decision making.	In MyITLab and in text
1G **MyITLab**	Combination of Objectives from Projects 1A and 1B	**1G Mastery (Grader Project)** **Mastery and Transfer of Learning** A demonstration of your mastery of the skills in Projects 1A and 1B with extensive decision making.	In MyITLab and in text
1H	Combination of Objectives from Projects 1A and 1B	**1H GO! Fix It** **Critical Thinking** A demonstration of your mastery of the skills in Projects 1A and 1B by creating a correct result from a document that contains errors you must find.	Instructor Resource Center (IRC) and MyITLab
1I	Combination of Objectives from Projects 1A and 1B	**1I GO! Make It** **Critical Thinking** A demonstration of your mastery of the skills in Projects 1A and 1B by creating a result from a supplied picture.	IRC and MyITLab
1J	Combination of Objectives from Projects 1A and 1B	**1J GO! Solve It** **Critical Thinking** A demonstration of your mastery of the skills in Projects 1A and 1B, your decision-making skills, and your critical-thinking skills. A task-specific rubric helps you self-assess your result.	IRC and MyITLab
1K	Combination of Objectives from Projects 1A and 1B	**1K GO! Solve It** **Critical Thinking** A demonstration of your mastery of the skills in Projects 1A and 1B, your decision-making skills, and your critical thinking skills. A task-specific rubric helps you self-assess your result.	In text
1L	Combination of Objectives from Projects 1A and 1B	**1L GO! Think** **Critical Thinking** A demonstration of your understanding of the Chapter concepts applied in a manner that you would outside of college. An analytic rubric helps you and your instructor grade the quality of your work by comparing it to the work an expert in the discipline would create.	In text
1M	Combination of Objectives from Projects 1A and 1B	**1M GO! Think** **Critical Thinking** A demonstration of your understanding of the Chapter concepts applied in a manner that you would outside of college. An analytic rubric helps you and your instructor grade the quality of your work by comparing it to the work an expert in the discipline would create.	IRC and MyITLab
1N	Combination of Objectives from Projects 1A and 1B	**1N You and GO!** **Critical Thinking** A demonstration of your understanding of the Chapter concepts applied in a manner that you would in a personal situation. An analytic rubric helps you and your instructor grade the quality of your work.	IRC and MyITLab
1O	Combination of Objectives from Project 1A and 1B	**1O Collaborative Team Project for ACCESS Chapter 1 Critical Thinking** A demonstration of your understanding of concepts and your ability to work collaboratively in a group role-playing assessment, requiring both collaboration and self-management.	IRC and MyITLab

GLOSSARY

GLOSSARY OF CHAPTER KEY TERMS

Append To add on to the end of an object; for example, to add records to the end of an existing table.

AutoNumber data type A data type that describes a unique sequential or random number assigned by Access as each record is entered and that is useful for data that has no distinct field that can be considered unique.

Best Fit An Access command that adjusts the width of a column to accommodate the column's longest entry.

Blank desktop database A database that has no data and has no database tools—you must create the data and tools as you need them; the database is stored on your computer or other storage device.

Caption A property setting that displays a name for a field in a table, query, form, or report different from the one listed as the field name.

Common field A field included in two or more tables that stores the same data.

Currency data type An Access data type that describes monetary values and numeric data that can be used in mathematical calculations involving values with one to four decimal places.

Custom web app A database that you can publish and share with others over the Internet.

Data Facts about people, events, things, or ideas.

Data source The table or tables from which a query, form, or report gathers its data.

Data type Classification identifying the kind of data that can be stored in a field, such as numbers, text, or dates.

Database An organized collection of facts about people, events, things, or ideas related to a specific topic or purpose.

Database management system (DBMS) Database software that controls how related collections of data are stored, organized, retrieved, and secured; also known as a DBMS.

Database template A preformatted database that contains prebuilt tables, queries, forms, and reports that perform a specific task, such as tracking events.

Datasheet view The Access view that displays data organized in columns and rows similar to an Excel worksheet.

DBMS An acronym for database management system.

Design view An Access view that displays the detailed structure of a table, query, form, or report. For forms and reports, may be the view in which some tasks must be performed, and only the controls, and not the data, display in this view.

Destination table The table to which you import or append data.

Export The process of copying data from one file into another file, such as an Access table into an Excel spreadsheet.

Field A single piece of information that is stored in every record; represented by a column in a database table.

Field properties Characteristics of a field that control how the field displays and how data can be entered in the field; vary for different data types.

First principle of good database design A principle of good database design stating that data is organized in tables so that there is no redundant data.

Flat database A simple database file that is not related or linked to any other collection of data.

Form An Access object you can use to enter new records into a table, edit or delete existing records in a table, or display existing records.

Form view The Access view in which you can view records, but you cannot change the layout or design of the form.

Import The process of copying data from another file, such as a Word table or an Excel workbook, into a separate file, such as an Access database.

Information Data that is accurate, timely, and organized in a useful manner.

Layout view The Access view in which you can make changes to a form or report while the data from the underlying data source displays.

Link A connection to data in another file.

Multiple-items form A form that enables you to display or enter multiple records in a table.

Navigation area An area at the bottom of the Access window that indicates the number of records in the table and contains controls in the form of arrows that you click to move among the records.

Navigation Pane An area of the Access window that displays and organizes the names of the objects in a database; from here, you open objects for use.

Normalization The process of applying design rules and principles to ensure that your database performs as expected.

Number data type An Access data type that represents a quantity, how much or how many, and may be used in calculations.

Object tab In the object window, a tab that identifies the object and which enables you to make an open object active.

Object window An area of the Access window that displays open objects, such as tables, queries, forms, or reports; by default, each object displays on its own tab.

Objects The basic parts of a database that you create to store your data and to work with your data; for example, tables, queries, forms, and reports.

Populate The action of filling a database table with records.

Primary key A required field that uniquely identifies a record in a table; for example, a Student ID number at a college.

Property Sheet A list of characteristics—properties—for fields or controls on a form or report in which you can make precise changes to each property associated with the field or control.

Query A database object that retrieves specific data from one or more database objects—either tables or other queries—and then, in a single datasheet, displays only the data you specify.

Record All of the categories of data pertaining to one person, place, event, thing, or idea; represented by a row in a database table.

Record selector bar The bar at the left edge of a record when it is displayed in a form, and which is used to select an entire record.

Record selector box The small box at the left of a record in Datasheet view that, when clicked, selects the entire record.

Redundant In a database, information that is duplicated in a manner that indicates poor database design.

Relational database A sophisticated type of database that has multiple collections of data within the file that are related to one another.

Report A database object that summarizes the fields and records from a table or query in an easy-to-read format suitable for printing.

Run The process in which Access searches the records in the table(s) included in the query design, finds the records that match the specified criteria, and then displays the records in a datasheet; only the fields that have been included in the query design display.

Second principle of good database design A principle stating that appropriate database techniques are used to ensure the accuracy and consistency of data as it is entered into the table.

Select query A type of Access query that retrieves (selects) data from one or more tables or queries, displaying the selected data in a datasheet; also known as a simple select query.

SharePoint A Microsoft application used for setting up websites to share and manage documents.

Short Text data type An Access data type that describes text, a combination of text and numbers, or numbers that are not used in calculations, such as the Postal Code.

Simple select query Another name for a select query.

Single-record form A form that enables you to display or enter one record at a time from a table.

Source file When importing a file, refers to the file being imported.

Structure In Access, the underlying design of a table, including field names, data types, descriptions, and field properties.

Table A format for information that organizes and presents text and data in columns and rows; the foundation of a database.

Tables and Related Views An arrangement in the Navigation Pane that groups objects by the table to which they are related.

Truncated Data that is cut off or shortened because the field or column is not wide enough to display all of the data or the field size is too small to contain all of the data.

Wizard A feature in Microsoft Office that walks you step by step through a process.

Apply **1A** skills from these Objectives:

1 Identify Good Database Design

2 Create a Table and Define Fields in a Blank Desktop Database

3 Change the Structure of Tables and Add a Second Table

4 Create a Query, Form, and Report

5 Close a Database and Exit Access

Skills Review **Project 1C College Administrators**

In the following Skills Review, you will create a database to store information about the administrators of Texas Lakes Community College and their departments. Your completed database objects will look similar to Figure 1.51.

PROJECT FILES

For Project 1C, you will need the following files:

Blank desktop database

a01C_Administrators (Excel workbook)

a01C_Departments (Excel workbook)

You will save your database as:

Lastname_Firstname_1C_College_Administrators

PROJECT RESULTS

Build From Scratch

FIGURE 1.51

Access 2016, Windows 10, Microsoft Corporation

(Project 1C College Administrators continues on the next page)

Skills Review Project 1C College Administrators (continued)

1 Start Access. In the Access opening screen, click **Blank desktop database**. In the **Blank desktop database** dialog box, to the right of the **File Name** box, click **Browse**. In the **File New Database** dialog box, navigate to your **Access Chapter 1** folder. In the **File New Database** dialog box, click in the **File name** box, type **Lastname_ Firstname_1C_College_Administrators** and then press Enter. In the **Blank desktop database** dialog box, click **Create**.

a. **Close** the **Navigation Pane**. In the field names row, click in the text *Click to Add*, and then click **Short Text**. Type **Title** and then press Enter.

b. In the third field name box, click **Short Text**, type **Last Name** and then press Enter. In the fourth field name box, click **Short Text**, type **First Name** and then press Enter. Create the remaining fields shown in **Table 1**, pressing Enter after the last field name. All of the data is typed on one line.

c. If necessary, scroll to bring the first column into view, and then click the **ID** field name. On the **Fields**

tab, in the **Properties group**, click **Name & Caption**. In the **Name** box, change *ID* to **Employee ID** and then click **OK**. On the ribbon, in the **Formatting group**, click the **Data Type arrow**, and then click **Short Text**.

d. In the new record row, click in the **Employee ID** field, type **ADM-9200** and press Enter. In the **Title** field, type **Vice President** and press Enter. Continue entering data in the fields shown in **Table 2**, pressing Enter or Tab to move to the next field and to the next row.

e. On the Quick Access Toolbar, click **Save**. In the **Save As** dialog box, in the **Table Name** box, using your own name, replace the selected text by typing **Lastname Firstname 1C Administrators** and then click **OK**.

f. In the new record row, enter the data for two college administrators shown in Table 3, pressing Enter or Tab to move from field to field and to the next row.

TABLE 1

Data Type		Short Text	Short Text	Short Text	Short Text	Short Text	Short Text	Short Text	Short Text	Short Text	Short Text	Currency
Field Name	ID	Title	Last Name	First Name	Middle Initial	Address	City	State	Postal Code	Phone Number	Department ID	Salary

(Return to Step 1c)

TABLE 2

Last Name	First Name	Middle Initial	Address	City	State	Postal Code	Phone Number	Department ID	Salary
Shaffer	Lonnie	J	489 Ben Ave	Austin	TX	78734	(512) 555-6185	AS	123500

(Return to Step 1e)

TABLE 3

Employee ID	Title	Last Name	First Name	Middle Initial	Address	City	State	Postal Code	Phone Number	Department ID	Salary
ADM-9201	Associate Vice President	Holtz	Diann	S	8416 Spencer Ln	Georgetown	TX	78627	(512) 555-1069	AS	101524
ADM-9202	Director, Enrollment Services	Fitchette	Sean	H	3245 Deer Trl	Spicewood	TX	78669	(512) 555-9012	SS	45070

(Return to Step 1g)

(Project 1C College Administrators continues on the next page)

g. **Close** your **1C Administrators** table. On the **External Data tab**, in the **Import & Link group**, click **Excel**. In the **Get External Data – Excel Spreadsheet** dialog box, click **Browse**. In the **File Open** dialog box, navigate to your student data files, and then double-click the **a01C_Administrators** Excel file.

h. Click the **Append a copy of the records to the table** option button, and then click **OK**. In the **Import Spreadsheet Wizard**, click **Next**, and then click **Finish**. In the **Get External Data – Excel Spreadsheet** dialog box, click **Close**.

i. **Open** the Navigation Pane. Resize the Navigation Pane so that the entire table name displays. In the **Navigation Pane**, double-click your **1C Administrators** table to open it, and then **Close** the Navigation Pane—there are 30 records in this table.

2 Click the **Home tab**, and then in the **Views group**, click the top of the **View** button to switch to **Design** view. In the **Field Name** column, to the left of **Middle Initial**, click the row selector box to select the entire row. On the **Design tab**, in the **Tools group**, click **Delete Rows**. In the message box, click **Yes**.

a. Click in the **Employee ID** field name box. Under **Field Properties**, click **Field Size** to select the existing text. Type **8** and then in the **Employee ID** field row, click in the **Description** box. Type **Eight-character Employee ID** and then press Enter.

b. Click in the **State** field name box. In the **Field Properties** area, click **Field Size**, and then type **2** In the **State Description** box, type **Two-character state abbreviation** and then press Enter.

c. **Save** the design changes to your table, and in the message box, click **Yes**. On the **Design tab**, in the **Views group**, click the top of the **View** button to switch to **Datasheet** view.

d. On the ribbon, click the **External Data tab**, and then in the **Import & Link group**, click **Excel**. In the **Get External Data – Excel Spreadsheet** dialog box, to the right of the **File name** box, click **Browse**. In the **File Open** dialog box, navigate to your student data files, and then double-click **a01C_Departments**. Be sure that the **Import the source data into a new table in the current database** option button is selected, and then click **OK**.

e. In the upper left corner of the wizard, select the **First Row Contains Column Headings** check box, and then click **Next**. Click **Next** again. Click the **Choose my own primary key** option button, be sure that **Department ID** displays, and then click **Next**. In the **Import to Table** box, type **Lastname Firstname 1C Departments** and then click **Finish**. In the **Get External Data – Excel Spreadsheet** dialog box, click **Close**.

f. **Open** the Navigation Pane, double-click your **1C Departments** table, and then **Close** the Navigation Pane. There are 12 records in your **1C Departments** table.

g. To the left of the **Department** field name, click **Select All**. On the ribbon, click the **Home tab**, and in the **Records group**, click **More**, and then click **Field Width**. In the **Column Width** dialog box, click **Best Fit**. Click in any field to cancel the selection, and then **Save** your table. In the object window, click the **object tab** for your **1C Administrators** table. Using the techniques you just practiced, apply **Best Fit** to the columns, cancel the selection, and then **Save** the table.

h. With your **1C Administrators** table displayed, on the ribbon, click the **File tab**, click **Print**, and then click **Print Preview**. On the **Print Preview tab**, in the **Page Layout group**, click **Landscape**. Create a paper printout or PDF electronic image as directed by your instructor—two pages result. On the ribbon, click **Close Print Preview**, and then **Close** your **1C Administrators** table.

i. With your **1C Departments** table displayed, view the table in **Print Preview**. Change the orientation to **Landscape**, and then create a paper printout or PDF electronic image as directed by your instructor—one page results. Click **Close Print Preview**, and then **Close** your **1C Departments** table.

3 On the ribbon, click the **Create tab**, and then in the **Queries group**, click **Query Wizard**. In the **New Query** dialog box, be sure **Simple Query Wizard** is selected, and then click **OK**. In the wizard, click the **Tables/Queries arrow**, and then click your **Table: 1C Administrators**.

a. Under **Available Fields**, click **Last Name**, and then click **Add Field** to move the field to the **Selected Fields** list on the right. Double-click the **First Name** field to move it to the **Selected Fields** list. By using **Add Field** or by double-clicking the field name, add

(Project 1C College Administrators continues on the next page)

the following fields to the **Selected Fields** list in the order specified: **Title**, **Department ID**, and **Phone Number**. This query will answer the question, *What is the last name, first name, title, Department ID, and phone number of every administrator?*

b. In the wizard, click **Next**. Click in the **What title do you want for your query?** box. Using your own name, edit as necessary so that the query name is **Lastname Firstname 1C All Administrators Query** and then click **Finish**. If necessary, apply Best Fit to the columns, and then Save the query. Display the query in **Print Preview**, and then create a paper printout or PDF electronic image as directed—one page results. Click **Close Print Preview**, and then **Close** the query.

c. **Open** the **Navigation Pane**, right-click your **1C Administrators** table, and then click **Open** to display the table in the object window. **Close** the **Navigation Pane**. Notice that the table has 11 fields. On the ribbon, click the **Create tab**, and in the **Forms group**, click **Form**. On the Quick Access Toolbar, click **Save**. In the **Save As** dialog box, click in the **Form Name** box, edit to name the form **Lastname Firstname 1C Administrator Form** and then click **OK**.

d. In the navigation area, click **Last Record**, and then click **Previous Record** two times to display the record for *Diann Holtz*. By using the instructions in Activity 1.15, print or create a PDF electronic image of only this record on one page. **Close** the form object, saving it if prompted. Your **1C Administrators** table object remains open.

e. **Open** the **Navigation Pane**, open your **1C Departments** table by double-clicking the table name or by right-clicking the table name and clicking Open. **Close** the **Navigation Pane**. On the **Create tab**, in the **Reports group**, click **Report**.

f. Click the **Department ID** field name, and then on the ribbon, under **Report Layout Tools**, click the **Arrange tab**. In the **Rows & Columns group**, click **Select Column**, and then press Del. Using the same technique, delete the **Department Email** field.

g. Click the **Department Phone** field name. Hold down Shift, and then click the **Suite Number** field name to select the last three field names. In the **Rows & Columns group**, click **Select Column**. On the ribbon, click the **Design tab**, and then in the **Tools group**, click **Property Sheet**. In the **Property Sheet**, on the **Format tab**, click **Width**, type **1.5** and then press Enter. **Close** the **Property Sheet**.

h. Click the **Department Name** field name. On the ribbon, click the **Home tab.** In the **Sort & Filter group**, click **Ascending** to sort the report in alphabetic order by *Department Name*. At the bottom of the report, on the right side, click **Page 1 of 1**, and then press Del.

i. **Save** the report as **Lastname Firstname 1C Departments Report** and then click **OK**. Display the report in **Print Preview**, and then create a paper printout or PDF electronic image of the report as directed. Click **Close Print Preview**. In the object window, right-click any **object tab**, and then click **Close All** to close all open objects, leaving the object window empty.

4 **Open** the **Navigation Pane**. If necessary, increase the width of the Navigation Pane so that all object names display fully. On the right side of the title bar, click **Close** to close the database and to close Access. As directed by your instructor, submit your database and the paper printouts or PDF electronic images of the five objects—two tables, one query, one form, and one report—that are the results of this project. Specifically, in this project, using your own name, you created the following database and printouts or PDF electronic images:

1. Lastname_Firstname_1C_College_Administrators	Database file
2. Lastname Firstname 1C Administrators	Table
3. Lastname Firstname 1C Departments	Table
4. Lastname Firstname 1C All Administrators Query	Query
5. Lastname Firstname 1C Administrator Form	Form
6. Lastname Firstname 1C Departments Report	Report

END | You have completed Project 1C

Skills Review   Project 1D Certification Events

Apply **1B** skills from these Objectives:

6 Use a Template to Create a Database

7 Organize Objects in the Navigation Pane

8 Create a New Table in a Database Created with a Template

9 Print a Report and a Table

In the following Skills Review, you will create a database to store information about certification test preparation events at Texas Lakes Community College. Your completed report and table will look similar to Figure 1.52.

PROJECT FILES

For Project 1D, you will need the following files:

Desktop event management template
a01D_Certification_Events (Excel workbook)

You will save your database as:

Lastname_Firstname_1D_Certification_Events

PROJECT RESULTS

Build From Scratch

Lastname Firstname 1D All Events   Tuesday, July 28, 2015   12:49:58 AM

Title	Start Time	End Time	Location
Word 2016	7/9/2021 10:00:00 AM	7/9/2021 4:00:00 PM	Southwest Campus
Office 2016			
Excel 2016	7/16/2021 10:00:00 AM	7/16/2021 4:00:00 PM	Northeast Campus
Office 2016			
Access 2016	7/23/2021 12:00:00 PM	7/23/2021 6:00:00 PM	Southeast Campus
Office 2016			
PowerPoint 2016	7/30/2021 9:00:00 AM	7/30/2016 3:00:00 PM	Northwest Campus
Office 2016			
Word 2016	8/5/2021 10:00:00 AM	8/5/2021 4:00:00 PM	Southeast Campus
Office 2016			
Windows Server	8/6/2021 8:00:00 AM	8/6/2021 2:00:00 PM	Northeast Campus
Networking			
Excel 2016	8/12/2021 3:00:00 PM	8/12/2021 9:00:00 PM	Southeast Campus
Office 2016			
Windows 10	8/13/2021 10:00:00 AM	8/13/2021 4:00:00 PM	Southwest Campus
Networking			
Access 2016	8/19/2021 9:00:00 AM	8/19/2021 3:00:00 PM	Northeast Campus
Office 2016			
A+	8/19/2021 12:00:00 PM	8/19/2021 6:00:00 PM	Southwest Campus
Networking			
PowerPoint 2016	8/26/2021 1:00:00 PM	8/26/2021 7:00:00 PM	Northwest Campus
Office 2016			
Network+	8/26/2021 9:00:00 AM	8/26/2021 3:00:00 PM	Northwest Campus
Networking			

Page 1 of 1

Lastname Firstname 1D Cert Prep Locations   6/1/2015

Lab ID	Campus Location	Lab	# Computers	Additional Equipment
NE-L01	Northeast Campus	F32	40	4 printers, smart board, instructor touch screen
NW-L01	Northwest Campus	H202	35	3 printers, DVD player
SE-L01	Southeast Campus	E145	25	Projector, document camera, smart board
SE-L02	Southeast Campus	A225	25	Projector, white board, instructor touch screen
SW-L01	Southwest Campus	G332	30	Projector, 4 digital display

Page 1

Access 2016, Windows 10, Microsoft Corporation

FIGURE 1.52

(Project 1D Certification Events continues on the next page)

1 Start Access. In the Access opening screen, click in the **Search** box, type **event** and then press Enter to search for a template to manage events. Click the **Desktop event management** template. In the **Desktop event management** dialog box, to the right of the **File Name** box, click **Browse**, and then navigate to your **Access Chapter 1** folder. In the **File New Database** dialog box, click in the **File name** box to select the existing text. Using your own name, type **Lastname_Firstname_1D_ Certification_Events** and then press Enter. In the **Desktop event management** dialog box, click **Create** to download the template and to save the database. Under the ribbon, on the **Message Bar**, click **Enable Content**.

a. In the first row, click in the **Title** field, type **Word 2016** and then press Tab. In the **Start Time** field, type **7/9/21 10a** and then press Tab. In the **End Time** field, type **7/9/21 4p** and then press Tab. In the **Description** field, type **Office 2016** and then press Tab. In the **Location** field, type **Southwest Campus** and then press Tab three times to move to the **Title** field in the new record row.

b. In the form, directly above the field names row, click **New Event** to open the **Event Details** single-record form. Using Tab to move from field to field, enter the record shown in Table 1. Press Tab three times to move from the **End Time** field to the **Description** field.

c. In the **Events Detail** form, click **Close**. Using either the **Event List** multiple-items form or the **Event Details** single-record form, enter the records shown in Table 2. If you use the Events Detail form, be sure to Close it after entering records to display the records in the Event List form.

d. **Close** the **Event List** form. On the ribbon, click the **External Data tab**, and in the **Import & Link group**, click **Excel**. In the **Get External Data – Excel Spreadsheet** dialog box, click **Browse**. Navigate to your student data files, and then double-click **a01D_Certification_Events**. Click the second option button—**Append a copy of the records to the table**—and then click **OK**.

e. In the **Import Spreadsheet Wizard**, click **Next**, and then click **Finish**. In the **Get External Data – Excel Spreadsheet** dialog box, click **Close**. **Open** the **Navigation Pane**, and then double-click **Event List** to open the form that displays data stored in the Events table—12 total records display. **Close** the **Navigation Pane**.

f. To the left of the **ID** field name, click **Select All**. In the field names row, point to the right edge of any of the selected columns to display the ✛ pointer, and then double-click to apply Best Fit to all of the columns. Click in any field to cancel the selection, and then **Save** the form.

2 Open the **Navigation Pane**. At the top of the Navigation Pane, click **More**. On the list, under **Navigate To Category**, click **Tables and Related Views**.

a. In the **Navigation Pane**, point to **Events: Table**, right-click, and then click **Open** to display the records in the underlying table. In the **Navigation Pane**, double-click the **Current Events** *report* (green icon) to view this predesigned report. From the **Navigation Pane**, open the **Events by Week** report to view this predesigned report.

TABLE 1

Title	Location	Start Time	End Time	Description
Excel 2016	**Northeast Campus**	**7/16/21 10a**	**7/16/21 4p**	**Office 2016**

→ (Return to Step 1c)

TABLE 2

ID	Title	Start Time	End Time	Description	Location
3	**Access 2016**	**7/23/21 12p**	**7/23/21 6p**	**Office 2016**	**Southeast Campus**
4	**PowerPoint 2016**	**7/30/21 9a**	**7/30/21 3p**	**Office 2016**	**Northwest Campus**

→ (Return to Step 1d)

(Project 1D Certification Events continues on the next page)

Skills Review | **Project 1D Certification Events** (continued)

b. In the object window, right-click any of the **object tabs**, and then click **Close All**. **Close** the **Navigation Pane**.

3 On the ribbon, click the **Create tab**, and in the **Tables group**, click **Table**.

a. In the field names row, click **Click to Add**, click **Short Text**, type **Campus Location** and then press Enter. In the third column, click **Short Text**, type **Lab** and then press Enter. In the fourth column, click **Number**, type **# Computers** and then press Enter. In the fifth column, click **Short Text**, type **Additional Equipment** and then press ↓.

b. Right-click the **ID** field name, and then click **Rename Field**. Type **Lab ID** and then press Enter. On the **Fields tab**, in the **Formatting group**, click the **Data Type arrow**, and then click **Short Text**.

c. In the new record row, click in the **Lab ID** field, and then enter the records shown in Table 3, pressing Enter or Tab to move from one field to the next.

d. In the **Views group**, click the upper portion of the **View** button to switch to **Design** view. In the **Save As** dialog box, in the **Table Name** box, using your own name, type **Lastname Firstname 1D Cert Prep Locations** and then click **OK**. Notice that the **Lab ID** field is the **Primary Key**. On the **Design tab**, in the **Views group**, click the upper portion of the **View** button to switch to **Datasheet** view.

e. To the left of the **Lab ID** field name, click **Select All** to select all of the columns and rows in the table. On the **Home tab**, in the **Records group**, click **More**, and then click **Field Width**. In the **Column Width** dialog box, click **Best Fit**. Click

in any field to cancel the selection, and then **Save** the changes to the table. **Close** the table, and then **Open** the **Navigation Pane**. Increase the width of the **Navigation Pane** so that your entire table name displays.

4 In the **Navigation Pane**, double-click the **All Events** report to open it in the object window. **Close** the **Navigation Pane**. On the **Home tab**, in the **Views group**, click the top of the **View** button to switch to **Layout** view. At the top of the report, click the title—*All Events*—to display a colored border around the title. Click to the left of the letter *A* to place the insertion point there. Using your own name, type **Lastname Firstname 1D** and then press Spacebar. Press Enter, and then **Save** the report.

a. On the right side of the status bar, click **Print Preview**, and notice that the report will print on one page. Create a paper printout or PDF electronic image as instructed. Click **Close Print Preview**, and then **Close** the report.

b. **Open** the **Navigation Pane**, double-click your **1D Cert Prep Locations** table, and then **Close** the **Navigation Pane**. On the ribbon, click the **File tab**, click **Print**, and then click **Print Preview**. On the **Print Preview tab**, in the **Page Layout group**, click **Landscape**. Create a paper printout or PDF electronic image as directed, and then click **Close Print Preview**. Close your **1D Cert Prep Locations** table.

c. **Open** the **Navigation Pane**. On the right side of the title bar, click **Close** to close the database and to close Access. As directed by your instructor,

TABLE 3

Lab ID	Campus Location	Lab	# Computers	Additional Equipment
NW-L01	Northwest Campus	H202	35	3 printers, DVD player
SE-L01	Southeast Campus	E145	25	Projector, document camera, smart board
NE-L01	Northeast Campus	F32	40	4 printers, smart board, instructor touch screen
SW-L01	Southwest Campus	G332	30	Projector, 4 digital display
SE-L02	Southeast Campus	A225	25	Projector, white board, instructor touch screen

(Return to Step 3d)

(Project 1D Certification Events continues on the next page)

submit your database and the paper printouts or PDF electronic images of the two objects—one report and one table—that are the results of this project.

Specifically, in this project, using your own name, you created the following database and printouts or PDF electronic images:

1. Lastname_Firstname_1D_Certification_Events	Database file
2. Lastname Firstname 1D Cert Prep Locations	Table
3. Lastname Firstname 1D All Events	Report

END | You have completed Project 1D

Mastering Access Project 1E Kiosk Inventory

In the following Mastering Access project, you will create a database to track information about the inventory of items for sale in the kiosk located in the Snack Bar at the Southeast Campus of Texas Lakes Community College. Your completed database objects will look similar to Figure 1.53.

PROJECT FILES

For Project 1E, you will need the following files:

Blank desktop database

a01E_Inventory (Excel workbook)

a01E_Inventory_Storage (Excel workbook)

You will save your database as:

Lastname_Firstname_1E_Kiosk_Inventory

PROJECT RESULTS

Build From Scratch

Access 2016, Windows 10, Microsoft Corporation

FIGURE 1.53

(Project 1E Kiosk Inventory continues on the next page)

1 Start Access. Create a **Blank desktop database** in your **Access Chapter 1** folder. Name the database **Lastname_Firstname_1E_Kiosk_Inventory** and then **Close** the **Navigation Pane**. Create the fields shown in **Table 1**.

2 For the **ID** field, change the **Data Type** to **Short Text**, rename the field to **Item ID** and then enter the records shown in **Table 2**.

3 Save the table as **Lastname Firstname 1E Inventory** and then **Close** the table. From your student data files, import and then **Append** the data in the Excel file **a01E_ Inventory** to your **1E Inventory** table. After importing, open your **1E Inventory** table—17 records display.

4 In **Design** view, delete the **Campus** field, which is redundant data. For the **Category** field, change the **Field Size** to **25** and enter a **Description** of **Enter the category of the item** For the **Item ID** field, change the **Field Size** to **10** and then **Save** the changes to your table. Switch to **Datasheet** view, apply **Best Fit** to all of the fields in the table, and then **Save** your changes. Display the table in **Print Preview**, change the orientation to **Landscape**, and then create a paper printout or PDF electronic image as directed by your instructor. **Close Print Preview**, and then **Close** the table.

5 From your student data files, import the **Excel** file **a01E_Inventory_Storage** into the database as a new table; designate the first row as column headings and the **Category** field as the primary key. In the wizard, name the table **Lastname Firstname 1E Inventory Storage** and then open your **1E Inventory Storage** table—five records display. In **Design** view, for the **Location Detail** field,

change the **Field Size** to **35** and enter a **Description** of **Room and bin number or alternate location of inventory item** Save the design changes, switch to **Datasheet** view, apply **Best Fit** to all of the fields, and then **Save** your changes. Display the table in **Print Preview**, create a paper printout or PDF electronic image as directed, **Close Print Preview**, and then **Close** the table.

6 Create a **Simple Query**, by using the **Query Wizard**, based on your **1E Inventory** table. Include only the three fields that will answer the question, *For all items, what is the storage location and quantity in stock?* In the wizard, accept the default name for the query. Display the query in **Print Preview**, create a paper printout or PDF electronic image as directed, **Close Print Preview**, and then **Close** the query.

7 Open your **1E Inventory** table, and then **Create** a **Form** for this table. **Save** the form as **Lastname Firstname 1E Inventory Form** and then display and select the fifth record. By using the instructions in Activity 1.15, create a paper printout or PDF electronic image of only this record on one page as directed by your instructor. **Close** the form object, saving changes if prompted.

8 With your **1E Inventory** table open, **Create** a **Report**. Delete the **Category** and **Price** fields, and then sort the **Item ID** field in **Ascending** order. Using the **Property Sheet**, for the **Item ID** field, change the **Width** to **0.75** and then for the **Storage Location** field, change the **Width** to **1.5** Scroll to display the bottom of the report, if necessary, and then delete the page number— **Page 1 of 1**. Save the report as **Lastname Firstname 1E**

TABLE 1

Data Type		Short Text	Short Text	Short Text	Short Text	Currency	Number
Field Name	ID	**Item**	**Category**	**Campus**	**Storage Location**	**Price**	**Quantity in Stock**

(Return to Step 2)

TABLE 2

Item ID	Item	Category	Campus	Storage Location	Price	Quantity in Stock
C-1	**Chocolate Bar**	**Candy**	**Southeast**	**SE100A**	.89	250
C-2	**Lollipop**	**Candy**	**Southeast**	**SE100A**	.5	500
T-1	T-shirt	**Clothing**	**Southeast**	**SE100B**	17.5	100

(Return to Step 3)

(Project 1E Kiosk Inventory continues on the next page)

Mastering Access | Project 1E Kiosk Inventory (continued)

Inventory Report and then display the report in **Print Preview**. Create a paper printout or PDF electronic image as directed. Click **Close Print Preview.**

9 ▶ **Close All** open objects. **Open** the **Navigation Pane** and be sure that all object names display fully. **Close** the database, and then **Close** Access. As directed by your instructor, submit your database and the paper printouts or PDF electronic images of the five objects—two tables, one query, one form, and one report—that are the results of this project. Specifically, in this project, using your own name, you created the following database and printouts or PDF electronic images:

1. Lastname_Firstname_1E_Kiosk_Inventory	Database file
2. Lastname Firstname 1E Inventory	Table
3. Lastname Firstname 1E Inventory Storage	Table
4. Lastname Firstname 1E Inventory Query	Query
5. Lastname Firstname 1E Inventory Form	Form
6. Lastname Firstname 1E Inventory Report	Report

END | You have completed Project 1E

MyITLab® grader

Mastering Access Project 1F Recruiting Events

Apply 1B skills from these Objectives:

6 Use a Template to Create a Database

7 Organize Objects in the Navigation Pane

8 Create a New Table in a Database Created with a Template

9 Print a Report and a Table

In the following Mastering Access project, you will create a database to store information about the recruiting events that are scheduled to attract new students to Texas Lakes Community College. Your completed report and tables will look similar to Figure 1.54.

PROJECT FILES

For Project 1F, you will need the following files:

Desktop event management template
a01F_Recruiting_Events (Excel workbook)

You will save your database as:

Lastname_Firstname_1F_Recruiting_Events

PROJECT RESULTS

Build From Scratch

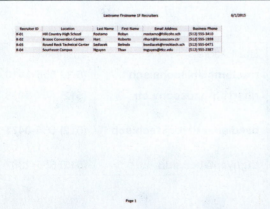

Access 2016, Windows 10, Microsoft Corporation

FIGURE 1.54

(Project 1F Recruiting Events continues on the next page)

Mastering Access   Project 1F Recruiting Events (continued)

1 Start Access. In the Access opening screen, search for **event** and then click the **Desktop event management** template. Save the database in your **Access Chapter 1** folder as **Lastname_Firstname_1F_Recruiting_Events** and on the **Message Bar**, click **Enable Content**.

2 In the **Event List** multiple-items form or the **Event Details** single-record form—open by clicking New Event on the Event List form—enter the records shown in Table 1.

3 Close the **Event List** form. From your student data files, import and **Append** the data from the **Excel** file **a01F_Recruiting_Events** to the **Events** table. **Open** the **Navigation Pane**, organize the objects by **Tables and Related Views**, and then open the **Events** table to display 13 records. **Close** the table, and then **Close** the **Navigation Pane**.

4 **Create** a new **Table** defining the new fields shown in Table 2.

5 For the **ID** field, change the **Data Type** to **Short Text**, rename the field to **Recruiter ID** and then enter the records shown in Table 3.

6 Apply **Best Fit** to all of the columns. **Save** the table as **Lastname Firstname 1F Recruiters** and then **Close** the table.

7 From the **Navigation Pane**, open the **Event Details** *report* (green icon). Switch to **Layout** view. In the report, click in the title—*Event Details*—and then click to position the insertion point to the left of the word *Event*. Using your own type, type **Lastname Firstname 1F** and then press Spacebar and Enter. If necessary, decrease the font size of the title so that the title does not overlap the date on the right side or does not extend to two lines.

TABLE 1

ID	Title	Start Time	End Time	Description	Location
1	Health Professions	6/1/21 8a	6/1/21 12p	Science Students	Hill Country High School
2	New Students	6/1/21 10a	6/1/21 3p	College Fair	Brazos Convention Center
3	Information Technology	6/2/21 9a	6/2/21 12p	Technical Students	Round Rock Technical Center
4	International Students	6/2/21 2p	6/2/21 5p	Open House	Southeast Campus

(Return to Step 3)

TABLE 2

Data Type		Short Text	Short Text	Short Text	Short Text	Short Text
Field Name	ID	Location	Last Name	First Name	Email Address	Business Phone

(Return to Step 5)

TABLE 3

Recruiter ID	Location	Last Name	First Name	Email Address	Business Phone
R-01	Hill Country High School	Rostamo	Robyn	rrostamo@hillcohs.sch	(512) 555-3410
R-02	Brazos Convention Center	Hart	Roberto	rlhart@brazosconv.ctr	(512) 555-1938
R-03	Round Rock Technical Center	Sedlacek	Belinda	bsedlacek@rrocktech.sch	(512) 555-0471
R-04	Southeast Campus	Nguyen	Thao	tnguyen@tlcc.edu	(512) 555-2387

(Return to Step 6)

(Project 1F Recruiting Events continues on the next page)

Mastering Access   Project 1F Recruiting Events (continued)

Save the report, and then display it in **Print Preview**. If directed to create a paper printout, in the **Print group**, click **Print**. In the **Print** dialog box, under **Print Range**, to the right of **Pages**, click in the **From** box, type **1** and then click in the **To** box and type **1** and then click **OK** to print only the first page. If directed to create a PDF electronic image, in the **Publish as PDF or XPS** dialog box, click **Options**, and then under **Range**, click the **Page(s)** option button, and then click **OK**. **Close Print Preview**, and then **Close** the report.

8 From the **Navigation Pane**, open the **Events** table, select all of the columns, and then apply **Best Fit** to all of the columns by double-clicking the right edge of any of the selected columns. Cancel the selection, and then **Save** the table. Display the table in **Print Preview**, change the orientation to **Landscape**, change the **Margins** to **Normal**, and then create a paper printout or PDF electronic image as directed. **Close Print Preview**, and then **Close** the table.

9 From the **Navigation Pane**, open your **1F Recruiters** table. Display the table in **Print Preview**, change the orientation to **Landscape**, and then create a paper printout or PDF electronic image as directed. **Close Print Preview**, and then **Close** the table.

10 Open the **Navigation Pane**, and be sure that all object names display fully. **Close** Access. As directed by your instructor, submit your database and the paper printouts or PDF electronic images of the three objects—one report and two tables—that are the results of this project. Specifically, in this project, using your own name, you created the following database and printouts or PDF electronic images:

1. Lastname_Firstname_1F_Recruiting_Events	Database file
2. Lastname Firstname 1F Event Details	Report
3. Lastname Firstname 1F Events	Table
4. Lastname Firstname 1F Recruiters	Table

END | You have completed Project 1F

Mastering Access | Project 1G College Construction

In the following Mastering Access project, you will create one database to store information about construction projects for Texas Lakes Community College and a second database to store information about the public events related to the construction projects. Your completed database objects will look similar to Figure 1.55.

Apply 1A and 1B skills from these Objectives:

1 Identify Good Database Design

2 Create a Table and Define Fields in a Blank Desktop Database

3 Change the Structure of Tables and Add a Second Table

4 Create a Query, Form, and Report

5 Close a Database and Exit Access

6 Use a Template to Create a Database

7 Organize Objects in the Navigation Pane

8 Create a New Table in a Database Created with a Template

9 Print a Report and a Table

> **NOTE** | Project 1G Differs from the MyITLab Project
>
> If you are completing this project in the MYITLab Grader system, your results will differ from the following project. In Grader, the steps are all completed in one database instead of two in the project below.

PROJECT FILES

For Project 1G, you will need the following files:

Blank desktop database
a01G_Projects (Excel workbook)
a01G_Contractors (Excel workbook)
Desktop event management template

You will save your databases as:

Lastname_Firstname_1G_College_Construction
Lastname_Firstname_1G_Public_Events

Build From
Scratch

PROJECT RESULTS

FIGURE 1.55

(Project 1G College Construction continues on the next page)

Access 2016, Windows 10, Microsoft Corporation

Mastering Access Project 1G College Construction (continued)

1 Start Access. Create a **Blank desktop database** in your **Access Chapter 1** folder. Name the database **Lastname_Firstname_1G_College_Construction** and then **Close** the **Navigation Pane**. Create the fields shown in **Table 1**.

2 For the **ID** field, change the **Data Type** to **Short Text**, rename the field to **Project ID** and then enter the three records shown in **Table 2**.

3 **Save** the table as **Lastname Firstname 1G Projects** and then **Close** the table. From your student data files, import and then **Append** the data in the **Excel** file **a01G_Projects** to your **1G Projects** table. After importing, open your **1G Projects** table—eight records display.

4 In **Design** view, for the **Project ID** field, change the **Field Size** to **5** and then enter a **Description** of **Enter the Project ID using the format P-###** Save the changes to your table. Switch to **Datasheet** view, apply **Best Fit** to all of the fields in the table, and then **Save** your changes. Display the table in **Print Preview**, change the orientation to **Landscape**, and then create a paper printout or PDF electronic image as directed by your instructor. **Close Print Preview**, and then **Close** the table.

5 From your student data files, import the **Excel** file **a01G_Contractors** into the database as a new table; designate the first row as column headings and the **ID** field as the primary key. In the wizard, name the table **Lastname Firstname 1G Contractors** and then open

your **1G Contractors** table—four records display. Apply **Best Fit** to all of the fields, and then **Save** your changes. Display the table in **Print Preview**, change the orientation to **Landscape**, and then create a paper printout or PDF electronic image as directed. **Close Print Preview**, and then **Close** the table.

6 **Create**, by using the **Query Wizard**, a **Simple Query** based on your **1G Projects** table. Include only the three fields that will answer the question, *For every site, what is the building project and the budget amount?* In the wizard, accept the default name for the query. Display the query in **Print Preview**, create a paper printout or PDF electronic image as directed, **Close Print Preview**, and then **Close** the query.

7 Open your **1G Projects** table, and then **Create** a **Form** for this table. **Save** the form as **Lastname Firstname 1G Project Form** and then display and select the seventh record. By using the instructions in Activity 1.15, create a paper printout or PDF electronic image of only this record on one page as directed by your instructor. **Close** the form object, saving changes if prompted.

8 With your **1G Projects** table open, **Create** a **Report**. Delete the **Budget Amount** field, and then sort the **Building Project** field in **Ascending** order. For the **Building Project**, **Site**, and **Contractor** fields, using the **Property Sheet**, change the **Width** of all three fields to **2** At the bottom of the report, delete the page

TABLE 1

Data Type		Short Text	Short Text	Short Text	Currency
Field Name	ID	**Building Project**	**Site**	**Contractor**	**Budget Amount**

(Return to Step 2)

TABLE 2

Project ID	Building Project	Site	Contractor	Budget Amount
P-356	**Student Center, 3-story**	**Northeast Campus**	**RR Construction**	**61450000**
P-823	**Student Center, 2-story**	**Southeast Campus**	**RR Construction**	**41960000**
P-157	**Health Professions Center**	**Northwest Campus**	**Marshall Ellis Construction**	**42630000**

(Return to Step 3)

(Project 1G College Construction continues on the next page)

number—**Page 1 of 1**. **Save** the report as **Lastname Firstname 1G Projects Report** and then display the report in **Print Preview**. Create a printout or PDF electronic image as directed. **Close Print Preview.**

9 ▶ **Close All** open objects. **Open** the **Navigation Pane**, arrange the objects by **Tables and Related Views**, and be sure that all object names display fully. **Close** the database, but do *not* close Access.

10 ▶ In the Access opening screen, search for **event** and then click the **Desktop Event management** template. Save the database in your **Access Chapter 1** folder as **Lastname_Firstname_1G_Public_Events** and on the **Message Bar**, click **Enable Content**.

11 ▶ In the **Event List** multiple-items form or the **Event Details** single-record form—open by clicking New Event on the Event List form—enter the three records shown in **Table 3**.

12 ▶ **Close** the **Event List** form. **Open** the **Navigation Pane**, organize the objects by **Tables and Related Views**,

and then open the **Current Events** *report* (green icon). Switch to **Layout** view. In the report, click in the title—*Current Events*—and then click to position the insertion point to the left of the letter *C*. Using your own name, type **Lastname Firstname 1G** and then press Spacebar and Enter. If necessary, decrease the font size of the title so that the title does not overlap the date on the right side or does not extend to two lines. **Save** the report, display it in **Print Preview**, and then create a paper printout or PDF electronic image as directed. **Close Print Preview**, and then **Close** the report.

13 ▶ Open the **Navigation Pane**, and be sure that all object names display fully. **Close** Access. As directed by your instructor, submit your database and the paper printouts or PDF electronic images of the six objects—two tables, one query, one form and two reports—that are the results of this project. Specifically, in this project, using your own name, you created the following database and printouts or PDF electronic images:

1. Lastname_Firstname_1G_College_Construction	Database file
2. Lastname_Firstname_1G_Public_Events	Database file
3. Lastname Firstname 1G Projects	Table
4. Lastname Firstname 1G Contractors	Table
5. Lastname Firstname 1G Projects Query	Query
6. Lastname Firstname 1G Project Form	Form
7. Lastname Firstname 1G Projects Report	Report
8. Lastname Firstname 1G Current Events	Report

TABLE 3

ID	Title	Start Time	End Time	Description	Location
1	Groundbreaking	6/13/21 10a	6/13/21 11a	Student Center groundbreaking	Northeast Campus
2	Dedication	8/26/21 12:30 p	8/26/21 2p	Gymnasium building dedication	Southwest Campus
3	Community Arts Expo	10/5/21 6p	10/5/21 9p	Book and Art Expo at Library	Southeast Campus

(Return to Step 12)

END | You have completed Project 1G

GO! Fix It	**Project 1H Scholarships**	**MyITLab**
GO! Make It	**Project 1I Theater Events**	**MyITLab**
GO! Solve It	**Project 1J Athletic Scholarships**	**MyITLab**
GO! Solve It	**Project 1K Student Activities**	

Apply a combination of the **1A** and **1B** skills.

 PROJECT FILES

Build From Scratch

For Project 1K, you will need the following files:

Desktop event management template
a01K_Student_Activities (Word document)

You will save your database as:

Lastname_Firstname_1K_Student_Activities

Use the Desktop event management template to create a database, and save it in your Access Chapter 1 folder as **Lastname_Firstname_1K_Student_Activities** From your student data files, use the information in the Word document a01K_Student_Activities to enter data into the Event List multiple-items form. Each event begins at 7 p.m. and ends at 10 p.m.

After entering the records, close the form, and arrange the Navigation Pane by Tables and Related Views. Open the Event Details *report*, and then add **Lastname Firstname 1K** to the beginning of the report title. If necessary, decrease the font size of the title so that it does not overlap the date and displays on one line. Create a paper printout or PDF electronic image as directed. As directed, submit your database and the paper printout or PDF electronic image that results.

Performance Level

Performance Criteria	Exemplary: You consistently applied the relevant skills	Proficient: You sometimes, but not always, applied the relevant skills	Developing: You rarely or never applied the relevant skills
Create database using Desktop event management template and enter data	Database created using the correct template, named correctly, and all data entered correctly.	Database created using the correct template, named correctly, but not all data entered correctly.	Database created using the correct template, but numerous errors in database name and data.
Modify report	Event Details report title includes name and project on one line.	Event Details report title includes name and project, but not on one line.	Event Details report title does not include name and project and does not display on one line.
Create report printout	Event Details report printout is correct.	Event Details printout is incorrect.	Event Details report printout not created.

END | You have completed Project 1K

RUBRIC

The following outcomes-based assessments are open-ended assessments. That is, there is no specific correct result; your result will depend on your approach to the information provided. Make Professional Quality your goal. Use the following scoring rubric to guide you in how to approach the problem and then to evaluate how well your approach solves the problem.

The *criteria*—Software Mastery, Content, Format & Layout, and Process—represent the knowledge and skills you have gained that you can apply to solving the problem. The *levels of performance*—Professional Quality, Approaching Professional Quality, or Needs Quality Improvements—help you and your instructor evaluate your result.

	Your completed project is of Professional Quality if you:	Your completed project is Approaching Professional Quality if you:	Your completed project Needs Quality Improvements if you:
1-Software Mastery	Choose and apply the most appropriate skills, tools, and features and identify efficient methods to solve the problem.	Choose and apply some appropriate skills, tools, and features, but not in the most efficient manner.	Choose inappropriate skills, tools, or features, or are inefficient in solving the problem.
2-Content	Construct a solution that is clear and well organized, contains content that is accurate, appropriate to the audience and purpose, and is complete. Provide a solution that contains no errors of spelling, grammar, or style.	Construct a solution in which some components are unclear, poorly organized, inconsistent, or incomplete. Misjudge the needs of the audience. Have some errors in spelling, grammar, or style, but the errors do not detract from comprehension.	Construct a solution that is unclear, incomplete, or poorly organized, contains some inaccurate or inappropriate content, and contains many errors of spelling, grammar, or style. Do not solve the problem.
3-Format and Layout	Format and arrange all elements to communicate information and ideas, clarify function, illustrate relationships, and indicate relative importance.	Apply appropriate format and layout features to some elements, but not others. Overuse features, causing minor distraction.	Apply format and layout that does not communicate information or ideas clearly. Do not use format and layout features to clarify function, illustrate relationships, or indicate relative importance. Use available features excessively, causing distraction.
4-Process	Use an organized approach that integrates planning, development, self-assessment, revision, and reflection.	Demonstrate an organized approach in some areas, but not others; or, use an insufficient process of organization throughout.	Do not use an organized approach to solve the problem.

Apply a combination of the **1A** and **1B** skills.

OUTCOMES-BASED ASSESSMENTS (CRITICAL THINKING)

GO! Think Project 1L Student Clubs

Build From Scratch

PROJECT FILES

For Project 1L, you will need the following files:

Blank desktop database
a01L_Clubs (Word document)
a01L_Student_Clubs (Excel workbook)
a01L_Club_Presidents (Excel workbook)

You will save your database as

Lastname_Firstname_1L_Student_Clubs

Dr. Daniel Martinez, Vice President of Student Services, needs a database that tracks information about student clubs. The database should contain two tables—one for club information and one for contact information for the club presidents.

Create a desktop database, and save the database in your Access Chapter 1 folder as **Lastname_Firstname_1L_Student_Clubs** From your student data files, use the information in the Word document a01L_Clubs to create the first table and to enter two records. Name the table appropriately to include your name and 1L, and then append the 23 records from the Excel workbook a01L_Student_Clubs to your table. For the Club ID and President ID fields, add a description and change the field size.

Create a second table in the database by importing 25 records from the Excel workbook a01L_Club_Presidents, and name the table appropriately to include your name and 1L. For the State and Postal Code fields, add a description and change the field size. Be sure that the field data types are correct—recall that numbers that are not used in calculations should have a data type of Short Text. Be sure all of the data and field names display in each table.

Create a simple query based on the Clubs table that answers the question, *What is the club name, meeting day, meeting time, campus, and Room ID for all of the clubs?* Create a form based on the Clubs table, saving it with an appropriate name that includes your name and 1L. Create a report based on the Presidents table, saving it with an appropriate name that includes your name and 1L, that displays the president's last name (in ascending order), the president's first name, and the phone number of every president. Change the width of the three fields so that there is less space between them, but being sure that each record prints on a single line.

Create paper printout or PDF electronic images of the two tables, the query, only Record 21 of the form, and the report as directed being sure that each object prints on one page. Organize the objects on the Navigation Pane by Tables and Related Views, and be sure that all object names display fully. As directed, submit your database and the paper printouts or PDF electronic images of the five objects—two tables, one query, one form, and one report—that are the results of this project.

END | You have completed Project 1L

GO! Think Project 1M Faculty Training **MyItLab**

Build From Scratch

You and GO! Project 1N Personal Contacts **MyItLab**

Build From Scratch

GO! Collaborative Team Project Project 1O Bell Orchid Hotels **MyItLab**

Introducing Microsoft PowerPoint 2016

Surpasspro/Fotolia

PowerPoint 2016: Introduction

Communication skills are critical to your success in a business career, and when it comes to communicating *your* ideas, presentation is everything! Whether you are planning to deliver your presentation in person or online—to a large audience or to a small group—Microsoft PowerPoint 2016 is a versatile business tool that will help you create presentations that make a lasting impression. Additionally, collaborating with others to develop a presentation is easy because you can share the slides you create by using your free Microsoft OneDrive cloud storage.

Microsoft PowerPoint 2016 includes a variety of themes that you can apply to a new presentation. Each theme includes several theme variants that coordinate colors, fonts, and effects. The benefit of this approach is that the variations evoke different moods and responses, yet the basic design remains the same. As a result, you can use a similar design within your company to brand your presentations, while still changing the colors to make the presentation appropriate to the audience and topic. You do not have to determine which colors work well together in the theme you choose, because professional designers have already done that for you. So you can concentrate on how best to communicate your message. Focus on creating dynamic, interesting presentations that keep your audience engaged!

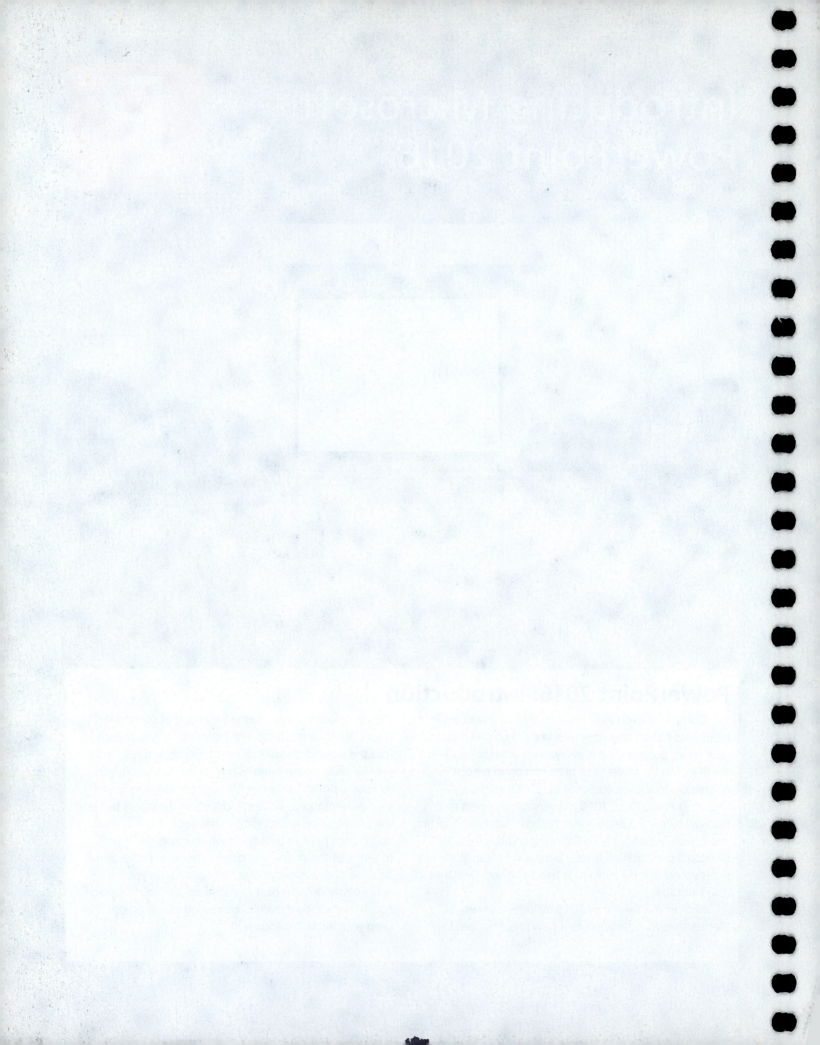

Getting Started with Microsoft PowerPoint

PROJECT 1A

OUTCOMES
Create a company overview presentation.

OBJECTIVES
1. Create a New Presentation
2. Edit a Presentation in Normal View
3. Add Pictures to a Presentation
4. Print and View a Presentation

PROJECT 1B

OUTCOMES
Create a new product announcement presentation.

OBJECTIVES
5. Edit an Existing Presentation
6. Format a Presentation
7. Use Slide Sorter View
8. Apply Slide Transitions

Jeff McGraw/Fotolia

In This Chapter

GO! to Work with PowerPoint

In this chapter, you will study presentation skills, which are among the most important skills you will learn. Good presentation skills enhance your communications—written, electronic, and interpersonal. In this technology-enhanced world, communicating ideas clearly and concisely is a critical personal skill. Microsoft PowerPoint 2016 is presentation software with which you create electronic slide presentations. Use PowerPoint to present information to your audience effectively. You can start with a new, blank presentation and add content, pictures, and themes, or you can collaborate with colleagues by inserting slides that have been saved in other presentations.

The projects in this chapter relate to **Kodiak West Travel**, which is a travel agency with offices in Juneau, Anchorage, and Victoria. Kodiak West Travel works closely with local vendors to provide clients with specialized adventure travel itineraries. The company was established in 2001 in Juneau and built a loyal client base that led to the expansion into Anchorage and Victoria. As a full-service travel agency, Kodiak West Travel agents strive to provide their clients with travel opportunities that exceed their expectations. The company works with all major airlines, cruise lines, hotel chains, and vehicle rental companies as well as with small, specialized, boutique hotels.

PROJECT ACTIVITIES

In Activities 1.01 through 1.16, you will create the first five slides of a new presentation that Kodiak West Travel tour manager Ken Dakano is developing to introduce the tour services that the company offers. Your completed presentation will look similar to Figure 1.1.

PROJECT FILES

 If your instructor wants you to submit Project 1A in the MyITLab Grader system, log in to MyITLab, locate Grader Project1A, and then download the files for this project.

For Project 1A, you will need the following files:

New blank PowerPoint presentation
p01A_Glacier
p01A_Bay

You will save your presentation as:

Lastname_Firstname_1A_KWT_Overview

PROJECT RESULTS

Build From
Scratch

GO!
Walk Thru
Project 1A

PowerPoint 2016, Windows 10, Microsoft Corporation

FIGURE 1.1 Project 1A KWT Overview

NOTE	If You Are Using a Touchscreen
Tap an item to click it.	
Press and hold for a few seconds to right-click; release when the information or command displays.	
Touch the screen with two or more fingers and then pinch together to zoom out or stretch your fingers apart to zoom in.	
Slide your finger on the screen to scroll—slide left to scroll right and slide right to scroll left.	
Slide to rearrange—similar to dragging with a mouse.	
Swipe to select—slide an item a short distance with a quick movement—to select an item and bring up commands, if any.	

Objective 1 | Create a New Presentation

GO! Learn How
Video P1-1

Microsoft PowerPoint 2016 is software you can use to present information to your audience effectively. You can edit and format a blank presentation by adding text, a presentation theme, and pictures. When you start PowerPoint, presentations you have recently opened, if any, display on the left. On the right you can select either a blank presentation or a *theme*—a set of unified design elements that provides a look for your presentation by applying colors, fonts, and effects. A presentation consists of one or more slides. Similar to a page in a document—a presentation *slide* can contain text, pictures, tables, charts, and other multimedia or graphic objects.

Activity 1.01 | Identifying Parts of the PowerPoint Window

> **ALERT!** **To submit as an autograded project, log into MyITLab, download the files for this project, and begin with those files instead of a new blank presentation.**

1.1.1

In this Activity, you will start PowerPoint and identify the parts of the PowerPoint window.

1 Start PowerPoint. On the right, click **Facet** to view a preview of the Facet theme and the color variations associated with this theme. Below the theme preview, click either the left- or right-pointing **More Images** ◀ and ▶ arrows to view how various types of slides in this theme display. To the right of the preview, click each of the color variations. After you have viewed each color, click the original green color.

2 On either the left or right side of the preview window, notice the arrow, and then compare your screen with Figure 1.2.

You can use the arrows to the left and right of the preview window to scroll through the available themes.

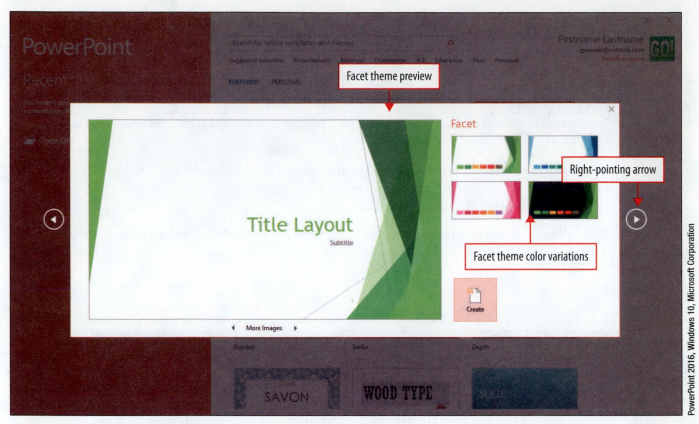

Facet theme preview

Right-pointing arrow

Facet theme color variations

Title Layout

Subtitle

Create

More Images

PowerPoint 2016, Windows 10, Microsoft Corporation

FIGURE 1.2

3 Click the right- or left-pointing arrow several times to view other available themes, and then return to the **Facet** theme. In the lower right area of the preview window, click **Create** to begin a new presentation using the **Facet** theme.

4 Compare your screen with Figure 1.3, and then take a moment to study the parts of the PowerPoint window described in the table in Figure 1.4.

The presentation displays in ***Normal view***, which is the primary editing view in PowerPoint where you write and design your presentations. On the left, a pane displays miniature images—***thumbnails***—of the slides in your presentation. On the right, the ***Slide pane*** displays a larger image of the active slide.

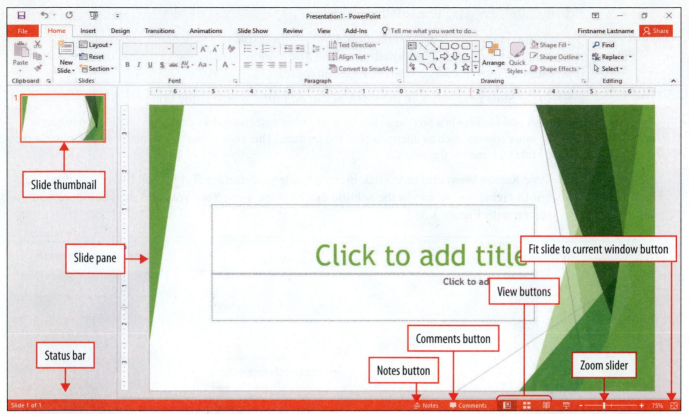

FIGURE 1.3

PowerPoint 2016, Windows 10, Microsoft Corporation

MICROSOFT POWERPOINT SCREEN ELEMENTS	
SCREEN ELEMENT	**DESCRIPTION**
Slide pane	Displays a large image of the active slide.
Slide thumbnails	Miniature images of each slide in the presentation. Clicking a slide thumbnail displays the slide in the Slide pane.
Status bar	Displays, in a horizontal bar at the bottom of the presentation window, the current slide number, number of slides in a presentation, Notes button, Comments button, View buttons, Zoom slider, and Fit slide to current window button; you can customize this area to include additional information.
Notes button	When clicked, displays an area below the Slide pane in which presentation notes can be typed.
Comments button	When clicked, displays a Comments pane to the right of the Slide pane, in which reviewers can type comments.
View buttons	Controls the look of the presentation window with a set of commands.
Zoom slider	Zooms the slide displayed in the Slide pane, in and out.
Fit slide to current window button	Fits the active slide to the maximum view in the Slide pane.

FIGURE 1.4

Activity 1.02 | Entering Presentation Text

When you create a new presentation, PowerPoint displays a new blank presentation with a single slide—a title slide in Normal view. The *title slide* is usually the first slide in a presentation; it provides an introduction to the presentation topic.

1 In the **Slide pane**, click in the text *Click to add title*, which is the title placeholder.

A *placeholder* is a box on a slide with dotted or dashed borders that holds title and body text or other content such as charts, tables, and pictures. This slide contains two placeholders, one for the title and one for the subtitle.

2 Type **Kodiak West** and then click in the subtitle placeholder. Type **Your Travel** and then press Enter to create a new line in the subtitle placeholder. Type **Your Way** and then compare your screen with Figure 1.5.

FIGURE 1.5

3 On the **Quick Access Toolbar**, click **Save** 🖫. Under **Save As**, click **Browse**. Navigate to the location where you are saving your files for this chapter, and then create and open a new folder named **PowerPoint Chapter 1** In the **File name** box, using your own name, replace the existing text with **Lastname_Firstname_1A_KWT_Overview** and then click **Save**.

Activity 1.03 | Applying a Presentation Theme

A theme is a set of unified design elements that provides a look for your presentation by applying colors, fonts, and effects. After you create a presentation, you can change the look of your presentation by applying a different theme. Kodiak West Travel wants a theme that evokes a feeling of nature.

1 On the ribbon, click the **Design tab**. In the **Themes group**, click **More** ⊽ to display the **Themes** gallery. Compare your screen with Figure 1.6.

The themes displayed on your system may differ from Figure 1.6.

FIGURE 1.6

PowerPoint 2016, Windows 10, Microsoft Corporation

2 ▸ Under **Office**, point to several of the themes and notice that a ScreenTip displays the name of each theme, and the Live Preview feature displays how each theme would look if applied to your presentation.

The first theme that displays is the Office Theme.

3 ▸ Use the ScreenTips to locate the **Organic** theme shown in Figure 1.7.

FIGURE 1.7

PowerPoint 2016, Windows 10, Microsoft Corporation

4 ▸ Click **Organic** to change the presentation theme and then **Save** 🖫 your presentation.

Objective 2   Edit a Presentation in Normal View

GO! Learn How
Video P1-2

Editing is the process of modifying a presentation by adding and deleting slides or by changing the contents of individual slides.

Activity 1.04 │ Inserting a New Slide

1.2.1

Your presentation consists of a single slide. You can insert additional slides in any order. If you have more than one slide, to insert a new slide in a presentation, display the slide that will come before the slide that you want to insert.

1 ▸ On the **Home tab**, in the **Slides group**, point to the **New Slide arrow**—the lower part of the New Slide button. Compare your screen with Figure 1.8.

The New Slide button is a ***split button***—a type of button in which clicking the main part of the button performs a command and clicking the arrow opens a menu, list, or gallery. The upper, main part of the New Slide button, when clicked, inserts a slide without displaying any options. The lower part—the New Slide arrow—when clicked, displays a gallery of slide *layouts*— the arrangement of elements, such as title and subtitle text, lists, pictures, tables, charts, shapes, and movies, on a slide.

FIGURE 1.8

PowerPoint 2016, Windows 10, Microsoft Corporation

2 ▸ In the **Slides group**, click the lower portion of the **New Slide** button—the **New Slide arrow**—to display the gallery, and then compare your screen with Figure 1.9.

FIGURE 1.9

3 ▸ In the gallery, click the **Panoramic Picture with Caption** layout to insert a new slide. Notice that the new blank slide displays in the **Slide pane**, and a slide thumbnail displays at the left. Compare your screen with Figure 1.10.

🔄 **BY TOUCH**   In the gallery, tap the desired layout to insert a new slide.

New Panoramic Picture with Caption slide displays

Slide thumbnail

PowerPoint 2016, Windows 10, Microsoft Corporation

FIGURE 1.10

4 On the new slide, below the picture placeholder, click the text *Click to add title*, and then type **Your Dreams**

5 Below the title placeholder, click in the text placeholder. Type **Whether you want to trek on a glacier or spend your time in quiet solitude, Kodiak West Travel can make your dream a reality.** Compare your screen with Figure 1.11.

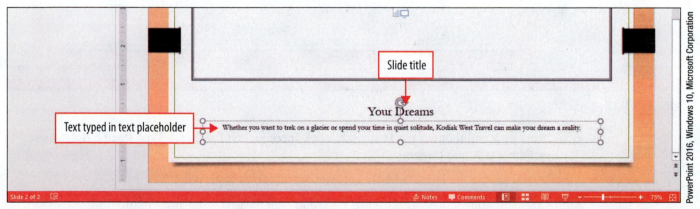

Slide title

Text typed in text placeholder

PowerPoint 2016, Windows 10, Microsoft Corporation

FIGURE 1.11

6 On the **Home tab**, in the **Slides group**, click the **New Slide arrow** to display the gallery, and then click **Title and Content**. In the title placeholder, type **Our Expertise** and then below the title placeholder, click in the content placeholder. Type **Over 20 years of experience in the travel industry**

7 **Save** 🖫 your presentation.

Activity 1.05 | Increasing and Decreasing List Levels

You can organize text in a PowerPoint presentation according to *list levels*. List levels, each represented by a bullet symbol, are similar to outline levels. On a slide, list levels are identified by the bullet style, indentation, and the size of the text. The first level on an individual slide is the title.

Increasing the list level of a bullet point increases its indent and results in a smaller text size. Decreasing the list level of a bullet point decreases its indent and results in a larger text size.

1 On **Slide 3**, if necessary, click at the end of the last bullet point after the word *industry*, and then press Enter to insert a new bullet point.

2 Press Tab, and then notice that the bullet is indented. Type **Certified Travel Associates**

By pressing Tab at the beginning of a bullet point, you can increase the list level and indent the bullet point.

3 Press Enter, and then notice that a new bullet point displays at the same level as the previous bullet point.

4 On the **Home tab**, in the **Paragraph group**, click **Decrease List Level** ⬜. Type **Specializing in land and sea travel** and then compare your screen with Figure 1.12.

The indent is removed and the size of the text increases.

FIGURE 1.12

5 Press Enter, and then on the **Home tab**, click **Increase List Level** ⬜. Type **Pacific Northwest including U.S. and Canada**

You can use the Increase List Level button to indent the bullet point.

6 Compare your screen with Figure 1.13, and then **Save** 💾 your presentation.

FIGURE 1.13

PowerPoint 2016, Windows 10, Microsoft Corporation

Activity 1.06 | Adding Speaker Notes to a Presentation

The **Notes pane** is an area of the Normal view window that displays below the Slide pane with space to type notes regarding the active slide. You can refer to these notes while making a presentation, reminding you of the important points that you want to discuss.

1 With **Slide 3** displayed, in the **Status bar**, click **Notes** ▇, and then notice that below the Slide pane, the Notes pane displays. Click in the **Notes pane**, and then type **Kodiak West Travel has locations in Juneau, Anchorage, and Victoria.**

2 Compare your screen with Figure 1.14, and then **Save** 🖫 your presentation.

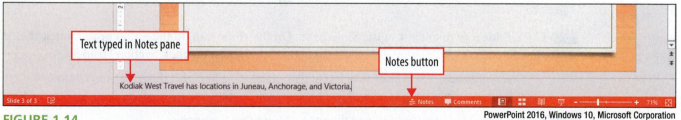

FIGURE 1.14

PowerPoint 2016, Windows 10, Microsoft Corporation

Activity 1.07 | Displaying and Editing Slides in the Slide Pane

1 At the left side of the PowerPoint window, look at the slide thumbnails, and then notice that the presentation contains three slides. At the right side of the PowerPoint window, in the vertical scroll bar, point to the scroll box, and then hold down the left mouse button to display a ScreenTip indicating the slide number and title.

2 Drag the scroll box up until the ScreenTip displays *Slide: 2 of 3 Your Dreams*. Compare your screen with Figure 1.15, and then release the mouse button to display **Slide 2**.

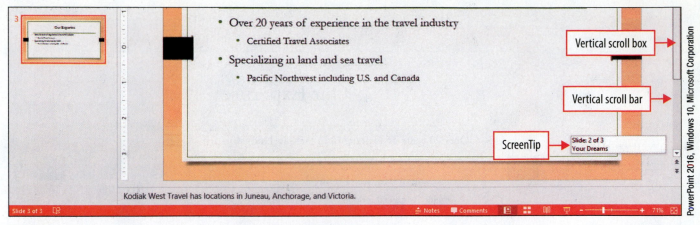

FIGURE 1.15

3 At the bottom of the slide, in the content placeholder, click at the end of the sentence, after the period. Press [Spacebar], and then type **If you can dream it, we can help you get there.**

4 On the left side of the PowerPoint window, in the slide thumbnails, point to **Slide 3**, and then notice that a ScreenTip displays the slide title. Compare your screen with Figure 1.16.

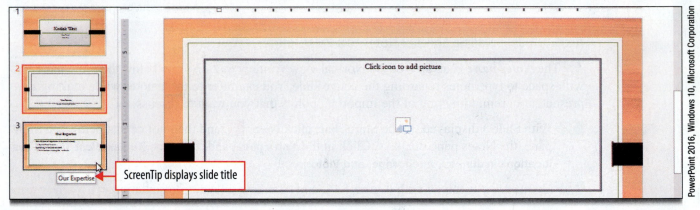

FIGURE 1.16

5 Click **Slide 3** to display it in the Slide pane. On the **Home tab**, in the **Slides group**, click the **New Slide arrow** to display the **Slide Layout** gallery, and then click **Section Header**.

A *section header* is a type of slide layout that changes the look and flow of a presentation by providing text placeholders that do not contain bullet points.

6 Click in the title placeholder, and then type **About Our Company**

7 Click in the content placeholder below the title, and then type **Kodiak West Travel was established in May of 2001 by Ken Dakona and Mariam Dorner, two Alaska residents whose sense of adventure and commitment to ecotourism is an inherent aspect of their travel itineraries.** Compare your screen with Figure 1.17.

The placeholder text is resized to fit within the placeholder. The AutoFit Options button displays.

FIGURE 1.17

PowerPoint 2016, Windows 10, Microsoft Corporation

8 ▸ Click **AutoFit Options** ⊞, review the AutoFit options, and then click outside the menu to close it.

The *AutoFit Text to Placeholder* option keeps the text contained within the placeholder by reducing the size of the text. The *Stop Fitting Text to This Placeholder* option turns off the AutoFit option so that the text can flow beyond the placeholder border; the text size remains unchanged. You can also choose to split the text between two slides, continue on a new slide, or divide the text into two columns.

9 ▸ In the slide thumbnails, click **Slide 1** to display it in the **Slide pane**, and then in the slide title, click at the end of the word *West*. Press ⎵Spacebar, and then type **Travel**

Clicking a slide thumbnail is the most common method used to display a slide in the Slide pane.

10 ▸ **Save** ⊟ your presentation.

Objective 3 ▸ Add Pictures to a Presentation

GO! Learn How
Video P1-3

Photographic images add impact to a presentation and help the audience visualize your message.

Activity 1.08 │ Inserting a Picture from a File

Many slide layouts in PowerPoint accommodate digital picture files so that you can easily add pictures you have stored. The agency has a collection of photographs to be inserted in the presentation that highlight the beauty of the region.

1 ▸ Display **Slide 2**, and then compare your screen with Figure 1.18.

In the center of the picture placeholder, the *Pictures* button displays.

FIGURE 1.18

> **2** In the picture placeholder, click **Pictures** to open the **Insert Picture** dialog box. Navigate to the location where your student data files are stored, click **p01A_Glacier**, and then click **Insert** to insert the picture in the placeholder. Compare your screen with Figure 1.19.

> Small circles—*sizing handles*—surround the inserted picture and indicate that the picture is selected and can be modified or formatted. The *rotation handle*—a circular arrow above the picture—provides a way to rotate a selected image. The Picture Tools are added to the ribbon, providing picture formatting commands.

FIGURE 1.19

> **3** Display **Slide 3**. On the **Home tab**, in the **Slides group**, click the **New Slide arrow**, and then click **Title and Content**. In the title placeholder, type **Your Vacation**

> **4** In the content placeholder, click **Pictures**. Navigate to your student data files, and then click **p01A_Bay**. Click **Insert**, and then compare your screen with Figure 1.20. **Save** the presentation.

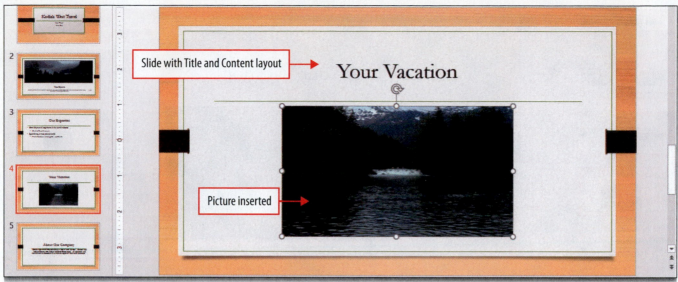

FIGURE 1.20

Activity 1.09 | Applying a Style to a Picture

MOS
2.3.3

When you select a picture, the Picture Tools display, adding the Format tab to the ribbon. The Format tab provides numerous styles that you can apply to your pictures. A *style* is a collection of formatting options that you can apply to a picture, text, or an object.

1 With **Slide 4** displayed, if necessary, click the picture to select it. On the ribbon, notice that the *Picture Tools* are active and the *Format* tab displays.

2 On the **Format tab**, in the **Picture Styles group**, click **More** ⊽ to display the **Picture Styles** gallery, and then compare your screen with Figure 1.21.

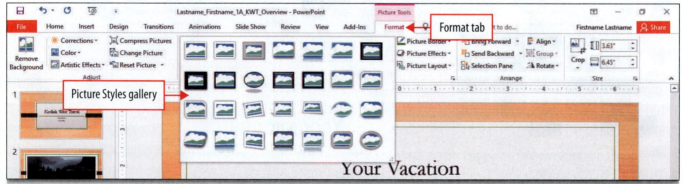

FIGURE 1.21

3 In the gallery, point to several of the picture styles to display the ScreenTips and to view the effect on your picture. In the second row, click the second style—**Simple Frame, Black**. Click in a blank area of the slide, compare your screen with Figure 1.22, and then **Save** 🖫 the presentation.

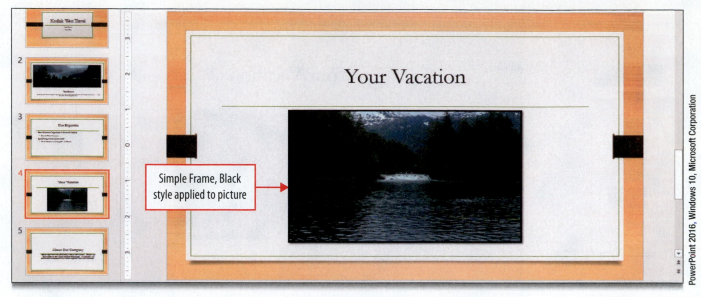

FIGURE 1.22

Activity 1.10 | Applying and Removing Picture Artistic Effects

MOS
2.3.3

Artistic effects are formats applied to images that make pictures resemble sketches or paintings.

1 On **Slide 4**, click the picture to select it. On the **Format tab**, in the **Adjust group**, click **Artistic Effects** to display the **Artistic Effects** gallery. Compare your screen with Figure 1.23.

FIGURE 1.23

2 In the gallery, point to several of the artistic effects to display the ScreenTips and to have Live Preview display the effect on your picture. Then, in the second row, click the **Glow Diffused** effect.

3 With the picture still selected, on the **Format tab**, in the **Adjust group**, click **Artistic Effects** again to display the gallery. In the first row, click the first effect—**None**—to remove the effect from the picture and restore the previous formatting.

4 **Save** the presentation.

GO! Learn How
Video P1-4

There are several print options in PowerPoint. For example, you can print full page images of your slides, presentation handouts to provide your audience with copies of your slides, or Notes pages displaying speaker notes below an image of the slide.

Activity 1.11 | Viewing a Slide Show

When you view a presentation as an electronic slide show, the entire slide fills the computer screen, and an audience can view your presentation if your computer is connected to a projection system.

1 On the ribbon, click the **Slide Show tab**. In the **Start Slide Show group**, click **From Beginning**. Compare your slide with Figure 1.24.

The first slide fills the screen, displaying the presentation as the audience would see it if your computer was connected to a projection system.

ANOTHER WAY Press F5 to start the slide show from the beginning. Or, display the first slide you want to show and click the Slide Show button on the lower right side of the status bar.

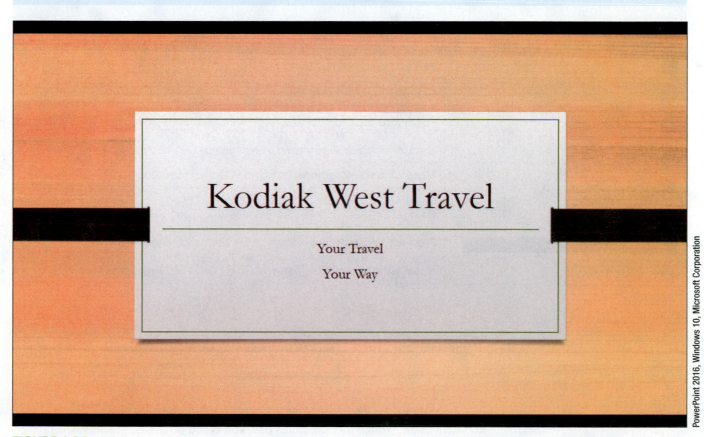

PowerPoint 2016, Windows 10, Microsoft Corporation

FIGURE 1.24

2 Click the left mouse button or press Spacebar to advance to the second slide.

3 Continue to click or press Spacebar until the last slide displays, and then click or press Spacebar one more time to display a **black slide**—a slide that displays after the last slide in a presentation indicating that the presentation is over.

4 With the black slide displayed, click the left mouse button to exit the slide show and return to the presentation.

ANOTHER WAY   Press [Esc] to exit the slide show.

Activity 1.12 | Using Presenter View

Presenter View shows the full-screen slide show on one monitor or projection screen for the audience to see, while enabling the presenter to view a preview of the next slide, notes, and a timer on another monitor.

1 On the **Slide Show tab**, in the **Monitors** group, if necessary, select the **Use Presenter View** check box. Hold down [Alt] and press [F5]. Take a moment to study the parts of the PowerPoint Presenter View window described in the table in Figure 1.25.

If you do not have two monitors, you can practice using Presenter View by pressing [Alt] + [F5]. You will only see the presenter's view—not the audience view—in this mode.

MICROSOFT POWERPOINT PRESENTER VIEW ELEMENTS	
SCREEN ELEMENT	**DESCRIPTION**
0:00:00 II ↺	**Timer:** running time, pause timer, and reset timer options
✎	**Pen and laser pointer tools:** point to or annotate slides during a presentation
▦	**See all slides:** display all slides on the screen to easily navigate between them
🔍	**Zoom into the slide:** focus on a part of a slide while presenting
▨	**Black or unblack slide show:** hide or unhide the presentation
⊙	**More slide show options:** including hide presenter view, help, pause, and end show
◀ and ▶	**Navigation buttons:** move back and forth through the presentation
SHOW TASKBAR DISPLAY SETTINGS ▼ END SLIDE SHOW	**Presenter View ribbon:** control slide presentation display options
A⁺ or A˙	**Notes pane text size adjustment:** make notes text larger or smaller

FIGURE 1.25

PowerPoint 2016, Windows 10, Microsoft Corporation

2 Below the current slide, click the **Advance to the next slide arrow** ⊙ to display **Slide 2**.

BY TOUCH   Advance to the next slide by swiping the current slide to the left.

3 In the upper right corner of the **Presenter View** window, point to the next slide—*Our Expertise*—and then click. Notice that the notes that you typed on **Slide 3** display. Compare your screen with Figure 1.26.

Clicking the image of the next slide advances the presentation.

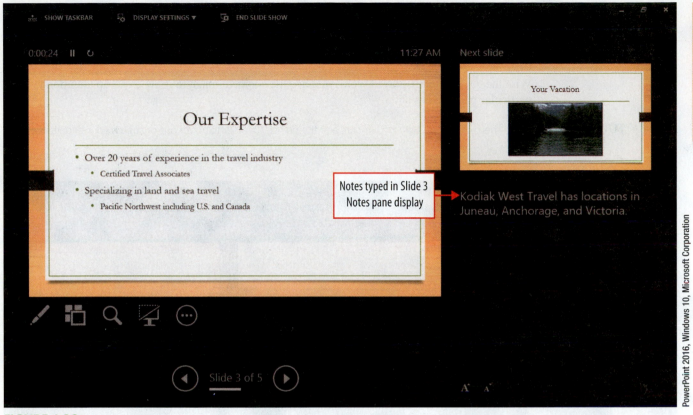

FIGURE 1.26

4 ▶ Below the notes, click **Make the text larger** 🅰 to increase the font size of the notes in Presenter view to make the notes easier to read.

5 ▶ Below the current slide, click the second button—**See all slides** 🔲. Compare your screen with Figure 1.27.

A thumbnail view of all of the slides in your presentation displays. Here you can quickly move to another slide, if, for example, you want to review a concept or answer a question related to a slide other than the current slide.

FIGURE 1.27

6 Click **Slide 4** to make Slide 4 the current slide in Presenter View. Below the current slide, click the third button—**Zoom into the slide** 🔍. Move the 🔍 pointer to the middle of the picture on the current slide, and then click to zoom in on the picture. Notice that the 🖐 pointer displays. Compare your slide with Figure 1.28.

With the 🖐 pointer displayed, you can move the zoomed image to draw close-up attention to a particular part of your slide.

🔄 **BY TOUCH**   Touch the current slide with two fingers and then pinch together to zoom out or stretch your fingers apart to zoom in.

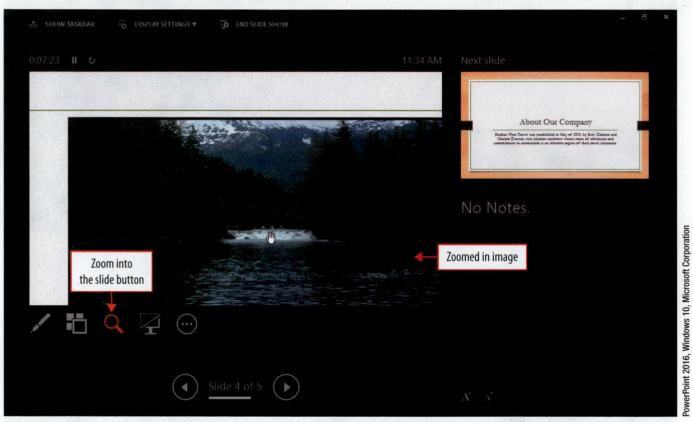

FIGURE 1.28

7 Below the current slide, click the **Advance to the next slide arrow** ▶ to display **Slide 5.** At the top of the Presenter View window, click **END SLIDE SHOW** to return to your presentation.

Activity 1.13 | Inserting Headers and Footers on Slide Handouts

1.2.7

A *header* is text that prints at the top of each sheet of *slide handouts* or *notes pages*. Slide handouts are printed images of slides on a sheet of paper. Notes pages are printouts that contain the slide image on the top half of the page and notes that you have created in the Notes pane in the lower half of the page.

In addition to headers, you can insert *footers*—text that displays at the bottom of every slide or that prints at the bottom of a sheet of slide handouts or notes pages.

1 Click the **Insert tab**, and then in the **Text group**, click **Header & Footer** to display the **Header and Footer** dialog box.

2 In the **Header and Footer** dialog box, click the **Notes and Handouts tab**. Under **Include on page**, select the **Date and time** check box, and as you do so, watch the Preview box in the upper right corner of the Header and Footer dialog box.

The two narrow rectangular boxes at the top of the Preview box are placeholders for the header text and date. When you select the Date and time check box, the placeholder in the upper right corner is outlined, indicating the location in which the date will display.

3 Be sure that the **Update automatically** option button is selected so that the current date prints on the notes and handouts each time the presentation is printed. If it is not selected, click the Update automatically option button.

4 Verify that the **Page number** check box is selected and select it if it is not. If necessary, clear the Header check box to omit this element. Notice that in the **Preview** box, the corresponding placeholder is not selected.

5 Select the **Footer** check box, and then click in the **Footer** box. Using your own name, type **Lastname_Firstname_1A_KWT_Overview** so that the file name displays as a footer, and then compare your dialog box with Figure 1.29.

PowerPoint 2016, Windows 10, Microsoft Corporation

FIGURE 1.29

6 In the lower right corner of the dialog box, click **Apply to All**. **Save** 💾 your presentation.

Activity 1.14 | Inserting Slide Numbers on Slides

MOS
1.2.7

In this Activity, you will insert the slide numbers on the presentation slides.

1 Display **Slide 1**. On the **Insert tab**, in the **Text group**, click **Header & Footer** to display the **Header and Footer** dialog box.

2 In the **Header and Footer** dialog box, if necessary, click the Slide tab. Under **Include on slide**, select the **Slide number** check box, and then select the **Don't show on title slide** check box. Verify that all other check boxes are cleared, and then compare your screen with Figure 1.30.

Selecting the *Don't show on title slide* check box omits the slide number from the first slide in a presentation.

Check boxes selected

FIGURE 1.30

3 Click **Apply to All**, and then notice that on the first slide, the slide number does not display.

4 Display **Slide 2**, and then notice that the slide number displays in the lower right area of the slide. Display each slide in the presentation and notice the placement of the slide number.

The position of the slide number and other header and footer information is determined by the theme applied to the presentation.

Activity 1.15 | Printing Presentation Handouts

N O T E	**What Does Your Instructor Require for Submission? A Paper Printout of Your Slide Handouts, an Image That Looks Like Printed Handouts, or Your PowerPoint File?**

In this Activity, you can produce a paper printout of your Slides Handouts or an electronic image of your handouts that looks like a printed document. Or, your instructor may want only your completed PowerPoint file.

1.6.3, 1.5.3, 1.6.4

Use Backstage view to preview the arrangement of slides and to print your presentation.

1 Display **Slide 1**. Click the **File tab** to display **Backstage** view, and then click **Print**.

The Print tab in Backstage view displays the tools you need to select your settings and also to view a preview of your presentation. On the right, Print Preview displays your presentation exactly as it will print. If your system is not connected to a color printer, your slide may display in black and white.

2 Under **Settings**, click **Full Page Slides**, and then compare your screen with Figure 1.31.

The gallery displays either the default print setting—Full Page Slides—or the most recently selected print setting. This button might indicate the presentation Notes Pages, Outline, or one of several arrangements of slide handouts—depending on the most recently used setting.

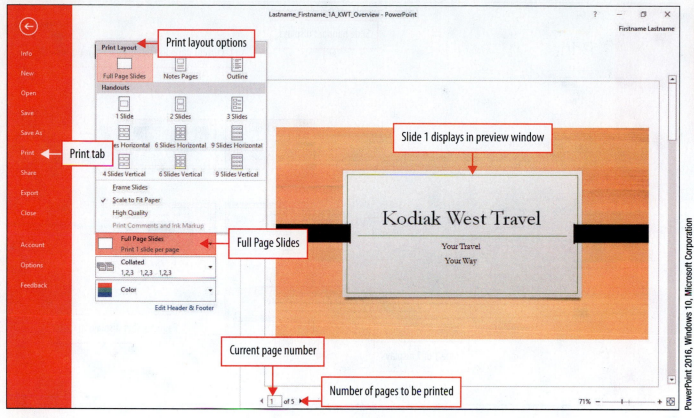

Print layout options

Print tab

Slide 1 displays in preview window

Full Page Slides

Kodiak West Travel

Your Travel
Your Way

Current page number

Number of pages to be printed

PowerPoint 2016, Windows 10, Microsoft Corporation

FIGURE 1.31

3 In the gallery, under **Handouts**, click **6 Slides Horizontal**. Notice that the **Print Preview** on the right displays the slide handout, and that the current date, file name, and page number display in the header and footer. Compare your screen with Figure 1.32.

In the Settings group, the Portrait Orientation option displays; here you can change the print orientation from Portrait to Landscape. The Portrait Orientation option does not display when Full Page Slides is chosen.

FIGURE 1.32

4 ▶ To create an electronic image of your handouts that looks like printed handouts, skip this step and continue to Step 5. To print your handout document on paper using the default printer on your system, in the upper left portion of the screen, click **Print**.

> The handout will print on your default printer—on a black and white printer, the colors will print in shades of gray. To save the cost of color ink, you can print in grayscale by clicking the Color button. Backstage view closes and your file redisplays in the PowerPoint window.

5 ▶ To create an electronic image of your document that looks like a printed document, on the left click **Export**. On the right, click the **Create PDF/XPS** button to display the **Publish as PDF or XPS** dialog box.

6 ▶ In the **Publish as PDF or XPS** dialog box, click **Options**. Under **Publish what**, click the **Slides arrow**, and then click **Handouts**. Be sure **Slides per page** is set to **6**, and **Order** is set to **Horizontal**. Click **OK**.

> **🔄 ANOTHER WAY**   Under Printer, click the printer arrow, click Print as a PDF, and then click Print to print your presentation to a PDF file. Microsoft Print to PDF is an automatically installed printer option in Windows 10, which enables you to create an image that looks like a printed document.

7 ▶ Navigate to your **PowerPoint Chapter 1** folder, and then click **Publish**. If your Adobe Acrobat or Reader program displays your PDF, close the PDF file. If your PDF displays in Microsoft Edge (on a Windows 10 computer), in the upper right corner click Close ☒. Notice that your presentation redisplays in PowerPoint.

MOS

1.6.2

Activity 1.16 │ **Printing Speaker Notes**

1 ▶ On the **File tab**, click **Print**. Under **Settings**, click **6 Slides Horizontal**, and then under **Print Layout**, click **Notes Pages** to view the presentation notes for **Slide 1**; recall that you created notes for **Slide 3**.

> Indicated below the Notes page are the current slide number and the number of pages that will print when Notes Pages is selected. You can use the Next Page and Previous Page arrows to display each Notes page in the presentation.

2 At the bottom of the **Print Preview**, click **Next Page** ▶ two times so that **Page 3** displays. Notice that the notes that you typed for Slide 3 display below the image of the slide. Compare your screen with Figure 1.33.

FIGURE 1.33

3 Under **Settings**, click in the **Slides box**. Type **3** and then click **Notes Pages**. In the lower section, click **Frame Slides**. Under **Printer**, click the printer arrow, click **Print as a PDF**, and then click **Print** to print your presentation to a PDF file.

Microsoft Print to PDF is an automatically installed printer option in Windows 10, which enables you to create an image that looks like a printed document.

> **ALERT!** **No Print as a PDF Printer Option Available**
>
> If you are using Windows 7 or 8, select the Microsoft XPS Document Writer printer instead to print your presentation to the XPS format, a Microsoft file format that also creates an image of your document and that opens in the XPS viewer.

4 Navigate to the location where you store your files for this chapter, name the file **Lastname_Firstname_1A_KWT_Overview_Notes**, and then click **Save**.

5 Redisplay **Backstage** view. On the right, at the bottom of the **Properties** list, click **Show All Properties**. On the list of **Properties**, click to the right of **Tags**, and then type **company overview**

6 Click to the right of **Subject**, and then type your course name and section number. Under **Related People**, be sure that your name displays as the author, and edit if necessary.

7 Click **Save**. On the right end of the title bar, click **Close** ✕ to close the presentation and close PowerPoint.

END | You have completed Project 1A

GO! With Google

Build From
Scratch

> **ALERT!** **Working with Web-Based Applications and Services**
>
> Computer programs and services on the web receive continuous updates and improvements, so the steps to complete this web-based activity may differ from the ones shown. You can often look at the screens and the information presented to determine how to complete the activity.
>
> If you do not already have a Google account, you will need to create one before you begin this activity. Go to http://google.com and in the upper right corner, click Sign In. On the Sign In screen, click Create Account. On the Create your Google Account page, complete the form, read and agree to the Terms of Service and Privacy Policy, and then click Next step. On the Welcome screen, click Get Started.

Activity | Creating a Company Overview Presentation in Google Slides

In this Activity, you will use Google Slides to create a presentation similar to the one you created in Project 1A.

1 From the desktop, open your browser, navigate to **http://google.com**, and then sign in to your Google account. Click **Google Apps**, and then click **Drive**. Open your **GO! Web Projects** folder—or click New to create and then open this folder if necessary.

2 In the left pane, click **NEW**, and then click **Google Slides**. In the **Themes** pane, click **Tropic**. If this theme is not available, select another theme. **Close** the **Themes** pane.

3 At the top of the window, click **Untitled presentation** and then, using your own name, type **Lastname_Firstname_1A_Web** as the file name and then press Enter.

4 In the title placeholder, type **Kodiak West Travel** and then in the subtitle placeholder type **Your Travel - Your Way**

5 On the **toolbar**, click the **New slide arrow** [+], and then click **Caption**.

6 On the **toolbar**, click **Image**. In the **Insert image** dialog box, click **Choose an image to upload**. Navigate to your student data files, and then click **p01_1A_Web_Glacier**. Click **Open**.

7 Type **Your Dreams** in the text placeholder.

8 On the **toolbar**, click the **New slide arrow** [+], and then click **Title and body**. Type **Our Expertise** in the title placeholder.

9 Click in the content placeholder. On the toolbar, if necessary, click **More** [More ▾], click **Bulleted list**. In the placeholder, type **Over 20 years of experience in the travel industry** and then press Enter. Press Tab. Type **Certified Travel Associates** and then press Enter. On toolbar, if necessary, click More, and then click **Decrease indent**. Type **Specializing in land and sea travel** and then press Enter. Press Tab and then type **Pacific Northwest including U.S. and Canada**

10 Below the slide, click in the Notes pane. Type **Kodiak West Travel has locations in Juneau, Anchorage, and Victoria.** Compare your screen to Figure A.

11 In the upper right, click the **Present arrow**, click **Present from beginning**. Click the left mouse button to progress through the presentation. When the last slide displays, press Esc or click **Exit**.

12 Your presentation will be saved automatically. If you are instructed to submit your file, click the File menu, point to Download as, and then click Microsoft PowerPoint, PDF Document, or another format as directed by your instructor. The file will download to your default download folder as determined by your browser settings. Sign out of your Google account and close your browser.

(GO! With Google continues on the next page)

FIGURE A

PROJECT ACTIVITIES

In Activities 1.17 through 1.33, you will combine two presentations that the marketing team at Kodiak West Travel developed describing itinerary ideas when visiting Seattle before or after a cruise. You will insert slides from one presentation into another, and then you will rearrange and delete slides. You will also apply font formatting and slide transitions to the presentation. Your completed presentation will look similar to Figure 1.34.

PROJECT FILES

 If your instructor wants you to submit Project 1B in the MyITLab Grader system, log in to MyITLab, locate Grader Project1B, and then download the files for this project.

For Project 1B, you will need the following files:

p01B_Seattle
p01B_Slides

You will save your presentation as:

Lastname_Firstname_1B_Seattle

PROJECT RESULTS

GO!
Walk Thru
Project 1B

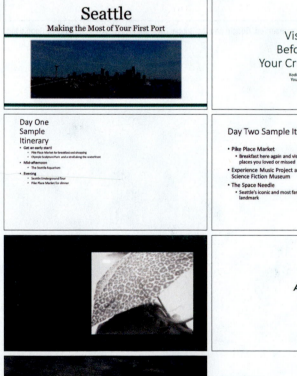

FIGURE 1.34 Project 1B Seattle

Objective 5   Edit an Existing Presentation

GO! Learn How
Video P1-5

1.5.1

Recall that editing refers to the process of adding, deleting, and modifying presentation content. You can edit presentation content in either the Slide pane or in the presentation outline.

Activity 1.17 | Changing Slide Size

ALERT!   **To submit as an autograded project, log into MyITLab, download the files for this project, and begin with these files instead of the student data files.**

Presentations created with one of the new themes in PowerPoint 2016 default to a widescreen format using a 16:9 *aspect ratio*—the ratio of the width of a display to the height of the display. This slide size is similar to most television and computer monitor screens. PowerPoint 2010 and earlier versions of PowerPoint used a squarer format with a 4:3 aspect ratio. The widescreen format utilizes screen space more effectively.

1 ▶ Start PowerPoint. On the left, under the list of recent presentations, click **Open Other Presentations**. Under **Open**, click **Browse**. In the **Open** dialog box, navigate to your student data files, and then click **p01B_Seattle**. Click **Open**. On the **File tab**, click **Save As**, navigate to your **PowerPoint Chapter 1** folder, and then using your own name, save the file as **Lastname_ Firstname_1B_Seattle**

2 ▶ Notice that **Slide 1** displays in a square format.

3 ▶ On the **Design tab**, in the **Customize group**, click **Slide Size**, and then click **Widescreen (16:9)**. Compare your screen with Figure 1.35, and notice that the slide fills the slide pane. **Save** 🖫 the presentation.

FIGURE 1.35

Activity 1.18 | Inserting Slides from an Existing Presentation

Presentation content is commonly shared among group members in an organization. Rather than re-creating slides, you can insert slides from an existing presentation into the current presentation. In this Activity, you will insert slides from an existing presentation into your 1B_Seattle presentation.

1 With **Slide 1** displayed, on the **Home tab**, in the **Slides group**, click the **New Slide arrow** to display the **Slide Layout** gallery and additional commands for inserting slides. Compare your screen with Figure 1.36.

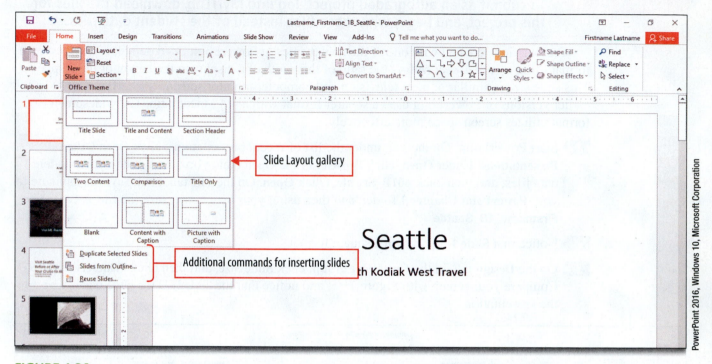

FIGURE 1.36

2 Below the gallery, click **Reuse Slides** to open the Reuse Slides pane on the right side of the PowerPoint window.

3 In the **Reuse Slides** pane, click **Browse**, and then click **Browse File**. In the **Browse** dialog box, navigate to the location where your student data files are stored, and then double-click **p01B_Slides** to display the slides from this presentation in the Reuse Slides pane.

4 At the bottom of the **Reuse Slides** pane, be sure that the **Keep source formatting** check box is *cleared*, and then compare your screen with Figure 1.37.

When the *Keep source formatting* check box is cleared, the theme formatting of the presentation into which the slides are inserted is applied. When the *Keep source formatting* check box is selected, you retain the formatting of the slides when inserted into the presentation.

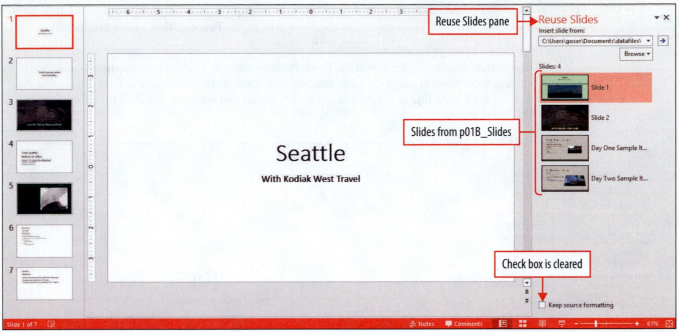

FIGURE 1.37

PowerPoint 2016, Windows 10, Microsoft Corporation

5 ▶ In the **Reuse Slides** pane, point to each slide to view a ScreenTip displaying the file name and the slide title.

6 ▶ In the **Reuse Slides** pane, click the first slide to insert the slide after **Slide 1** in your Seattle presentation. Notice that the inserted slide adopts the color of your Seattle presentation theme.

> **NOTE**   Inserting Slides
>
> You can insert slides into your presentation in any order; remember to display the slide that will come before the slide that you want to insert.

7 ▶ In your **1B_Seattle** presentation, in the slide thumbnails, click **Slide 7** to display it in the **Slide pane**.

8 ▶ In the **Reuse Slides** pane, click the fourth slide to insert it after **Slide 7**.

Your presentation contains nine slides. When a presentation contains a large number of slides, a scroll box displays to the right of the slide thumbnails so that you can scroll and then select the thumbnails.

9 ▶ **Close** ✕ the **Reuse Slides** pane, and then **Save** 🖫 the presentation.

> **More Knowledge**   Inserting All Slides
>
> You can insert all of the slides from an existing presentation into the current presentation at one time. In the Reuse Slides pane, right-click one of the slides that you want to insert, and then click Insert All Slides.

Activity 1.19 | Displaying and Editing the Presentation Outline

Outline View displays the presentation outline to the left of the Slide pane. You can use the outline to edit the presentation text. Changes that you make in the outline are immediately displayed in the Slide pane.

1 To the right of the slide thumbnails, if necessary, drag the scroll box up, and then click **Slide 1** to display it in the Slide pane. On the **View tab**, in the **Presentation Views group**, click **Outline View**. Compare your screen with Figure 1.38.

The outline displays at the left of the PowerPoint window in place of the slide thumbnails. Each slide in the outline displays the slide number, slide icon, and the slide title in bold. Slides that do not display a slide title in the outline use a slide layout that does not include a title, for example, the Blank layout.

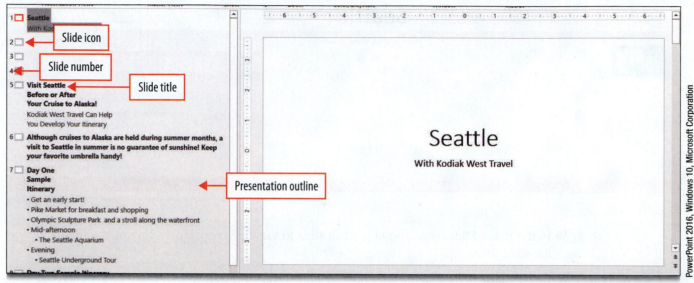

FIGURE 1.38

2 In the **Outline**, in **Slide 7**, drag to select the text of the second and third bullet points—*Pike Market for breakfast and shopping*, and *Olympic Sculpture Park and a stroll along the waterfront*. Compare your screen with Figure 1.39.

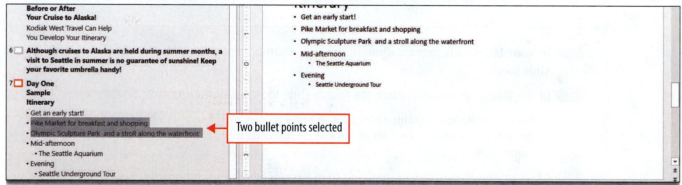

FIGURE 1.39

PowerPoint 2016, Windows 10, Microsoft Corporation

3 On the **Home tab**, in the **Paragraph group**, click **Increase List Level** one time to increase the list level of the selected bullet points.

When you type in the outline or change the list level, the changes also display in the Slide pane.

4 In the **Outline**, in **Slide 7**, click at the end of the last bullet point after the word *Tour*. Press Enter to create a new bullet point at the same list level as the previous bullet point. Type **Pike Place Market for dinner** and then compare your screen with Figure 1.40.

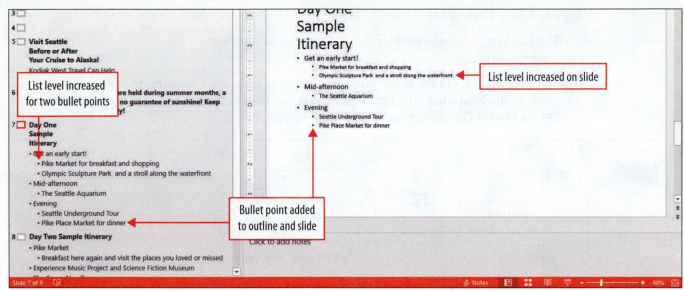

FIGURE 1.40

5 ▸ In the **Status bar**, click **Normal** 🔲 to close Outline View and redisplay the slide thumbnails. **Save** 🔲 the presentation.

> You can type text in the Slide pane or in the Outline. Displaying the Outline enables you to view the entire flow of the presentation text.

MOS
1.2.4

Activity 1.20 | Deleting and Moving a Slide

1 ▸ To the right of the slide thumbnails, locate the vertical scroll bar and scroll box. If necessary, drag the scroll box down so that **Slide 9** displays in the slide thumbnails. Click **Slide 9** to display it in the Slide pane. Press Delete to delete the slide from the presentation.

> Your presentation contains eight slides.

2 ▸ If necessary, scroll the slide thumbnails so that **Slide 4** displays. Point to **Slide 4**, hold down the left mouse button, and then drag down to position the **Slide 4** thumbnail below the **Slide 8** thumbnail. Release the mouse button, and then compare your screen with Figure 1.41. **Save** 🔲 the presentation.

> You can easily rearrange your slides by dragging a slide thumbnail to a new location in the presentation.

🔄 **BY TOUCH**   Use your finger to drag the slide you want to move to a new location in the presentation.

FIGURE 1.41

Activity 1.21 | Finding and Replacing Text

The Replace command enables you to locate all occurrences of specified text and replace it with alternative text.

1 Display **Slide 1**. On the **Home tab**, in the **Editing group**, click **Replace**. In the **Replace** dialog box, in the **Find what** box, type **Pike Market** and then in the **Replace with** box, type **Pike Place Market** Compare your screen with Figure 1.42.

Text typed in Replace with box

Text typed in Find what box

With Kodiak West Travel

FIGURE 1.42

2 In the **Replace** dialog box, click **Replace All** to display a message box indicating that two replacements were made.

3 In the message box, click **OK**. **Close** the **Replace** dialog box, and then click **Save** 🖫.

Objective 6 Format a Presentation

GO! Learn How
Video P1-6

Formatting refers to changing the appearance of the text, layout, and design of a slide.

Activity 1.22 | Applying a Theme Variant

Recall that a theme is a set of unified design elements that provides a look for your presentation by applying colors, fonts, and effects. Each PowerPoint theme includes several *variants*—variations on the theme style and color. The themes and variants that are available on your system may vary.

1 On the **Design tab**, in the **Variants group**, notice that four variants of the current theme display and the second variant is applied.

2 Point to each of the variants to view the change to **Slide 1**.

If you do not see the same variants, refer to the figures for this activity.

3 With **Slide 1** displayed, in the **Variants group**, point to the **third variant**, and then right-click. Compare your screen with Figure 1.43.

The shortcut menu displays options for applying the variant.

Shortcut menu displays options for applying Variant

FIGURE 1.43

4 Click **Apply to Selected Slides** to apply the variant to **Slide 1** only.

5 In the **Variants group**, right-click the **second variant**. On the shortcut menu, click **Apply to All Slides** so that the original variant color is applied to all of the slides in the presentation. Compare your screen with Figure 1.44. **Save** 🖫 your presentation.

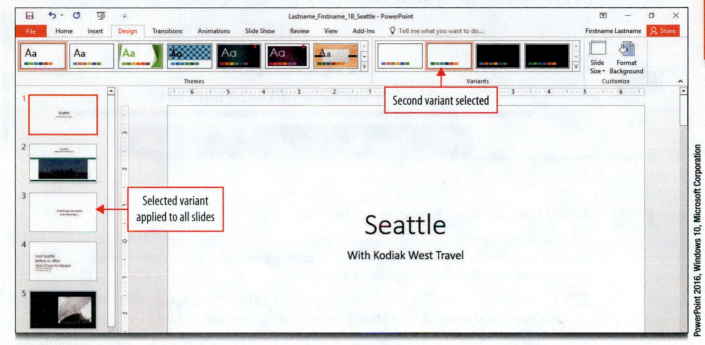

FIGURE 1.44

🔄 **ANOTHER WAY**   Click Undo to remove the variant you applied in step 4.

2.1.2

Activity 1.23 | Changing Fonts and Font Sizes

A font is a set of characters with the same design and shape, and fonts are measured in points. Font styles include bold, italic, and underline, and you can apply any combination of these styles to presentation text. Font styles and font color are useful to provide emphasis and are a visual cue to draw the reader's eye to important text.

1 Display **Slide 2**. Select all of the text in the title placeholder, point to the mini toolbar, and then click the **Font arrow** to display the available fonts. Scroll the font list, and then click **Georgia**.

2 Select the first line of the title—*Seattle*. On the mini toolbar, click the **Font Size arrow** and then click **80**.

3 Select the second line of the title—*Making the Most of Your First Port*. On the **Home tab**, in the **Font group**, click the **Font Size arrow**, and then click **36**. Click in a blank area of the slide to cancel your selection, and then compare your screen with Figure 1.45. **Save** 🖫 your presentation.

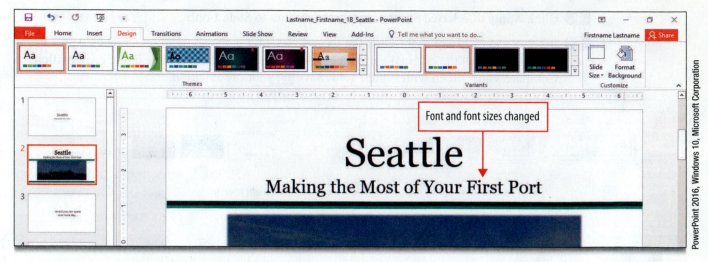

FIGURE 1.45

PowerPoint 2016, Windows 10, Microsoft Corporation

MOS
2.1.2

Activity 1.24 | Changing Font Styles and Font Colors

Font styles include bold, italic, and underline, and you can apply any combination of these styles to presentation text. Font styles and font color are useful to provide emphasis and are a visual cue to draw the reader's eye to important text.

1 ▶ Display **Slide 3**, and then select both lines of text. On the **Home tab**, in the **Font group**, click the **Font Color arrow** ▲ ▼ and then compare your screen with Figure 1.46.

The colors in the top row of the color gallery are the colors associated with the presentation theme. The colors in the rows below the first row are light and dark variations of the theme colors.

FIGURE 1.46

PowerPoint 2016, Windows 10, Microsoft Corporation

2 ▶ Point to several of the colors and notice that a ScreenTip displays the color name and Live Preview displays the selected text in the color to which you are pointing.

3 In the fifth column of colors, click the last color—**Dark Green, Accent 1, Darker 50%**—to change the font color. Notice that on the **Home tab**, the lower part of the **Font Color** button displays the most recently applied font color— *Dark Green, Accent 1, Darker 50%*.

When you click the Font Color button instead of the Font Color button arrow, the color displayed in the lower part of the Font Color button is applied to selected text without displaying the color gallery.

4 With the two lines of text still selected, right-click within the selected text to redisplay the mini toolbar, and then from the mini toolbar, apply **Bold** and **Italic**.

5 Display **Slide 4**, and then select the title—*Visit Seattle Before or After Your Cruise to Alaska!* On the mini toolbar, click **Font Color** to apply the font color **Dark Green, Accent 1, Darker 50%** to the selection. Select the subtitle—*Kodiak West Travel Can Help You Develop Your Itinerary*—and then change the **Font Color** to **Dark Green, Accent 1, Darker 50%**. Click anywhere on the slide to cancel the selection, and then compare your screen with Figure 1.47. **Save** your presentation.

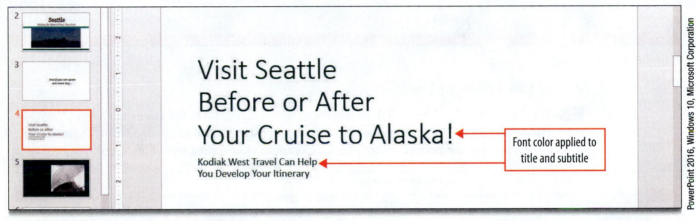

FIGURE 1.47

Activity 1.25 | Aligning Text

In PowerPoint, *text alignment* refers to the horizontal placement of text within a placeholder. You can align text left, centered, right, or justified.

1 Display **Slide 5**, and then, click anywhere in the paragraph. On the **Home tab**, in the **Paragraph group**, click **Center** to center the text within the placeholder.

2 Display **Slide 4**, and then click anywhere in the slide title. Press Ctrl + E to use the keyboard shortcut to center the text.

3 On **Slide 4**, using one of the methods that you practiced, **Center** the subtitle. Click in a blank area of the slide. Compare your screen with Figure 1.48 and then **Save** the presentation.

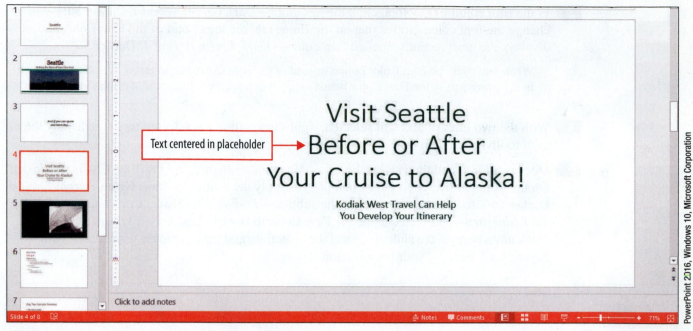

FIGURE 1.48

Activity 1.26 | Changing Line Spacing

1 Display **Slide 5**, and then click anywhere in the paragraph. On the **Home tab**, in the **Paragraph group**, click **Line Spacing** ⬚▾. In the list, click **2.0** to change from single spacing to double spacing between lines of text. Compare your screen with Figure 1.49.

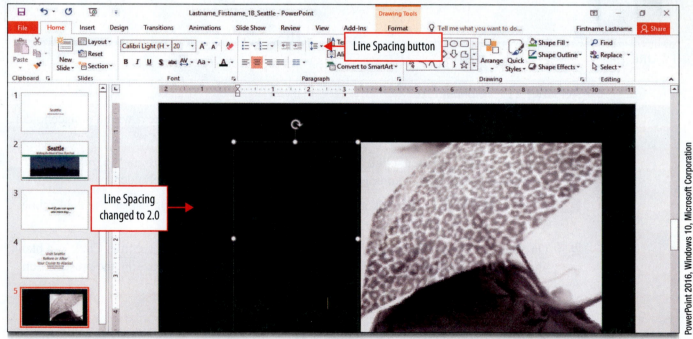

FIGURE 1.49

2 **Save** ⬚ your presentation.

Activity 1.27 | Changing the Slide Layout

The slide layout defines the placement of the content placeholders on a slide. PowerPoint includes predefined layouts that you can apply to your slide for the purpose of arranging slide elements. For example, a Title Slide contains two placeholder elements—the title and the subtitle. When you design your slides, consider the content that you want to include, and then choose a layout with the elements that will display the message you want to convey in the best way.

1 Display **Slide 1**. On the **Home tab**, in the **Slides group**, click **Layout** to display the **Slide Layout** gallery. Notice that *Title Slide* is selected, indicating the layout of the current slide.

2 Click **Section Header** to change the slide layout. Compare your screen with Figure 1.50, and then **Save** 🔲 your presentation.

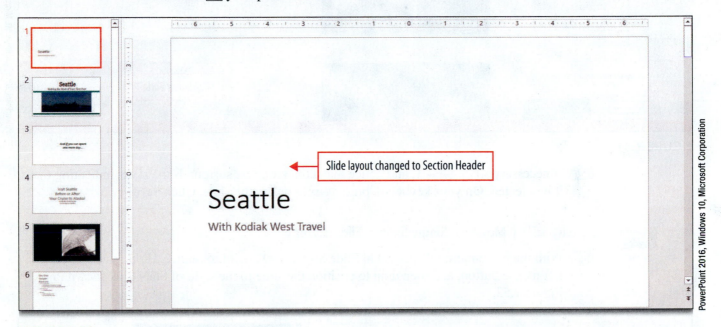

Slide layout changed to Section Header

PowerPoint 2016, Windows 10, Microsoft Corporation

FIGURE 1.50

Objective 7   Use Slide Sorter View

GO! Learn How
Video P1-7

Slide Sorter view displays thumbnails of all of the slides in a presentation. Use Slide Sorter view to rearrange and delete slides and to apply formatting to multiple slides.

1.2.4, 1.5.2

Activity 1.28 | Deleting Slides in Slide Sorter View

1 In the lower right corner of the PowerPoint window, click **Slide Sorter** ▦ to display all of the slide thumbnails. Compare your screen with Figure 1.51.

Your slides may display larger or smaller than those shown in Figure 1.51.

ANOTHER WAY   On the View tab, in the Presentation Views group, click Slide Sorter.

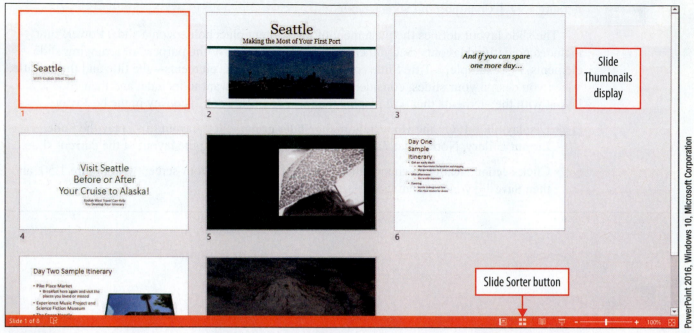

FIGURE 1.51

2 If necessary, click **Slide 1**, and notice that a thick outline surrounds the slide, indicating that it is selected. On your keyboard, press Delete to delete the slide. Click **Save** 🖫.

MOS
1.4.2

Activity 1.29 | Moving a Single Slide in Slide Sorter View

1 With the presentation displayed in Slide Sorter view, point to **Slide 2**. Hold down the left mouse button, and then drag to position the slide to the right of **Slide 6**, as shown in Figure 1.52.

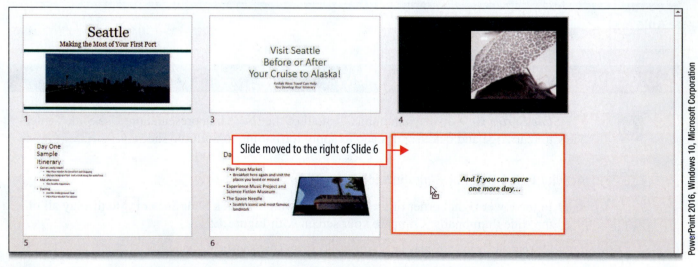

FIGURE 1.52

2 Release the mouse button to move the slide to the **Slide 6** position in the presentation. **Save** 🖫 your presentation.

Activity 1.30 | Selecting Contiguous and Noncontiguous Slides and Moving Multiple Slides

Contiguous slides are slides that are adjacent to each other in a presentation. *Noncontiguous slides* are slides that are not adjacent to each other in a presentation.

1 Click **Slide 2**, hold down Ctrl, click **Slide 4**, release Ctrl. Notice that both slides are selected.

> The noncontiguous slides—Slides 2 and 4—are outlined, indicating that both are selected. By holding down Ctrl, you can select noncontiguous slides.

2 Click **Slide 3**, so that only Slide 3 is selected. Hold down Shift, click **Slide 5**, and then release Shift. Compare your screen with Figure 1.53.

> The contiguous slides—Slides 3, 4, and 5—are outlined, indicating that all three slides are selected. By holding down Shift, you can create a group of contiguous selected slides.

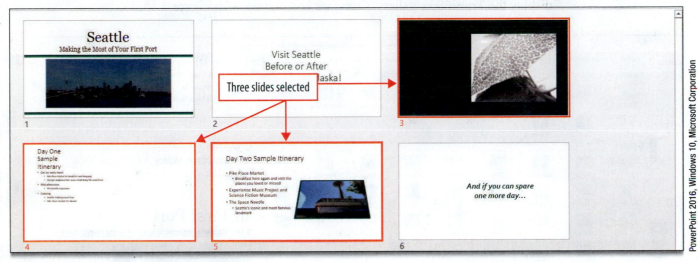

FIGURE 1.53

3 With **Slides 3, 4,** and **5** selected, hold down Ctrl, and then click **Slide 3**. Notice that only **Slides 4** and **5** are selected.

> With a group of selected slides, you can press Ctrl and then click a selected slide to *deselect* it.

4 Point to either of the selected slides, hold down the left mouse button, and then drag to position the two slides to the right of **Slide 2**. Compare your screen with Figure 1.54.

> The selected slides are dragged as a group, and the number 2 in the upper left area of the selected slides indicates the number of slides that you are moving.

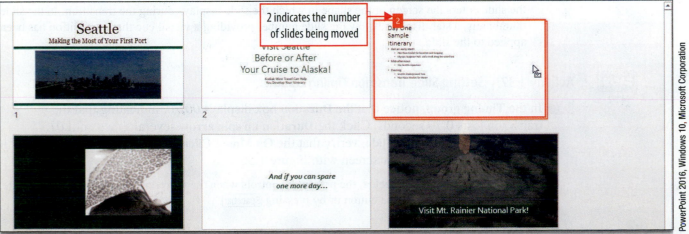

FIGURE 1.54

5 ▶ In the status bar, click **Normal** to return to Normal view. **Save** 🖫 your presentation.

Objective 8 Apply Slide Transitions

Slide transitions are the motion effects that occur in Slide Show view when you move from one slide to the next during a presentation. You can choose from a variety of transitions, and you can control the speed and method with which the slides advance.

GO! Learn How
Video P1-8

4.1.1

Activity 1.31 | Applying Slide Transitions to a Presentation

1 ▶ Display **Slide 1**. On the **Transitions tab**, in the **Transition to This Slide group**, click **More** ⊡ to display the **Transitions** gallery. Compare your screen with Figure 1.55.

FIGURE 1.55

2 ▶ Under **Subtle**, click **Fade** to apply and view the transition. In the **Transition to This Slide group**, click **Effect Options** to display the way the slide enters the screen. Click **Smoothly**. In the **Timing group**, click **Apply To All** to apply the *Fade, Smoothly* transition to all of the slides in the presentation. **Save** 🖫 your presentation.

> The Effect Options vary depending on the selected transition and include the direction from which the slide enters the screen or the shape in which the slide displays during the transition. In the slide thumbnails, a star displays below the slide number providing a visual cue that a transition has been applied to the slide.

4.1.2

Activity 1.32 | Setting Slide Transition Timing Options

1 ▶ In the **Timing group**, notice that the **Duration** box displays *00.70*, indicating that the transition lasts 0.70 seconds. Click the **Duration up spin arrow** several times until *01.75* displays. Under **Advance Slide**, verify that the **On Mouse Click** check box is selected; select it if necessary. Compare your screen with Figure 1.56.

> With On Mouse Click selected, the presenter controls when the current slide advances to the next slide by clicking the mouse button or by pressing Spacebar.

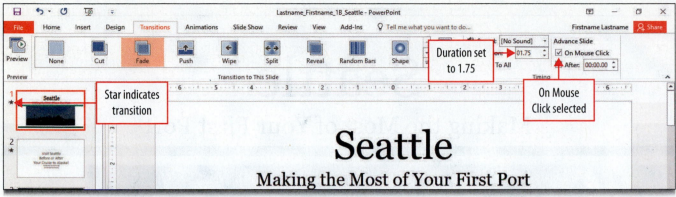

FIGURE 1.56

PowerPoint 2016, Windows 10, Microsoft Corporation

2 In the **Timing group**, click **Apply To All** so that the Duration of *1.75* seconds transition is applied to all of the slides in the presentation.

3 Click the **Slide Show tab**. In the **Start Slide Show group**, click **From Beginning**, and then view your presentation, clicking the mouse button to advance through the slides. When the black slide displays, click the mouse button one more time to display the presentation in Normal view. **Save** 🖫 your presentation.

More Knowledge | **Applying Multiple Slide Transitions**

You can apply more than one type of transition in your presentation by displaying the slides one at a time, and then clicking the transition that you want to apply instead of clicking Apply To All.

MOS

1.5.2

Activity 1.33 | Displaying a Presentation in Reading View

Organizations frequently conduct online meetings when participants are unable to meet in one location. The *Reading view* in PowerPoint displays a presentation in a manner similar to a slide show but the taskbar, title bar, and status bar remain available in the presentation window. Thus, a presenter can easily facilitate an online conference by switching to another window without closing the slide show.

1 In the lower right corner of the PowerPoint window, click **Reading View** . Compare your screen with Figure 1.57.

In Reading view, the status bar contains the Next and Previous buttons, which are used to navigate in the presentation, and the Menu button, which is used to print, copy, and edit slides.

🔄 **ANOTHER WAY**   On the View tab, in the Presentation Views group, click Reading View.

FIGURE 1.57

PowerPoint 2016, Windows 10, Microsoft Corporation

2 Press **Spacebar** to display **Slide 2**. Click the left mouse button to display **Slide 3**. In the status bar, click **Previous** ◀ to display **Slide 2**.

3 In the status bar, click **Menu** 📖 to display the Reading view menu, and then click **End Show** to return to Normal view.

🔄 **ANOTHER WAY**   Press **Esc** to exit Reading view and return to Normal view.

4 On the **Insert tab**, in the **Text group**, click **Header & Footer**, and then click the **Notes and Handouts tab**. Under **Include on page**, select the **Date and time** check box, and if necessary, select Update automatically. If necessary, select the **Page number** check box and clear the **Header** check box. Select the **Footer** check box, in the **Footer** box, using your own name, type **Lastname_Firstname_1B_Seattle** and then click **Apply to All**.

5 Display **Backstage** view, and then on the right, at the bottom of the **Properties** list, click **Show All Properties**. On the list of properties, click to the right of **Tags**, and then type **Seattle** To the right of **Subject**, type your course name and section number. Under **Related People**, be sure that your name displays as the author; edit if necessary.

6 On the left, scroll up as necessary, and then click **Save**. As directed by your instructor, create and submit a paper printout or an electronic image of your presentation that looks like a printed document; or, submit your completed PowerPoint file.

7 **Close** ✕ PowerPoint.

◀ **END | You have completed Project 1B**

GO! With Google

Objective   Create an Itinerary Presentation in Google Slides

ALERT!   **Working with Web-Based Applications and Services**

Computer programs and services on the web receive continuous updates and improvements, so the steps to complete this web-based activity may differ from the ones shown. You can often look at the screens and the information presented to determine how to complete the activity. If you do not already have a Google account, you will need to create one before you begin this activity.

Activity | Creating an Itinerary Presentation in Google Slides

In this Activity, you will use Google Slides to create a presentation similar to the one you created in Project 1B.

1 From the desktop, open your browser, navigate to **http://google.com**, and then sign in to your Google account. Click **Google Apps** and then click **Drive**. Open your **GO! Web Projects** folder—or create and then open this folder if necessary.

2 In the left pane, click **NEW**, and then click **File upload**. Navigate to your student data files, click **p01_1B_Web**, and then click **Open**.

3 Wait a moment for the upload to complete, point to the uploaded file **p01_1B_Web.pptx**, and then right-click. On the shortcut menu, click **Rename**. Delete the existing text, and then using your own last name and first name, type **Lastname_Firstname_ 1B_Web** Click **OK** to rename the file.

4 Right-click the file that you just renamed, point to **Open with**, and then click **Google Slides**.

5 On **Slide 1**, in the Title placeholder, drag to select the two lines of text. On the **toolbar**, click the **Font arrow** and then click **Georgia**.

6 Select the text *Making the Most of Your First Port*. On the **toolbar**, click the **Font Size arrow**, and then click **24**.

7 Click **Slide 2**. Click the **Edit menu**, and then click **Delete** to remove the slide from the presentation.

8 With **Slide 2**—*Seattle Weather*—displayed, press Delete to remove the slide from your presentation. Notice that the presentation contains 7 slides.

9 Display **Slide 3**, and then click in the paragraph on the left side of the slide. Drag to select the text, and then on the **toolbar**, click the **Text color arrow** [A]. Under **Theme**, click the second color—**Theme Color white**. With the paragraph still selected, on the toolbar, click **Bold** [B] and **Italic** [I]. Click the **Align** button [≡] and click **Center** [≡]. Click anywhere in a blank area of the slide to cancel the selection and view your changes.

10 In the slide thumbnails, point to **Slide 4**, hold down the left mouse button, and then drag up slightly. Notice that a black bar displays above **Slide 4**. Continue to drag up until the black bar displays above **Slide 3**. Release the mouse button to move the slide.

11 Using the technique that you just practiced, move **Slide 5** to position it above **Slide 4**.

12 Display **Slide 6**. Select all three lines of text. Click the **Align** button [≡], and then click **Center** [≡]. Click anywhere on the slide to cancel the selection. Click **Slide 1** and compare your screen with Figure A.

(GO! With Google continues on the next page)

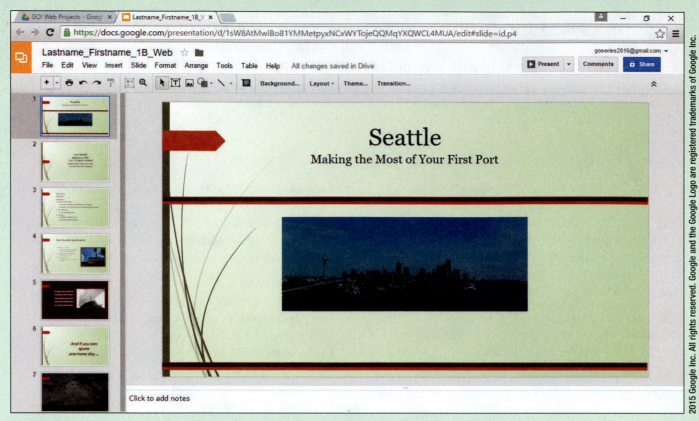

FIGURE A

13 At the right end of the toolbar, click **Transition** to open the **Animations** pane. On the right, in the Animations pane, click the **No transition button**, click **Slide from right**, and then click **Apply to all slides**.

14 To the right of the **menu bar**, click the **Present button arrow**, and then click **Present from beginning**. If necessary, click Allow. Click the left mouse button to

progress through the presentation. When the last slide displays, press Esc or in the lower left corner, click **Exit**.

15 Your presentation will be saved automatically. Download as Microsoft PowerPoint, PDF Document, or another format and submit as directed by your instructor. Sign out of your Google account and close your browser.

GO! To Work

MICROSOFT OFFICE SPECIALIST (MOS) SKILLS IN THIS CHAPTER	
PROJECT 1A	**PROJECT 1B**
1.1.1 Create a new presentation	**1.2.4** Delete slides
1.2.1 Insert specific slide layouts	**1.2.5** Apply a different slide layout
1.2.7 Insert slide headers, footers, and page numbers	**1.4.2** Modify slide order
1.5.3 Set file properties	**1.5.1** Change slide size
1.6.2 Print notes pages	**1.5.2** Change views of a presentation
1.6.3 Print handouts	**2.1.2** Apply formatting and styles to text
1.6.4 Print in color, grayscale, or black and white	**4.1.1** Insert slide transitions
1.7.4 Present a slide show by using Presenter View	**4.1.2** Set transition effect options
2.1.1 Insert text on a slide	**5.1.1** Insert slides from another presentation
2.3.3 Apply styles and effects	

BUILD YOUR E-PORTFOLIO

An E-Portfolio is a collection of evidence, stored electronically, that showcases what you have accomplished while completing your education. Collecting and then sharing your work products with potential employers reflects your academic and career goals. Your completed documents from the following projects are good examples to show what you have learned: 1G, 1K, and 1L.

GO! FOR JOB SUCCESS

Video: Managing Priorities and Workspace

Your instructor may assign this video to your class, and then ask you to think about, or discuss with your classmates, these questions:

FotolEdhar / Fotolia

What kind of scheduling tool do you use? Is it on your computer, your cell phone, or other electronic device, or do you write in a notebook or physical calendar? Which kind of scheduling tool will be most effective for you and why?

Name one lifestyle change that you can make today that will help you create more time for your work projects.

What is the one touch rule and how do you think it will help you be more efficient?

END OF CHAPTER

SUMMARY

In this chapter, you started a new presentation in PowerPoint. You inserted slides with various layouts and you entered, edited, and formatted text. You also inserted text from another PowerPoint file.

Use a presentation theme to establish a unified presentation design. You can change the color of the presentation theme by applying one of the predefined variants that are supplied with each theme.

Presentations are often organized in a manner similar to outlines. List levels represent outline levels and are identified by the bullet style, indentation, and text size.

Slide layout defines the placement of content placeholders on a slide. Each presentation theme includes predefined layouts that you can apply to slides for the purpose of arranging slide elements.

GO! LEARN IT ONLINE

Review the concepts, key terms, and MOS skills in this chapter by completing these online challenges, which you can find at **MyITLab**.

Matching and Multiple Choice: Answer matching and multiple choice questions to test what you learned in this chapter.

Lessons on the GO!: Learn how to use all the new apps and features as they are introduced by Microsoft.

MOS Prep Quiz: Answer questions to review the MOS skills that you practiced in this chapter.

GO! COLLABORATIVE TEAM PROJECT (Available in **MyITLab** and Instructor Resource Center)

If your instructor assigns this project to your class, you can expect to work with one or more of your classmates—either in person or by using Internet tools—to create work products similar to those that you created in this chapter. A team is a group of workers who work together to solve a problem, make a decision, or create a work product. Collaboration is when you work together with others as a team in an intellectual endeavor to complete a shared task or achieve a shared goal.

PROJECT GUIDE FOR POWERPOINT CHAPTER 1

Your instructor will assign Projects from this list to ensure your learning and assess your knowledge.

	Project Guide for Powerpoint Chapter 1		
Project	**Apply Skills from These Chapter Objectives**	**Project Type**	**Project Location**
1A MyITLab	Objectives 1–4 from Project 1A	**1A Instructional Project (Grader Project)** Guided instruction to learn the skills in Project 1A.	In MyITLab and in text
1B MyITLab	Objectives 5–8 from Project 1B	**1B Instructional Project (Grader Project)** Guided instruction to learn the skills in Project 1B.	In MyITLab and in text
1C	Objectives 1–4 from Project 1A	**1C Skills Review (Scorecard Grading)** A guided review of the skills from Project 1A.	In text
1D	Objectives 5–8 from Project 1B	**1D Skills Review (Scorecard Grading)** A guided review of the skills from Project 1B.	In text
1E MyITLab	Objectives 1–4 from Project 1A	**1E Mastery (Grader Project)** **Mastery and Transfer of Learning** A demonstration of your mastery of the skills in Project 1A with extensive decision making.	In MyITLab and in text
1F MyITLab	Objectives 5–8 from Project 1B	**1F Mastery (Grader Project)** **Mastery and Transfer of Learning** A demonstration of your mastery of the skills in Project 1B with extensive decision making.	In MyITLab and in text
1G MyITLab	Objectives 1–8 from Projects 1A and 1B	**1G Mastery (Grader Project)** **Mastery and Transfer of Learning** A demonstration of your mastery of the skills in Projects 1A and 1B with extensive decision making.	In MyITLab and in text
1H	Combination of Objectives from Projects 1A and 1B	**1H GO! Fix It(Scorecard Grading)** **Critical Thinking** A demonstration of your mastery of the skills in Projects 1A and 1B by creating a correct result from a document that contains errors you must find.	Instructor Resource Center (IRC) and MyITLab
1I	Combination of Objectives from Projects 1A and 1B	**1I GO! Make It (Scorecard Grading)** **Critical Thinking** A demonstration of your mastery of the skills in Projects 1A and 1B by creating a result from a supplied picture.	IRC and MyITLab
1J	Combination of Objectives from Projects 1A and 1B	**1J GO! Solve It (Rubric Grading)** **Critical Thinking** A demonstration of your mastery of the skills in Projects 1A and 1B, your decision-making skills, and your critical thinking skills. A task-specific rubric helps you self-assess your result.	IRC and MyITLab
1K	Combination of Objectives from Projects 1A and 1B	**1K GO! Solve It (Rubric Grading)** **Critical Thinking** A demonstration of your mastery of the skills in Projects 1A and 1B, your decision-making skills, and your critical thinking skills. A task-specific rubric helps you self-assess your result.	In text
1L	Combination of Objectives from Projects 1A and 1B	**1L GO! Think (Rubric Grading)** **Critical Thinking** A demonstration of your understanding of the chapter concepts applied in a manner that you would outside of college. An analytic rubric helps you and your instructor grade the quality of your work by comparing it to the work an expert in the discipline would create.	In text
1M	Combination of Objectives from Projects 1A and 1B	**1M GO! Think (Rubric Grading)** **Critical Thinking** A demonstration of your understanding of the chapter concepts applied in a manner that you would outside of college. An analytic rubric helps you and your instructor grade the quality of your work by comparing it to the work an expert in the discipline would create.	IRC and MyITLab
1N	Combination of Objectives from Projects 1A and 1B	**1N You and GO! (Rubric Grading)** **Critical Thinking** A demonstration of your understanding of the chapter concepts applied in a manner that you would in a personal situation. An analytic rubric helps you and your instructor grade the quality of your work.	IRC and MyITLab
1O	Combination of Objectives from Projects 1A and 1B	**1O Collaborative Team Project for PowerPoint Chapter 1** **Critical Thinking** A demonstration of your understanding of concepts and your ability to work collaboratively in a group role-playing assessment, requiring both collaboration and self-management.	IRC and MyITLab

GLOSSARY

GLOSSARY OF CHAPTER KEY TERMS

Artistic effects Formats applied to images that make pictures resemble sketches or paintings.

Aspect ratio The ratio of the width of a display to the height of the display.

Black slide A slide that displays after the last slide in a presentation, indicating that the presentation is over.

Contiguous slides Slides that are adjacent to each other in a presentation.

Editing The process of modifying a presentation by adding and deleting slides or by changing the contents of individual slides.

Footer Text that displays at the bottom of every slide or that prints at the bottom of a sheet of slide handouts or notes pages.

Formatting The process of changing the appearance of the text, layout, and design of a slide.

Header Text that prints at the top of each sheet of slide handouts or notes pages.

Layout The arrangement of elements, such as title and subtitle text, lists, pictures, tables, charts, shapes, and movies, on a slide.

List level An outline level in a presentation represented by a bullet symbol and identified in a slide by the indentation and the size of the text.

Noncontiguous slides Slides that are not adjacent to each other in a presentation.

Normal view The primary editing view in PowerPoint where you write and design your presentations.

Notes page A printout that contains the slide image on the top half of the page and notes that you have created on the Notes pane in the lower half of the page.

Notes pane An area of the Normal view window that displays below the Slide pane with space to type notes regarding the active slide.

Outline view A PowerPoint view that displays the presentation outline to the left of the Slide pane.

Placeholder A box on a slide with dotted or dashed borders that holds title and body text or other content such as charts, tables, and pictures.

Presenter view A view that shows the full-screen slide show on one monitor or projection screen while enabling the presenter to view a preview of the next slide, notes, and a timer on another monitor.

Reading view A view in PowerPoint that displays a presentation in a manner similar to a slide show but in which the taskbar, title bar, and status bar remain available in the presentation window.

Rotation handle A circular arrow that provides a way to rotate a selected image.

Section header A type of slide layout that changes the look and flow of a presentation by providing text placeholders that do not contain bullet points.

Sizing handles Small circles surrounding a picture that indicate that the picture is selected.

Slide A presentation page that can contain text, pictures, tables, charts, and other multimedia or graphic objects.

Slide handout Printed images of slides on a sheet of paper.

Slide pane A PowerPoint screen element that displays a large image of the active slide.

Slide Sorter view A presentation view that displays thumbnails of all of the slides in a presentation.

Slide transitions Motion effects that occur in Slide Show view when you move from one slide to the next during a presentation.

Split button A type of button in which clicking the main part of the button performs a command and clicking the arrow opens a menu, list, or gallery.

Style A collection of formatting options that you can apply to a picture, text, or an object.

Text alignment The horizontal placement of text within a placeholder.

Theme A set of unified design elements that provides a look for your presentation by applying colors, fonts, and effects.

Thumbnails Miniature images of presentation slides.

Title slide A slide layout—most commonly the first slide in a presentation—that provides an introduction to the presentation topic.

Variant A variation on the presentation theme style and color.

Apply 1A skills from these Objectives:

1 Create a New Presentation
2 Edit a Presentation in Normal View
3 Add Pictures to a Presentation
4 Print and View a Presentation

Skills Review Project 1C Glaciers

In the following Skills Review, you will create a new presentation by inserting content and pictures, adding notes and footers, and applying a presentation theme. Your completed presentation will look similar to Figure 1.58.

PROJECT FILES

For Project 1C, you will need the following files:

New blank PowerPoint presentation
p01C_Glacier_Bay
p01C_Ice
p01C_Ship

Build From Scratch

You will save your presentation as:

Lastname_Firstname_1C_Glaciers

PROJECT RESULTS

FIGURE 1.58

PowerPoint 2016, Windows 10, Microsoft Corporation

(Project 1C Glaciers continues on the next page)

1 ▶ Start PowerPoint. On the right, click **Ion**, and then click **Create**. In the **Slide pane**, click in the text *Click to add title*. Type **Glacier Bay** and then click in the subtitle placeholder. Type **Part One in a Series of Alaskan Passage Adventures**

a. On the **Quick Access Toolbar**, click **Save**. Under **Save As**, click **Browse**. Navigate to your **PowerPoint Chapter 1** folder. In the **File name** box, using your own name, replace the existing text with **Lastname_Firstname_1C_Glaciers** and then click **Save**.

b. On the **Home tab**, in the **Slides group**, click the **New Slide arrow**, and then in the gallery, click **Two Content**. Click the text *Click to add title*, and then type **About the Park**

2 ▶ On the left side of the slide, click in the content placeholder. Type **Located in the Southeast Alaskan Wilderness** and then press ⏎. Press ⇥. Type **3.3 million acres** and then press ⏎. Type **A national park and preserve** and then press ⏎.

a. On the **Home tab**, in the **Paragraph group**, click **Decrease List Level**. Type **Visitor season** and then press ⏎. On the **Home tab**, in the **Paragraph group**, click **Increase List Level**. Type **May to September**

b. On the **Home tab**, in the **Slides group**, click the **New Slide arrow**, and then in the gallery, click **Panoramic Picture with Caption**. In the lower portion of the slide, click the text **Click to add title**, and then type **Prepare to be Amazed!**

c. Click in the text placeholder. Type **Before you reach Glacier Bay, walk around your cruise ship to find the best viewing locations. Make sure your camera battery is charged!**

d. On the **Home tab**, in the **Slides group**, click the **New Slide arrow**, and then in the gallery, click **Content with Caption**. In the title placeholder, type **Learn More!**

e. Click in the text placeholder, and then type **A national park ranger will board your ship during your visit to Glacier Bay. Check your ship's itinerary for presentation information and locations.**

3 ▶ With **Slide 4** displayed, in the **Status bar**, click **Notes**. Click in the **Notes pane**, and then type **Your cruise ship will spend between 6 and 8 hours in Glacier Bay.**

a. On the left side of the PowerPoint window, in the slide thumbnails, click **Slide 1**. Click in the subtitle placeholder after the *n* in *ALASKAN*. Press ⎵, and then type **Inside**

b. In the slide thumbnails, click **Slide 2**, and then click at the end of the last bullet point after the word *September*. Press ⏎, and then type **Be prepared for rain**

4 ▶ With **Slide 2** displayed, in the placeholder on the right side of the slide, click **Pictures**. Navigate to your student data files, and then click **p01C_Glacier_Bay**. Click **Insert**.

a. With the picture selected, on the **Format tab**, in the **Picture Styles group**, click **More** ⏷ to display the **Picture Styles** gallery. In the second row, click the third style—**Beveled Oval, Black**.

b. Display **Slide 3**. In the Picture placeholder, click **Pictures**. Navigate to your student data files, and then click **p01C_Ice**. Click **Insert**.

c. Display **Slide 4**. In the content placeholder on the right side of the slide, click **Pictures**. Navigate to your student data files, and then insert **p01C_Ship**. On the **Format tab**, in the **Picture Styles group**, click **More** ⏷ to display the **Picture Styles** gallery. In the third row, click the sixth style—**Soft Edge Oval**.

d. With the picture still selected, on the **Format tab**, in the **Adjust group**, click **Artistic Effects** to display the gallery. In the fourth row, click the third effect—**Crisscross Etching**.

5 ▶ On the **Slide Show tab**, in the **Start Slide Show group**, click **From Beginning**.

a. Click the left mouse button or press ⎵ to advance to the second slide. Continue to click or press ⎵ until the last slide displays, and then click or press ⎵ one more time to display a black slide.

b. With the black slide displayed, click the left mouse button or press ⎵ to exit the slide show and return to the presentation.

6 ▶ Click the **Insert tab**, and then in the **Text group**, click **Header & Footer** to display the **Header and Footer** dialog box.

a. In the **Header and Footer** dialog box, click the **Notes and Handouts tab**. Under **Include on page**, select the **Date and time** check box. If necessary,

(Project 1C Glaciers continues on the next page)

click the Update automatically option button so that the current date prints on the notes and handouts.

b. Select the **Page number** check box. If necessary, clear the Header check box to omit this element. Select the **Footer** check box. In the **Footer** box, type **Lastname_Firstname_1C_Glaciers** and then click **Apply to All**.

c. In the upper left corner of your screen, click the **File** tab to display **Backstage** view. On the right, at the bottom of the **Properties list**, click **Show All Properties**.

d. On the list of Properties, click to the right of **Tags** to display an empty box, and then type **Glacier Bay** Click to the right of **Subject** to display an empty box, and then type your course name and section number. Under **Related People**, be sure that your name displays as the author; edit if necessary.

e. **Save** your presentation. As directed by your instructor, create and submit a paper printout or an electronic image of your presentation that looks like a printed document; or, submit your completed PowerPoint file. **Close** PowerPoint.

END | You have completed Project 1C

Skills Review Project 1D Photography

In the following Skills Review, you will edit an existing presentation by inserting slides from another presentation, applying font and slide formatting, and applying slide transitions. Your completed presentation will look similar to Figure 1.59.

PROJECT FILES

For Project 1D, you will need the following files:

p01D_Photography
p01D_Photography_Slides

You will save your presentation as:

Lastname_Firstname_1D_Photography

PROJECT RESULTS

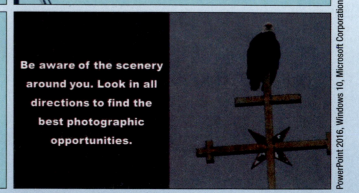

FIGURE 1.59

(Project 1D Photography continues on the next page)

PowerPoint 2016, Windows 10, Microsoft Corporation

1 Start PowerPoint. On the left, under the list of recent presentations, click **Open Other Presentations**. Under **Open**, click **Browse**. Navigate to your student data files, and then click **p01D_Photography**. Click **Open**. On the **File tab**, click **Save As**, navigate to your **PowerPoint Chapter 1** folder, and then using your own name, save the file as **Lastname_Firstname_1D_Photography**

a. On the **Design tab**, in the **Customize group**, click **Slide Size**, and then click **Widescreen (16:9)**.

b. With **Slide 1** displayed, on the **Home tab**, in the **Slides group**, click the **New Slide arrow**, and then click **Reuse Slides**. In the **Reuse Slides** pane, click **Browse**, and then click **Browse File**. In the **Browse** dialog box, navigate to your student data files, and then double-click **p01D_Photography_Slides** to display the slides from this presentation in the **Reuse Slides** pane.

c. At the bottom of the **Reuse Slides** pane, be sure that the **Keep source formatting** check box is *cleared*. In the **Reuse Slides** pane, click the first slide to insert the slide after Slide 1.

d. At the left of your screen, in the slide thumbnails, click **Slide 6** to display it in the **Slide pane**. In the **Reuse Slides** pane, click the second slide to insert it after **Slide 6**. **Close** the **Reuse Slides** pane.

2 Display **Slide 1**. On the **View tab**, in the **Presentation Views group**, click **Outline View**.

a. In the **Outline**, in **Slide 7**, drag to select the second and third bullet points—beginning with *Never approach* and ending with *animal's home*.

b. On the **Home tab**, in the **Paragraph group**, click **Decrease List Level** one time.

c. In the **Outline**, in the same slide, click at the end of the first bullet point after the word *sense*. Press Spacebar, and then type **when photographing wildlife**

d. In the **Status bar**, click **Normal** to display the slide thumbnails.

3 Display **Slide 8**, and then press Delete to delete the slide from the presentation.

a. Display **Slide 1**. On the **Home tab**, in the **Editing group**, click **Replace**. In the **Replace** dialog box, in the **Find what** box, type **home** and then in the **Replace with** box, type **habitat**

b. In the **Replace** dialog box, click **Replace All** to display a message box indicating that one

replacement was made. In the message box, click **OK**. **Close** the **Replace** dialog box.

c. On the **Design tab**, in the **Variants group**, right-click the third variant. On the shortcut menu, click **Apply to All Slides** so that the variant color is applied to all of the slides in the presentation.

4 Display **Slide 5**. Select all of the text in the placeholder. On the **Home tab**, in the **Font group**, click the **Font arrow**, scroll the font list, and then click **Arial Black**. Click the **Font Size arrow**, and then click **32**. In the **Paragraph group**, click **Line Spacing**, and then click **1.5**.

a. Display **Slide 2**. On the **Home tab**, in the **Slides group**, click **Layout** to display the **Slide Layout** gallery. Click **Title Slide** to change the slide layout.

b. On **Slide 2**, select the title—*Alaskan Wildlife*. On the **Home tab**, in the **Font group**, click the **Font Color arrow**. In the fourth column, click the first color— **Dark Teal, Text 2**.

c. Display **Slide 3**, and then select the title—*Lights, Camera, Action*. On the mini toolbar, click **Font Color** to apply the font color **Dark Teal, Text 2**.

d. Display **Slide 4**, and then, click anywhere in the text. On the **Home tab**, in the **Paragraph group**, click **Center** to center the text within the placeholder.

e. Display **Slide 6**, and then select the subtitle. From the mini toolbar, apply **Bold** and **Italic**.

f. In the slide thumbnails, point to **Slide 7**, hold down the left mouse button, and then drag up to position the slide between **Slides 3** and **4**.

5 In the lower right corner of the PowerPoint window, click **Slide Sorter** to display all of the slide thumbnails. Click **Slide 1**, so that it is selected. On your keyboard, press Delete to delete the slide.

a. Click **Slide 4**, and then hold down Ctrl and click **Slide 5**. With both slides selected, point to either of the selected slides, hold down the left mouse button, and then drag to position the two slides to the right of **Slide 6**. Release the mouse button to move the two slides. In the status bar, click **Normal** to return to Normal view.

b. Display **Slide 1**. On the **Transitions tab**, in the **Transition to This Slide group**, click **More** to display the **Transitions** gallery.

(Project 1D Photography continues on the next page)

Skills Review Project 1D Photography (continued)

c. Under **Exciting**, click **Gallery** to apply and view the transition. In the **Transition to This Slide group**, click **Effect Options**, and then click **From Left**. In the **Timing group**, click **Apply To All** to apply the *Gallery, From Left* transition to all of the slides in the presentation.

d. In the **Timing group**, click the **Duration up spin arrow** so that *01.75* displays. Under **Advance Slide**, verify that the **On Mouse Click** check box is selected; select it if necessary. In the **Timing group**, click **Apply To All**.

e. Click the **Slide Show tab**. In the **Start Slide Show group**, click **From Beginning**, and then view your presentation, clicking the mouse button to advance through the slides. When the black slide displays, click the mouse button one more time to display the presentation in Normal view.

6 On the **Insert tab**, in the **Text group**, click **Header & Footer** to display the **Header and Footer** dialog box.

a. In the **Header and Footer** dialog box, click the **Notes and Handouts tab**. Under **Include on page**, select the **Date and time** check box. If necessary,

click the Update automatically option button so that the current date prints on the notes and handouts.

b. Select the **Page number** check box. If necessary, clear the Header check box to omit this element. Select the **Footer** check box. In the **Footer** box, type **Lastname_Firstname_1D_Photography** and then click **Apply to All**.

c. In the upper left corner of your screen, click the **File** tab to display **Backstage** view. On the right, at the bottom of the **Properties list**, click **Show All Properties**.

d. On the list of Properties, click to the right of **Tags**, and then type **photography** Click to the right of **Subject**, and then type your course name and section number. Under **Related People**, be sure that your name displays as the author. If necessary, right-click the author name, click Edit Property, type your name, and click OK.

e. **Save** your presentation. As directed by your instructor, create and submit a paper printout or an electronic image of your presentation that looks like a printed document; or, submit your completed PowerPoint file. **Close** the presentation.

END | You have completed Project 1D

Mastering PowerPoint | Project 1E Juneau

Apply 1A skills from these Objectives:

1 Create a New Presentation
2 Edit a Presentation in Normal View
3 Add Pictures to a Presentation
4 Print and View a Presentation

Build From Scratch

In the following Mastering PowerPoint project, you will create a new presentation that Kodiak West Travel will use in their promotional materials to describe activities in the city of Juneau. Your completed presentation will look similar to Figure 1.60.

PROJECT FILES

For Project 1E, you will need the following files:

New blank PowerPoint presentation
p01E_Aerial_View
p01E_Whale
p01E_Falls

You will save your presentation as:

Lastname_Firstname_1E_Juneau

PROJECT RESULTS

PowerPoint 2016, Windows 10, Microsoft Corporation

FIGURE 1.60

(Project 1E Juneau continues on the next page)

Mastering PowerPoint Project 1E Juneau (continued)

1 Start PowerPoint and create a presentation using the **Integral** theme. Use the default color variant.

2 As the title of this presentation type **Juneau Highlights** and as the subtitle type **Kodiak West Travel** Save the presentation in your **PowerPoint Chapter 1** folder as **Lastname_Firstname_1E_Juneau**

3 Insert a **New Slide** using the **Content with Caption** layout. In the title placeholder, type **The View from Above**

4 In the content placeholder on the right side of the slide, from your student data files, insert the picture **p01E_Aerial_View**. Format the picture with the **Beveled Matte, White** picture style.

5 In the text placeholder on the left, type **View a glacial ice field from above by plane or helicopter. If you are more adventurous, try glacier trekking in Juneau where you can land on a glacier and climb an ice wall.**

6 Insert a **New Slide** using the **Two Content** layout. In the title placeholder, type **On Land and Sea**

7 In the content placeholder on the left, type the following text, increasing and decreasing the list level as shown below. In this presentation theme, the first level bullet points do not include a bullet symbol.

On the water
    Whale watching
    Kayaking
Mount Roberts tramway
    Spectacular views of Juneau
    Recreational hiking trails

8 In the content placeholder on the right, from your student data files, insert the picture **p01E_Whale**. Apply the **Rotated, White** picture style.

9 Insert a new slide with the **Picture with Caption** layout. In the title placeholder, type **Mendenhall Glacier** and then in the picture placeholder, from your student data files, insert the picture **p01E_Falls**.

10 In the text placeholder, type **Walk to Mendenhall Glacier from the Visitor Center to get a close-up view of Nugget Falls.**

11 In the **Notes pane**, type **Mendenhall Glacier is the most famous glacier in Juneau and in some years is visited by over 400,000 people.**

12 Insert a **Header & Footer** on the **Notes and Handouts**. Include the **Date and time** updated automatically, the **Page number**, and a **Footer**—using your own name—with the text **Lastname_Firstname_1E_Juneau** and apply to all the slides.

13 Display the **Document Properties**. As the **Tags** type **Juneau** As the **Subject** type your course and section number. Be sure your name is indicated as the Author.

14 **Save** your presentation, and then view the slide show from the beginning. As directed by your instructor, create and submit a paper printout or an electronic image of your presentation that looks like a printed document; or, submit your completed PowerPoint file. **Close** PowerPoint.

END | You have completed Project 1E

Mastering PowerPoint Project 1F Refuge

Apply 1B skills from these Objectives:

5 Edit an Existing Presentation

6 Format a Presentation

7 Use Slide Sorter View

8 Apply Slide Transitions

In the following Mastering PowerPoint project, you will edit a presentation regarding a wildlife refuge where Kodiak West Travel conducts tours. Your completed presentation will look similar to Figure 1.61.

PROJECT FILES

For Project 1F, you will need the following files:

p01F_Refuge
p01F_Excursions

You will save your presentation as:

Lastname_Firstname_1F_Refuge

PROJECT RESULTS

FIGURE 1.61

(Project 1F Refuge continues on the next page)

Mastering PowerPoint   Project 1F Refuge (continued)

1 Start PowerPoint, and then from your student data files, open the file **p01F_Refuge**. In your **PowerPoint Chapter 1** folder, **Save** the file as **Lastname_Firstname_1F_Refuge**

2 Change the **Slide Size** to **Widescreen (16:9)**.

3 Display the presentation **Outline**. In the **Outline**, on **Slide 2**, increase the list level of the third and the fifth bullet points. Click at the end of the last bullet point after the word *roads*, and then type **or facilities**

4 Return the presentation to **Normal view**, and then display **Slide 4**. Display the **Reuse Slides** pane. Browse to open from your student data files, **p01F_Excursions**. Make sure the **Keep source formatting** check box is *cleared*. With **Slide 4** in your presentation displayed, insert the last two slides from the **Reuse Slides** pane.

5 Display **Slide 1**, and then change the layout to **Title Slide**.

6 Select the subtitle—*Experience Alaska with Kodiak West Travel*. Change the **Font** to **Arial**, and the **Font Size** to **28**. Change the **Font Color** to **Black, Text 1**. **Center** the title and the subtitle.

7 Display **Slide 5**, and then select the paragraph in the content placeholder. Apply **Bold** and **Italic**, and then change the **Font Size** to **16**.

8 **Center** the paragraph text, and then change the **Line Spacing** to **1.5**. **Center** the slide title.

9 In **Slide Sorter** view, delete **Slide 3**. Move **Slide 5** to position it after **Slide 2**.

10 Move **Slide 4** to the end of the presentation.

11 In **Normal** view, display **Slide 1**. Apply the **Split** transition and change the **Effect Options** to **Horizontal Out**. Change the **Duration** to **1.75** and apply the transition to all of the slides in the presentation. View the slide show from the beginning.

12 **Insert** a **Header & Footer** on the **Notes and Handouts**. Include the **Date and time** updated automatically, the **Page number**, and a **Footer** with the text **Lastname_Firstname_1F_Refuge**

13 Display the **Document Properties**. As the **Tags** type **refuge, tours** As the **Subject** type your course and section number. Be sure your name is indicated as the Author.

14 **Save** your presentation, create and submit a paper printout or an electronic image of your presentation that looks like a printed document; or, submit your completed PowerPoint file as directed by your instructor. **Close** PowerPoint.

END | You have completed Project 1F

grader

Mastering PowerPoint Project 1G Northern Lights

Apply 1A and 1B skills from these Objectives:

1 Create a New Presentation
2 Edit a Presentation in Normal View
3 Add Pictures to a Presentation
4 Print and View a Presentation
5 Edit an Existing Presentation
6 Format a Presentation
7 Use Slide Sorter View
8 Apply Slide Transitions

In the following Mastering PowerPoint project, you will edit an existing presentation that describes the Northern Lights and ideal viewing areas. Your completed presentation will look similar to Figure 1.62.

PROJECT FILES

For Project 1G, you will need the following files:

p01G_Northern_Lights
p01G_Lights
p01G_Slides

You will save your presentation as:

Lastname_Firstname_1G_Northern_Lights

PROJECT RESULTS

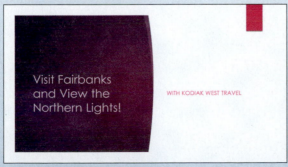

PowerPoint 2016, Windows 10, Microsoft Corporation

FIGURE 1.62

(Project 1G Northern Lights continues on the next page)

Mastering PowerPoint Project 1G Northern Lights (continued)

1 Start PowerPoint, and then from your student data files, open the file **p01G_Northern_Lights**. In your **PowerPoint Chapter 1** folder, **Save** the file as **Lastname_Firstname_1G_Northern_Lights**

2 Replace all occurrences of the text **North** with **Northern** and then change the layout of **Slide 1** to **Title Slide**.

3 Apply the **Ion Boardroom** theme, with the default purple variant option.

4 Change the **Slide Size** to **Widescreen (16:9)**.

5 Display **Slide 2**, open the **Reuse Slides** pane, and then from your student data files browse for and open the presentation **p01G_Slides**. If necessary, clear the Keep source formatting check box, and then insert the last two slides from the **p01G_Slides** file.

6 Display **Slide 2**. In either the slide pane or in the slide outline, click at the end of the first bullet point after the word *time*. Add the words **for viewing** and then in the same slide, increase the list level of the second and third bullet points.

7 With **Slide 2** still displayed, select the title and change the **Font Size** to **32**. In the **Notes pane**, type the following notes: **The lights reach their peak in September and March.**

8 Display **Slide 3**. Select the paragraph of text, and then change the **Font Color** to **Purple, Accent 6, Lighter 60%**—in the last column, the third color. Change the **Font Size** to **16**, and then apply **Bold**.

9 Change the paragraph **Line Spacing** to **1.5**, and then **Center** the paragraph and the slide title.

10 With **Slide 3** still displayed, format the picture with the **Soft Edge Rectangle** picture style and the **Marker** artistic effect.

11 Display **Slide 4**. In the content placeholder on the right, from your student data files, insert the picture **p01G_Lights**. Apply the **Reflected Rounded Rectangle** picture style.

12 Move **Slide 3** between **Slides 1** and **2**.

13 Display **Slide 4**. Insert a **New Slide** with the **Section Header** layout. In the title placeholder type **Visit Fairbanks and View the Northern Lights!** In the text placeholder type **With Kodiak West Travel**

14 Apply the **Uncover** transition and change the **Effect Options** to **From Top**. Change the **Timing** by increasing the **Duration** to **01.25**. Apply the transition effect to all of the slides. View the slide show from the beginning.

15 **Insert** a **Header & Footer** on the **Notes and Handouts**. Include the **Date and time** updated automatically, the **Page number**, and a **Footer**, using your own name, with the text **Lastname_Firstname_1G_Northern_Lights**

16 Display the **Document Properties**. As the **Tags** type **northern lights, Fairbanks** As the **Subject** type your course and section number. Be sure your name is indicated as the Author.

17 **Save** your presentation, create and submit a paper printout or an electronic image of your presentation that looks like a printed document; or, submit your completed PowerPoint file as directed by your instructor. **Close** PowerPoint.

END | You have completed Project 1G

Apply a combination of the **1A** and **1B** skills.	GO! Fix It	Project 1H Rain Forest	MyITLab
	GO! Make It	Project 1I Eagles	MyITLab
	GO! Solve It	Project 1J Packrafting	MyITLab
	GO! Solve It	Project 1K Packing	

PROJECT FILES

For Project 1K, you will need the following file:

p01K_Packing

You will save your presentation as:

Lastname_Firstname_1K_Packing

Open the file p01K_Packing and save it as **Lastname_Firstname_1K_Packing** Complete the presentation by applying a theme and changing the variant. Format the presentation by applying appropriate font formatting and by changing text alignment and line spacing. Change the layout of the last slide to an appropriate layout. On Slide 2, insert a picture that you have taken yourself, or use one of the pictures in your student data files that you inserted in other projects. Apply a style to the picture. Apply slide transitions to all of the slides in the presentation, and then insert a header and footer that includes the date and time updated automatically, the file name in the footer, and the page number. Add your name, your course name and section number, and the tags **packing, weather** to the properties. Save and print or submit as directed by your instructor.

Performance Level

Performance Criteria		Exemplary: You consistently applied the relevant skills	Proficient: You sometimes, but not always, applied the relevant skills	Developing: You rarely or never applied the relevant skills
	Apply a theme and a variant	An appropriate theme and variant were applied to the presentation.	A theme was applied but the variant was not changed.	Neither a theme nor the variant theme were applied.
	Apply font and slide formatting	Font and slide formatting is attractive and appropriate.	Adequately formatted but difficult to read or unattractive.	Inadequate or no formatting.
	Use appropriate pictures and apply styles attractively	An appropriate picture was inserted and a style is applied attractively.	A picture was inserted but a style was not applied.	Picture was not inserted.
	Apply appropriate slide layout to Slide 4	An appropriate layout was applied to the last slide.	The slide layout was changed but is not appropriate for the type of slide.	The slide layout was not changed.

END | You have completed Project 1K

RUBRIC

The following outcomes-based assessments are open-ended assessments. That is, there is no specific correct result; your result will depend on your approach to the information provided. Make Professional Quality your goal. Use the following scoring rubric to guide you in how to approach the problem and then to evaluate how well your approach solves the problem.

The *criteria*—Software Mastery, Content, Format and Layout, and Process—represent the knowledge and skills you have gained that you can apply to solving the problem. The *levels of performance*—Professional Quality, Approaching Professional Quality, or Needs Quality Improvements—help you and your instructor evaluate your result.

	Your completed project is of Professional Quality if you:	Your completed project is Approaching Professional Quality if you:	Your completed project Needs Quality Improvements if you:
1-Software Mastery	Choose and apply the most appropriate skills, tools, and features and identify efficient methods to solve the problem.	Choose and apply some appropriate skills, tools, and features, but not in the most efficient manner.	Choose inappropriate skills, tools, or features, or are inefficient in solving the problem.
2-Content	Construct a solution that is clear and well organized, contains content that is accurate, appropriate to the audience and purpose, and is complete. Provide a solution that contains no errors in spelling, grammar, or style.	Construct a solution in which some components are unclear, poorly organized, inconsistent, or incomplete. Misjudge the needs of the audience. Have some errors in spelling, grammar, or style, but the errors do not detract from comprehension.	Construct a solution that is unclear, incomplete, or poorly organized; contains some inaccurate or inappropriate content; and contains many errors in spelling, grammar, or style. Do not solve the problem.
3-Format & Layout	Format and arrange all elements to communicate information and ideas, clarify function, illustrate relationships, and indicate relative importance.	Apply appropriate format and layout features to some elements, but not others. Overuse features, causing minor distraction.	Apply format and layout that does not communicate information or ideas clearly. Do not use format and layout features to clarify function, illustrate relationships, or indicate relative importance. Use available features excessively, causing distraction.
4-Process	Use an organized approach that integrates planning, development, self-assessment, revision, and reflection.	Demonstrate an organized approach in some areas, but not others; or, use an insufficient process of organization throughout.	Do not use an organized approach to solve the problem.

Apply a combination of the 1A and 1B skills.

GO! Think **Project 1L Bears**

PROJECT FILES

For Project 1L, you will need the following files:

Build From Scratch

New blank PowerPoint presentation
p01L_Bear

You will save your presentation as:

Lastname_Firstname_1L_Bears

Cindy Barrow, Tour Operations Manager for Kodiak West Travel, is developing a presentation describing brown bear viewing travel experiences that the company is developing. In the presentation, Cindy will be describing the brown bear habitat and viewing opportunities.

Kodiak bears are the largest known size of brown bears on record; they can weigh as much as 2,000 pounds and can get as large as polar bears. Kodiak bears are active during the day and are generally solitary creatures. The Kodiak Bear Travel Experience is a small, personalized travel adventure available to only eight participants at a time. It is an opportunity to peer into the life of these majestic mammals.

The adventure takes place on Kodiak Island near a lake with a high concentration of salmon, making it the perfect natural feeding ground for the Kodiak bears. Travelers can view the bears from boats, kayaks, and recently constructed viewing platforms, and guides are available.

This is a true wildlife experience as the area is home to deer, fox, and river otter. Accommodations are available at the Kodiak West Breakfast Inn from mid-June to the end of August. Peak season is early August and reservations can be made up to one year in advance. The cost is $1,800 per person for one week, and includes all meals, use of watercraft, and guided tours.

Using the preceding information, create a presentation that Cindy can show at a travel fair. The presentation should include four to six slides describing the travel experience. Apply an appropriate theme and use slide layouts that will effectively present the content. Insert at least one picture and apply appropriate picture formatting. You may use your own image file, search for one online, or from your student data files, use the file p01L_Bear. Apply font formatting and slide transitions, and modify text alignment and line spacing as necessary.

Save the file as **Lastname_Firstname_1L_Bears** and then, on the Notes and Handouts, insert a header and footer that include the date and time updated automatically, the file name in the footer, and the page number. Add your name, your course name and section number, and the tags **bears, tours** to the properties. Save and print or submit as directed by your instructor.

END | You have completed Project 1L

Build From Scratch

GO! Think **Project 1M Sitka** **MyITLab**

Build From Scratch

You and GO! **Project 1N Travel** **MyITLab**

GO! Collaborative Team Project **Project 2O Bell Orchid Hotels** **MyITLab**

Glossary

Absolute cell reference A cell reference that refers to cells by their fixed position in a worksheet; an absolute cell reference remains the same when the formula is copied.

Accounting Number Format The Excel number format that applies a thousand comma separator where appropriate, inserts a fixed U.S. dollar sign aligned at the left edge of the cell, applies two decimal places, and leaves a small amount of space at the right edge of the cell to accommodate a parenthesis for negative numbers.

Active cell The cell, surrounded by a border, ready to receive data or be affected by the next Excel command.

Alignment The placement of text or objects relative to the left and right margins.

Alignment guides A green vertical or horizontal line that displays when you are moving or sizing an object to assist you with object placement.

Alt text Another name for alternative text.

Alternative text Text added to a picture or object that helps people using a screen reader understand what the object is.

App The shortened version of the term *application*, and which typically refers to a smaller application designed for a single purpose, is self-contained, and that run on smartphones and other mobile devices.

Append To add on to the end of an object; for example, to add records to the end of an existing table.

Apps for Office A collection of downloadable apps that enable you to create and view information within Office programs and that combine cloud services and web technologies within the user interface of Office.

Arithmetic operators The symbols +, −, *, /, %, and ^ used to denote addition, subtraction (or negation), multiplication, division, percentage, and exponentiation in an Excel formula.

Artistic effects Formats applied to images that make pictures resemble sketches or paintings.

Aspect ratio The ratio of the width of a display to the height of the display.

Auto Fill An Excel feature that generates and extends values into adjacent cells based on the values of selected cells.

AutoCalculate A feature that displays three calculations in the status bar by default—Average, Count, and Sum—when you select a range of numerical data.

AutoComplete A feature that speeds your typing and lessens the likelihood of errors; if the first few characters you type in a cell match an existing entry in the column, Excel fills in the remaining characters for you.

AutoFit An Excel feature that adjusts the width of a column to fit the cell content of the widest cell in the column.

AutoNumber data type A data type that describes a unique sequential or random number assigned by Access as each record is entered and that is useful for data that has no distinct field that can be considered unique.

AutoSum A button that provides quick access to the SUM function.

Backstage tabs The area along the left side of Backstage view with tabs to display screens with related groups of commands.

Backstage view A centralized space for file management tasks; for example, opening, saving, printing, publishing, or sharing a file. A navigation pane displays along the left side with tabs that group file-related tasks together.

Best Fit An Access command that adjusts the width of a column to accommodate the column's longest entry.

Black slide A slide that displays after the last slide in a presentation, indicating that the presentation is over.

Blank desktop database A database that has no data and has no database tools—you must create the data and tools as you need them; the database is stored on your computer or other storage device.

Bookmark A command that identifies a word, section, or place in a document so that you can find it quickly without scrolling.

Bulleted list A list of items with each item introduced by a symbol such as a small circle or check mark, and which is useful when the items in the list can be displayed in any order.

Bullets Text symbols such as small circles or check marks that precede each item in a bulleted list.

Caption A property setting that displays a name for a field in a table, query, form, or report different from the one listed as the field name.

Category axis The area along the bottom of a chart that identifies the categories of data; also referred to as the x-axis.

Category labels The labels that display along the bottom of a chart to identify the categories of data; Excel uses the row titles as the category names.

Cell (Excel) The intersection of a column and a row.

Cell address Another name for a cell reference.

Cell content Anything typed into a cell.

Cell reference The identification of a specific cell by its intersecting column letter and row number.

Cell style A defined set of formatting characteristics, such as font, font size, font color, cell borders, and cell shading.

Center alignment The alignment of text or objects that is centered horizontally between the left and right margin.

Chart The graphic representation of data in a worksheet; data presented as a chart is usually easier to understand than a table of numbers.

Chart Elements button A button that enables you to add, remove, or change chart elements such as the title, legend, gridlines, and data labels.

Chart Filters button A button that displays options for changing the data displayed in a chart.

Chart layout The combination of chart elements that can be displayed in a chart such as a title, legend, labels for the columns, and the table of charted cells.

Chart style A set of predefined formats applied to a chart, including colors, backgrounds, and effects.

Chart Styles button A button that displays options for setting the style and color scheme for a chart.

Chart Styles gallery A group of predesigned chart styles that you can apply to an Excel chart.

Chart types Various chart formats used in a way that is meaningful to the reader; common examples are column charts, pie charts, and line charts.

Check Accessibility A command that checks the document for content that people with disabilities might find difficult to read.

Check Compatibility A command that searches your document for features that may not be supported by older versions of Office.

Clipboard A temporary storage area for information that you have copied or moved from one place and plan to use somewhere else.

Cloud computing Applications and services that are accessed over the Internet, rather than accessing applications that are installed on your local computer.

Cloud storage Storage space on an Internet site that may also display as a drive on your computer.

Collaborate To work with others as a team in an intellectual endeavor to complete a shared task or to achieve a shared goal.

Column A vertical group of cells in a worksheet.

Column chart A chart in which the data is arranged in columns and that is useful for showing data changes over a period of time or for illustrating comparisons among items.

Column heading The letter that displays at the top of a vertical group of cells in a worksheet; beginning with the first letter of the alphabet, a unique letter, or combination of letters identifies each column.

Comma Style The Excel number format that inserts thousand comma separators where appropriate and applies two decimal places; Comma Style also leaves space at the right to accommodate a parenthesis when negative numbers are present.

Commands Instructions to a computer program that cause an action to be carried out.

Common field A field included in two or more tables that stores the same data.

Compressed file A file that has been reduced in size and that takes up less storage space and can be transferred to other computers faster than uncompressed files.

Constant value Numbers, text, dates, or times of day that you type into a cell.

Content app An app for Office that integrates web-based features as content within the body of a document.

Context menus Menus that display commands and options relevant to the selected text or object; also called *shortcut menus*.

Context sensitive commands A command associated with the currently selected or active object; often activated by right-clicking a screen item.

Contextual tabs Tabs that are added to the ribbon automatically when a specific object, such as a picture, is selected, and that contain commands relevant to the selected object.

Contiguous slides Slides that are adjacent to each other in a presentation.

Copy A command that duplicates a selection and places it on the Clipboard.

Creative Commons A nonprofit organization that enables sharing and use of images and knowledge through free legal tools.

Currency data type An Access data type that describes monetary values and numeric data that can be used in mathematical calculations involving values with one to four decimal places.

Custom web app A database that you can publish and share with others over the Internet.

Cut A command that removes a selection and places it on the Clipboard.

Data (Access) Facts about people, events, things, or ideas.

Data (Excel) Text or numbers in a cell.

Data marker A column, bar, area, dot, pie slice, or other symbol in a chart that represents a single data point; related data points form a data series.

Data point A value that originates in a worksheet cell and that is represented in a chart by a data marker.

Data series Related data points represented by data markers; each data series has a unique color or pattern represented in the chart legend.

Data source The table or tables from which a form, query, or report retrieves its data.

Data type Classification identifying the kind of data that can be stored in a field, such as numbers, text, or dates.

Database An organized collection of facts about people, events, things, or ideas related to a specific topic or purpose.

Database management system (DBMS) Database software that controls how related collections of data are stored, organized, retrieved, and secured; also known as a DBMS.

Database template A preformatted database that contains prebuilt tables, queries, forms, and reports that perform a specific task, such as tracking events.

Datasheet view The Access view that displays data organized in columns and rows similar to an Excel worksheet.

DBMS An acronym for database management system.

Default The term that refers to the current selection or setting that is automatically used by a computer program unless you specify otherwise.

Deselect The action of canceling the selection of an object or block of text by clicking outside of the selection.

Design view An Access view that displays the detailed structure of a table, query, form, or report. For forms and reports, it may be the view in which some tasks must be performed, and only the controls, and not the data, display in this view.

Desktop app A computer program that is installed on the hard drive of a personal computer and that requires a computer operating system like Microsoft Windows or Apple OSX to run.

Destination table The table to which you import or append data.

Dialog Box Launcher A small icon that displays to the right of some group names on the ribbon and that opens a related dialog box or pane providing additional options and commands related to that group.

Displayed value The data that displays in a cell.

Document properties Details about a file that describe or identify it, including the title, author name, subject, and keywords that identify the document's topic or contents; also known as *metadata*.

Dot leader A series of dots preceding a tab that guides the eye across the line.

Drag The action of moving something from one location on the screen to another while holding down the left mouse button; the action of dragging includes releasing the mouse button at the desired time or location.

Drawing objects Graphic objects, such as shapes, diagrams, lines, or circles.

Edit The process of making changes to text or graphics in an Office file.

Editing The process of modifying a presentation by adding and deleting slides or by changing the contents of individual slides.

Ellipsis A set of three dots indicating incompleteness; an ellipsis following a command name indicates that a dialog box will display if you click the command.

Embed code A code that creates a link to a video, picture, or other type of rich media content.

Enhanced ScreenTip A ScreenTip that displays more descriptive text than a normal ScreenTip.

Excel pointer An Excel window element with which you can display the location of the pointer.

Expand Formula Bar button An Excel window element with which you can increase the height of the Formula Bar to display lengthy cell content.

Expand horizontal scroll bar button An Excel window element with which you can increase the width of the horizontal scroll bar.

Export The process of copying data from one file into another file, such as an Access table into an Excel spreadsheet.

Field (Access) A single piece of information that is stored in every record; represented by a column in a database table.

Field properties Characteristics of a field that control how the field displays and how data can be entered in the field; vary for different data types.

Fill The inside color of an object.

Fill handle The small square in the lower right corner of a selected cell.

First principle of good database design A principle of good database design stating that data is organized in tables so that there is no redundant data.

Flat database A simple database file that is not related or linked to any other collection of data.

Floating object A graphic that can be moved independently of the surrounding text characters.

Font styles Formatting emphasis such as bold, italic, and underline.

Font A set of characters with the same design and shape.

Footer Text that displays at the bottom of every slide or that prints at the bottom of a sheet of slide handouts or notes pages.

Form An Access object you can use to enter new records into a table, edit or delete existing records in a table, or display existing records.

Form view The Access view in which you can view, modify, delete, or add records in a table but you cannot change the layout or design of the form.

Format Changing the appearance of cells and worksheet elements to make a worksheet attractive and easy to read.

Formatting The process of establishing the overall appearance of text, graphics, and pages in an Office file—for example, in a Word document.

Formatting marks Characters that display on the screen, but do not print, indicating where the Enter key, the Spacebar, and the Tab key were pressed; also called *nonprinting characters*.

Formula An equation that performs mathematical calculations on values in a worksheet.

Formula Bar An element in the Excel window that displays the value or formula contained in the active cell; here, you can also enter or edit values or formulas.

Function A predefined formula—a formula that Excel has already built for you—that performs calculations by using specific values in a particular order or structure.

Gallery An Office feature that displays a list of potential results instead of just the command name.

General format The default format that Excel applies to numbers; this format has no specific characteristics—whatever you type in the cell will display, with the exception that trailing zeros to the right of a decimal point will not display.

Gradient fill A fill effect in which one color fades into another.

Graphics Pictures, charts, or drawing objects.

Groups On the Office ribbon, the sets of related commands that you might need for a specific type of task.

Header (PowerPoint) Text that prints at the top of each sheet of slide handouts or notes pages.

Header (Word) A reserved area for text or graphics that displays at the top of each page in a document.

Import The process of copying data from another file, such as a Word table or an Excel workbook, into a separate file, such as an Access database.

Info tab The tab in Backstage view that displays information about the current file.

Information Data that is accurate, timely, and organized in a useful manner.

Inline object An object or graphic inserted in a document that acts like a character in a sentence.

Insertion point A blinking vertical line that indicates where text or graphics will be inserted.

Inspect Document A command that searches your document for hidden data or personal information that you might not want to share publicly.

Interactive media Computer interaction that responds to your actions; for example, by presenting text, graphics, animation, video, audio, or games. Also referred to as rich media.

Justified alignment An arrangement of text in which the text aligns evenly on both the left and right margins.

Keyboard shortcut A combination of two or more keyboard keys, used to perform a task that would otherwise require a mouse.

KeyTip The letter that displays on a command in the ribbon and that indicates the key you can press to activate the command when keyboard control of the Ribbon is activated.

Keywords Custom file properties in the form of words that you associate with a document to give an indication of the document's content; used to help find and organize files. Also called *tags*.

Label Another name for a text value, and which usually provides information about number values.

Landscape orientation A page orientation in which the paper is wider than it is tall.

Layout The arrangement of elements, such as title and subtitle text, lists, pictures, tables, charts, shapes, and movies, on a slide.

Layout Options A button that displays when an object is selected and that has commands to choose how the object interacts with surrounding text.

Layout view The Access view in which you can make changes to a form or report while the data from the underlying data source displays.

Leader character Characters that form a solid, dotted, or dashed line that fills the space preceding a tab stop.

Left alignment The cell format in which characters align at the left edge of the cell; this is the default for text entries and is an example of formatting information stored in a cell.

Legend A chart element that identifies the patterns or colors that are assigned to the categories in the chart.

Lettered column headings The area along the top edge of a worksheet that identifies each column with a unique letter or combination of letters.

Line spacing The distance between lines of text in a paragraph.

Link A connection to data in another file.

List level An outline level in a presentation represented by a bullet symbol and identified in a slide by the indentation and the size of the text.

Live Layout A feature that reflows text as you move or size an object so that you can view the placement of surrounding text.

Live Preview A technology that shows the result of applying an editing or formatting change as you point to possible results—*before* you actually apply it.

Location Any disk drive, folder, or other place in which you can store files and folders.

Mail app An app for Office that displays next to an Outlook item.

Margins The space between the text and the top, bottom, left, and right edges of the paper.

Merge & Center A command that joins selected cells in an Excel worksheet into one larger cell and centers the contents in the merged cell.

Metadata Details about a file that describe or identify it, including the title, author name, subject, and keywords that identify the document's topic or contents; also known as *document properties*.

Mini toolbar A small toolbar containing frequently used formatting commands that displays as a result of selecting text or objects.

MRU Acronym for *most recently used*, which refers to the state of some commands that retain the characteristic most recently applied; for example, the Font Color button retains the most recently used color until a new color is chosen.

Multiple-items form A form that enables you to display or enter multiple records in a table.

Name Box An element of the Excel window that displays the name of the selected cell, table, chart, or object.

Navigation area An area at the bottom of the Access window that indicates the number of records in the table and contains controls in the form of arrows that you click to move among the records.

Navigation Pane (Access) An area of the Access window that displays and organizes the names of the objects in a database; from here, you open objects for use.

Noncontiguous slides Slides that are not adjacent to each other in a presentation.

Nonprinting characters Characters that display on the screen, but do not print, indicating where the Enter key, the Spacebar, and the Tab key were pressed; also called *formatting marks*.

Normal view (Excel) A screen view that maximizes the number of cells visible on your screen and keeps the column letters and row numbers close to the columns and rows.

Normal view (PowerPoint) The primary editing view in PowerPoint where you write and design your presentations.

Normalization The process of applying design rules and principles to ensure that your database performs as expected.

Notes page A printout that contains the slide image on the top half of the page and notes that you have created on the Notes pane in the lower half of the page.

Notes pane An area of the Normal view window that displays below the Slide pane with space to type notes regarding the active slide.

Number data type An Access data type that represents a quantity, how much or how many, and may be used in calculations.

Number format A specific way in which Excel displays numbers in a cell.

Number values Constant values consisting of only numbers.

Numbered list A list of items preceded by numbers, which indicate sequence or rank of the items. Sometimes called an *ordered list*.

Numbered row headings The area along the left edge of a worksheet that identifies each row with a unique number.

Object A text box, picture, table, or shape that you can select and then move and resize.

Object anchor The symbol that indicates to which paragraph an object is attached.

Object tab In the object window, a tab that identifies the object and which enables you to make an open object active.

Object window An area of the Access window that displays open objects, such as tables, queries, forms, or reports; by default, each object displays on its own tab.

Objects The basic parts of a database that you create to store your data and to work with your data; for example, tables, queries, forms, and reports.

Office 365 A version of Microsoft Office to which you subscribe for an annual fee.

Office Store A public marketplace that Microsoft hosts and regulates on Office.com.

OneDrive A free file storage and file-sharing service provided by Microsoft when you sign up for a free Microsoft account.

Open dialog box A dialog box from which you can navigate to, and then open on your screen, an existing file that was created in that same program.

Operators The symbols with which you can specify the type of calculation you want to perform in an Excel formula.

Option button In a dialog box, a round button that enables you to make one choice among two or more options.

Options dialog box A dialog box within each Office application where you can select program settings and other options and preferences.

Outline view A PowerPoint view that displays the presentation outline to the left of the Slide pane.

Page Width A view that zooms the document so that the width of the page matches the width of the window. Find this command on the View tab, in the Zoom group.

Paragraph symbol The symbol ¶ that represents the end of a paragraph.

Paste The action of placing cell contents that have been copied or moved to the Clipboard into another location.

Paste Options gallery A gallery of buttons that provides a Live Preview of all the Paste options available in the current context.

PDF The acronym for *Portable Document Format*, which is a file format that creates an image that preserves the look of your file, but that cannot be easily changed; a popular format for sending documents electronically, because the document will display on most computers.

Picture effects Effects that enhance a picture, such as a shadow, glow, reflection, or 3-D rotation.

Picture element A point of light measured in dots per square inch on a screen; 64 pixels equals 8.43 characters, which is the average number of characters that will fit in a cell in an Excel worksheet using the default font.

Pixel The abbreviated name for a picture element.

Placeholder text Nonprinting text that holds a place in a document where you can type.

Placeholder A box on a slide with dotted or dashed borders that holds title and body text or other content such as charts, tables, and pictures.

Point and click method The technique of constructing a formula by pointing to and then clicking cells; this method is convenient when the referenced cells are not adjacent to one another.

Pointer Any symbol that displays on your screen in response to moving your mouse and with which you can select objects and commands.

Points A measurement of the size of a font; there are 72 points in an inch.

Populate The action of filling a database table with records.

Portable Document Format A file format that creates an image that preserves the look of your file, but that cannot be easily changed; a popular format for sending documents electronically, because the document will display on most computers; also called a *PDF*.

Portrait orientation A page orientation in which the paper is taller than it is wide.

Presenter view A view that shows the full-screen slide show on one monitor or projection screen while enabling the presenter to view a preview of the next slide, notes, and a timer on another monitor.

Primary key A required field that uniquely identifies a record in a table; for example, a Student ID number at a college.

Print Preview A view of a document as it will appear when you print it.

Property Sheet A list of characteristics—properties—for fields or controls on a form or report in which you can make precise changes to each property associated with the field or control.

Protected View A security feature in Office 2016 that protects your computer from malicious files by opening them in a restricted environment until you enable them; you might encounter this feature if you open a file from an e-mail or download files from the Internet.

pt The abbreviation for *point*; for example, when referring to a font size.

Query A database object that retrieves specific data from one or more database objects—either tables or other queries—and then, in a single datasheet, displays only the data you specify.

Quick Access Toolbar In an Office program window, the small row of buttons in the upper left corner of the screen from which you can perform frequently used commands.

Quick Analysis Tool A tool that displays in the lower right corner of a selected range, with which you can analyze your data by using Excel tools such as charts, color-coding, and formulas.

Range Two or more selected cells on a worksheet that are adjacent or nonadjacent; because the range is treated as a single unit, you can make the same changes or combination of changes to more than one cell at a time.

Range finder An Excel feature that outlines cells in color to indicate which cells are used in a formula; useful for verifying which cells are referenced in a formula.

Reading view A view in PowerPoint that displays a presentation in a manner similar to a slide show but in which the taskbar, title bar, and status bar remain available in the presentation window.

Read-only A property assigned to a file that prevents the file from being modified or deleted; it indicates that you cannot save any changes to the displayed document unless you first save it with a new name.

Recommended Charts An Excel feature that displays a customized set of charts that, according to Excel's calculations, will best fit your data based on the range of data that you select.

Record All of the categories of data pertaining to one person, place, event, thing, or idea; represented by a row in a database table.

Record selector bar The bar at the left edge of a record when it is displayed in a form, and which is used to select an entire record.

Record selector box The small box at the left of a record in Datasheet view that, when clicked, selects the entire record.

Redundant In a database, information that is duplicated in a manner that indicates poor database design.

Relational database A sophisticated type of database that has multiple collections of data within the file that are related to one another.

Relative cell reference In a formula, the address of a cell based on the relative positions of the cell that contains the formula and the cell referred to in the formula.

Report A database object that summarizes the fields and records from a query or table in an easy-to-read format suitable for printing.

Rich media Computer interaction that responds to your actions; for example, by presenting text, graphics, animation, video, audio, or games. Also referred to as interactive media.

Right alignment An arrangement of text in which the text aligns at the right margin, leaving the left margin uneven.

Right-click The action of clicking the right mouse button one time.

Rotation handle A symbol with which you can rotate a graphic to any angle; displays above the top center sizing handle.

Rounding A procedure in which you determine which digit at the right of the number will be the last digit displayed and then increase it by one if the next digit to its right is 5, 6, 7, 8, or 9.

Row A horizontal group of cells in a worksheet.

Row heading The numbers along the left side of an Excel worksheet that designate the row numbers.

Run The process in which Access looks at the records in the table(s) included in the query design, finds the records that match the specified criteria, and then displays the records in a datasheet; only the fields included in the query design display.

Sans serif font A font design with no lines or extensions on the ends of characters.

Scaling The process of shrinking the width and/or height of printed output to fit a maximum number of pages.

Screen reader Software that enables visually impaired users to read text on a computer screen to understand the content of pictures.

ScreenTip Useful information that displays in a small box on the screen when you perform various mouse actions, such as pointing to screen elements or dragging.

Second principle of good database design A principle stating that appropriate database techniques are used to ensure the accuracy and consistency of data as it is entered into the table.

Section header A type of slide layout that changes the look and flow of a presentation by providing text placeholders that do not contain bullet points.

Select All box A box in the upper left corner of the worksheet grid that, when clicked, selects all the cells in a worksheet.

Select query A type of Access query that retrieves (selects) data from one or more tables or queries, displaying the selected data in a datasheet; also known as a simple select query.

Selecting Highlighting, by dragging with your mouse, areas of text or data or graphics, so that the selection can be edited, formatted, copied, or moved.

Series A group of things that come one after another in succession; for example, January, February, March, and so on.

Serif font A font design that includes small line extensions on the ends of the letters to guide the eye in reading from left to right.

Shapes Lines, arrows, stars, banners, ovals, rectangles, and other basic shapes with which you can illustrate an idea, a process, or a workflow.

Share button Opens the Share pane from which you can save your file to the cloud—your OneDrive—and then share it with others so you can collaborate.

SharePoint Collaboration software with which people in an organization can set up team sites to share information, manage documents, and publish reports for others to see.

Sheet tab scrolling buttons Buttons to the left of the sheet tabs used to display Excel sheet tabs that are not in view; used when there are more sheet tabs than will display in the space provided.

Sheet tabs The labels along the lower border of the workbook window that identify each worksheet.

Short Text data type An Access data type that describes text, a combination of text and numbers, or numbers that are not used in calculations, such as the Postal Code.

Shortcut menu A menu that displays commands and options relevant to the selected text or object; also called a *context menu*.

Show Formulas A command that displays the formula in each cell instead of the resulting value.

Simple select query Another name for a select query.

Single-record form A form that enables you to display or enter one record at a time from a table.

Sizing handles Small circles surrounding a picture that indicate that the picture is selected.

Slide A presentation page that can contain text, pictures, tables, charts, and other multimedia or graphic objects.

Slide handout Printed images of slides on a sheet of paper.

Slide pane A PowerPoint screen element that displays a large image of the active slide.

Slide Sorter view A presentation view that displays thumbnails of all of the slides in a presentation.

Slide transitions Motion effects that occur in Slide Show view when you move from one slide to the next during a presentation.

SmartArt A designer-quality visual representation of your information that you can create by choosing from among many different layouts to effectively communicate your message or ideas.

Source file When importing a file, refers to the file being imported.

Sparkline A tiny chart in the background of a cell that gives a visual trend summary alongside your data; makes a pattern more obvious.

Spin box A small box with an upward- and downward-pointing arrow that lets you move rapidly through a set of values by clicking.

Split button A button that has two parts—a button and an arrow; clicking the main part of the button performs a command and clicking the arrow opens a menu with choices.

Spreadsheet Another name for a worksheet.

Status bar The area along the lower edge of the Excel window that displays, on the left side, the current cell mode, page number, and worksheet information; on the right side, when numerical data is selected, common calculations such as Sum and Average display.

Structure In Access, the underlying design of a table, including field names, data types, descriptions, and field properties.

Style A group of formatting commands, such as font, font size, font color, paragraph alignment, and line spacing that can be applied to a paragraph with one command.

SUM function A predefined formula that adds all the numbers in a selected range of cells.

Switch Row/Column A charting command to swap the data over the axis—data being charted on the vertical axis will move to the horizontal axis and vice versa.

Synchronization The process of updating computer files that are in two or more locations according to specific rules—also called *syncing*.

Syncing The process of updating computer files that are in two or more locations according to specific rules—also called *synchronization*.

Tab stop A specific location on a line of text, marked on the Word ruler, to which you can move the insertion point by pressing the Tab key, and which is used to align and indent text.

Table (Access) A format for information that organizes and presents text and data in columns and rows; the foundation of a database.

Tables and Related Views An arrangement in the Navigation Pane that groups objects by the table to which they are related.

Tabs (ribbon) On the Office ribbon, the name of each task-oriented activity area.

Tags Custom file properties in the form of words that you associate with a document to give an indication of the document's content; used to help find and organize files. Also called *keywords*.

Task pane app An app for Office that works side-by-side with an Office document by displaying a separate pane on the right side of the window.

Tell Me A search feature for Microsoft Office commands that you activate by typing what you are looking for in the Tell Me box.

Tell me more A prompt within a ScreenTip that opens the Office online Help system with explanations about how to perform the command referenced in the ScreenTip.

Template An existing document that you use as a starting point for a new document; it opens a copy of itself, unnamed, and then you use the structure—and possibly some content, such as headings—as the starting point for new a document.

Text alignment The horizontal placement of text within a placeholder.

Text box A movable resizable container for text or graphics.

Text effects Decorative formats, such as shadowed or mirrored text, text glow, 3-D effects, and colors that make text stand out.

Text string A sequence of characters.

Text values Constant values consisting of only text, and which usually provide information about number values; also referred to as labels.

Text wrapping The manner in which text displays around an object.

Theme A predesigned set of colors, fonts, lines, and fill effects that look good together and that can be applied to all of the objects in the database or to individual objects in the database.

Thumbnails (PowerPoint) Miniature images of presentation slides.

Title bar The bar at the top edge of the program window that indicates the name of the current file and the program name.

Title slide A slide layout—most commonly the first slide in a presentation—that provides an introduction to the presentation topic.

Toggle button A button that can be turned on by clicking it once, and then turned off by clicking it again.

Toolbar In a folder window, a row of buttons with which you can perform common tasks, such as changing the view of your files and folders or burning files to a CD.

Triple-click The action of clicking the left mouse button three times in rapid succession.

Truncated Data that is cut off or shortened because the field or column is not wide enough to display all of the data or the field size is too small to contain all of the data.

Trusted Documents A security feature in Office that remembers which files you have already enabled; you might encounter this feature if you open a file from an e-mail or download files from the Internet.

Underlying formula The formula entered in a cell and visible only on the Formula Bar.

Value Another name for a constant value.

Value axis A numerical scale on the left side of a chart that shows the range of numbers for the data points; also referred to as the Y-axis.

Variant A variation on the presentation theme style and color.

Windows apps An app that runs on all Windows device families—including PCs, Windows phones, Windows tablets, and the Xbox gaming system.

Wizard A feature in Microsoft Office that walks you step by step through a process.

WordArt An Office feature in Word, Excel, and PowerPoint that enables you to change normal text into decorative stylized text.

Wordwrap The feature that moves text from the right edge of a paragraph to the beginning of the next line as necessary to fit within the margins.

Workbook An Excel file that contains one or more worksheets.

Worksheet The primary document that you use in Excel to work with and store data, and which is formatted as a pattern of uniformly spaced horizontal and vertical lines.

X-axis Another name for the horizontal (category) axis.

XML Paper Specification A Microsoft file format that creates an image of your document and that opens in the XPS viewer.

XPS The acronym for XML Paper Specification—a Microsoft file format that creates an image of your document and that opens in the XPS viewer.

Y-axis Another name for the vertical (value) axis.

Zoom The action of increasing or decreasing the size of the viewing area on the screen.

Index